"While reading this book, I sensed the tectonic plates of sociological theorizing shift. The collected essays highlight exciting new directions for Black feminist sociological inquiry. Though grounded in sociology, the vision and relevance of this volume extend beyond those disciplinary borders. This spectacular collection is a must have for anyone teaching about Black feminisms."

Michele Tracy Berger, *Department of Women's and Gender Studies, University of North Carolina-Chapel Hill*

"Luna and Pirtle have pulled together the definitive volume on Black feminist sociology of our time. The pieces in this book root Black feminist sociology in its activist and intellectual origins, trace its development, help us to understand the contemporary period, and urge us to look forward. The thinkers and writers represented in this book range from retired founders of Black Feminist Thought and the most influential contemporary scholars in Black feminist sociology to the up and coming next generation of Black feminist intellectuals. This book is a masterpiece and a model for how to do a field-defining edited volume."

Joyce Bell, *Department of Sociology, the University of Chicago*

"Intergenerational, interdisciplinary, and all around fierce! *Black Feminist Sociology* is a collection that is long-overdue but well worth the wait. Luna and Pirtle have given us a treasure of reflection, instruction, and future mandate. Their vision of a foundational Black feminist praxis will make all of our scholarship better and bolder. This text will be referenced for decades to come."

Mary Pattillo, *Department of Sociology, Northwestern University*

"Black women's scholarship has always been theoretically, methodologically, and epistemologically foundational to the discipline of sociology. This collection of essays is a scholarly, communal Black feminist gathering that tends carefully and poignantly to the multiple legacies of Black feminist work in the field. Calling back to Black feminist sociological histories, naming our place and showing our work now, and anticipating Black feminist futures, it offers crucial insight into Black feminist sociological scholarship that is essential reading in the ever-persistent call for the U.S. to 'listen to Black women.'"

Zandria Robinson, *Department of African American Studies, Georgetown University*

Black Feminist Sociology

Black Feminist Sociology offers new writings by established and emerging scholars working in a Black feminist tradition. The book centers Black feminist sociology (BFS) within the sociology canon and widens it to feature Black feminist sociologists both outside the US and the academy. Inspired by a BFS lens, the essays are critical, personal, political and oriented toward social justice. Key themes include the origins of BFS, expositions of BFS orientations to research that extend disciplinary norms, and contradictions of the pleasures and costs of such an approach both academically and personally. Authors explore their own sociological legacy of intellectual development to raise critical questions of intellectual thought and self-reflexivity. The book highlights the dynamism of BFS so future generations of scholars can expand upon and beyond the book's key themes.

Zakiya Luna is Associate Professor of Sociology and Dean's Distinguished Professorial Scholar at Washington University in Saint Louis. Her research, teaching and community work are in the areas of social movements, human rights and health. Her research on the reproductive justice movement includes the book *Reproductive Rights as Human Rights: Women of Color and the Fight for Reproductive Justice* (NYU Press).

Whitney N. Laster Pirtle is Assistant Professor of Sociology and McArthur Foundation Chair in International Justice and Human Rights at the University of California, Merced, where she directs the Sociology of Health and Equity (SHE) Lab. She is a critical race, Black feminist scholar currently studying disparities in COVID-19, racial formation in South Africa and racism on college campuses.

Sociology Re-Wired

Edited by Jodi O'Brien, Seattle University, and Marcus Hunter,
University of California, Los Angeles

Sociology Re-Wired captures this combustible moment in American and
global societies with new books that innovate and re-configure social
and political issues. This hybrid series publishes timely, relevant, original
research and textbooks that address significant social issues informed by
critical race theory, Black feminism and Queer Studies traditions. Series
books are written in a publicly accessible, multi-vocal style broadening the
reach and impact of significant scholarly contributions beyond traditional
academic audiences.

Some titles published in this series were published under an earlier series
name and a different editorship.

Published

All Media Are Social
Sociological Perspectives on Mass Media
by Andrew Lindner and Stephen R. Barnard

Incarceration without Conviction
Pretrial Detention and the Erosion of Innocence in American
Criminal Justice
by Mikaela Rabinowitz

Transforming Scholarship
Why Women's and Gender Studies Students Are Changing
Themselves and the World
by Michele Tracy Berger and Cheryl Radeloff

Black Feminist Sociology
Perspectives and Praxis
edited by Zakiya Luna and Whitney N. Laster Pirtle

For a full list of available titles please visit: www.routledge.com

Black Feminist Sociology

Perspectives and Praxis

Edited by
Zakiya Luna and
Whitney N. Laster Pirtle

Routledge
Taylor & Francis Group

NEW YORK AND LONDON

First published 2022
by Routledge
605 Third Avenue, New York, NY 10158

and by Routledge
2 Park Square, Milton Park, Abingdon, Oxon, OX14 4RN

Routledge is an imprint of the Taylor & Francis Group, an informa business

Library of Congress Cataloging-in-Publication Data
Names: Luna, Zakiya, editor. | Pirtle, Whitney, editor.
Title: Black feminist sociology : perspectives and praxis /
    edited by Zakiya Luna and Whitney Pirtle.
Description: New York, NY : Routledge, [2021] | Includes
    bibliographical references and index.
Identifiers: LCCN 2021015765 (print) | LCCN 2021015766
    (ebook) | ISBN 9781032057798 (hbk) | ISBN 9781032057538
    (pbk) | ISBN 9781003199113 (ebk)
Subjects: LCSH: Feminist theory. | African American feminists.
    | Sociology.
Classification: LCC HQ1190 .B574 2021 (print) | LCC HQ1190
    (ebook) | DDC 305.4201—dc23
LC record available at https://lccn.loc.gov/2021015765
LC ebook record available at https://lccn.loc.gov/2021015766

ISBN: 978-1-032-05779-8 (hbk)
ISBN: 978-1-032-05753-8 (pbk)
ISBN: 978-1-003-19911-3 (ebk)

DOI: 10.4324/9781003199113

Typeset in Garamond
by Apex CoVantage, LLC

We dedicate this to the Black feminist sociologists past, present and future.

Contents

Contributors

Shaonta' E. Allen is Mellon Faculty Fellow in the Department of Sociology and an affiliate of the African and African American Studies Program at Dartmouth College. Her research examines how Black resistance to racial inequality varies across social institutions. She specifically explores Black resistive practices within religion, higher education, pop culture and sports to theorize contemporary strategies for navigating racial and gender hierarchies.

Subini Ancy Annamma is an associate professor at Stanford University whose research positions multiply marginalized youth as knowledge generators to inform how intersectional injustice impacts education. Dr. Annamma's book, *The Pedagogy of Pathologization*, focuses on the education trajectories of incarcerated disabled girls of color and has won the 2019 Association of Educational Services Agencies Critic's Choice Book Award and the 2018 National Women's Studies Association Alison Piepmeier Book Prize.

Freeden Blume Oeur is an associate professor of sociology and education at Tufts University. His research interests are in the areas of Black politics, Black feminism, masculinity and K-12 education. Blume Oeur is the author of *Black Boys Apart: Racial Uplift and Respectability in All-Male Public Schools* (Minnesota, 2018) and coeditor of *Unmasking Masculinities: Men and Society* (Sage, 2017).

Alicia D. Bonaparte is Associate Professor of Sociology at Pitzer College and trained as a medical sociologist with a specialization in reproductive health, health disparities and female crime and deviance. Her publications and research interests examine the gendered social hierarchy within American medicine as well as the intersection of race and gender in healthcare practices and racial disparities. She is also coeditor of the anthology *Birthing Justice: Black Women, Pregnancy, and Childbirth* and contributed to Routledge's *Motherhood Companion* (2019) examining the collusion of race, class and gender regarding choices about midwife-attended births.

Rose M. Brewer, PhD, is The Morse Alumni Distinguished Teaching Professor and past chairperson of the Department of African American & African Studies, University of Minnesota-Twin Cities. A social activist and scholar, Brewer publishes extensively on Black feminism, political economy, social movements, race, class, gender and social change. Her current work on Black life looks deeply at the impact of late capitalism.

Kenly Brown is a postdoctoral fellow in the Department of African and African American Studies at Washington University in St. Louis. Her work problematizes the relationship between Black girlhood, institutional violence and alternative schooling. She started the Black Girlhood Studies Lab supported by the Center for Race, Ethnicity and Equity at Washington University in St. Louis. This research is supported by the Ford Foundation and American Educational Research Association Minority Fellowship.

Melissa Brown is a postdoctoral research fellow at the Clayman Institute for Gender Research at Stanford University. Her dissertation, "The Jezebel Speaks: Black Women's Erotic Labor in the Digital Age," was defended in May 2019. She enjoys using her free time to play and cuddle with her pug, Frank Lucas.

Blu Buchanan is a PhD candidate in sociology, with a designated emphasis in feminist theory and research at the University of California, Davis. Their academic work falls along two parallel lines, the collection and archiving of Black trans oral histories and the study of gay right-wing organizations, interrogating the nature of political and intracommunity violence. Outside of the university, they organize around Black, trans and labor justice movements.

Mali Collins is a PhD candidate in the English Department and an NEH NextGen Fellow with the African American Public Humanities Initiative at the University of Delaware. Her dissertation project examines representations of Black mother-child separation in contemporary literature and visual art to form a critique of current political and social crises that directly affect Black mothers.

Patricia Hill Collins is Distinguished University Professor Emerita at the University of Maryland, College Park, and at the University of Cincinnati. She is the author of ten books, including *Black Feminist Thought* (1990, 2000), *Black Sexual Politics* (2004) and *Intersectionality as Critical Social Theory* (2019). In 2008, she became the 100th President of the American Sociological Association.

LeConté J. Dill is an associate professor of Black Feminisms, Genders, and Sexualities Studies in the Department of African American and African Studies at Michigan State University. She holds degrees from

Spelman College, UCLA and UC Berkeley. Guided by Black Feminist epistemologies, she engages in qualitative, arts-based and community-accountable research methods to examine urban Black girls' strategies of resilience, safety and wellness.

Mercedez Dunn received her BA in sociology from Spelman College and a master of public health and PhD in sociology from the University of Michigan. She is a postdoctoral research fellow at University of Maryland, Baltimore County in the department of sociology, anthropology, and public health. Her research lies at the intersection of gender, race, class, sexual relationships, and health.

Brittany Friedman is an assistant professor of sociology at the University of Southern California. She holds a PhD in sociology from Northwestern University. She is currently writing her first book, which is under contract with the University of North Carolina Press, Chapel Hill, and listed in the special series Justice, Power and Politics. Her work advances critical race theory in the areas of punishment, incarceration and prison order. She is an avid student of nature, loves writing poetry and getting lost in music.

Ashley Garner is a doctoral student in the Department of Sociology at the University of Massachusetts, Amherst. She studies race, religion and eldercare. Out of office, Ashley enjoys baking, gardening, and reading and reviewing fiction.

Saida Grundy is an assistant professor of sociology and African American studies at Boston University. She is a feminist scholar whose research focuses on campus sexual assault and gender and sexuality within the Black middle class. Grundy is the author of *Manhood Within the Margins: Promise, Peril, and Paradox at the Historically Black College for Men* (California, forthcoming).

Endia Louise Hayes is a doctoral student in sociology at Rutgers University, the State University of New Jersey. She studies the epistemological contribution of Black formerly enslaved women, specifically Afro-Texan women. Endia posits these Afro-Texan women as avenues through which Black women can assist the discipline in adequately revisiting the past, unpacking the present and better integrating slavery into contemporary sociological work.

Brooklynn K. Hitchens holds a PhD in sociology from Rutgers University, the State University of New Jersey. Her work centers on the lived experiences of low-income Black women and girls with violence and crime in urban communities. She enjoys debating the State of Black America, mentoring women of color moving through the doctorate and speaking truth to power whenever necessary.

Ashley E. Hollingshead is a doctoral student of sociology at Rutgers University, the State University of New Jersey, New Brunswick. Her work focuses on Black women's experiences with policing and surveillance in gentrified communities. Ashley mentors young Black women and men on character development, honoring her past.

Ayotunde Khyree Ikuku is pursuing a double major in sociology and ethnic studies with a focus on LGBTQ+ perspectives at Los Rios Community Colleges in Sacramento, CA. Within academia, their main desire is disciplinary transformation—away from the distant, spectacle-like practice so common to sociology and toward a kind of sociology invested in developing tangible resources, change, and accountability for the perpetually marginalized. They also do intersectional organizing with both local and online community organizers/activists, with a focus on centering the needs and knowledge of the most marginalized people.

Jennifer Elyse James is an assistant professor at the University of California, San Francisco. She is a qualitative researcher and Black feminist scholar whose research lies at the intersection of race, gender and health. Her past work has focused on the lived experience of cancer, and she is now studying experiences of health and illness for women who have been incarcerated.

Maria S. Johnson, PhD, is Founder and Chairperson of the Black Women and Girls Fund (BWGF). BWGF awards grants to projects that support Black women and girls. Johnson is completing a book titled *Black Daughters, Black Fathers: Understanding Complex Family Relationships* (under contract with NYU Press). She earned a PhD from the University of Michigan and a BA from Hampton University.

Jalia L. Joseph is a graduate student in the Department of Sociology at Texas A & M University, additionally obtaining a graduate certificate in Africana Studies. Their work centers around race/ethnicity, social movements, feminisms and critical race theory. Their research appears in a coauthored paper in *Women's Studies in Communication*, and a solo-authored debate article in *Ethnic and Racial Studies*.

Jasmine Kelekay is an Afro-Finland-Swedish researcher and activist focusing on anti-Black racism and Black activism in the Nordics. She is a PhD candidate at the University of California, Santa Barbara, and a visiting researcher at the Centre for Multidisciplinary Studies on Racism (CEMFOR) at Uppsala University.

Zakiya Luna, MSW, PhD, is Associate Professor of Sociology and Dean's Distinguished Professorial Scholar at Washington University in Saint Louis. Her research, teaching and community work are in the areas of social movements, human rights and health. Her research on the reproductive justice movement includes the book *Reproductive Rights as Human Rights: Women of Color and the Fight for Reproductive Justice* (NYU Press).

Mandisi Majavu holds a PhD from the University of Auckland, New Zealand. Dr Majavu is Senior Lecturer in the Department of Politics and International Studies at Rhodes University. Majavu's research ranges widely across political histories of race in settler societies such as Australia, New Zealand and South Africa. He is author of the book *Uncommodified Blackness* (Palgrave Macmillan, 2017).

Lori Latrice Martin is Professor of Sociology and African and African American Studies at Louisiana State University. Dr. Martin is also the faculty athletic representative. Dr. Martin earned her doctoral degree from the University at Albany. Her most recent books include *Black Women as Leaders, Big Box Schools* and *Black Asset Poverty and the Enduring Racial Divide*.

Mignon R. Moore is Professor of Sociology at Barnard College and Columbia University, the 2021 President of the Sociologists for Women in Society and Vice President-Elect of the American Sociological Association. Her first book, *Invisible Families: Gay Identities, Relationships and Motherhood among Black Women*, is a study of family formation and lesbian identity in a Black racial context. She is completing a new book, which uses historical archives and interviews to analyze the development of Black lesbian community in the context of the Great Migration. It is tentatively titled *In the Shadow of Sexuality: Social Histories of African American Lesbian and Gay Elders, 1950–1979*.

Jennifer C. Nash is Associate Professor of African American Studies and Gender and Sexuality Studies. Her second book, *Black Feminism Reimagined: After Intersectionality* (Duke University Press, 2019), rewrites black feminist theory's engagement with intersectionality, an innovation that is often celebrated as black feminism's primary intellectual and political contribution to feminist theory and related fields.

Carolette Norwood is Professor and Department Chair of Sociology and Criminology at Howard University. She earned a PhD in sociology from the University of Nebraska-Lincoln and was an Andrew W. Mellon fellow in African Demography at the Université de Montréal. Dr. Norwood's current research interests include exploring the simultaneity and particularities of feminism(s) in the African Diaspora within and across geographical and local contexts; reproductive justice and sexual health disparities; gendered violence; stress, trauma and mental health; and spatial distribution of STIs and HIV across the Cincinnati MSA. Dr. Norwood is finalizing a book project tentatively entitled, *Jim Crow*

Geographies: Mapping the Intersections of Gender, Race, and Sexuality in Urban Space.

Julia Chinyere Oparah is Provost and Vice President for Academic Affairs at the University of San Francisco. She has published extensively on Black maternal health, decarceral politics, research justice and transnational Black feminisms. Most recently, she launched #BattlingOverBirth, a book and campaign about the crises of Black women's health and maternal health. Oparah loves the redwoods, yoga, gospel and family playtime.

Mona Taylor Phillips is a professor of sociology at Spelman College, where she also coordinates the Ida B. Wells-Barnett/Social Justice Distinguished Lecture and Performance Series. Dr. Phillips received her BA degree from Spelman College and her MA and PhD degrees from the University of Michigan. Her research focuses on pedagogy and on the social contexts of Black women's health.

Whitney N. Laster Pirtle, PhD, is an assistant professor of sociology and McArthur Foundation Chair in International Justice and Human Rights at the University of California, Merced, where she directs the Sociology of Health and Equity (SHE) Lab. She is a critical race, Black feminist scholar currently studying disparities in COVID-19, racial formation in South Africa and racism on college campuses. She was a 2018 Ford Foundation Postdoc awardee and receivedthe 2020 A. Wade Smith Award for Teaching, Mentoring, and Service from the Association of Black Sociologists.

Jomaira Salas Pujols is a doctoral candidate in the Department of Sociology at Rutgers University, where she studies Black girlhood and identity formation in educational spaces. She is a National Science Foundation Graduate Research fellow and a youth worker. Jomaira loves swimming and warm sunny days.

Assata Richards is Founding Director of the Sankofa Research Institute, as well as Founding Board President of the Houston Community Land Trust, the Third Ward Cooperative Community Builders, the Community Care Cooperative and the Emancipation Economic Development Council. She is committed to repaying the debt paid by her ancestors and doing all she can to end white supremacy and patriarchy.

Dorothy Roberts is the 14th Penn Integrates Knowledge Professor, George A. Weiss University Professor of Law & Sociology, and Raymond Pace & Sadie Tanner Mossell Alexander Professor of Civil Rights at the University of Pennsylvania. An internationally acclaimed scholar, activist and social critic, she has written and lectured extensively on the interplay of gender, race and class in legal issues concerning reproduction, bioethics and child welfare.

She has authored multiple books and published more than 100 articles and essays in books and scholarly journals, including *Harvard Law Review*, *Yale Law Journal*, *Stanford Law Review* and *Signs*.

Nzali Scales received her BA in sociology from Spelman College. As UNCF-Mellon Mays Undergraduate Fellow and Social Justice Fellow at Spelman, her research and activism focused on the intersection of race, class and gender in the lives of Black girls. She is currently a PhD student in sociology at Northwestern University.

Cynthia Neal Spence is an associate professor of sociology, Director of the UNCF/Mellon Programs, and Director of the Social Justice Fellows Program at Spelman College. She received her BA from Spelman College and her MA and PhD from Rutgers University. Issues of service learning, gender role socialization and violence against women frame her research, writing and public service.

Aisha A. Upton is an assistant professor of sociology at Susquehanna University. Her research agenda is centered broadly around race, gender, social movements, and Black civic engagement. Aisha's work has focused on Black women's organizations interactions with Black radical movements.

Tashelle Wright is a McNair Scholar alumni and a member of the Graduate Dean's Advisory Council on Diversity at the University of California, Merced. Tashelle has worked for a health department in the Office of Health Disparities and as a Certified Nursing Assistant. As a PhD student, she is interested in aging and cognition, older adults, chronic disease and addressing preventable health disparities, specifically within African, African American and Hispanic/Latino populations.

Foreword

The scene was the Association of Black Sociologists' 48th three-day annual meeting. The theme was *The New Black Sociologists*. Underneath a rising summer moon in Philly in 2018, legendary poet-professor-activist Sonia Sanchez commanded the power of love and Blackness until it swept through the hearts, minds and spirits of every person in the room. All in attendance were moved to tears and to hugs and to laughter. A deep stillness took over the room which then exploded into joyous applause, whistles and snaps for the loving wisdom she shared. That light burned through the evening and for the days ahead. So much so that by the time the pioneering sociologist-activist-Black feminist-legal scholar Dorothy Roberts completed the final words of her closing keynote, this was an audience on fire.

Those three days in August marked the ascension of Routledge's newest edited volume, *The New Black Sociologists: Historical and Contemporary Perspectives*—a manifesto of reflection and direction in the spirit of Black sociologists Joyce Ladner and James Blackwell. Those same three days were also the impetus for an inspired collaboration between Dr. Zakiya Luna and Dr. Whitney N. Laster Pirtle. *Black Feminist Sociology*, a necessary, brave and unprecedented collection, is the outcome of their bold vision, which took shape in that inspired summer. In this book, the editors have convened and amplified a broad universe of multivocal, multigenerational praxis, principles, peoples and concepts. Taken together the book's contents constitute the collective light, fire and purpose emergent within Black feminist sociological thought and endeavors. Luna and Pirtle's *Black Feminist Sociology* is a gift to the discipline of sociology specifically, and to the world over more generally. Underscored by powerful contributions that make plain the ontological and epistemological imports of Black feminist sociology, this book will be an immediate resource in the present and well into the future.

Marcus Anthony Hunter, Coeditor
Jodi O'Brien, Coeditor
Sociology Re-Wired

Acknowledgements

First and foremost, we would like to thank the many people before us who made this possible: our ancestors and family. There is a proclamation that many Black people of a certain generation heard at different Black celebrations: the repetition of the idea of Ubuntu, "I am because we are." This was sometimes followed by everyone singing the Black National Anthem, "Lift Every Voice and Sing." These are simultaneously meaningful and dated practices that do not seem to fit with contemporary insistence on Black futurity, especially for those wary of religion or patriotism. But it is not an accident that they reappeared at places like Beyoncé's record-breaking Coachella performance. They remind us that time is not linear and what makes it possible for any person to read the words on these pages, and particularly Black people of the diaspora, is so many named and unnamed people who believed in a future where Black people could be free. As we and others in this book describe, this project is formally an edited volume, but informally it is a community and reminder of the creativity and reach of those who dare embrace Black feminist thought.

Marcus Anthony Hunter was outgoing president of the Association of Black Sociologists (ABS) at a thrilling conference that generated many ideas. He had also developed a relationship between ABS and Routledge Press so ABS members could get an inside look at the publishing process, thereby sharing the knowledge that still remains too often in the hands of a lucky few. He did not hesitate when at the end of ABS we proposed this volume. His Sociology Re-Wired series coeditor, Jodi O'Brien, took on guiding this project with humor. Her consistent check-ins were filled with affirmation and she was sure to remind us of her belief in our capacity to carry out our vision. Dean Birkenkamp, our Routledge editor, helped nourish the project into fruition—once literally as we all met for breakfast when attending the Pacific Sociological Association conference in Oakland.

Patricia Hill Collins has inspired many of us at different points in our career, and witnessing her Author Meets Legacy session at ABS was another experience where she filled us with fire. As we updated authors, she would ask a logistical question then tell us that what we were doing was "an ambitious and much needed project." Each time she sent us an update on her chapter was mind-blowing—her version of revision is to reimagine for the better.

Early on in the project, we reached out to some of the Black feminist sociologists we admired. We are thankful to Nikki Jones and Joyce Bell for pledging their support and graciously offering to help us review abstracts. They gave us the confirmation we needed.

Jasmine Kelekay and Tashelle Wright were invaluable, enthusiastic graduate editorial assistants with a motivation for the project even when we were not fully sure of its direction. They brought their energy and ideas to the process so the learning could be reciprocal. Well before the pandemic we were making use of everyone's new best friend, Zoom, often across seas and time zones. They embodied Black girl magic and it is a thrill to watch their journeys as Black feminist scholars.

We look forward to working with Melissa Brown, given how stunned she left us in meeting with her to discuss Black feminist sociology in the digital realm. She was the person we both independently and secretly hoped might join the team, yet she reached out to us on her own accord—we call it divine.

We thank the UCSB undergraduates that transcribed Dorothy Roberts's remarks and the UC Merced Center for Humanities that provided funding for parts of the project and a book symposium.

The authors in this volume came along for the ride that is an edited volume—delays and shifts. They were also open to the other elements we brought to the process of creative connecting—meals at a conference, letting us know when they would be at a conference so we could say hello, sharing names of editors, online yoga classes and more. We learned so much from each author in engaging with their work and their voices. Your writing brought us laughter, tears, snaps and sometimes snatched edges. We share difference nationalities, gender identities, academic disciplines and attachment to universities, but we represent the best of Black feminist sociology. To the many people whose submitted work we could not move forward, please know your submissions inspired us.

We knew people were cheering for us from afar, even if we didn't actually know who. Somehow, we could always feel the energy and excitement. This is a project of both honor and passion for us too, and the positive vibrations always fueled our fire.

If we forgot your name, please forgive us. You are in our hearts therefore in this book.

Editorial Assistants' Reflection

As editorial assistants for *Black Feminist Sociology: Perspectives and Praxis*, we had the opportunity to work collaboratively with Drs Zakiya Luna and Whitney N. Laster Pirtle. Volumes such as this support and promote the powerful research and perspectives of Black and Brown scholars throughout the world and provide needed space to have crucial conversations about inequalities and injustices in and outside of academia.

Our role in this edited volume allowed us both to delve deeper into the discipline of Black feminist sociology and provided a space for us to gain valuable experience reviewing, critiquing and providing feedback on abstracts and ideas submitted. We participated in periodic editorial meetings, checking and responding to emails, and gained insider knowledge about book editing and publishing. We also had the opportunity to disseminate and share the call for abstracts with personal and professional networks.

As budding social scientists—and as Black feminists—it has been a joy and a privilege to be a part of the making of this book. Throughout our education and academic training, we have been searching for ways to integrate our disciplines with the theoretical, political and empirical lessons from ethnic studies, feminist studies, the Black radical tradition and especially Black feminism. While there is a long tradition of incredibly talented scholars engaging in and talking about Black feminist sociology (some of whose work graces the pages of this text), we have never come across an explicitly Black feminist collection of sociological writing.

In many ways, what this volume has become is a resource that we wish would have existed when we were first students. It not only engages with the long tradition of Black feminist sociologists but also puts them in conversation with dynamic new research that is taking the field in exciting and important directions. The breadth of content and variety of form across the pieces also enriches our understanding of the praxis and possibilities of Black feminist sociology. Indeed, what has been most pleasurable about working on this book has been the ways in which the coeditors have been adamant about taking Black feminism seriously as a praxis—both in terms of how we have conceived of the volume and in how we have worked together.

Jasmine Kelekay & Tashelle Wright
BFS Editorial Assistants

Introduction

Black Feminist Sociology Is the Past, Present and Future of Sociology. Period.

Zakiya Luna and Whitney N. Laster Pirtle

Black Feminist Sociology: Perspectives and Praxis is a project we needed for ourselves. The initial ideas for this book took shape on a humid August evening in Philadelphia, Pennsylvania, during a carpool to the famed South restaurant. Empty warehouses and street murals on storefronts started to dot the street amidst tall brick buildings. Looking across to the stated address, the passengers were skeptical of the GPS's insistence they had arrived to their dinner location. A placard pointed to the entrance around the corner. A tiny one-way street with cars backed up. Jazz music wafting in from side dining room mixed with laughter and the clink of glasses.

At a long table sat 11 Black women of different ages, colors, sizes, hairstyles, backgrounds and sexualities. We had decided to meet for dinner after a year of Facebook conversations. On Facebook, a few sociologists who are included in this volume proposed they could name every Black woman on the US sociology tenure track since there were so few of us . . . and they could. They then created a private Facebook group and arranged to meet in person during the sociological conference season in Philadelphia.[1] One on hand, this gathering was unremarkable since Philadelphia is a large city with many Black women and the restaurant was a popular one. On the other hand, this was a remarkable dinner. All the women had PhDs, were trained in sociology, and were attending the 2018 disciplinary conferences of the Association of Black Sociologists (ABS) and/or the American Sociological Association (ASA) and the Society for the Study of Social Problems. The ABS conference was themed "The New Black Sociologists," and would have Black feminists as two primary plenary speakers. The ASA conference was themed "Feeling Race" and featured sessions on Du Boisian thought, the role of Historically Black Colleges and Universities in developing the discipline of sociology, racism within the study of sexuality, and global formations of Blackness. On Saturday of the conference, in a fabulous mini campaign led by one of the coeditors, hundreds of people wore shirts declaring #CiteBlackWomen (referencing a larger campaign and collective started by anthropologist Christen A. Smith).[2]

DOI: 10.4324/9781003199113-1

Dinner proved magical. Black women make up less than 3 percent of the US professoriate,[3] and according to ASA's own data there are only 544 members across all stages of their careers who identify as Black and women in ASA's 11,500-plus membership.[4] It was rare—and invigorating—to be surrounded by so many Black women who were early career sociologists; we had to make something more concrete of the conference and convening. And thus, the idea for an edited volume showcasing Black feminist sociology was proposed. We, the prospective editors, exchanged contact information. With support from ABS President Marcus Anthony Hunter and Vice President Zandria Robinson, our plan was in motion. We didn't let up on the plan until a book contract was signed three months later, thanks to the editors of the Sociology Re-Wired series, Jodi O'Brien and Marcus Hunter.

Where We're Coming From—BFS's Historical Roots

This volume proceeds from the foundational understanding that Black feminist theorizing is the present and future of sociology. The foundations for what we're now calling Black feminist sociology (BFS)[5] were curated by Black feminist scholars and activists long before the academy had a name for it. In a 1989 essay "Black women and Feminist Sociology" in *American Sociologist*, Rose M. Brewer shared her vision for an emerging Black feminist sociology centered in the intersection of race, class, and gender. She concluded, "Without a black, feminist, class perspective that goes further than existing frameworks, sociological theory and praxis is permanently stifled."[6] A project that challenges the whiteness of sociological theorizing as supposedly "generalizable" must also acknowledge its maleness. Brewer was part of a Black feminist intelligentsia, which included Patricia Hill Collins, who had already analyzed the "outsider within" experience of being a Black woman in sociology, and legal scholar Kimberlé Crenshaw who articulated the dynamic concept of "intersectionality." In her critical essay, Brewer applies this concept as a corrective to feminist sociology, which omitted race as well as race relations perspectives that overlooked gender. Thirty years later, in her keynote address to the ABS 2018 conference, Patricia Hill Collins reminded the audience that "the terrain of theory sets the agenda."[7]

Where are we now with this project of a Black feminist approach as a foundation for a sociology that more fully speaks to our times? In her 2018 presidential address to the Sociologists for Women in Society, Adia Harvey Wingfield reminded the audience that "reclaiming our time" as Black women is occurring despite overwhelming odds and at great cost to our intellectual productivity and bodies.[8] Like Harvey Wingfield, we are heartened by sociology's reckoning with its too oft-erased history, for instance situating Du Boisian sociology and the Atlantic School as central. Yet, as Wingfield writes, the field has yet to acknowledge the persistent and significant contributions of Black women: "black women were also early originators of sociological arguments and knowledge. Yet systemic racism and patriarchal norms limited the extent to which their analyses were widely disseminated and/or taken seriously."[9]

Despite the inroads in this area, such as the *New Black Sociologists'* (NBS) chapters covering Anna Julia Cooper and Zora Neale Hurston, and Shaonta' E. Allen's chapter in this volume on Ida B. Wells, we need to do more.[10] We must, for instance, also look to activist and theorist Joyce Ladner and her *Tomorrow's Tomorrow: The Black Woman*, a pioneer study about Black women and girls. We must also celebrate the likes of Delores Aldridge, the first Black woman hired at Emory University and the founder of the first African American and African studies program in the US South, who laid out roots by profiling five Black women sociology firsts in her book *Imagine a World: Pioneering Black Women Sociologists*.[11] We are glad that the ASA recently created an award named after her to honor her scholarship and activism.[12]

Black feminist sociology is also interdisciplinary and draws from multiple ways of knowing and understanding. Our ranks include historians, Black studies scholars, and anthropologists. Activists have also contributed importantly to our current theorizing. For instance, the Combahee River Collective outlined how building coalitions that support the freedom and well-being of Black women would allow all of us to get free.[13] Contemporary Black women activists, such as Alicia Garza, Patrisse Cullors and Opel Tometi, are emphasizing this unifying rallying call again, through the Black Lives Matter movement.[14]

Given the inherent exclusion of rigid canons, knowledge and insight cultivated in fields of oppression takes many forms. Collins has always encouraged us to uphold ordinary Black women, including poets, song-stresses, politicians, organizers, and activists. Our theorizing is also informed by those whose names are known only to us, like the midwives who catch us and the women who style our hair, those who raise us and who teach us. A Black feminist sociology recognizes that people as varied as Ida B. Wells (see chapter 2) and Remy Ma have insights to offer the field and the world. For instance, with an average of 2.6 million monthly listeners on Spotify, Remy Ma, who earned an associate's degree in sociology while incarcerated, influences millions. Remy Ma's life path, including her six-year incarceration, is familiar to many Black listeners; thus, even without having read a peer-reviewed article they know Remy Ma beat the odds when she "left the big house to a bigger house."[15] These figures are all part of a Black feminist sociological legacy.

Our overview is non-comprehensive and intentionally leaves space for you, the reader, to reflect on what you don't know and then to do the work to learn. But we encourage you to look to Rose M. Brewer's 1989 article on Black feminist sociology, "Black Women and Feminist Sociology: The Emerging Perspective," which laid out organizing principals such as drawing on interpretive paradigms, incorporation of larger structural forces to understanding biographies, and deeper delineations of hierarchical intersections. Her work, along with Patricia Hill Collins's *Black Feminist Thought*, helped lay the theoretical groundwork and guiding orientations of a critical, reflective, feminist sociology and has been foundational for training a new generation of Black feminist sociologists. Collins's text marked a turning point in sociology in offering a framework for considering an ethics of care in research, analyzing controlling images of Black women, identifying the constraints of disciplines, and introducing a field-changing theory of the matrix of domination, all within one volume. According to Collins, "Black feminist thought consists of specialized knowledge created by African-American women which clarifies a standpoint of and for Black women. In other words, Black feminist thought encompasses theoretical interpretations of Black women's reality by those who live it."[16] Centering the knowledge production of those who live it is a hallmark.[17]

As Brewer and others in this volume discuss, while there has been progress since those words were published, many of the same problems with sociological thought remain. Countless sociologists still analyze surveys that show, once again, the level of discrimination racial and ethnic minorities experience, or for a more "humane" approach, they "embed" themselves in communities of color for an amount of time, gather data, then leave to write articles and books that reveal the "secrets" of what decades of institutional and social disinvestment produce. Meanwhile, many of us live these oppressions. Irrespective of the bodies producing the research, much of this research draws on classical sociological theory and therefore brings with it white supremacist, masculinist assumptions about the ways that power can be measured, how families "should" look, and what makes work meaningful. This affects the analyses produced and the vision offered of the groups under study.

BFS is not simply everything that White sociology is not—that would be a derivative approach that continues to center whiteness and white logics. When it came to writing about White sociology's engagement with Black subjects, it posed a challenge to us: their work riddled with racist misconceptions, it's painful to read how these scholars thought—and think—of us. Joyce Ladner published *The Death of White Sociology: Essays on Race and Culture* in 1973, reflecting on how Black sociology conceptualizes our communities differently.[18] Echoing Ladner, we have chosen to not spend additional ink on White sociology, focusing instead on framing sociology's new day/way forward as grounded in Black feminist sociology.

Our dedication is to Black feminist epistemologies and praxes. Collins, in writing about Black feminist epistemology, explains that

> As a critical social theory, U.S. Black feminist thought reflects the interests and standpoint of its creators. Tracing the origin and diffusion of Black feminist thought or any comparable body of specialized knowledge reveals its affinity to the power of the group that created it.[19]

This is the same for general social theories, though they reflect elite white men, meaning, therefore, that "U.S. Black women's experiences as well as those of women of African descent transnationally have been routinely distorted within or excluded from what counts as knowledge."[20] Not only is this a call to the death of white sociology, then, but it is also a call to unequivocally demand that Black feminist thought is validated knowledge and in fact the present and future of sociology.

With that, we present the mission for the book: To use Black feminist ethics to produce an edited volume that reflects the breadth and magnitude of contemporary Black feminist sociology for the discipline and praxis.

The guiding questions for the BFS project are:

- What is Black feminist sociology? How does it differ from Black critical thought and feminist theory?
- What role did Black feminism have in shaping sociological thought? Who should be included in the Black feminist sociological cannon?
- What role does Black feminism have in shaping sociology in the 21st century?
- In what new directions are Black feminist sociologists taking the field?
- How can we best do Black feminist sociology? What are the guiding principles, theories, methods, and practical applications of Black feminist sociology?
- What are the risks and rewards for practicing Black feminist sociology?

Because the writers of the following chapters use the BFS lens, work here is inherently critical, personal, political, and oriented towards social justice. *Black Feminist Sociology* brings together a diverse set of scholars and activists for a timely, accessible, and intellectually stimulating conversation regarding the foundations and state of Black feminist sociological thought.

We put forth the understanding of Black feminist sociological epistemology as a framing orientation that is inclusive and vast, but finds grounding in its reflexivity, community centeredness and intentional praxis. Black feminist sociology theorizes about the value of everyday life and all that it entails, including imagination, health and well-being, gender expressions, sexualities, religiosity, political engagement, scholarship, restoration and more. Through this theorizing, BFS questions the multiple and intersectional forces that harm these lived experiences, and, importantly, envisions broad systematic changes to make life better for everyone. It is grounded in living and archived history but remains forward-thinking toward not only equity but also abolition. As we show in this volume, BFS is not only contained in the bodies of Black women. From its earliest iterations, radical Black feminists identified that "we" included different classes, sexualities and genders. No one in the Black community was disposable. This is the spirit a younger generation is insisting on for their Black feminism: a diverse community-based model that does not rely on, in the words of Audre Lorde, the master's tool. Black feminist sociology is creative, undefined, transformative, humanizing and loving.

Demystifying Processes, Expanding Opportunities

We share the BFS origin story and mission because truth-telling and community have been at the center of this endeavor. In fact, along every step of the way to create this book we have received valuable lessons about what Black feminist sociology really means. The process of knowledge production is not separate from the product, so in the following we explain more of our process. For us, the process of co-creating this volume was a lesson in what Black feminist sociological projects might be, and the impact that they can surely have on us, our communities, and the academy.

At every point of the creation process for this book we reflected on the BFS tradition and our mission and used that to guide our decisions, seeking to trust our truths and the truths laid out before us. Speaking our truths is why we have learned to trust Black women.[21] Speaking truth to power is telling our truths to those who haven't wanted to listen to Black women.[22] Being transparent about our truths entails both care and clarity; a sort of bringing to the table talk that directly cares for people that includes directly challenging them when needed.[23] Truth and transparency mean listening to and trusting in ourselves, our team, our supporters, and our communities.

A goal of a Black feminist sociological project, then, must be to have a far reach; to spread knowledge and critique as well as spread joy and uplift, and to do so through multilateral pathways. To fight against insularity, we had to reckon with ourselves and ask, often, *Who has a seat at the table?* This impacted our decisions on whether we would have a call for abstracts, how we disseminated that call, and our review process. Early on in our proposal we were explicit in our desire to include established scholars, graduate student scholars, scholars in nonacademic positions, and scholars working outside of the US. Though a quicker way to produce a volume is to draw from a small network, we knew this also to be a narrower approach, and one that limited full access; one that would not reflect our BFS. Thus, the aim for a far reach informed our decision to amplify an open, transnational call for abstracts.

To start our process as a larger team, all team members (re-)read the same guiding texts. We needed to be sure our foundations were strong, so that as we entered into conversations with authors who were grounded in the BFS tradition we were also in conversation with ourselves. Nonetheless, we often had hard conversations about the submissions and chapters regarding whether a reading unsettled the literature or unsettled ourselves. With a strong foundation, though, we were able to better think through the new thoughts from a place of respect for both. We sought to balance between reverence for the foundations and encouragement for future visioning. We sat with our own comfort, or not, with the arguments before us. Our feedback ranged from congratulating the authors on their profound thoughts, sometimes simply with the comment "*yassss!*" or asking the authors to question what assumptions their writing was making. We trusted the authors to sharpen their voices throughout the process.

The reflexive nature of the scholarship also made us circle back to the question we posed in the first principle, *Who has a seat at the table?* In this principle, however, the focus is not only on the positionality of the author but also on the scholarship produced. We wanted to know what areas were missing in a conversation about Black feminist sociology. We returned this question to our team, and in conversation realized, for instance, that we didn't have work related to critical disability studies. This shaped our decision to invite additional authors into the conversation. We expect that later editions of this book will include other areas we missed here, and are excited to hear about the conversations that questions might elicit in this phase.

The more we worked on this project, the more clarity we gained about what we came to see as guiding principles of Black feminist sociology. We write these sentences mindful of the words of Nikki Jones, one of our senior advisors: "Black feminist epistemologies value various forms of knowledge production; therefore, avoid claims about reaching consensus or definitive ideas on the 'right' way to do Back feminist sociology."[24] These are not epistemological tenets or concepts, though varying perspectives of epistemologies are uncovered throughout this text, but rather guiding ethics for how we might frame BFS projects. We share these in this introduction and provide examples of how they emerged throughout the book's evolution.

Ethics of truth and transparency fill the pages of this book. The scholarship produced is coming from a place of personal reflection and honesty as well as deep engagement with literatures and debates. In line with Collins's conceptualization of the "outsider within,"[25] *BFS* seeks to divulge not only what is behind the veil, but reveals what personhoods, motivations, challenges, and triumphs lie underneath the surface of standard, positivist approaches to sociology and beyond academic walls and ivory towers. We often pushed the authors to situate their piece with their own positionality so that readers could see how one's lived experience informs the knowledge they produce. The truths reflected come from a breadth of sources—love letters, Twitter feeds, community conversations, in-depth interviews, and more—revealing that both questions and answers come from those places we engage with, expected or not. Black feminist sociology trusts Black women and is unapologetic in doing so.

Creating and Connecting Community

Community and collaboration is at the core of BFS. Contrary to the individualist practices and expectations that define White academe, Black scholars have long understood that knowledge is a collective process. In one submission, an author wrote about sociology "opening the doors" to Black women. Luna disagreed, noting in a comment,

> I don't know many Black feminist scholars of my generation or older who think the academy "opened its doors." The door[s] were pried open with a crowbar and blood, sweat and lives—and some of those people and white allies have been able to [open] it a little wider but the forces on the other side trying to close it are stronger than ever. [U]sing our ideas and bodies is not the same as being open.

The history of notably show rates of Black women gaining access, advancement, and voice in academe, despite comparatively high rates of pursuing PhDs; the way institutions leave Black women and gender nonconforming academics to fend for themselves when publicly attacked for our scholarship (or existence); and many more examples are reminders of why we have to cultivate community.

Expanding opportunities and cultivating mentorship—up, down, sideways, and around—must be at the core of any BFS project. As Carolette Norwood notes in this volume,

> The spaces that we construct and that construct us (terrains of transgression and resistance) shape who we are and determine if and how we access resources and what knowledge is available to us. Sociologists need to follow the lead of Black feminists in recognizing the intersectional nature of spatiality.

Cultivating mentorship includes learning from ourselves, our peers, our students, our ancestors, our collaborators, our senior scholars, and so on.

Critically, building all around recognizes that community-building goes together with our knowledge creation projects.

We started this project as two assistant professors with an idea and a passion but knew right away we needed a team to help us through. We thought we needed a senior scholar to lead the project and usher us in and reached out to a few people with the plea. Though every senior scholar told us no, they also told us they believed in our project and in us to complete it and offered to help in other ways. Our series editor, Jodi O'Brien, agreed. It took hearing this a few times and checking in with one another to accept that we would co-edit alone. Yet, we weren't alone. We had an advisory board of trusted scholars whom we could check in with when needed—thank you, Joyce Bell and Nikki Jones.[26] We also had people on the "dream team" who, in responding to some query, would write something that probably seemed unremarkable to them but buoyed us.

We also wanted to bring in students whom we could train along the way, and help our team grow. What could we honestly offer them? What could we ask of them? What would set up the project expectations and relationships? We put out a call at our universities and brought on two Black women graduate students in the social sciences, Jasmine Kelekay and Tashelle Wright. We created a resource guide to onboard the team, all reading essential works, like those by Brewer and Collins, to share perspectives on how they could ground our work, and we talked explicitly about collaborative experiences, including what had worked well or challenged us on prior projects. We were sure to begin every meeting with personal check-ins, which for us is part of the work. As the book process continued, our meetings shifted from merely being at different campuses to being in different countries. We included visibility practices to acknowledge the graduate students' work, like including their names on the *BFS* email signature line or showing screenshots of team meetings when presenting at large conference panels. And, on the suggestion of our editor, we placed the reflection we asked them to write for a subsection of our introduction as a standalone in the book's front matter.

In discussing the tremendous response to the call for papers (over 80 abstracts, with even more coming in after the deadline) with our series editor and Routledge editor, multiple ideas emerged. Our editors suggested an additional project—a handbook that would serve as a reference book at libraries, similar to others, that would cover key areas regarding methods and subfields in sociology (and related fields). Though we did not have the capacity to take the lead on a project of this size, we curated an interest list for those who might take it on to support them in the major endeavor of collective knowledge creation. Our discussions with the press also led to consideration of the digital presence this book could have. It is one thing to know how to tweet; it is another to "think digital," as became clear after our first meeting with Melissa Brown, then a PhD student and founder of BlackFeminisms.

com, who had responded to our inquiry about anyone wanting to help create a linked *BFS* website and thus became our digital editor. As our digital editor, she asked questions that before the call we had thought we knew the answers to, and we later laughed at our limited understanding of online spaces. It is both humbling and inspiring to be able to engage with a range of generations throughout this process and learn from all.

Once we narrowed the list of contributors to the volume, we considered how to build community. We first attempted to do this through taking advantage of conference time to share space with each other. We orchestrated this by sending calls prior to the conference, encouraging folks to show up at one another's sessions, and planning meetups when possible. At ASA in 2019 we hosted a breakfast for those who could attend (see Appendix A). We encouraged cross-citing throughout the volume by sharing the authors' titles with one another and adding editorial comments about connections between pieces when we saw them. The digital space has also been a place of connection—for example, one contributor hosts online yoga for people of color, which opened other contributors to different embodied possibilities even before the pandemic.

Along the way we've also been supported by a few "savvy tricksters," the white allies who understand their place as gatekeepers in white-dominated academe and who actively use their institutional authority to disrupt the entrenched practices of the dominant group.[27] We hope to have made a community within this volume that continues to grow and shape spaces beyond the pages of the book.

We are also reflective about who we are and the privileges we carry that helped make this book a reality. What does it mean that both *NBS* and *BFS* are edited by faculty who graduated from doctoral programs at well-resourced R1/Carnegie "very high research productivity" institutions? How did that allow us to engage with the discipline in ways that led to the accumulation of resources, including visibility? How does our current location in California shape our experience and view of race, Blackness, and knowledge? How does us both embodying some levels of advantage—lighter skin, "good hair," cisgender, straight(ish) and many others—position us to be able to pursue a volume like this? At the same time, how does the fact that those advantages did not keep some of our colleagues from engaging in myriad unprofessional behaviors directed at us perfectly position us to pursue this project? Whose stories have we missed, and how will we make sure we leave the door open for them? Questions and tensions continue throughout our work and are reflected in this volume.

Layout of the Volume

There were many ways for us to organize this volume. We encourage deep engagement with the volume, though each part and essay can be enjoyed on its own. In creating the structure, we emphasized what Black feminist sociology does for us as individuals, scholars, and interpretive communities.

In Part 1 we revisit legacies of Black feminist sociology and explore *how they ground us*. In Part 2 we delve into Black feminist sociological communities and share *how they speak to us*. Part 3 covers Black feminist sociology epistemologies and uncovers *what they reveal to us*. Part 4 then moves to Black feminist sociological methodologies and describes *what they teach us*. Finally, Part 5 encourages us to imagine Black feminist sociological futures and envision *what they create for us*.

Love, Joy and Fun

In a Black feminist sociological project, we conceive of love consistent with the ethos of agape—a way of doing that seeks to minimize the load we carry and escalate kindness, grace, support, uplift, reflection, and care. To do so means you have to be open to extending love and embracing love. A BFS love moves beyond words into actionable items, but it also includes joy and flat-out fun.

We loved doing this work, but it was not always easy. We had to set boundaries and revisit them if they weren't upheld. We sometimes got things wrong—whether it be a missed deadline, canceled meeting or over-sharing of information—and when we recognized it, we apologized and did our best to avoid it in the future. We extended grace to ourselves and those involved in this project; we rejected perfectionism. We did not bite our tongues, but even in those moments of correction we centered our words on love. We focused on listening until we understood. Reading these abstracts, extended abstracts, and chapters was a joy even if the topic wasn't something that interested us personally. It was just exciting to see all this work in one place. The idea of a creating a Spotify playlist comprising songs that each author identified with their chapter emerged.

We mostly celebrated; we found joy in other's joy. This means we were purposeful in rejoicing. We toasted virtually when we signed our contract, and in person when we received good news. We pushed each other to take breaks, or to meet a deadline, or to find time to run three miles during a busy conference. We sent memes that would make one another laugh out loud, international postcards, and a celebratory "Tenured AF" mug. We built friendships that are hard to find in the academy and that will be cherished for years to come. We put love into every step of this project and we hope others fall in love with the project too. *we love to see it*

Moving Forward When the World Is Too Much

Amid finalizing this volume, we are contending with a deadly pandemic, a racial uprising in response to more publicized police murders and the historic election of US Vice President Kamala Harris for the Democratic Party during a time when so much is at stake with our political offices. This time represents new realities shaped by long-standing problems. A time when again people have to contend with differences between representation and dismantling systems of oppression.[28]

Initially in the pandemic there were flurries of activity and moments of reflection at educational institutions and calls to be mindful of the mental health of students given the context. Then . . . back to business as usual, the business of the academy, or at least the "new normal." A new normal of signing liability forms and designating another faculty member to take over your course in case you get sick (or die). A new normal where sheltering in place means you might be safe from the pandemic but not wildfires (and definitely not police). A time when male-identified academics are sending out more articles than ever, whereas women and mothers are suffering.[29] A time when White people, including some sociologists, "discovered" that racism exists, and suddenly became qualified to do research on it and garner grants, even as they have spent years ignoring the racism perpetuated in their own departmental hallways.[30] When inequity is identified, but un-interrogated. As activist Sonya Renee Taylor said of the attempts to return to "normal":

> We will not go back to normal. Normal never was. Our pre-corona existence was never normal other than we normalized greed, inequity, exhaustion, depletion, extraction, disconnection, confusion, rage, hoarding, hate and lack. We should not long to return, My friends. We are being given the opportunity to stitch a new garment. One that fits all of humanity and nature.[31]

This time tells us, unequivocally, that we must recognize the present and future of our discipline is a Black feminist sociology. We are the way forward.

Notes

1. The name draws on bell hooks. 1993. *Sisters of the Yam: Black Women and Self-Recovery*. Boston, MA: South End Press.
2. See Cite Black Women. www.citeblackwomencollective.org/. Accessed August 20, 2020.
3. US Department of Education, National Center for Education Statistics. 2017. *The Condition of Education 2017* (NCES 2017–144), Characteristics of Postsecondary Faculty. Washington, DC: Author.
4. Email correspondence with Teresa Ciabattari, director of academic and professional affairs, American Sociological Association. September 11, 2018.
5. *Black Feminist Sociology* is capitalized as the title of the volume, whereas Black feminist sociology (BFS) represents a larger framework as explained in this introduction.
6. Rose M. Brewer. 1989. "Black Women and Feminist Sociology: The Emerging Perspective." *The American Sociologist* 20(1): 57–70, 68. https://doi.org/10.1007/BF02697787.

7. Patricia Hills Collins's 2018 remarks can be found on the Association of Black Sociologists' Facebook page: www.facebook.com/61066513769/videos/1015657 5934383770.

8. US Representative Maxine Waters (D-California) used the phrase "Reclaiming my time" in a July 2017 Finance hearing when the Secretary of the Treasury began to answer a direct question from Waters with appreciation for her service. Waters repeated the phrase and insisted on an answer to her question. "Reclaiming my time" is the official phrase for use in hearings but Waters's use of it was memefied and became the subject of many opinion pieces and internet songs. Vanessa Williams. 2017. "Maxine Waters Inspires a New Anthem: 'Reclaiming My Time.'" *Washington Post* (blog). www. washingtonpost.com/news/post-nation/wp/2017/08/01/maxine-waters-inspires-a-new-anthem-reclaiming-my-time/. Accessed September 6, 2018.

9. Adia Harvey Wingfield. 2019. "Does Sociology Silence Black Women?" *Gender & Society* (blog). June 4, 2019. https://gendersociety.wordpress.com/2019/06/04/does-sociology-silence-black-women/.

10. Part One of *The New Black Sociologists* uncovers "hidden figures." See Hedwig Less and Christina Hughes. "#SayHerName: Why Black Women Matter in Sociology." In *The New Black Sociologists*, edited by Marcus Anthony Hunter, 3–17. New York: Routledge; Ashanté Reese. 2018. "Zora Neale Hurston and Ethnography of Black Life." In *The New Black Sociologists*, edited by Marcus Anthony Hunter, 62–68. New York: Routledge; Tennille Nicole Allen. "Poking and Prying with a Purpose: Zora Neal Hurston and Black Feminist Sociology." In *The New Black Sociologists*, edited by Marcus Anthony Hunter, 69–86. New York: Routledge, as well as Shaonta' E. Allen's chapter in this volume, "Black Feminist Scholar-Activism & the Crusade for Justice: Lessons from Ida B. Wells-Barnett."

11. For more names see, Amber Joy Powell and Caity Curry, https://thesocietypages.org/trot/2019/02/28/unearthing-black-womens-early-contributions-to-sociology/.

12. https://www.asanet.org/about/awards/cox-johnson-frazier-award

13. See Cite Black Women.

14. As Crystal Fleming reminded the audience during the Cite Black Women panel at ASA 2019, rigid canons are inherently exclusionary. She named a plethora of Black scholars as well as our mothers and ancestors as canonical to our knowledge, the recorded panel is on the Cite Black Women podcast: https://soundcloud.com/user-211649525/s1e9-centering-and-celebrating.

15. Fat Joe and Remy Ma. 2016. "All the Way Up." *Plata O Plomo*. RNG and Empire. Retrieved from https://open.spotify.com/album/7vzvohRzBtrnr3miUJrpAk?highlight=spotify:track:61QSuw5VlC0LTS8WMO356g

16. Patricia Hill Collins. 1990. *Black Feminist Thought: Knowledge, Consciousness, and the Politics of Empowerment*, 22. Boston, MA: Unwin Hyman.

17. Collin's providing a guide for others, like Mignon Moore to write about their experiences within the matrix in the academy. See "Women of Color in the Academy: Navigating Multiple Intersections and Multiple Hierarchies." 2017. *Social Problems*. https://academic.oup.com/socpro/article/64/2/200/3231961

18. Joyce A. Ladner. 1973. *The Death of White Sociology White Sociology*. New York: Random House.

19. Collins 1990, 251.

20. Ibid.

21. SisterSong Women of Color Reproductive Justice Collective started the Trust Black Women campaign in mobilizing against anti-abortion billboards placed in predominately Black neighborhoods: https://trustblackwomen.org/our-roots/.

22. For example, sociologist Crystal Fleming overviews the long-understood yet slim practice of listening to Black women in her book. Crystal Fleming. 2018. "Listen to Black Women." In *How to Be Less Stupid About Race*, 49–75. New York: Beacon Press.

23. See Tami Navarro, Bianca Williams, and Attiya Ahmad. 2013. "Sitting at the Kitchen Table: Fieldnotes from Women of Color in Anthropology." *Cultural Anthropology* 28(3): 443–463. https://doi.org/10.1111/cuan.12013; Lynn Bolles. 2013. "Telling the Story Straight: Black Feminist Intellectual Through in Anthropology." *Transforming Anthropology* 21(1): 57–71. https://doi.org/10.1111/traa.12000.
24. Email correspondence.
25. Patricia Hill Collins. 1986. "Learning from the Outsider Within: The Sociological Significance of Black Feminist Thought." *Social Problems* 33(6): S14–S32. https://doi.org/10.2307/800672. According to the journal's website, this article remains its most read.
26. Bell and Jones are so esteemed that when, after making our selections, we informed the final authors they had assisted us in selection, one author gave thanks we had not told her their role beforehand because she would have been too intimidated to submit.
27. Jodi O'Brien. 2020. "Can I Charge My Therapy to the University?" In *Presumed Incompetent II: Race, Class, Power, and Resistance of Women in Academia*, edited by Y. F. Niemann, G. G. Muhs, and C. G. González, 95–105. Boulder: University Press of Colorado.
28. For instance, where in the same election, Kamala Harris and Stacey Abrams represent two different approaches to politics and getting free.
29. As editor Elizabeth Crooks pointed out to us, there is a lot of complexity here. It is not only that women-identified academics are sending out fewer articles, but that many women and mothers have been pushed out of a plethora of jobs and/or roles because they had no alternative for their presumed caretaking responsibilities. See this piece that Pirtle is quoted in about how the pandemic impacted women academics; Caroline Kitchener. 2020. "Women Academics Seem to be Submitting Fewer Papers During Coronavirus. 'Never Seen Anything Like it,' Says One Editor." *The Lily*. April 24, 2020. www.thelily.com/women-academics-seem-to-be-submitting-fewer-papers-during-coronavirus-never-seen-anything-like-it-says-one-editor/.
30. Courtney Cogburn. 2020. "Who Produces Science During Crisis?" *Items* (blog). September 17, 2020. https://items.ssrc.org/covid-19-and-the-social-sciences/society-after-pandemic/who-produces-science-during-crisis/.
31. Sonya Renee Taylor. 2020. "Sonya Renee Taylor on Instagram: 'We Will Not Go Back to Normal. Normal Never Was. Our Pre-Corona Existence Was Never Normal Other than We Normalized Greed, Inequity, . . .'" *Instagram*. April 2, 2020. www.instagram.com/p/B-fc3ejAlvd/.

References

Allen, Tennille Nicole. 2018. "Poking and Prying with a Purpose: Zora Neal Hurston and Black Feminist Sociology." In *The New Black Sociologists*, edited by Marcus Anthony Hunter, 69–86. New York: Routledge.

Anon. n.d. "Cite Black Women." www.citeblackwomencollective.org/. Accessed August 20, 2020.

Bolles, Lynn. 2013. "Telling the Story Straight: Black Feminist Intellectual Thought in Anthropology." *Transforming Anthropology* 21(1): 57–71. https://doi.org/10.1111/traa.12000.

Brewer, Rose M. 1989. "Black Women and Feminist Sociology: The Emerging Perspective." *American Sociologist* 20(1): 57–70. https://doi.org/10.1007/BF02697787.

Cogburn, Courtney. 2020. "Who Produces Science During Crisis?" *Items*. https://items.ssrc.org/covid-19-and-the-social-sciences/society-after-pandemic/who-produces-science-during-crisis/. Accessed November 23, 2020.

Collins, Patricia Hill. 1986. "Learning from the Outsider Within: The Sociological Significance of Black Feminist Thought." *Social Problems* 33(6): S14–S32. https://doi.org/10.2307/800672.

Collins, Patricia Hill. 1990. *Black Feminist Thought: Knowledge, Consciousness, and the Politics of Empowerment*. Boston, MA: Unwin Hyman.

Fleming, Crystal. 2018. "Listen to Black Women." In *How to Be Less Stupid About Race*, 49–75. New York: Beacon Press.

hooks, bell. 1993. *Sisters of the Yam: Black Women and Self-Recovery*. Brooklyn, NY: South End Press.

Hunter, Marcus A. (ed.). 2018. *The New Black Sociologists: Historical and Contemporary Perspectives*. New York: Routledge.

Kitchener, Caroline. 2020. "Women Academics Seem to Be Submitting Fewer Papers During Coronavirus. 'Never Seen Anything Like it,' Says One Editor." *The Lily*. April 24, 2020. www.thelily.com/women-academics-seem-to-be-submitting-fewer-papers-during-coronavirus-never-seen-anything-like-it-says-one-editor/

Ladner, Joyce A. 1973. *The Death of White Sociology: Essays on Race and Culture*. New York: Random House.

Lee, Hedwig, and Christina Hughes. 2018 "#SayHerName: Why Black Women Matter in Sociology." In *The New Black Sociologists*, edited by Marcus Anthony Hunter, 3–17. New York: Routledge.

McClaurin, Irma (ed.). 2001. *Black Feminist Anthropology: Theory, Politics, Praxis, and Poetics*. New Brunswick, NJ: Rutgers University Press.

Navarro, Tami, Bianca Williams, and Attiya Ahmad. 2013. "Sitting at the Kitchen Table: Fieldnotes from Women of Color in Anthropology." *Cultural Anthropology* 28(3): 443–463. https://doi.org/10.1111/cuan.12013.

O'Brien, Jodi. 2020. "Can I Charge My Therapy to the University?" In *Presumed Incompetent II: Race, Class, Power, and Resistance of Women in Academia*, edited by Y. F. Niemann, G. G. Muhs, and C. G. González, 95–105. Boulder: University Press of Colorado.

Powell, Amber Joy, and Caity Curry. 2019. "Best of 2019: Unearthing Black Women's Early Contributions to Sociology." *The Society Pages*. https://thesocietypages.org/trot/2019/02/28/unearthing-black-womens-early-contributions-to-sociology/. Accessed September 19, 2020.

Reese, Ashanté. 2018. "Zora Neale Hurston and Ethnography of Life." In *The New Black Sociologists*, edited by Marcus Anthony Hunter, 62–68. New York: Routledge.

Taylor, Sonya Renee. 2020. "Sonya Renee Taylor on Instagram: 'We Will Not Go Back to Normal. Normal Never Was. Our Pre-Corona Existence Was Never Normal Other than We Normalized Greed, Inequity, ...'" *Instagram*. www.instagram.com/p/B-fc3ejAlvd/. Accessed November 24, 2020.

US Department of Education, National Center for Education Statistics. 2017. *The Condition of Education 2017* (NCES 2017–144). Characteristics of Postsecondary Faculty. Washington, DC: Author.

Williams, Vanessa. 2017. "Maxine Waters Inspires a New Anthem: 'Reclaiming My Time.'" *Washington Post* (blog). www.washingtonpost.com/news/post-nation/wp/2017/08/01/maxine-waters-inspires-a-new-anthem-reclaiming-my-time/. Accessed September 6, 2018.

Wingfield, Adia Harvey. 2019. "Does Sociology Silence Black Women?" *Gender & Society*. https://gendersociety.wordpress.com/2019/06/04/does-sociology-silence-black-women/. Accessed November 24, 2020.

Part 1

Revisiting Legacies of Black Feminist Sociology and How They Ground Us

Chapter 1

Black Feminist Sociology
An Interview With Patricia Hill Collins

Patricia Hill Collins

Whitney Pirtle (W. P.): In 1986, you published "Learning from the Outsider-Within: The Sociological Significance of Black Feminist Thought" to argue that Black women are marginalized within academia.[1] Nearly 14 years later, in 2009, you were elected as the first Black woman president of the American Sociological Association, and *Black Feminist Thought* has over twenty thousand citations. In what ways do you see the marginalization of Black women still manifest in sociology today?

Patricia Hill Collins (P. H. C.): I wrote "Learning from the Outsider Within" because I could not see space for the kinds of arguments that I wanted to make in my own work within sociology as it was then organized. I wanted to create space for Black feminist thought as a discourse, whether it was in sociology or not. The subtitle of the article, "The Sociological Significance of Black Feminist Thought," speaks to the substance of my argument. I argue that Black women's social location both inside and outside academia fosters an important form of knowledge that is important in and of its own right. My analysis explained how the lived experiences of Black women within racism, sexism, and class exploitation, specifically, the journeys of Black domestic workers between their home spaces and the homes of their white employers, created outsider within spaces. From these spaces, Black women cultivated angles of vision on social phenomena that grew from these lived experiences.

The fact that this edited volume on Black feminist sociology exists is evidence that Black women in sociology are no longer marginalized in the same way. But getting here has not been easy and staying here is not guaranteed. Even the best argument is meaningless if it never gets published or ignored because it strays too far from conventional wisdom. In writing "Learning from the Outsider Within," I had to be mindful of sociological gatekeeping in *how* I made the then-radical argument that ordinary Black women could think and had something important to say. Strategically, I used sociological tools to make my case in terms that would be recognized within sociology. I certainly aimed to gain

DOI: 10.4324/9781003199113-3

legitimacy for Black feminist thought within sociology. But because Black feminist thought is bigger than sociology, my sights were far more ambitious than convincing sociologists. By suggesting that sociology contributed important ideas and methodologies to my approach to Black feminism and that sociology might benefit from attending to Black feminist thought, I hoped to carve out a space within sociology.

But doing sociological work need not be confined within the discipline of sociology. The longstanding exclusion of Black women intellectuals from sociology meant that most Black women intellectuals worked outside sociology across a variety of fields. "Learning from the Outsider Within" spoke to them as well. There is space for my outsider-within argument to travel into political science, anthropology, performance studies and other fields of study. The piece both criticizes sociology for the absence of these arguments and offers a way of remedying that situation. I was not trying to present either myself or Black women as marginalized victims that needed special treatment. That article aimed to create space for Black feminist thought and legitimate Black feminist thought.

W. P.: How do you respond to claims of "racial progress" within the academy and sociology that use your success to back their claims?

P. H. C.: Changing the terms of the debate is the best way to respond to this claim. I know that we should not conflate the success of a few Black women worthies in sociology with the continued oppression of the many Black women who struggle on a daily basis for survival and basic human dignity. Most Black feminist sociologists already know this. It should be clear to us that one biography, in this case, my trajectory in sociology, is no substitute for historical understanding of the bona fide progress of Black women in the sociology as a group as well as the hidden barriers that persist within academia. Clearly these claims rest on assumptions that the system is fair, and all we have to do is work hard enough or have enough talent to excel. What are we *not* doing when we try and answer this question without first putting forth our own analysis of the problem? And our analysis has to rest on our own research.

We need to research the questions that are important to and for Black women, and that often means doing research that is neither trendy, flashy, nor fun. In 1998, I published a chapter titled "On Race, Gender, and Science: Black Women as Objects and Agents of Sociological Knowledge" in *Fighting Words: Black Women and the Search for Justice* that refutes these claims.[2] Building on my earlier argument of Black women's knowledge as an outsider-within perspective, I sketched out a preliminary genealogy of Black women in sociology, naming and emphasizing the important contributions of Black women with doctorates in sociology who preceded me, e.g., Adelaide Cromwell Hill, Cora

Bagley Marrett, Jacqueline Johnson Clarke Jackson and Joyce Ladner. I offer a structural argument that traces the trajectory of when Black women were included in sociology as a discipline, the kind of scholarship they produced, and how that inclusion in turn influenced sociology. Though I wrote this chapter twelve years after "Learning from the Outsider Within" was published, this chapter provides the context for my earlier argument. We have to know our history in order to make informed judgments about the present. When it comes to social justice scholarship, there is no one-and-done stance. Deepening analyses takes time, effort, and resources. And it is a collective effort.

I work in the sociology of knowledge, that space between questions of who gets to do intellectual work and what kinds of things they say. This is one reason that I remain so vigilant concerning the theoretical frameworks that are imposed on us that uphold someone else's agenda, and the kinds of questions that keep us spinning our wheels. Quite frankly, given the small numbers of Black women in sociology when I was an undergraduate and a graduate student ten years later, I look at the numbers of Black women in sociology today as a victory. Yet exclusion is no longer the problem, but rather one of inclusion on whose terms and at what cost. Structural oppression gets at these dynamics. We are sociologists—we have data and we should use it. The treatment of Black women in sociology may be neither equitable nor comfortable, but the arc is trending in the right direction. This is slow, incremental, hard-fought social change, capturing positions one person at a time, and maintaining forward motion. Right now, I'm in the front of the line. I will not always be there.

W. P.: In your ABS remarks, you stated that you felt "smothered in sociology" when you were writing "Learning from the Outsider Within." When you were being smothered in and by sociology, what did you do for a release?

P. H. C.: That word *smothered* really stood out for you. At the time of the 2018 ABS session, I was reading Black feminist philosopher Kristie Dotson's analysis of *testimonial smothering* as a form of epistemic oppression.[3] Her work has been extremely helpful for analyzing what I was experiencing when I wrote "Learning from the Outsider Within." Dotson is part of a progressive cohort of Black feminist philosophers whose edited volume, *Convergences: Black Feminism and Continental Philosophy*, has similar goals for philosophy as those for this volume[4] as well as a broader community of philosophers who study epistemic oppression and epistemic resistance. For Black women, testimonial quieting aims to silence Black women by ignoring, ridiculing, or dismissing what we say. In contrast, *testimonial smothering* occurs when we remain silent because we *anticipate* impending testimonial quieting.

Testimonial smothering is a form of self-censorship that silences us before we open our mouths to speak. Dotson identifies testimonial quieting and testimonial smothering as silencing strategies that are used to suppress Black women's authority to testify in our own behalf, create our own self-defined knowledge, and speak for ourselves. In an ideal world, we should not need the approval of others to speak and to have our ideas heard. But we do not live in that world yet and have to figure out how to navigate this one. Epistemic oppression remains powerful, regardless of how we are positioned within sociology or how nicely people now treat us, because it silences us and possibilities for Black feminist thought.

These silencing strategies never go away, no matter how high you rise in sociology. For me, it has been easier to see how other people are trying to silence or "quiet" me that recognizing how I self-censor myself or "smother" my own ideas. Let me give you a recent example. Before I read *The Racial Order*, I agreed to write a book review of it for a major sociological journal.[5] The standard framework for a book review is straightforward: identify the author's goals, evaluate a book based on how well he/she met them, and then offer an informed critique of the argument and evidence. I was more than prepared to write this particular book review, but I just could not bring myself to do it. Within the parameters of established sociology, this book laid out a seemingly innovative new direction for racial theory. But that was exactly the problem. Its fundamental premise violated a tenet of critical race scholarship that we *challenge* the parameters of disciplinary knowledge, especially the standard sociological theory from which the book took inspiration. In the opening pages of *The Racial Order*, Emirbayer and Desmond simply ignored the vast critical race scholarship that was produced *outside* of sociology as not relevant to their argument. Their argument only worked by excluding copious countervailing evidence in other disciplines, the entire field of African American Studies, and the corpus of work by Du Bois as being theoretically unrecognizable to them. The very name of the book summed it up. With hindsight, I see why I never wrote that review. Avoiding the kind of self-censorship (or testimonial smothering) that I would have endured to write the review was an act of self-care.

Dotson's analysis of the silencing strategies has been helpful to me to explain not just how they worked early in my career (the "Learning from the Outsider Within" phase) but how these strategies suppress the ideas of subordinated people in general. My use of the term smothering in my talk comes from a litany of experiences such as these. To be frank, the work of philosophers on epistemic oppression works has illuminated patterns in my scholarship and that of others. We all smother ourselves to some degree without knowing it. I have yet to find that safe space where I can say, without filters, exactly what I think using the language of my choice to say it. If you read between the lines of my published work, I often offer trenchant criticism of other people's work, but in coded language that may not read as criticism at all. What I don't say can speak volumes for those who know the code.

Zakiya Luna (Z. L.): What is the most surprising aspect of being retired that you wish someone had told you when you started on the tenure track?

P. H. C.: Here is the advice that I would give my junior colleagues: *The tenure track is an institutional arrangement that disciplines you to fit into existing norms. You are not the same thing as your job. Do not use being on the tenure track as shorthand for being a Black feminist scholar. You have to constantly work at becoming a Black feminist intellectual. That is a lifelong commitment.*

I cannot emphasize enough the distinction between my life's work as intellectual activism and my academic positions within the colleges and universities that have employed me. My life's work is committed to using the power of ideas as part of a broader social justice struggle. Much of that life's work is grounded in the experiences of African American women, but t hat work has meant that I had to ask hard questions about how racism, heteropatriarchy, capitalism, nationalism, and similar systems of power harm people and, conversely, the meaning of resistance. In contrast, working my way up the tenure ladder has been important because it provides me with a platform for ideas as well as a site for working for institutional transformation. There's always a tension between the two—trying to cultivate and protect the power of a free mind within colleges and universities that drag their heels at efforts for institutional transformation. While I have assertively sought out and been fortunate to hold academic positions that further my intellectual work, I do not conflate the two.

Because I view higher education as a battleground for institutional change, I cannot think of anything more that anyone could have told me that would have helped me with my tenure track decisions. I arrived with a healthy sense of skepticism gleaned from seeing how my father had been denied an education (he never graduated from high school), how my mother was repeatedly passed over for promotions (she had to train the white men who became her new bosses), and my own battle scars from getting an elite education within my Philadelphia public high school (those four years required serious testimonial smothering). Just as I had arrived in college motivated, self-disciplined, as prepared as I could be, and skeptical, I entered my tenure-line job with the same orientation. What I needed was information and opportunities, not hand-picked institutional mentors who "looked like me" and could help me assimilate into a system that was not set up with me in mind; or that infantilized me because they assumed that, because I was a Black woman from a working-class background, I needed help with my attitude, my work skills, or my assumedly inadequate academic preparation. The delicate dance here is being brutally honest with yourself about your own personal qualities—motivation, self-discipline, and preparation, while seeking out people who really do want to help you, even if it means giving you bad news.

Some things definitely surprise me about being retired from my day job, but I really have no regrets about the path I followed. I am quite happy to not have an academic day job because I am freed from institutional restraints or, as a colleague of mine who retired puts it, becoming *de-institutionalized*. So much of being on the tenure track is constantly being evaluated by others, learning to fit into a discipline, and being disciplined to academic routines. Testimonial quieting and smothering are part of that routine for students and junior faculty. Yet this disciplinary process often become less visible over time because it is incremental, ongoing, and relentless. I find it ironic that in sociology we apply Goffman's framework of total institutions to mental hospitals, prisons, and other places where people are incarcerated, yet fail to see how our own institutions so discipline our everyday lives. Yet for many of my junior colleagues, the academic departments where they work within higher education are well on the way to becoming total institutions that become their lives, if they allow them to be so. Thinking for yourself is challenging. It has been difficult, but I can honestly say that I can celebrate my own successes because I have been brutally honest with myself about my own mistakes. Standing on the bedrock of your own decisions is empowering.

Z. L.: What do you define as the most important aspect of your legacy?

P. H. C.: My work is broad and interdisciplinary, written in dense academic prose, in accessible language, though talks, and with the advent of COVID-19, through media (see, e.g., Oge Egbuonu's 2020 film on Black women titled *(In)Visible Portraits*). Thematically, it reaches out in so many different directions—intersectionality, Black nationalism, popular culture, Black sexual politics, critical race theory, epistemology, Black activism, and critical education. Black feminist sociology is one piece of this broader legacy. My vita details the list of accomplishments that reflect the institutional concerns of my day job. It provides one sense of my life's work.

In contrast, my legacy lies in all the ways that people have thus far received my ideas and how those ideas will travel into the future. I want to be an active participant in shaping my own legacy. If I do not tell my story, others will do so for me, and I may not like what they have to say. I seem to be at that moment in my life where Audre Lorde's words, "your silence will not protect you," ring eerily true. My goal now is to say everything that I want to say while I still can. And when I can no longer do this work, it is the responsibility of those who have used my work to take it up and take it forward. This is especially important for Black feminist sociology. If you do not nurture Black feminist sociology, it will fail and join the littered landscape of progressive projects that have come and gone when they no longer fit the commodity needs of the capitalist marketplace. Black feminist sociology is not something to be consumed in the here and now. It is something to leave behind for others to find.

Z. L.: You advise the audience to not cede intersectionality or Blackness. Could you say more about why that might be important for Black feminist sociology?

P. H. C.: When I say not to cede Blackness or intersectionality, I mean do not cede either *term* to projects that do not take social justice into consideration. Refusing to cede Blackness is fundamental, because as Black women intellectuals, we bring our total selves into all of our work, including Blackness, whether we want to or not. For me, Blackness is not an adjective, a descriptive word that modifies me—as in "I am a woman who happens to be Black"—it is me as in "I am a Black woman." When it comes to Black women's collective knowledge, Black feminism is not simply an expression of a more universal (white) feminism. Rather, Black feminism arises from Black political and intellectual struggles with race and gender as essential intersections of Black women's experiences. In a similar vein, Black feminist sociology is not simply an add-on to mainstream sociology. It cannot nor should not be assimilated into the existing canon. The advice to check Blackness at the door is both bad for us and compromises the integrity of our work.

The refusal to cede Blackness, the sense of being unapologetically Black, is what I really enjoy about contemporary Black women's intellectual work. In the 1950s and 1960s, expressions such as "I'm Black and I'm proud" and "To be young, gifted and Black" claimed Blackness as an expression of self-definition with important political consequences. It is difficult to keep this as a front-stage persona within contemporary academic work, but if a commitment to Black people underlies our work, we do not need to wear our commitment to Black people on our sleeve. If I know that I am committed, there is no need to perform the persona of the "committed Black woman intellectual." In fact, if that becomes yet another controlling image, it may be dangerous to do so.

We misrecognize committed Black people all the time, especially in a period of time where style often masquerades as substance. So how do we recognize Blackness, at least the kind of political Blackness that we all seem to think we possess, when we claim it unapologetically? How do we perform sophisticated versions of Black womanhood in settings that are so varied? I am the same Black woman for myself from one situation to the next, and yet I have to perform different versions of myself from one situation to the next. I have to manage my performance of Black womanhood, especially in situations where being misrecognized is dangerous.

My 23 years in African American studies, as well as my five years working in the community school's movement and my five years as director of the African American Center at Tufts University, have been different sites for both performing and not ceding Blackness. No matter how annoyed I might be with how a Black male colleague treats me, as long as he is not dangerous, I will work with him. That does not mean that I automatically go to a subordinate position. Rather, despite the reality of patriarchy, I recognize that being Black is a shared fate that mandates a shared reaction. In contrast, commitment to Black people has been far less consistent among white men, white women, and other people of color. That is the reality of the situation. No one is going care more about you or your family than you do. And if you are a Black person who does not care about Black people, why would you expect anyone else to do so?

Z. L.: You also advise the audience to not cede intersectionality. Yet you also say that the salient intersections to investigate around a particular question that interests us may not include race. The idea of intersectionality not including race in certain analyses is a controversial idea for many people as they see examples of how some mainstream sociologists take up intersectionality to avoid saying "racism" or "oppression." How do you reconcile these ideas?

P. H. C.: For some time, several of us have recognized the need to protect the radical potential of intersectionality as a critical social theory that can bring multiple groups together in a common struggle. But having a common political struggle does not mean having homogenous experiences. Sometimes, we have to challenge how our allies are using the term itself. For example, in her book *Undermining Intersectionality*, Barbara Tomlinson criticizes the strategies that feminists use to accept intersectionality yet undermine its radical potential.[6] In *Intersectionality as Critical Social Theory*, I also defend intersectionality by presenting an analysis of intersectionality as a social justice project. The issue here is to be quite clear about the necessity of claiming intersectionality on our own terms.

For me, intersectionality attends to intersecting systems of power; it acknowledges the important influence of social movement activism on intersectionality's critical analysis and praxis; and it claims ethical, aspirational goals such as democracy, freedom, equality and social justice as central to intersectionality's mission. Politically, however, a variety of people invoke intersectionality for diverse scholarly and political projects, often knowing little about the term that they use so freely. Micromanaging how people use the term intersectionality will not solve the problem of how easily some people, especially those on the Far-Right, seem to take up the term as a way of rejecting its ideas. When it comes to intersectionality, what exactly is being invoked when "race" is required? Not racist scholarship, for example. There is considerable race scholarship in sociology that you would not want to see in inter-sectionality. Moreover, intersectionality and race are not the same thing. Using one term does not automatically invoke the other. They are not substitutes. So, what is the issue?

I make a similar argument about Blackness and race. They also are not the same thing. To conflate the two sends us off in the wrong direction, especially when it comes to the critical potential of intersectionality. Insisting that people use the term race in their scholarship will not nec-essarily make intersectional scholarship anti-racist or progressive, and it certainly does not mean that such scholarship addresses the interests of Black people or Black feminism. Conversely, condemning all intersec-tional projects that do not contain a racial analysis as inherently flawed or incomplete is also not going to produce scholarship that is supportive of social justice agendas. For example, to address the concerns of women and youth, my colleagues in Poland and Kosovo advance intersectional analyses that look at gender, age and class. Should I ignore their projects because they fail to mention race? How American-centric (nationalist) would that response be? Closer to home, some white Evangelicals criti-cize intersectionality as a new religion. Should I advise them to beef up their racial analysis in ways that would make their arguments stronger? Our response to the absence of race within intersectionality may be one outcome of how we are disciplined within Western institutions to interpret absence as exclusion and marginalization. The fear seems to be that if we don't say race, then the argument is nonracial, or that if a Black woman isn't in the room, then the activity cannot possibility benefit Black people.

There is amazing work on Black women, much of it from elsewhere in the African Diaspora, that does not use the term race. Why should it? It does use other categories such as those of nation and sexuality to pre-sent intersectional, Black feminist analyses. Black feminism in the US is enhanced by this work, as it reminds us to look beyond our own blind spots. Dialogue within intersectional scholarship is like that. There is no such thing as a finished intersectional project, one to which we can use a checklist to ascertain its value. Instead, intersectionality is a project in the making. Developing intersectionality as a form of critical inquiry and praxis requires a deeper analysis of the substance of our own work and that of others. There are no short cuts here. I refuse to cede the possibilities of the radical potential of intersectionality.

Z. L.: I have been thinking about transitions, exits (reading Sarah Lawrence-Lightfoot's book *Exit: The Ending That Set Us Free*): death (of mom, or the current refrain that right now we are in the death of democracy—as if it was robust before the election of 45!). At the end of *Black Feminist Thought*, you write about the importance of dialogue for development of Black feminist knowledge claims.[7] All of our dialogues will eventually end. When you know there is limited time in which to create dialogue, how do you decide in which direction to move forward first?

P. H. C.: One core question has guided my intellectual, political, and personal life—*what will it take for Black people to be free?* What a simple question with so many layers of complexity. This question serves as a touchstone for my decisions. It is a question of Black existence that will have no clear answer in my life. But I think it is the question I needed to ask. Any and all dialogues that might further that question have provided the particulars for prioritizing what I needed to do first and what could wait for later, assuming that I would get a later to do it. For me, dialogues are not superficial conversations on social media or with people who have no clue who I am. Dialogues are challenging ways of relating to one another, intellectually and politically, across differences, in order to deepen our humanity.

My work on intersectionality is grounded in this question of multiple dialogues. And, after over three decades of serious study and publishing about the complexities of intersecting oppressions and intersecting resistance, I am just coming to grasp the complexity of my very project. In *Intersectionality as Critical Social Theory*, I introduce the metaphor of the journey through dialogues as a methodology for intersectional theorizing.[8] I suggest no rules for where to start or how to decide where to start. Instead, I provide examples of what it means to be both grounded in race and to have a conversation with gender; or how being grounded in sexuality shapes dialogues with class. This notion of dialogical engagement is all very abstract until you realize that these kinds of dialogues lie at the heart of Black feminism. But the bottom line for all of us is that we are all continually choosing and rechoosing the path that lives our ethical commitments.[9]

Z. L.: In talking about *Intersectionality as Critical Social Theory*, you reflected, "In this case, there's a very good chance that the work that I'm doing now, the work that I'm taking into the future, is for a readership that I won't get to meet or see. I'll just have to assume that the next generation of Black women will be there and that my work will speak to them in some way. There's a trust element here, one of trusting in the beauty of the talent and the people who are in front of us, I trust in the fact that, if you oppress people, they will resist. They'll find a way." *How have you managed to find your way?*

P. H. C.: Without a sense of your own priorities, there is no way to answer this question. You never know how much time you will get. As Octavia Butler points out in *The Parable of the Sower*, the only lasting truth is change.[10] This means developing plans in a context of change and changing those plans as life unfolds. Bottom line—you have to live each day according to your priorities, all the while knowing that you will make mistakes and for-giving yourself when you do. Currently, I have a sense of urgency for each one of my current writing projects because it could very well be my last one. This is why I strive for excellence, even though I do not always achieve it. This book, paper, talk, or course offering may be my last one.

I was never expected to be doing what I have done—when you understand how power works, both through study and through your own expe-riences as a way of knowing, you understand how everything can be taken away from you so quickly. Money won't protect you; status won't protect you, your beauty, or your credentials—we have so many histori-cal examples of people who did everything right and who lost it all. That said, I am writing within and to the here and now. And since my work is on intellectual resistance, that's the part of the here and now to which I dedicate my time and talents. Taking shortcuts undermines excellence. You never know how good you could have been because you took the easy road. Moreover, you do a disservice to all those who depend on you if you take too many. We have enough leaders like that—why would we cultivate those qualities within ourselves?

W. P.: How have you approached self-care, individually or collectively?

P. H. C.: I definitely have been caring for myself throughout my career and have shared some strategies in this interview. As I used to say to my students in Africana Studies, "If I don't survive, I can't help you." No paycheck will ever be big enough to compensate you for abuse that undermines your survival. Self-care starts with your own survival, but it need not end there. In academic settings, my sense of self-care has centered on using my intellectual work to "write myself free" as it were. I make sure that my intellectual work energizes me and protects me from assault. In "Learning from the Outsider Within," I aimed to create a space for myself and others that would minimize testimonial quiet-ing and smothering. Preserving the power of a free mind is an essential aspect of self-care. This does not mean that I have no life outside aca-demia. Far from it, I live my life according to my priorities, and care for myself. Over my long career, being a faculty member was my day job—when it affirmed me, I thrived. When it did not, I fought to change my circumstances. And when my circumstances beat me down, I left.

W. P.: You started your comments at the 2018 ABS Author Meets Legacy panel by noting that the legacy of Black Feminist Thought is "you" (the audience). You ended your powerful remarks at ABS suggesting that our work becomes transformative by "imagining those possibilities, that we ourselves cannot live." What imaginations do you have for the future of Black feminist sociology?

P. H. C.: I think the future of Black feminist sociology lies in a pragmatic assessment of what kind of project it is and what kind of project it might become. We began this interview with the concept of outsider-within knowledge. The future of Black feminist sociology lies in its potential to remain an outsider-within project. As a knowledge project, it has a presence *within* sociology and has to navigate that. But it also has a presence *within* the broader context of a Black diasporic feminism that has been facilitated by new transportation and communication technologies. It is constantly crossing multiple borders. At the same time, Black feminist sociology has to craft its own independent project that stands apart from both sociology within the academy and Black feminism outside it. It is a form of local knowledge, the peculiar placement of Black women who were never meant to do intellectual work within structures that were not set up with us in mind.

What does it mean to imagine possibilities that we ourselves cannot live within these outsider-within spaces we create for ourselves? Our journeys are clearing the landscape so that we can breathe (or perhaps exhale) in the here and now. We are enjoying the results of the intellectual, political, physical, and emotional labor of Black women who came before us but who cannot be with us. As we move through the now, we lay a foundation for those who follow us. My imaginings take inspiration from your aspirations and actions. I hope to be able to listen to all the music and spoken word poetry both in the US and in the Diaspora that speaks from the soul of Black women. I hope to be able to see an effective critical Black feminist sociology whose science is so tight that the algorithms of oppression erode in the face of your brilliance. Talking about Black Girl Magic should be a starting place and not an ending place for Black women's self-care and self-affirmation. I want history rewritten now that we have the digital tools to do it in archives that were long off limits to us. I want to see enhanced literacy to be able to "read" anything that faces us. I want a Black feminist politics that is unapologetic, and a Black feminist sociology that understands what it needs to do and gets it done. The seeds of that future are already in our present because they have been lovingly given to us by our past. When I talk about Black women, I see that future in the faces of now. That is your talent and your beauty.

Notes

1. This chapter draws on Collins' transcribed talk from the Association of Black Sociologists 2018 meeting; Patricia Hill Collins. 1986. "Learning from the Outsider Within: The Sociological Significance of Black Feminist Thought." *Social Problems* 33(6): 14–32.
2. Patricia Hill Collins. 1998. *Fighting Words: Black Women and the Search for Justice*, 95–123. Minneapolis: University of Minnesota Press.
3. Kristie Dotson. 2014. "Conceptualizing Epistemic Oppression." *Social Epistemology* 14(March): 1–23.
4. Maria Del Guadalupe Davidson, Kathryn T. Gines, and Donna-Dale L. Marcano (eds.). 2010. *Convergences: Black Feminism and Continental Philosophy*. Albany, NY: State University of New York Press.
5. Mustafa Emirbayer and Matthew Desmond. 2015. *The Racial Order*. Chicago, IL: University of Chicago Press.
6. Barbara Tomlinson. 2019. *Undermining Intersectionality: The Perils of Powerblind Feminism*. Philadelphia, PA: Temple University Press.
7. Patricia Hill Collins. 2000. *Black Feminist Thought: Knowledge, Consciousness, and the Politics of Empowerment*. London: Routledge.
8. Patricia Hill Collins. 2019. *Intersectionality as Critical Social Theory*. Durham, NC: Duke University Press.
9. Ibid., 201–217.
10. Octavia E. Butler. 1993. *Parable of the Sower*. New York: Grand Central Publishing.

References

Butler, Octavia E. 1993. *Parable of the Sower*. New York: Grand Central Publishing.

Collins, Patricia Hill. 1986. "Learning from the Outsider Within: The Sociological Significance of Black Feminist Thought." *Social Problems* 33(6): 14–32.

Collins, Patricia Hill. 1998. *Fighting Words: Black Women and the Search for Justice*. Minneapolis: University of Minnesota Press.

Collins, Patricia Hill. 2000. *Black Feminist Thought: Knowledge, Consciousness, and the Politics of Empowerment*. New York: Routledge.

Collins, Patricia Hill. 2019. *Intersectionality as Critical Social Theory*. Durham, NC: Duke University Press.

Davidson, Maria Del Guadalupe, Kathryn T. Gines, and Donna-Dale L. Marcano (eds.). 2010. *Convergences: Black Feminism and Continental Philosophy*. Albany, NY: State University of New York Press.

Dotson, Kristie. 2014. "Conceptualizing Epistemic Oppression." *Social Epistemology* 14(March): 1–23.

Emirbayer, Mustafa, and Matthew Desmond. 2015. *The Racial Order*. Chicago, IL: University of Chicago Press.

Tomlinson, Barbara. 2019. *Undermining Intersectionality: The Perils of Powerblind Feminism*. Philadephia, PA: Temple University Press.

Chapter 2

The Black Feminist Roots of Scholar-Activism

Lessons From Ida B. Wells-Barnett

Shaonta' E. Allen

> Black women cannot afford to be fools of any type, for their devalued status denies them the protections that white skin, maleness, and wealth confer. This distinction between knowledge and wisdom, and the use of experience as the cutting edge dividing them, has been key to Black women's survival.
> —Patricia Hill Collins[1]

As a little Black girl growing up in Washington state, I was always eager to learn about Black history and culture. Where I'm from, the Black population was so small that the only other Black people I knew were immediate family members and friends from church. It became a hobby of mine to learn as much as I could about people who looked like me. Often, I would peruse through library aisles seeking books about Black girls and women. These stories about Black women particularly captivated my interest because the only Black woman I learned about in school was Rosa Parks and the amazing work she did to catalyze the Montgomery bus boycott. One weekly trip to the library would have a long-lasting impact on my trajectory as a Black girl and as a scholar. I pulled a book from the shelf about Ida B. Wells, and as I read her biography, I became very confused. Like Rosa Parks, she took a stand against racism while riding on public transportation. But she did it 71 years prior, yet I was never taught her name.[2] This deeply troubled me, even at a young age, and further ignited my spirit of curiosity about the told and untold stories of Black girls and women. As I've discovered more and more about Ida B. Wells-Barnett, I've been inspired by her legacy and have committed to using my sociological toolkit to continue the intellectual and applied work that she began so long ago for Black liberation.

Recent debates within the discipline have contested what it means to "do sociology" today. Black feminist sociologists, like myself, are uniquely implicated by these debates. Despite the strong tradition of using our words and our works to actualize Black liberation, epistemic injustice has resulted in the exclusion of many Black feminist foremothers from the cannon of classical sociologists.[3] Here, I intervene to reclaim the

DOI: 10.4324/9781003199113-4

Black feminist contributions to sociological praxis. I ask, what can Black feminist sociologists of the past teach Black feminist sociologists today? More specifically, what can our sociological foremothers teach us about the value of scholar-activism, an often-used yet rarely conceptualized term? To answer these questions, I draw attention to several foremothers but center and highlight prominent Black feminist sociologist, Ida B. Wells-Barnett. In doing so, I conduct historical analyses of notable events throughout her life to identify four lessons about contemporary scholar-activism. She is a premier case from which to theorize because, as Black feminist scholar and cultural critic Brittney Cooper notes, "Ida B. Wells is usually the race woman most associated with the work of racial agitation."[4] In the context of this agitation, Ida B. produced scholarship that orchestrated social change. Per her and others' example, Black feminist scholar-activists today know to use our bodies, our platforms, our research, and our organizations to comprehensively critique and actively deconstruct white-supremacist, capitalist, cis-heteropatriarchal systems.

For centuries our Black feminist foremothers have addressed the nuanced marginalization of Black womanhood. From the notable Anna Julia Cooper, Mary Church Terrell, Zora Neale Hurston, Pauli Murray, Maria Stewart, and Sojourner Truth to Patricia Hill Collins, Audre Lorde, bell hooks, the Combahee River Collective, Alice Walker, Kimberlé Crenshaw, and Angela Davis, among others[5]—these foremothers have articulated the ways race and gender work together to impact the lived experiences of Black women, even as some did not claim the term "feminist." Many texts weave together the genealogy of Black women's intellectual thought, such as Toni Cade Bambara's *The Black Woman*, Beverly Guy-Sheftall's *Words of Fire*, Kimberly Springer's *Still Lifting, Still Climbing*, Paula Giddings's *When and Where I Enter*, and most recently Brittney Cooper's *Beyond Respectability*. Despite these works detailing the succession of Black feminist thought, there are many scholars' and activists' names we are unable to say due to race- and gender-based erasure. Du Bois described this simultaneous sense of scholastic abandonment and wonder: "There are scattered in forgotten nooks and corners throughout the land, Negroes of some considerable training, of high minds, and high motives, who are unknown to their fellows, who exert far too little influence."[6] The influence of both named and unnamed foremothers, however, is carried on through Black feminist scholar-activism. I define Black feminist scholar-activism as the process of drawing on the strength, power, and traditions of Black feminist foremothers to inform and encourage the resistance practices of Black women scholars today.

Conceptualizing Scholar-Activism

The foremothers of Black feminist sociology embraced the significance of subjectivity, believing that social research could and should facilitate social action.[7] Black feminist scholar-activism is situated within this disposition as well. Specifically, it is an intellectual orientation that links the study of Black liberation with Black women's tendency to prioritize the "group survival" of the broader Black community. In many ways, doing Black feminist sociology prefigured what has more recently been referred to as "public sociology"[8] or, more specifically, the process of leveraging your status as a producer of knowledge to assess and respond to adverse social conditions.[9] The distinction lies in Black feminist scholar-activism's attention to the interlocking nature of oppression. With the oppression of Black women manifesting in multifaceted ways, there are likewise many options for Black feminist sociologists to embody resistance that will combat it.

Scholar-activism is premised on the ideal of lifting as one climbs. This slogan rose to prominence as the founding principle of the National Association of Colored Women in 1896, exemplifying that the only way to overcome our "linked fate" as Black women in a matrix of domination, was through linked faith in justice and equality for all.[10] We are still lifting and climbing today, as racial and gender structures merely evolve to take on new forms. We continue to prioritize ourselves by prioritizing our communities. Womanist theologian Marcia Riggs notes, "Black liberation requires *group* rather than *individual* progress,"[11] and I argue that through Black feminist scholar-activism, we can link our individual scholarship and our activism to the broader goals of the community.

In our roles as intellectuals, we are distinctly equipped to respond to the enduring issue of inequality. Black feminist scholars have consistently discussed the significance of intertwining scholarship with activism. For example, scholar and cultural critic bell hooks describes the relationship between knowledge and freedom, noting that "intellectual work is a necessary part of liberation struggle, central to the efforts of all oppressed and/or exploited people who would move from object to subject, who would decolonize and liberate their minds."[12] Julia Sudbury and Margo Okazawa-Rey encourage us to engage in activist scholarship, which they describe as "the production of knowledge and pedagogical practices through active engagements with, and in the service of, progressive social movements."[13] Patricia Hill Collins promotes engaging in intellectual activism, which she claims, translates experiential knowledge into an oppositional consciousness that, in turn, produces innovative survival tactics.[14] And, Nina Johnson claims:

> The role of the researcher is both scholar and activist—to make structural inequality visible and legible *and* to participate in its dismantling. . . . It is creating reciprocal relationships between academies and communities, between scholars and subjects, between ethics and practice that are characterized by accountability and are mutually generative and beneficial.[15]

Despite this foundation in the literature, many sociologists remain hesitant to embrace scholar-activism as a natural and longstanding byproduct of our discipline. Here, I aim to rectify this hesitation with evidence from a case study of Ida B. Wells-Barnett. I contend that, as one of the earliest scholar-activists, she has demonstrated how to use our intellectual capacities and subjugated knowledge to effectuate social change.

Lessons From Ida B.

Known as the "Princess of the Press," Ida B. Wells-Barnett cultivated a career out of dispersing her provocative perspectives on race relations in various Black newspapers across the nation. I survey the most notable events throughout her life as a public intellectual and sociocultural visionary to extract lessons that can guide our scholar-activism today.[16]

Lesson #1: Use Your Body

In 1884, on a train ride back to Memphis, Tennessee, Ida B. was verbally instructed and physically made to move from the ladies' train to the smoker car. Although she had purchased a first-class ticket, she was deemed unfit to sit in the "ladies" section because of her racial status. Ida B. refused to give up the seat she had paid for. The conductor then attempted to physically drag her off the train until she bit his hand in protest.[17] In response, he secured two additional men to assist him in forcing her out of the first-class section. Once back home in Memphis, Ida sought out legal counsel and began to compile her case. Upon suing the railroad company for discrimination and assault, Ida won her case and was awarded $500. This incident exemplifies the first lesson in Black feminist scholar-activism: *Use your body to stand up and speak out against inequality*. Ida B. was aware that her experience on that train was racist and sexist. She was not considered a "lady" deserving of dignity and respect because she was Black. Yet, she used her Black body to oppose her mistreatment.

While this incident involved physical altercations, Ida B.'s relentless response signifies how we as scholar-activists today can use our bodies in creative ways to challenge inequality. First, this lesson teaches us to unapologetically be ourselves in white spaces. Brittany Cooper refers to this process as embodied discourse and argues that Black women's bodies can be used to disrupt cultural notions of respectability.[18] Black women will always be hypervisible in a racialized and gendered society, so Cooper encourages us to use our bodies, through this process of embodied discourse, to articulate our ideas and social critiques. By taking her seat in the ladies' train, Ida B. challenged the notions of femininity that excluded Black women. Similarly, we should continue to wear our politics on our bodies, particularly in white spaces, to dismantle exclusive social norms.

Whether it be another #CitcBlackWomen t-shirt campaign during the annual sociology meetings or simply embracing our natural hair as we navigate classrooms and conferences. Our bodies can be used to complicate the politics of professionalism and in doing so create opportunities for change.

This lesson additionally teaches us that we must continue to disrupt the false dichotomy between emotions and reason. Hare argues that

> the Black scholar must reject absolutely the notion that it is 'not professional' ever to become "bitter." . . . If one is truly cognizant of adverse circumstances [s]he would be expected, through the process of reason, to experience some emotional response.[19]

Just as Ida B. demonstrates, we should embrace the emotional responses that our bodies produce. Rather than criticizing and suppressing these feelings, we should conceptualize them as a site of knowledge production and as a source of motivation to resist. Brittney Cooper's *Eloquent Rage* further explains the significance of reclaiming Black women's emotions by discussing and contextualizing Black women's anger, which is often misconstrued and misappropriated.[20] Black feminist scholar-activists today should use our bodies, while simultaneously working to preserve them,[21] to disrupt oppression by drawing on our emotions to produce emancipatory insights.

Lesson #2: Use Your Platforms

In 1891, Ida B. was employed as a school teacher in Memphis. While in this position, she noticed the school district was disproportionately allocating resources and favoring white schools in the area. As part owner of the *Memphis Free Speech* Black newspaper, she used this outlet to pen an exposé to reveal the institutionalized racism she had observed. Once her exposé circulated throughout the city, Ida B. was dismissed from her teaching position. This incident exemplifies the second lesson: *Use accessible platforms to vocalize subversive opinions in accessible ways.* When penning the whistleblowing article, Ida B. set the precedent for "naming inequality" or calling out inequities when we see them. She additionally emphasized the need to be accessible in both what we say and where we say it. Ida B. was particularly known for this. Even prior to establishing her own newspaper, she regularly wrote columns for other newspaper platforms. Biographies of Ida B. note that "her articles, about everything from compelling national issues to local community ones, became so popular that they were picked up by other Black newspapers throughout the country."[22] Accessibility was a significant aspect of her crusade for justice and should be a priority for contemporary scholar-activists, because in order to speak truth to power, you must first speak truth to the people.[23]

Being intentional about accessibility can take on a variety of forms. One mechanism is to utilize social media platforms. Literature suggests that contemporary activism must rely on new media forms to maximize success.[24] Using social media to disseminate subversive opinions and perspectives is particularly efficient. For example, academic blogs and vlogs are becoming increasing popular and allow scholars to translate their scholarship from academic jargon to publicly consumable material. Having academic Facebook, Twitter and Instagram accounts can also be useful in making your intellectual contributions more accessible by extending them beyond a written page to incorporate photos, videos, podcasts, memes, and gifs. Other options include conducting public talks and ensuring all published materials are not locked behind paywalls. Employing these strategies will convert your intellectual labor into an act of public service.[25] These considerations ultimately facilitate raising consciousness by providing people with the knowledge and language to articulate and make sense of their experiences with oppressive social conditions.

Lesson #3: Use Your Research

In 1892, Ida B. learned that her close friends Thomas Moss, Calvin McDowell and Henry Stuart had been lynched. As owners of the successful, People's Grocery Company, they posed a political and economic threat to white dominance and found themselves in a brawl with white store owners that ended in their deaths.[26] Knowing the positive reputations of these men, notice of their murder was extremely unsettling for Ida B., forcing her to criticize lynching as a distinct form of domestic terrorism even more deeply than she already had. This bereavement-based curiosity eventually evolved into an international anti-lynching campaign based on qualitative and quantitative assessments of racialized violence. This exemplifies the third lesson: *Use justice-focused methodologies to empirically measure the social implications of systemic oppression.* Giddings states, "Wells set out to find the truth by investigating every lynching she could. For months, she culled newspaper accounts, went to the scene of lynchings, interviewed eyewitnesses. All in all, she researched the circumstances of 728 lynchings."[27] This research not only demonstrates one of the first multisite, urban ethnographies conducted but further shows that we can and should investigate the injustices within our communities.

Specifically, Ida teaches us to reconceptualize the knowledge construction process. We must learn to value research topics and the methodological approaches necessary to rigorously examine them, even when the broader discipline neglects them. Black feminist scholar-activism requires us to decolonize ourselves from what Crystal Fleming refers to as white supremacist sociology. She urges us to rethink or let go of "exclusionary, elitist definitions of academic 'success.'"[28] Hare[29] similarly argues that a decolonization process is necessary: "On the shoulders of the Black scholar falls an enormous task. [S]he must decolonize [her] mind so that [s]he may effectively guide other intellectuals and students in their search for liberation."[30] Extrapolating this lesson to the present moment, we should, without hesitation, embrace "me-search" despite its stigma within the discipline. Critical research on Black women, by Black women, is powerful and contains liberative potential. So, we must refute the denigration of this scholarship. Patricia Hill Collins notes that "African-American women not only have developed distinctive interpretations of Black women's oppression, but have done so by using alternative ways of producing and validating knowledge itself."[31] It is up to Black feminist scholar-activists to continue this epistemological tradition. Just as Ida B. set out to determine for herself the circumstances of her friends' deaths, we should take up scholarly interest in the social conditions that impact our friends, families, and broader communities as well.[32]

Lesson #4: Use Your Network and Affiliations

Beginning in 1893, Wells-Barnett helped cofound several prominent organizations.[33] A few examples include the National Association of Colored Women and the National Association for the Advancement of Colored People. Some lesser known organizations she helped establish include the Alpha Suffrage Club and the Afro-American League. Her commitment to fostering unification among the Black community exemplifies the final lesson: *Create organizations and cultivate spaces where Black experiences are validated, and mobilization can occur.* Black feminist scholar-activists operating within academia occupy an "outsider-within" status. Patricia Hill Collins describes outsiders-within as "individuals whose marginality provide a distinctive angle of vision of these intellectual and political entities."[34] The outsider-within vantage point is often challenged and contested, so spaces where it is embraced and put into action remain necessary.

The historic moment when many Black organizations were founded is often referred to as the "club movement." Riggs notes that creating clubs was an "act of self-determination [for Black organizations] to address the particular concerns of Black women and all Black people."[35] These clubs encouraged radical knowledge production and used that knowledge to imagine solutions to social problems. Ida B. was committed to planting these organizations because she knew that within these spaces Black women would be "empowered to reinterpret the dominant racial, sexual, and class ideologies which oppressed them as women, while providing programs that addressed the oppression of Black people."[36]

To ensure that we continue to reinterpret social conditions, we must make it possible for those with various outsider-within statuses to share space. Today, scholars can seek membership in sociological organizations and sections/divisions that align with marginalized statuses and subversive ideologies. These include the Association of Black Sociologists, the Sociologists for Women in Society, and the Association of Humanist Sociology as well as the American Sociological Association's Section on Racial and Ethnic Minorities, and/or its Section on Race, Gender, and Class, and the Society for the Study of Social Problems Division on Racial and Ethnic Minorities. Another approach includes creating new organizations altogether or establishing spaces within existing academic conferences by organizing sessions that feature scholars who do justice-focused research. Some examples include the newly founded Cite Black Women Collective and the Black Women's Studies Association. The final suggestion is to use social networking apps and features to create electronic spaces, like private Facebook groups, Slack, or GroupMe chats, where solidarity and community can be built. Community organizations and spaces provided Ida B. with necessary resources to sustain her activist agenda. Similar resource-mobilization can occur today.

Conclusion: Lifting, Climbing, and Crusading for Justice

Our Black feminist foremothers have embodied theory as a form of resistance in many ways and in doing so have established radical intellectual traditions. Their scholarly and activist imprints abound. Ida B.'s legacy particularly informs our understanding of scholar-activism because, throughout her life, she utilized varied approaches to demonstrate radical resistance, reach diverse audiences, and emphasize the urgency of social justice work. She once stated, "Somebody must show that the Afro-American race is more sinned against than sinning, and it seems to have fallen upon me to do so."[37] It is with this same energy that scholar-activism thrives today as Black women continue to make contributions to social theory and social change. Ida B.'s embodied resistance teaches contemporary Black feminist sociologists how to convert gendered and racist exclusion into opportunities for change. Throughout this chapter, I've surveyed her actions to reveal the Black and feminist roots of scholar-activism while also extracting four lessons on how to do Black feminist sociology: (1) Use your body to stand up and speak out against inequality. (2) Use accessible platforms to vocalize subversive opinions in accessible ways. (3) Use justice-focused methodologies to empirically measure the social implications of systemic oppression. (4) Create organizations and cultivate spaces where Black experiences are validated and mobilization can occur. This is not an exhaustive list. The scholar-activist identity additionally requires reflexivity regarding one's approach toward teaching and serving as well. For example, scholar-activists must be intentional about formulating their pedagogical practices and their attitudes toward institutional service work, valuing the ability of both to significantly impact future generations of Black feminist and justice-focused scholars.

Although Black feminist scholar-activism particularly aims to produce emancipatory rewards for Black women, the fruits of such labor will undoubtedly extend beyond the Black community. As the preeminent Combahee River Collective statement proclaims, "If Black women were free, it would mean that everyone else would have to be free, since our freedom would necessitate the destruction of all systems of oppression."[38] Investment in Black feminist scholar-activism, then, is necessary to push the discipline of sociology toward fulfilling its radical potential. As Collins notes, "Public sociology demands that we consider the major issues of the day and that we bring tools of sociological analysis and empirical research to bear on them"[39]—doing so "breathes new life" into the discipline.

While sociology could undoubtedly benefit from inhaling a social-justice focus, as Black feminist scholar-activists, we must not fool ourselves into thinking that our discipline will be overtly welcoming to radical work. Sudbury and Okazawa-Rey note that "research with emancipatory intentions is inevitably troubled by unequal power relations."[40] Ida B. faced significant consequences and backlash for her uncompromising commitment to Black liberation. Speaking her truth to power often resulted in attacks on her newspaper's editorial office, and at times she received threats of physical harm, included lynching. For instance, the findings from her lynching investigation challenged the long-standing theory that lynched Black men were guilty of rape. She conversely proposed that white women were actively pursuing Black men and ultimately claimed that many Black men were lynched for being "weak enough" to accept white women's favors.[41] Upon publishing these conclusions, her newspaper office was burned down, forcing her to move out of town and seek refuge up north in Chicago.[42]

History further notes that Ida B. had a difficult time maintaining strong social bonds with her contemporaries, citing clashes with Mary Church Terrell, Frederick Douglass, Mary McLeoud Bethune, and W. E. B. Du Bois, due to her radical lifestyle.[43] Her eulogy in the National Association of Colored Women's newsletter states, "She was often criticized, misjudged, and misunderstood because she fought for justice as God gave her vision."[44] Black feminist sociologists interested in embracing a scholar-activist life should realize there are risks associated with doing this rewarding and important work. Some risks include being misunderstood and experiencing fractured relationships in their social and professional lives. The impact scholar-activism has on one's body should also be considered because much physical and mental exertion is required to engage in this pursuit of justice. These risks do not always accompany scholar-activism but are common enough that scholars with more power and protections should find ways to support Black feminist scholar-activists such as institutionalizing policies that would offer protections against these risks.

Despite these costs, Black feminist scholar-activists can remain confident in the utility of their efforts. Activism remains a powerful mechanism to bring about social change.[45] Further, Black feminist scholar-activism reconciles the long-held assumption that Black women are "all body and no mind" and instead illustrates that we are aware of the full capabilities of both our bodies and our minds.[46] As Black feminist sociologists, our scientific praxis involves interpreting social conditions with the moral intention to change them,[47] and we must continue to embrace this disposition today. Beverly Guy-Sheftall's words beautifully articulate what I've argued here: "Contemporary Black feminism is the outgrowth of countless generations of personal sacrifice, militancy, and work by our mothers and sisters."[48] Doing sociology in a way that honors this truth, by wielding strength and power from our Black feminist past, while also offering institutional and collective support to the Black feminists leading the charge, will equip our discipline to ask the necessary questions and do the analytic work required to realize an equitable future.

Notes

1. Patricia Hill Collins. 1989. "The Social Construction of Black Feminist Thought." *Signs* 14(4): 745–773, 759.
2. It wasn't until I was earning my MA in Sociology that I learned about Claudette Colvin, the teenager who also refused to give up her seat while riding public transportation *prior* to Rosa Parks but is rarely recognized for such bold resistance. See Danielle L. McGuire. 2010. *At the Dark End of the Street: Black Women, Rape, and Resistance—A New History of the Civil Rights Movement for Rosa Parks to the Rise of Black Power.* New York: Vintage Books, for more details about Claudette and how respectability politics contributed to her erasure from the history of the Civil Rights Movement.
3. See Miranda Fricker. 2007. *Epistemic Injustice: Power and the Ethics of Knowing.* New York: Oxford University Press.
4. Brittney C. Cooper. 2017. *Beyond Respectability: The Intellectual Thought of Race Women*, 64. Champaign: University of Illinois Press.
5. Here, I intentionally say their names because too often these women are erased and excluded from sociological conversations. Just as the #SayHerName movement intentionally shifted focus back to the women (cis- and transgender alike) who had been overlooked in the Black Lives Matter movement, it is my hope that this chapter will further emphasize the significance in shifting the discipline's focus back toward the canonical voices of Black women.
6. W. E. B. Du Bois. 1996 [1897]. *The Oxford W. E. B. Du Bois Reader*, edited by. Eric J. Sundquist, 45. Oxford: Oxford University Press.
7. See Tennille N. Allen. 2018. "Poking and Prying with a Purpose: Zora Neale Hurston and Black Feminist Sociology." In *The New Black Sociologists: Historical and Contemporary Perspectives*, edited by Marcus A. Hunter, 69–86. New York: Routledge.
8. See Herbert Gans. 2002. "More of Us Should Become Public Sociologists." *Footnotes* 30(July/August): 10; Michael Burawoy. 2005. "For Public Sociology." *American Sociological Review* 70(1): 4–28.

9. See Patricia H. Collins. 2013. *On Intellectual Activism*. Philadelphia, PA: Temple University Press; Adia H. Wingfield. 2016. "Public Sociology When the 'Public' Is Under Attack: Response to Hartmann." *Sociological Quarterly* 58(1): 24–27.

10. See Patricia H. Collins. 2000. *Black Feminist Thought: Knowledge, Consciousness, and the Politics of Empowerment*. London: Routledge.

11. Marcia Y. Riggs. 1994. *Awake, Arise, & Act: A Womanist Call for Black Liberation*, 12. Cleveland, OH: Pilgrim Press; emphasis in original.

12. bell hooks and Cornell West. 1991. *Breaking Bread: Insurgent Black Intellectual Life*, 150. Boston, MA: South End Press.

13. Julia Sudbury and Margo Okazawa-Rey (eds.). 2009. *Activist Scholarship: Antiracism, Feminism, and Social Change*, 3. New York: Routledge.

14. See Collins 2013.

15. Nina A. Johnson. 2018. "For, by and About: Notes on a Sociology of Black Liberation." In *The New Black Sociologists: Historical and Contemporary Perspectives*, edited by Marcus A. Hunter, 154. New York: Routledge.

16. See Ida B. Wells-Barnett. 2020 [1970]. *Crusade for Justice: The Autobiography of Ida B. Wells*. Edited by Michelle Duster. 2nd ed. Chicago, IL: University of Chicago Press.

17. Paula Giddings. 2001. *When and Where I Enter: The Impact of Black Women on Race and Sex in America*, 22. New York: Perennial.

18. See Cooper 2017.

19. Nathan Hare. 1973. "The Challenge of a Black Scholar." In *The Death of White Sociology: Essays on Race and Culture*, edited by Joyce A. Ladner, 67–68. Baltimore, MD: Black Classic Press.

20. Brittney C. Cooper. 2018. *Eloquent Rage: A Black Feminist Discovers Her Super Power*. New York: St. Martin's Press.

21. Audre Lorde reminded of us the sociopolitical significance of self-care: "Caring for myself is not self-indulgence, it is self-preservation, and that is an act of political warfare" (p. 130). See Audre Lorde, Sonia Sanchez, Jen Keenan. 2017. *A Burst of Light: And Other Essays*. New York: Ixia Press.

22. Giddings 2001, 24.

23. See Collins 2013.

24. See Randy Shaw. 2013. *The Archivist's Handbook: Winning Social Change in the 21st Century*. Berkeley: University of California Press.

25. See Collins 2013.

26. See Patricia M. Lengermann and Gillian Niebrugge. 1998. *The Women Founders: Sociology and Social Theory 1830–1930*. Long Grove, IL: Waveland Press, Inc.

27. Giddings 2001, 28.

28. Crystal M. Fleming. 2018. "No Fucks to Give: Dismantling the Respectability Politics of White Supremacist Sociology." In *The New Black Sociologists: Historical and Contemporary Perspectives*, edited by Marcus A. Hunter, 40, 131–146. New York: Routledge.

29. Hare utilizes a universal "he" to reference the general Black scholar. I have extended quotes from Hare to apply to Black women scholars as well. This extension not only reconciles the assumption that all Black scholars are men but additionally highlights the persistent erasure and exclusion of Black women's intellectual contributions.

30. Hare 1973, 68.

31. Collins 1989, 746.

32. See Joyce A. Ladner (ed.). 1998. *The Death of White Society: Essays on Race and Culture*. Baltimore, MD: Black Classic Press; Marcus A. Hunter (ed.). 2018. *The New Black Sociologists: Historical and Contemporary Perspectives*. New York: Routledge.

33. See Beverly Guy-Sheftall. 1995. *Words of Fire: An Anthology of African-American Feminist Thought*. New York: New Press; Lengermann and Niebrugge 1998; Giddings 2001.

34. Collins 2000, 12.
35. Riggs 1994, 63–64.
36. Ibid., 78.
37. Ida B. Wells-Barnett. 1892. *Southern Horrors: Lynch Law in All Its Phases*. New York: The New York Age Print.
38. The Combahee River Collective. 1982. "A Black Feminist Statement." In *But Some of Us Are Brave*, edited by Gloria T. Hull, Patricia B. Scott, and Barbara Smith, 13–22. New York: Feminist Press.
39. Collins 2013, 86.
40. Sudbury and Okazawa-Rey 2009, 3.
41. Giddings 2001, 28.
42. Ibid.
43. Ibid.
44. Ibid., 181.
45. See Shaw 2013.
46. Hooks and West 1991, 153.
47. See Riggs 1994.
48. Guy-Sheftall 1995, 233.

References

Allen, Tennille N. 2018. "Poking and Prying with a Purpose: Zora Neale Hurston and Black Feminist Sociology." In *The New Black Sociologists: Historical and Contemporary Perspectives*, edited by Marcus A. Hunter, 69–86. New York: Routledge.

Bambara, Toni C. 1970. *The Black Woman: An Anthology*. New York: Signet.

Burawoy, Michael. 2005. "For Public Sociology." *American Sociological Review* 70(1): 4–28.

Collins, Patricia H. 1989. "The Social Construction of Black Feminist Thought." *Signs* 14(4): 745–773.

Collins, Patricia H. 2000. *Black Feminist Thought: Knowledge, Consciousness, and the Politics of Empowerment*. New York: Routledge.

Collins, Patricia H. 2013. *On Intellectual Activism*. Philadelphia, PA: Temple University Press.

The Combahee River Collective. 1982. "A Black Feminist Statement." In *But Some of Us Are Brave*, edited by Gloria T. Hull, Patricia B. Scott, and Barbara Smith, 13–22. New York: Feminist Press.

Cooper, Brittney C. 2017. *Beyond Respectability: The Intellectual Thought of Race Women*. Champaign: University of Illinois Press.

Cooper, Brittney C. 2018. *Eloquent Rage: A Black Feminist Discovers Her Super Power*. New York: St. Martin's Press.

Du Bois, W. E. B. 1996 [1897]. *The Oxford W. E. B. Du Bois Reader*. Edited by Eric J. Sundquist. Oxford: Oxford University Press.

Fleming, Crystal M. 2018. "No Fucks to Give: Dismantling the Respectability Politics of White Supremacist Sociology." In *The New Black Sociologists: Historical and Contemporary Perspectives*, edited by Marcus A. Hunter, 131–146. New York: Routledge.

Fricker, Miranda. 2007. *Epistemic Injustice: Power and the Ethics of Knowing*. New York: Oxford University Press.

Gans, Herbert. 2002. "More of Us Should Become Public Sociologists." *Footnotes* 30(July/August): 10.

Giddings, Paula. 2001. *When and Where I Enter: The Impact of Black Women on Race and Sex in America*. New York: Perennial.

Guy-Sheftall, Beverly. 1995. *Words of Fire: An Anthology of African-American Feminist Thought*. New York: New Press.

Hare, Nathan. 1973. "The Challenge of a Black Scholar." In *The Death of White Sociology: Essays on Race and Culture*, edited by Joyce A. Ladner, 67–68. Baltimore, MD: Black Classic Press.

hooks, bell, and Cornell West. 1991. *Breaking Bread: Insurgent Black Intellectual Life*. Boston, MA: South End Press.

Hunter, Marcus A. (ed.). 2018. *The New Black Sociologists: Historical and Contemporary Perspectives*. New York: Routledge.

Johnson, Nina A. 2018. "For, by and about: Notes on a Sociology of Black Liberation." In *The New Black Sociologists: Historical and Contemporary Perspectives*, edited by Marcus A. Hunter, 149–162. New York: Routledge.

Ladner, Joyce A. (ed.). 1998. *The Death of White Sociology: Essays on Race and Culture*. Baltimore, MD: Black Classic Press.

Lengermann, Patricia M., and Gillian Niebrugge. 1998. *The Women Founders: Sociology and Social Theory 1830–1930*. Long Grove, IL: Waveland Press, Inc.

McGuire, Danielle L. 2010. *At the Dark End of the Street: Black Women, Rape, and Resistance—A New History of the Civil Rights Movement from Rosa Parks to the Rise of Black Power*. New York: Vintage Books.

Riggs, Marcia Y. 1994. *Awake, Arise, & Act: A Womanist Call for Black Liberation*. Cleveland, OH: Pilgrim Press.

Shaw, Randy. 2013. *The Activist's Handbook: Winning Social Change in the 21st Century*. Berkeley: University of California Press.

Springer, Kimberly. 1999. *Still Lifting, Still Climbing: African American Women's Contemporary Activism*. New York: New York University Press.

Sudbury, Julia, and Margo Okazawa-Rey (eds.). 2009. *Activist Scholarship: Antiracism, Feminism, and Social Change*. New York: Routledge.

Wells-Barnett, Ida B. 1892. *Southern Horrors: Lynch Law in All Its Phases*. New York: The New York Age Print.

Wells-Barnett, Ida B. 2020 [1970]. *Crusade for Justice: The Autobiography of Ida B. Wells*. Edited by Michelle Duster. 2nd ed. Chicago, IL: University of Chicago Press.

Wingfield, Adia H. 2016. "Public Sociology When the 'Public' Is Under Attack: Response to Hartmann." *Sociological Quarterly* 58(1): 24–27.

Chapter 3

The Radical Black Feminism Project

Rearticulating a Critical Sociology

Rose M. Brewer

Perhaps the best place to begin this discussion is with a brief visit to 20th-century sociological discourses on critical sociology. I contend that radical Black feminist sociology shifts the terrain on which we understand traditional critical sociology. I noted in my 1989 article "Black Women and Feminist Sociology: The Emerging Perspective" that "critical theorists such as Habermas presented an alternative view of sociological knowledge."[1] Also, the Gramscian idea of hegemony brought intellectuals into the processes of domination.[2] These thinkers critiqued intellectuals who failed to question power, domination, and the status quo and understood the critical Marxist insight that ideas bear an important relationship between interests and knowledge. Indeed, so long as conflict of interests exist, knowledge will remain affected and distorted by them.[3] This critical sociological tradition, found also in the work of radical thinkers such as W. E. B. Du Bois and C. Wright Mills, further articulated the idea that intellectuals have political and moral concerns; so, values are inevitable.[4]

The contention that values and interests are implicit in the evolution of sociological knowledge underpins the Black feminist critique of the field.[5] What the traditional critical sociologists did not interrogate was how racism and sexism articulate knowledge production. The erasure of women's knowledges runs through sociological thought. This absence anchored my discussion of the fourth critique of the field in a section focused on Black feminism and the "Intersection of Race, Class, and Gender." I asserted that this reworking of mainstream sociological thought was at the heart of the new Black feminist sociology.[6]

Thus by the time the 1989 article was written, it was increasingly apparent to me that the Eurocentric critical sociological frame was theoretically distorting. It was evident that given Black uprisings over the previous decade, the call to decolonize sociological knowledge and to end white sociology were core to changing the field.[7] Sociology was being challenged, and it was not surprising that the critical sociologists noted in the 1989 article could be interrogated through the lens of Black feminist sociology. The press to decolonize the field by articulating knowledge by those who

DOI: 10.4324/9781003199113-5

live it was a deep intervention.[8] Relevant here was the insight of eminent Black psychologist Kenneth Clark, "the tombs collect dust—from Johnson to Moynihan to the Kerner Commission. The solution is the creation of committed scholars of color who developed emancipatory paradigms."[9] Of course this point demands not just a race perspective but a race, class, and gender analysis. The erasure of race also characterized the increasingly visible white feminist sociology of the period.[10] The emergent Black feminist sociology rearticulated a critical sociology rooted in the knowledges of Black women.[11] Black writers such as Alice Walker and Toni Cade Bambara, too, were crafting the frame influencing Black feminist thinking. I read them voraciously.

When all is said and done it was the political economic underpinnings of Black women's lives that would deeply capture my radical Black feminist sensibilities. When I use the term radical Black feminist sociology, I lift up the transformational component of its logic given racial capitalism. It is not enough to integrate Black feminism into the *existing order* but to articulate a *praxis for fundamental change*. For me the "Combahee River Collective Statement" looms large in how I think about a transformational radical Black feminist sociology.[12] Radical Black feminism is a Black feminism which is anti-capitalism, anti-imperialist, anti-heteropatriarchal, and anti-white supremacist. It aligns with a critical sociology drawing upon Marxist insights while centering race and gender. Radical Black feminism articulates the simultaneity of these systems, challenges the masculinist frame, and presses for fundamental change of the racial capitalist patriarchal social order.

Disassembling Mainstream Critical Sociology

Drawing from Marxism, I contend that a number of strands in the radical Black feminist tradition rearticulates critical sociology. The theorization places front and center the simultaneities of gender/sexuality, race, class, and nation. This might be called a "reboot" and more of the critical sociological tradition. Radical Black feminist sociologists assert that systems of inequality are deeply imbricated with one another and social transformation requires ending all of these systems. This means a rupture with a critical sociology which only sees class or gender or race. The radical Black feminist sociological lens is embedded in political economy. This is an interpellation of political economy by centering gender in racial capitalism. Cedric Robinson articulated the idea of racial capitalism in his foundational analysis, *Black Marxism: The Making of the Black Radical Tradition* (1983). Robinson contends racism did not emerge out of western capitalism but was infused in the system from its very inception—racial capitalism. Gender, of course, was not centered in the Robinson analysis. Given this, the radical Black feminist theorization of political

economy ensures that Black women are made visible and epistemologically robust in the analysis. Labor is not simply at the point of production or a wage question but the expropriation of Black women's racialized
labor, simultaneously productive and reproductive. Violence occurs at the
state level, civil society, and in intimate relations. From enslavement to
the current period, profit is acquired through the intense expropriation
of Black women's labor. Given this, Black women's response is built and
oppositional to the system. The idea is to place at the center of sociological
practice an insurgent frame. Relatedly, theorists of the Black radical tradition have focused disproportionately on Black male radicals such as Du
Bois, Cabral, Malcolm X, to name a few. Centering the dispossession and
exploitation of Black women situated in a racialized gender dynamic and
our radical responses to exploitation fractures the idea of racial capitalism
rooted only in race and class.

Engendering Racial Capitalism: The Political Economic Turn

Early conceptualizations of Black feminist sociology did not consistently
articulate political economy. Critical sociologist William Wilson positioned deindustrialization and economic shifts on Black life in his analyses.
While racing the analysis, Wilson did not engender the argument except
for his tendency to lift up the cultural liabilities of Black men and women.
This is evident in his 1987 book, *The Truly Disadvantaged: The Inner City,
The Underclass, and Public Policy*. In contrast, the work of radical Black
feminist geographer Ruth Gilmore lifts up race, gender, class, and political economy. She directly takes on the gender, race, and class dialectic. In
Golden Gulag Gilmore detailing mass incarceration as a source of capitalist, flexible accumulation under neoliberalism.[13] The political economy of
capitalism matters in the radical Black feminist articulation.

The signature theoretical contribution of Black feminist sociology is
intersectionality. Here radical Black lesbian feminist thinker Audre Lorde's
words are striking, "there is no such thing as a single issue struggle because
we do not live single issue lives."[14] At the time of the publication of my
1989 article I did not have a full sense of how impactful the idea of intersectionality would be. As it turns out, it is a major contribution to theory
throughout the social sciences and humanities and informs the emergent
Black liberation struggles of the current period, including the Black Lives
Matter movement as well as Black Trans and Queer resistance.[15] The scholarship of Black feminist sociologists also correctly identified the through
line of 19th-century Black women's ideas even though the early thinkers
did not have access to the white academy. Even before Black feminism's
visibility in the halls of academe, there was a history of Black women act-
ing on both gender and race lines. Race women such as Anna J. Cooper

and Ida B. Wells-Barnett were active in race and gender struggles at the turn of the 20th century and the early years of that century.[16]

Intersectional thinkers point out that race, class, gender, and sexuality are complicated societal dynamics.[17] Despite its contributions, intersectional theory is not simple; nor is it uniformly practiced. For example, class and gender are central to Marxist and socialist feminist understandings, but, historically, these theoretical approaches have not been raced. Hence, for feminist theorists attempting to understand the mutually reinforcing impacts of race, gender, caste, and class, the challenge has been contending with the deep interrelationality of these social forces. Critical sociologists of the 20th century such as Oliver Cox, for example, argued for the tremendous leveling impact of capitalism despite its intense exploitation of workers.[18] Indeed, neither ethnic identities nor racial oppression would exist long in its wake, asserted Cox. Rather, workers would organize against the intense class exploitation that characterized industrial capitalist societies. Cox noted, "there seems to be every indication that this trend will continue." In *Caste, Class and Race* Cox argues quite cogently that the emergence of racism and capitalism were closely tied. Capitalism gave rise to racism. These two systems of oppression, in turn, became mutually reinforcing. Of course his analysis did not engender capitalism, and, the leveling that Cox spoke of has not happened under 21st-century "color-blind" neoliberal capitalism.[19]

In closing this section, the Du Boisian query (1898) of what, after all, has been accomplished speaks to my interrogation of a similar question regarding the impact of Black feminist sociology on the field of critical sociology 30 years ago. I discussed an emergent fourth critique of the field rooted in the theorization of Black feminist sociology. This fourth critique was deeply interventionist into the epistemological assumptions of sociology. It would incorporate the decolonizing move of Black sociology and extend beyond the gender-only articulation of white feminist sociology and a male-centered Black sociology.[20] This work, however, did not develop an anti-capitalist logic of social transformation.

Praxis

Radical Black feminist sociologists retain the notion of agency/activism largely by incorporating resistance into theorization and by participating in social change struggles.[21] Heteronormativity is deconstructed analytically and in organizing.[22] As noted, the radical Black feminist sociological approach is to think, reflect, resist, and organize for fundamental social transformation. Linda Burnham makes it quite clear that the historical origins of contemporary radical Black feminist theorizing, with an emphasis on the simultaneity of oppressions of race, class, and gender and the interlocking structures of dispossession can be traced to the activism of the Black women of the Student Non-Violent Coordinating Committee.[23] It was largely the insights and struggles of the Black Women's Liberation Committee of SNCC that were vital to the emergence of Black feminist insurgencies of the 1960s and 1970s. Here was the Black freedom struggle beyond a masculinist Black Power. I am clear that this theory/practice extends its reach into the current period and certainly impacts struggles on the ground and theorizing in the academy.[24]

My scholar activism is always deeply informed by theory and practice on the ground. The world is remade in the context of the dynamic interplay of theory and practice—praxis. This is a fundamental assertion of radical Black feminists. While sociology advances the tenet of going behind the appearance of things; it also too often accepts Anglo European conceptualizations—accepting behind this appearance whiteness as the unstated norm.[25] Thus, structural inequality is not dislodged foundationally in the field but remains the reality behind the appearance.

Today there is a carceral system filled with African Americans and a capitalist crisis of accumulation on which this incarceration can be understood.[26] A 21st-century Black freedom movement must be linked to multiple internal struggles for social transformation as well as global change. Black feminist thinkers in sociology have played a signature role in re-centering our understanding of race through an intersectional analysis: gender, sexuality, race, and class. But radical Black feminists name capitalism, articulating how racialized capitalist patriarchy profoundly structures Black life in the context of racism and white supremacy historically and today.[27]

As radical Black feminists assert, racism and capitalism are at the same time highly connected in American history, working in deep relationality with gender. Connecting male domination (patriarchy) to racism and capitalism is often unstated in analyses of Black inequality, but the intersection of capitalism, imperialism, racism, and patriarchy—means that "the race" must be understood in the context of complicated gender and class scripts. If the class and race debate characterized much of the intellectual tensions regarding Black life through the late 1970s and the 1980s, the absence of a systematic gender lens was hardly noticed by the combatants. It would take the emergence of a group of Black feminist activists and intellectuals to bring the issue of gender to the fore.

The discipline of sociology specializing in race relations, in theory, prepares one to research, theorize, and propose new policies. Rarely, however, does this specialty systematically examine gender, race, and class in political economy. Even conceptual standard bearers (for example Omi and Winant's work on racial formation, 2015) refer to but "undertheorize" race in the context of gender and class. They make the strong case for race being a central organizing principle of American society but separate it out from its deep embeddedness in heteronormativity, gender, and class. Omi and Winant have attempted to respond to this critique, but much work remains to be done.

As well, Black feminist theoretical moves have been grounded in the Black cultural experience in the US. It is the recognition of the agency of Black women as actors and movers in the world. Black feminist sociologists have inculcated in the theory the sociological dynamic of agency and social structure. Moreover, radical Black feminism anchors heteropatriarchy's intimate face as well as its political economy. As radical Black feminists Aston-Toure', Brewer, and Binta assert in "Living the Struggle for Marissa Alexander," capitalism and ideologies of male privilege and domination operate in dialectic with Black women's so-called incapacity and the ideological underpinning of male violence is forged.[28]

While the history of the expropriation of Black labor and Black bodies is the foundational context of racial capitalism, mass incarceration, police killings, and economic dispossession are its signature features today. The United States, which has less than 5 percent of the world's population, has 25 percent of its prisoners. This is the highest incarceration rate in the world. Over 2.4 million persons are in state or federal prisons and jails—a rate of 751 out of every 100,000.[29] Another 5 to 11 million are under some sort of correctional supervision such as probation or parole.[30] This reflects a dramatic escalation of the US prison population that has occurred in the past 40 years, a ten-fold increase since 1970.[31] The rate of incarceration for women escalated at an even more dramatic pace.[32] A race/class analysis that erases gender from political economy misses the gendered face of mass incarceration and the global working class. In the US this face is disproportionately Black, female, and located in the lower layers of the working class. The deindustrialization of much of the Black urban core has marginalized young Black men and women from work.[33] While capitalist patriarchy profoundly shapes and articulates gender(s), it is complicated by its deep embeddedness in racial dynamics, very specific anti-Black racism.[34] The missing anti-Black frame has largely come into the field from radical intellectuals outside of mainstream sociological thought. More specifically, while sociologists have articulated the social construction of racism, the idea of anti-Black racism is asserted in the context of on-the-ground struggles such as Black Lives Matter, by organic intellectuals, deepening our understanding of anti-Blackness.[35]

So Where Are We?

Racism and capitalism are at the same time highly connected in US American history, working in deep interplay with patriarchy. Connecting male domination (patriarchy) to white supremacy and capitalism is often unstated in analyses of Black inequality, but the intersection of capitalism, imperialism, racism, and patriarchy are constitutive of the social order.

This means that "the race" must be understood in the context of complicated gender and class scripts. If the class and race debate characterized much of the intellectual tensions regarding Black life through the late 1970s and the 1980s, the absence of a systematic gender lens demanded interruption. It would take the emergence of a group of Black feminist activists and intellectuals to bring the issue of gender to the fore.

As well, the caricatures that are deeply embedded in popular imagery reflect a simultaneous racial, gender, and class ideological logic. So, Black feminist theoretical moves have been grounded heavily in the Black cultural experience in the US. This involves lifting up the self-defining spaces of Black women's lives. This work identifies the agency of Black people as actors and movers in the world. Radical Black feminism is deeply linked to the sociology of agency and social structure. This is a feminist framework rooted in destabilizing white privilege and power simultaneously with broadscale social transformation. Even still, the complexities of multiplicity within Black communities, crosscut by age, region, ethnicity, and class, are real.

Concluding Observations

At the center of Black life today is a 21st-century transnational global capitalism, the social forces that keep the commitment for Black radical transformation alive. The ideological nature of neoliberal capitalism erases racism through the discourses of colorblindness and post racialism.[36] The ideology is reflected in the near disappearance of the public discourses for racial fairness and justice, the dismantling of affirmative action and the embrace of dismantling laws and government policies that support equality of opportunity by race. These retreats from racial justice characterize a good deal of societal racial realities today. Tellingly, the election of Donald Trump and his right-wing white nationalism has both unleashed and reflects the forces of white supremacy deeply embedded in American life. Thus there is a political crisis of legitimization and an economic crisis of dispossession. This crisis is the underpinning of the current political moment. Just as historically, we are confronting a rapacious profit-driven system. It is a world system. This means that the outsourcing and exploitation of workers globally are not disconnected from the economic devastation confronting Black workers in the US. Of course, segments of the white working class are experiencing the threat of economic dispossession and an ideology of white supremacy, as articulated in the right-wing nationalism of Trumpism, appeals to them domestically and across the European world globally. During a period of so-called economic recovery, millions of people in the US remain un/underemployed, most direly Black and Brown communities throughout this country.[37] Recent data from the Brookings Institution show that 53 million Americans currently make a median average income of $18,000 per year. This is 44 percent of the working age population who are living on the edge.[38]

Beyond the ideological and material realities of the current period, Black men, of course, experience excessive amounts of violence, state and interpersonal (as they are gendered as dangerous and expendable) but dramatically less domestic violence than Black women. State violence is expressed in the criminalization of poverty and the dismantling of the social wage. Black women and children are the primary victims of domestic violence, emotional and physical. It is in the home and community that the dispossession of Black women's personhood can be most profoundly contended.[39] Hence the articulation of white supremacist, patriarchal capitalism, unfolds at the micro and superstructural levels. Thus radical Black feminism is articulated through an intersective and dialectical logic, personal and political, state and personal, global and local. Indeed, patriarchal violence is part and parcel of this equation.

New global south immigrants, many of whom are Black women and children, have been forced from their lands through global capital's exploitative logic and are ideologically nested in discourses of racism, sexism, and classism. Indeed, the global struggle against this exploitation is the praxis of radical Black feminism. At its heart is a transformational vision. We must think dialectically, decentering the traditional ways of articulating sociological knowledge. We must understand and struggle against continued practices of heteropatriarchy, colonialisms: coloniality, neo, settler, and internal.

Indeed, my thinking about radical Black feminism is about deploying the frame in retheorizing critical sociology, movement building, and social transformations. These closing remarks flow from that space of energy, care, and a vision that extends beyond critique. Social transformation requires a different political dynamic and sensibility, a different meter if you will. It means a radical re-imagining, practice and theory of change—of how we move with and for ourselves—to create another world. It is personal, collective, but fundamentally systemic. It requires clarity and meaning rooted in the fact that we must be clear about this political moment. We must envision and transform our consciousness. We must be strategic and connected to create that new world. Thus social transformation is a deep process of praxis. That is, change does not happen linearly in the same degree or with the same tempo. Radical Black feminists from Claudia Jones to the Black lesbian feminists of the Combahee River Collective to the radical Black queer feminists of the 21st century understand this.[40] Radical Black feminism locates the imperative of the dispossessed in the center of the empire, as well as the world's people, coming together for change. This struggle must be at the core of our theory and practice.

In the movement for social transformation we simply cannot articulate race, class, and gender in reductionist terms but must move with a critical understanding of the deep interrelationality of social forces for fundamental social change. This articulation is at the heart of the radical praxis of Black feminism. I locate my activism and scholarship in this radical Black feminist tradition, always with an eye on emancipatory possibilities for the social transformation of a highly unequal US and global order.

Notes

1. David Glover and Sheelaugh Strawbridge. 1985. *The Sociology of Knowledge*. Lancashire: Causeway Press.
2. Antonio Gramsci. 2000. *The Antonio Gramsci Reader: Selected Writings, 1916–1935*. New York: New York University Press.
3. Glover and Strawbridge 1985.
4. W. E. B. Du Bois. 1903. *The Souls of Black Folk*. Chicago, IL: A.C. McClurg ad Company; Wright Mills. 1959. *The Sociological Imagination*. New York: Oxford University Press.
5. Rose M. Brewer. 1993. "Theorizing Race, Class and Gender: The New Scholarship of Black Feminist Intellectuals and Black Women's Labor." In *Theorizing Black Feminism: The Visionary Pragmatism of Black Women* edited by Stanlie M. James and Abena P. A. Busia, 13–30. London: Routledge.
6. Rose M. Brewer. 1989. "Black Women and Feminist Sociology: The Emerging Perspective." *The American Sociologist* 20 (Spring): 57–70.
7. Joyce Ladner (ed.). 1973. *The Death of White Sociology*. New York: Vintage Books.
8. Ibid.
9. James E. Blackwell and Morris Janowitz (eds.). 1974. Black Sociologists: Historical and Contemporary Perspectives. Chicago, IL: University of Chicago Press.
10. Janet Saltzman Chafetz. 1975. *Masculine/Feminine or Human? An Overview of the Sociology of Sex Roles*. San Francisco, CA: F. E. Peacock Publishers.
11. Bonnie Dill. 1979. "The Dialectics of Black Womanhood." *Signs* 4: 543–55; Patricia Hill Collins. 1990. *Black Feminist Thought*. Boston, MA: Unwin Hyman; LaFrances Rodgers-Rose. 1980. The Black Woman. Beverly Hills: Sage.
12. Combahee River Collective. 1977. "Combahee River Collective Statement." February 18, 2012. http://historyisaweapon.com/ defcon1/combrivercoll.html
13. Ruth Gilmore. 2007. *Golden Gulag: Prisons, Surplus, Crisis, and Opposition In Globalizing California*. Berkeley: University of California Press.
14. Audre Lorde. 2007. *Sister Outsider*. New York: Crossing Press.
15. Keeanga-Yamahtta Taylor. 2017. *How We Get Free*. Chicago, IL: Haymarket Books; Alicia Garza. 2014. "Accessed at A Herstory of the #BlackLivesMatter Movement by Alicia Garza." https://thefeministwire.com/2014/10/blacklivesmatter-2/
16. Joy James. 1997. *Transcending the Talented Tenth: Black Leaders and American Intellectuals*. New York: Routledge.
17. Kimberlé Crenshaw. 1989. "Demarginalizing the Intersection of Race and Sex: A Black Feminist Critique of Antidiscrimination Doctrine, Feminist Theory and Antiracist Politics." *University of Chicago Legal Forum*: 138–167; Collins 1990.
18. Oliver Cox. 1948. Caste, Class and Race: A Study in Social Dynamics. New York: Doubleday and Company.
19. Eduardo Bonilla-Silva. 2006. *Racism Without Racists: Color-Blind Racism and the Persistence of Racial Inequality in America*. 3rd ed. Lanham, MD: Rowman & Littlefield.
20. Dill 1979; Evelyn F. White. 2001. *Dark Continent of Our Bodies: Black Feminism and the Politics of Respectability*. Philadelphia, PA: Temple University Press.

21. Gloria Hull, Patricia Bell-Scott, and Barbara Smith. 1982. *All the Women Are White, All the Blacks Are Men, But Some of Us Are Brave: Black Women's Studies*. Old Westbury, NY: Feminist Press.
22. Lorde 2007; Charlene Carruthers. 2018. *Unapologetic: A Black, Queer and Feminist Mandate for Radical Movements*. Boston, MA: Beacon Press.
23. Linda Burnham. 2001. "The Wellspring of Black Feminist Theory." *Southern Law Review* 28(3): 265–270.
24. Jennifer C. Nash. 2019. *Black Feminism Reimagined after Intersectionality*. Chapel Hill: University of North Carolina.
25. William Roy. 2001. *Making Society: The Historical Construction of Our World*. Boston, MA: Pine Forge Press.
26. Gilmore 2007.
27. Evelyn F. White. 2001. *Dark Continent of Our Bodies: Black Feminism and the Politics of Respectability*. Philadelphia, PA: Temple University Press.
28. Austin-Ture, Aleta, Rose M. Brewer, and Ashaki Binta. 2014. "Living the Struggle for Marissa Alexander." *The Black Activist*, Issue 3(1): 70–77.
29. Michelle Alexander. 2010. *The New Jim Crow: Mass Incarceration in the Age of Color-blindness*. New York: The New Press.
30. Angela Davis. 2003. *Are Prisons Obsolete?* New York: Seven River Press.
31. Alexander 2010.
32. Davis 2010.
33. Brewer 2012.
34. Taylor 2017; bell hooks. 1984. *Feminist Theory: From Margin to Center*. Boston, MA: South End Press.
35. Garza 2014.
36. Bonilla-Silva 2006.
37. Brewer 2012.
38. Brookings Institution. 2019. "53 Million U.S. Workers Are Making Low Wages Despite Low National Unemployment." November 7. www.brookings.edu/wp-con tent/uploads/2019/11/201911_Brookings-MetroPressrelease_lowwageworkforce.pdf
39. Aleta, Brewer, and Binta 2014.
40. Davies, Carol Boyce. 2007. *Left of Marx: Political Life of a Black Communist*. Durham, NC: Duke University Press; Combahee River Collective 1977.

References

Alexander, Michelle. 2010. *The New Jim Crow: Mass Incarceration in the Age of Colorblindness*. New York: The New Press.

Austin-Ture, Aleta, Rose M. Brewer, and Ashaki Binta. 2014. "Living the Struggle for Marissa Alexander." *The Black Activist*, Issue 3(1): 70–77.

Blackwell, James E., and Morris Janowitz (eds.). 1974. *Black Sociologists: Historical and Contemporary Perspectives*. Chicago, IL: University of Chicago Press.

Bonilla-Silva, Eduardo. 2006. *Racism Without Racists: Color-Blind Racism and the Persistence of Racial Inequality in America*. 3rd ed. Lanham, MD: Rowman & Littlefield.

Brewer, Rose M. 1989. "Black Women and Feminist Sociology: The Emerging Perspective." *The American Sociologist*, 20(Spring): 57–70.

Brewer, Rose M. 1993. "Theorizing Race, Class and Gender: The New Scholarship of Black Feminist Intellectuals and Black Women's Labor." In *Theorizing Black Feminism: The Visionary Pragmatism of Black Women*, edited by Stanlie M. James and Abena P. A. Busia, 13–30. London: Routledge.

Brewer, Rose M. 2012. "21st Century Capitalism, Austerity and Educational Disposses-sion." *Souls* 14(3–4): 227–239.

Brookings Institution. 2019. "53 Million U.S. Workers Are Making Low Wages Despite Low National Unemployment." November 7. www.brookings.edu/wp-content/uploads/2019/11/201911_Brookings-MetroPressrelease_lowwageworkforce.pdf

Burnham, Linda. 2001. "The Wellspring of Black Feminist Theory." *Southern Law Review* 28(3): 265–270.

Carruthers, Charlene. 2018. *Unapologetic: A Black, Queer and Feminist Mandate for Radical Movements*. Boston, MA: Beacon Press.

Chafetz, Janet Saltzman. 1975. *Masculine/Feminine or Human? An Overview of the Sociology of Sex Roles*. San Francisco, CA: F.E. Peacock Publishers.

Collins, Patricia Hill. 1990. *Black Feminist Thought*. Boston, MA: Unwin Hyman.

Combahee River Collective. 1977. "Combahee River Collective Statement." February 18, 2012. http://historyisaweapon.com/defcon1/combrivercoll.html

Crenshaw, Kimberlé. 1989. "Demarginalizing the Intersection of Race and Sex: A Black Feminist Critique of Antidiscrimination Doctrine, Feminist Theory and Antiracist Politics." *University of Chicago Legal Forum*: 138–167.

Cox, Oliver. 1948. *Caste, Class and Race: A Study in Social Dynamics*. New York: Doubleday and Company.

Davies, Carol Boyce. 2007. *Left of Marx: Political Life of a Black Communist*. Durham, NC: Duke University Press.

Davis, Angela. 2003. *Are Prisons Obsolete?* New York: Seven River Press.

Dill, Bonnie. 1979. "The Dialectics of Black Womanhood." *Signs* 4: 543–555.

Du Bois, W. E. B. 1898. "The Study of the Negro Problems." *The Annals of the American Academy of Political and Social Science* 1 (January): 1–23.

Du Bois, W. E. B. 1903. *The Souls of Black Folk*. Chicago, IL: A.C. McClurg ad Company.

Garza, Alicia. 2014. "Accessed at A Herstory of the #BlackLivesMatter Movement by Alicia Garza." https://thefeministwire.com/2014/10/blacklivesmatter-2/

Gilmore, Ruth. 2007. *Golden Gulag: Prisons, Surplus, Crisis, and Opposition in Globalizing California*. Berkeley: University of California Press.

Glover, David, and Sheelaugh Strawbridge. 1985. *The Sociology of Knowledge*. Lancashire: Causeway Press.

Gramsci, Antonio. 2000. *The Antonio Gramsci Reader: Selected Writings, 1916–1935*. New York: New York University Press.

hooks, bell. 1984. *Feminist Theory: From Margin to Center*. Boston, MA: South End Press.

Hull, Gloria, Patricia Bell-Scott, and Barbara Smith. 1982. *All the Women Are White, All the Blacks Are Men, But Some of Us Are Brave: Black Women's Studies*. New York: Feminist Press.

James, Joy. 1997. *Transcending the Talented Tenth: Black Leaders and American Intellectuals*. New York: Routledge.

Ladner, Joyce (ed.). 1973. *The Death of White Sociology*. New York: Vintage Books.

Lorde, Audre. 2007. *Sister Outsider*. New York: Crossing Press.

Mills, C. Wright. 1959. *The Sociological Imagination*. New York: Oxford University Press.

Nash, Jennifer C. 2019. *Black Feminism Reimagined after Intersectionality*. Chapel Hill: University of North Carolina.

Omi, Michael and Howard Winant. 2015. *Racial Formation in the United States*. 3rd ed. New York: Routledge.

Robinson, Cedric. 1983. *Black Marxism: The Making of the Black Radical Tradition*. London: Zed Books.

Rodgers-Rose, LaFrances. 1980. *The Black Woman*. Beverly Hills: Sage.

Roy, William. 2001. *Making Society: The Historical Construction of Our World*. Boston, MA: Pine Forge Press.

Smith, Barbara. 1983. *Home Girls: A Black Feminist Anthology*. New Brunswick, NJ: Rutgers University Press.

Taylor, Keeanga-Yamahtta. 2017. *How We Get Free*. Chicago, IL: Haymarket Books.

White. Evelyn F. 2001. *Dark Continent of Our Bodies: Black Feminism and the Politics of Respectability*. Philadelphia, PA: Temple University Press.

Wilson, William. 1987. *The Truly Disadvantaged: The Inner City, The Underclass, and Public Policy*. Chicago, IL: University of Chicago Press.

Chapter 4

The Language Through Which Black Feminist Theory Speaks

A Conversation With Jennifer C. Nash

Mali Collins and Jennifer C. Nash

What Rose M. Brewer names the "fourth critique" of canonical sociology studies was much more than a Black feminist critique.[1] Black feminism and the "Black feminist intelligentsia" that fought for its undertaking amid myriad sociological debates permanently changed the language of the discipline and the value of this critique itself. Not only has the work of this intelligentsia transformed the discipline explored in this book volume, it heightened an attention to disciplinary, interdisciplinary and anti-disciplinary work that changed the stakes of Black Studies, Black Gender Studies, Visual Studies and more. Black feminism upended the mischaracterization of its radical thrust as a mere menacing appendage to sociology or even Women's Studies and rejected notions that it was a short-lived movement exploiting a "pick me" moment in the incorporation of growing demographic, political, and social changes occurring in the last decades of the 20th century. Black feminism, because of early Black feminist sociologists, in part, made way for contemporary methods, modes, and analytics to highlight Black women's affective locations as knowledge production[2] (Williams 2016)[3] and an "autonomous intellectual and political tradition" all on its own (Nash, 2019).[4]

Recent scholarly and public attentions are drawn to Black women-led initiatives in the Movement for Black Lives. Tarana Burke, a Black woman who began the MeToo Movement in 2006 drew attention to sexual harassment toward women and gender nonconforming people to form an international movement. Opal Tometi, Patrisse Cullors and Alicia Garza founded Black Lives Matter as political protest against the disproportionate rates of police and anti-Black violence in the country. Even the Black maternal and infant mortality crisis, which is attended to through a decentralized, but dedicated population of Black midwives and birth workers, is rarely included as a faction of the Movement for Black Lives. All of these women's work is erased in a larger schema of Black women's contributions to Black feminism.

Proper credit has yet to be given to these women and the long line of Black women activists from which they come. In the academy, we have

DOI: 10.4324/9781003199113-6

yet to fully recognize early Black feminist contributions to what is now referred to as "public humanities" or intellectual work committed to wrestling with the often raced and gendered language of institutional scholarship. In the 1990s, Dorothy E. Roberts and Barbara Omolade's work on Black motherhood helped develop language for how to fight systemic racism and sexism in homes and in classrooms. Indeed, the revitalized investment in diverse publics we see today is deeply indebted to their embrace of the slippery relationship with disciplinarity their work incited.

These activist-scholars inspire my work. They inspire how I live and how I conduct my research. But the value afforded to research on Black women's lives in the academy is abysmal. I'm a Black feminist scholar whose work centers on Black mothers and their creative archives and its reception indicates that Black mothers are a marginalized site of knowledge within Black feminist studies. The embodied and creative archives that Black mothers produce are obscured because they resist the logic of productive labors of which white supremacist capitalist heteropatriarchy can benefit. In other words, how we discover ourselves and document those discoveries resists the institutions that are complicit in our erasure. This includes the academy that divests in noninstitutional archives of Black women. Black women scholars participate in the project of Black feminist theory and practice to counter this erasure. I spoke recently with Jennifer C. Nash, Associate Professor of African American Studies and Gender & Sexuality Studies at Northwestern University, shortly after the publication of her second monograph, *Black Feminism Reimagined: After Intersectionality*, about what it means for Black feminist theory today to be both outside and within institutional boundaries. This conversation gives reverence to Black feminist sociologists, practitioners, and culture workers who made inter- and anti-disciplinary Black feminist work possible. It also honors Black feminist sociological formations as the bedrock of current Black feminist interventions widely made across scholarly discourses today. Here, we explore the standards set by Black feminist sociologists like Patricia Hill Collins, whose work continues to bolster emerging scholarship and the various theoretical contentions within Black studies. Isolating institutional location, the present political moment, and Black feminist activism, this conversation invites an expanded look at Brewer's notion of the "fourth critique" to trace the innovative traditions of knowledge production about and around the lives of Black women.

Mali Collins (M. C.): When I saw the call for submissions for this book, I immediately thought it was interesting how the editors were taking up the task of understanding Black feminism through the disciplinary machinations of sociology. It drew me to think of the ways that Black feminism is martialed differently in different disciplines. The call reminded me that Black feminism, as praxis and theory, provides different treatment to different disciplines and, in turn, receives different treatments from them.

Thinking about these various treatments through that disciplinary lens, how have Black feminist sociologists shaped your work as an interdisciplinary scholar? And who are those most influential people?

Jennifer C. Nash (J. C. N.): It was so funny because when you reached out to me, I was like "huh?" because I have such an ambivalent relationship with disciplines (laughs). This is an interesting question. You mentioned Patricia Hills Collins, whose work I think about in all of my research. In my first book on pornography, I was really interested in Collins's work on the "Hottentot Venus." She has that really short section in *Black Feminist Thought* where she is trying to tell the history of Black women's representation in pornography. That was sort of really foundational for me.[5] And then of course her work on the matrix of domination was foundational for me in thinking about intersectionality. I continue to puzzle over why it is that the term *intersectionality* has had this, kind of, cross-disciplinary life that the term *matrix of domination* hasn't. My new work is on Black motherhood, so I've been thinking a lot about Collins's work on other-mothering and community mothering. So, Collins is someone who I've been thinking alongside for a really long time. She's a crucial interlocutor for me.

M. C.: I think it's really interesting how we see folks like Dani McClain, a journalist, or Patrisse Cullors, an activist and visual artist, who are publishing in academic publications like the *Harvard Review* and *Signs* but are also generating critical work that appears outside of institutional bounds all while engaging in critical activism that is changing the social climates of our lives. And both their institutionally recognized writing and activism is done while citing people like Michelle Wallace or Patricia Hill Collins in *New York Times* articles, right?,[67]

J. C. N.: Totally.

M. C.: It's really interesting. How do you think work like that transforms through and beyond Black feminist sociology? You mentioned Black motherhood, but how does your work on pornography or the visual take up sociological practice in unexpected ways? How does Black feminism allow you to do that?

J. C. N.: Cards on the table: I'm someone who thinks of themselves as an interdisciplinary scholar. I went to a graduate program where we had to get a conventional disciplinary training, and so my conventional disciplinary training was in sociology, but I always felt, perhaps in the Patricia Hill Collins sense, like an *outsider-within*. It felt strange to me to be trained in an interdisciplinary theory and method and rooted in an interdisciplinary department, but also be told that I needed to get a disciplinary training. So, I'm always interested in how Black feminist scholarship—even as it might be rooted in conventional disciplines like Collins's Black feminist sociology—is always upending disciplinarity. When I think of someone like Collins, part of what I think makes her so foundational is that she traverses fields. I was reading Sabrina Strings's new book called *Fearing the Black Bodies: The Racial Origins of Fat Phobia*, and I've been following her work for some time because I've been trying to think about how Black women's imagined nonbreastfeeding is constructed as a crisis.[8] And, again, reading Strings's work I see her as a Black feminist social scientist who's thinking through a set of questions about embodiment and representation, and the construction of Black women's alterity that I feel like Black feminists have been thinking through for centuries. So there is always a larger question about the relationship between Black feminism and the conventional discipline, because for me Black feminism is this kind of anti-disciplinary project, a body of work that literally undoes disciplinary knowledge and the very construction of disciplines. (Laughs.)

***

As a literary scholar developing a Black feminist critique about the treatment of Black mothers who have been separated from their children through both natural and unnatural causes, my work unsettles an archive of Black feminist culture workers and their work. This unsettlement often raises questions of legibility that are above and beyond my own scholarship and certainly precedes my experience in graduate school. For instance, upon addressing the poetry and art/memorial installations of Tamir Rice's mother, Samaria Rice, as critical cultural objects of study, my choices are often questioned. Most critiques I receive are not unlike those made of us who study the lives and experiences of Black women: Is this critical *scholarship? Is work on Black women theoretical enough?*

M. C.: I'm trained in English, right. Even when I'm bringing in visual artwork I'm always getting like "How is this literary?" or "How is this an English project?" or "How are you going to sell this, let's say, on like a job market for English?" And my work, being a Black feminist scholar but also as a Black woman and a Black feminist is always questioned about whether it is "applicable" to some people or if people will understand it, as if I'm interested in being understood!

J. C. N.: (Laughs)

M. C.: How much do you think what you've said about your training has to do with Black feminism in general as kind of a framework or school of thought *or* you being a Black woman as a "monstrosity" in a disciplinary field?

J. C. N.: Yeah. I mean [I] think it's all of that. I think back again to my sociological training in graduate school where it was like we did the classical sociology theory course; we did the contemporary sociology theory course; we encountered no work by Black scholars; and we certainly never encountered Black feminist work, which was shocking, because then I thought, "What are we doing here?" And there was a way in which, well, we maybe feel like, could we at least read Du Bois, could we read Collins?

Those figures were seen as outside of the boundaries of sociology proper, even as those folks were also paradoxically claimed by those disciplines when they make an appeal to how they're "diverse." I think there are all of these collapses that happen where Black women's "monstrous" bodies, Black feminism's "monstrous" intellectual and political work, is seen as an interruption or a corrective rather than its own rich, generative body of thought and debate. I mean Collins is in these conversations and debates with other Black feminist scholars who are trying to think about the meaning of motherhood or standpoint epistemology or spirituality or Black sexual politics. There are debates happening among Black women about what all these key terms mean. But then there is a way in which conventional disciplines, I think, cannibalize someone like Collins, and they're like "Here's [what] a Black feminist has said about motherhood."

I think what's so interesting about this chorus of folks writing—Black feminists writing—on motherhood right now is that there are real fights among us, which are productive, right, like it's not as if there is a singular Black feminist perspective on mothering. There are generative and important arguments unfolding. So, I think conventional disciplines have a complicated relationship to Black women and to Black feminist scholarship, and I think in the contemporary academy it's a relationship that's marked by simultaneous disavowal and strategic consumption of that work. And as Black women who are interested in Black feminism, we get caught in the crosshairs of that battle.

M. C.: Absolutely. I'm thinking about the ways that your new book is eliciting a kind of emotional or affective rhetoric about your work in terms of passion or love or desire and care, rage, right, things that I've read in bell hooks's work. I think those terms are part of an answer to a question that scholars are afraid to ask: What are Black women *feeling*? And how can their feelings be critically incorporated into disciplinary scholarship? So much of the work produced about, through, on, and at its worst, *around* Black women is interested in a quantitative measure on how our lives can be summated after gendered, anti-Black violence. Rarely do we ask questions about what Black women's feelings are about their experiences. That's because scholarship that takes place *around* Black women is not actually interested in us as a site of knowledge. I'm curious how you think affective terms are changing the ways we think about academic work or research on Black women's experiences or Black mothers' experiences?

J. C. N.: I often teach a graduate seminar on affect and I teach it in Black studies. One of the things my students often say when they come to the class with is that affect theory has never thought about Black folks. I always say that there is this other genealogy of affect theory that is entirely about Black feminist scholarship. If we think about Patricia Williams or Saidiya Hartman or Toni Morrison or bell hooks, when we think about all of those folks together, they're asking us to think about rage, desire, love, passion, shame, friendship, they're asking us to think about the felt life, and about Black women's felt lives. These are also scholars who are writing in vulnerable ways that upend the genre conventions of academic writing. I really do think one of the ways to think about Black feminism is how does it ask us to understand or theorize emotion differently? How do we think about anger when we think about a Black woman's standpoint? Or how do we think about . . . how do Black feminists ask us to imagine love differently? And, in fact, I think entirely decenter romantic love, right? And ask us to think about love more capaciously as a fundamental political project. Or how do Black feminists ask us to think about vulnerability and risk as political ethic? So I think there is this way in which Black feminists have asked us these questions again and again, and have debated these questions, but maybe I think there is a way in which feminist theory writ large has only recently realized that this has been a long-standing preoccupation of Black feminists. There are obviously multiple ways of thinking about what constitutes a Black feminist intellectual tradition. Sometimes I want to think how I might characterize it as a spiritual tradition. Sometimes I want to think how might I want to characterize it as an affective tradition. I think of Bettina Judd's new piece in *Feminist Studies* about anger, and that for me was also really generative for thinking about Black feminism's affective commitments.[9] So I think there is a way in which Black feminists, the tradition writ large, asks us to think about both emotion and to go back to the thing about, sort of, disciplinary knowledge. It asks us to think about how we can't do the intellectual work we do without taking seriously feeling. So it's completely upending this idea that we are supposed to become rational subjects who research something that is entirely detached from what we do, from who we are, through an entirely objective methodology. Black feminists have jammed that, have jammed all those assumptions in really productive and self-conscious ways. I think of Ann duCille's "The Occult of True Black Womanhood," where she is so self-consciously reflecting on everything she's thinking at every moment.[10] That kind of intense self-consciousness is a Black feminist ethic. I think of Black feminists as, sort of, a vanguard of those questions.

***

Here, our conversation turned to a more explicit discussion of what it means to form a comprehensive Black feminist genealogy in our contemporary moment. Dr. Nash's previous comments on pedagogy and course-making compelled a question about interdisciplinary thinking and intra*disciplinary thinking that occurs within Black Studies.*

M. C.: You write in your newest book how Black studies has been preoccupied with Black death and/or afro-pessimism and then how Black feminism automatically seems to rise to this weird counterpoint, which I don't necessarily think it's always, for me, a counterpoint. It's just presenting this type of alternative rhetoric or other affective ways that we can think about Black life and Black death as coexisting. Here, I'm thinking more about Black kinship and when you offer for us to "think about love or kinship more capaciously." Much like Black women are called to "save" political elections or called upon socially to "read" folks in order to reset social situations that seem unjust, I'm concerned about the relationality Black feminism has with other theoretical pursuits taking place in Black studies right now. Just as Black women call into question the varying dynamics of relationality between a people and their country, how can Black feminism behave or coexist with other lines of inquiry within Black studies? Do you see space for coexistence in Black studies right now?

J. C. N.: I think the hard thing about taking the temperature of Black Studies is we're always shaped by our particular institutional locations. So I teach in an institution where Black studies is theoretically oriented in a way that is very different from where I did my graduate work. Many of our students come in with an interest in feminist theory, queer theory, gender, and sexuality. I'm exposed to a very particular iteration of Black studies, as I suspect we are all in our institutional homes.

I've become fascinated by the poles of Black death, i.e., afro-pessimism, and then ideas of Black futurity, Black hope, Black creativity, Black refusal, where Black feminism seems to be the stand-in for that. So, there's that tension and then there is I think a way in which Black studies as of late, i.e., like the last few years, has sort of lionized a particular set of Black feminist scholars, who all of my students have read—Spillers, Wynter, Sharpe, Hartman—and those are amazing scholars, right, but I think that that limited cannon can actually obscure exactly the kinds of debates that we're talking about that have unfolded in Black feminist scholarship for decades. I'll have moments where students will say, "I can't believe that any Black feminist scholar would engage law." And I'm like, "Well, Kimberlé Crenshaw is a legal scholar, Patricia Williams is a legal scholar, Angela Harris is a legal scholar. You have to have some conception of Black feminist theory that can attend to the variety of voices that have done work in the field." So, I think there is something really interesting happening in how Black studies has its own kind of really limited conception of what constitutes Black feminist theoretical work, as the field elevates certain Black feminist theorists to stand for the totality of Black feminist work.

And I see that as intimately tied to the rise of afro-pessimism, where I see Black studies as wanting to defend itself from the allegation that afro-pessimism has a gender problem by sort of saying, right, but we cite Hartman, Wynter, Spillers, so there's no gender problem with afro-pessimism. I find all that fascinating because Spillers herself entirely seems to disavow afro-pessimism even as she is hailed by afro-pessimist theorists.

M. C.: Absolutely. I agree that these scholars' contributions are valuable and play an important role in the Black feminist intellectual genealogy. And

I worry that their contributions to the project of Black feminism are only appreciated through the limitation of content, instead of appreciating their innovation of methods and genre, too. Hartman's *Wayward Lives, Beautiful Experiments* is engaging with a much larger project of genre-bending and collectivity that Black women scholars have been participating in for a long time.[11] Or, another question Omolade implicitly asks us in her 1995 chapter, "'Making Sense': Notes for Studying Black Teen Mothers" is, on what terms are we currently thinking Black women's lives through, and can we really understand them on those terms? In what ways can we penetrate conventional methods in qualitative and quantitative research to understand them outside terms of violence and violation? I know that you recall Patricia Williams often: Are there people who you think of, maybe not in the academy or not institutionally affiliated, performers and artists that you think are differently attending to Black studies?

J. C. N.: One of the questions I'm always interested in and probably ask everybody I meet is who do you feel like your students don't read? Who do you read that your students don't read or vice versa? Just to get a sense of how our collective conception of our socialization into our fields shift. So, this year I was teaching a class on the intellectual history of Black women, and each week was a different author, so we would just sort of singularly focus on a particular figure. And I find a set of texts that I read in graduate school, and what was really interesting to me was that most of them were texts that none of my students had encountered before, and I found that shift really interesting. So, we read Barbara Smith, June Jordan. My students who had read June Jordan had pretty much only read her poetry, so that was interesting. We read Alice Walker, which was fascinating, because it was at the same moment as her anti-Semitic comments, and so then we had to grapple with, like, what do we do with it—like, what is a Black feminist response to a figure like Alice Walker? What do we do when these figures espouse violent rhetoric? Williams as you mentioned is super important to me—oh!—we read Anita Hill, and my students know Anita Hill as a figure but not as a scholar. So that was really interesting. And actually to grapple with like some of Hill's more conservative writing, what do we do with these figures who we lionize in the moment of #MeToo, who actually had some political views that we might be like "hmm" that's a little more conservative than I might suspect. We read Ann duCille and Barbara Christian. We ended with bell hooks. And hooks was really interesting because when I was an undergrad, hooks was sort of the stand-in for Black feminism, and it was interesting because now most of my students know hooks because of her controversial comments about Beyoncé. Someone like hooks is so interesting because the sweep of her work is so huge, and she's written so much. And she's a public intellectual, but she's also been situated in universities in different moments, and so we were sort of reading samples from different moments in her life as a thinker. I think that was really fascinating for my students also because it's like, right, people change, their ideas change, their preoccupations change, right, like, suddenly you get a moment where hooks is writing like three books about love, well how do we make sense of that? So those were some of the folks who I think are really interesting. I always come back to Ann duCille, especially, "The Occult of True Black Womanhood," which I think is just an unbelievably rich and important article. And then I think [it] really anticipates the present moment where there is so much anxiety over who can do what work, over who gets to speak for Black women and who gets to speak for Black feminism. I think her work really suggests that that's an enduring debate. And then for my undergrad we always read *This Bridge Called My Back*. I always want them to think about the promise and peril of women of color as an analytic and what it does and doesn't make possible.

M. C.: You mentioned that when people read bell hooks, its read lockstep with these generational moments. I also think about your work as having seemingly disparate points but still engaged with particular political movements. One could read your premier book on pornography as part of a shift toward the erotic and a critical undertaking of the various lives of sex Black women make possible; and then subsequent work on "un-widowing" which responds to the murder of Trayvon Martin; and then intersectionality, which is a term you argue requires a more direct engagement with Black feminism despite its good- and bad-faith efforts in and outside the academy.[12] How do you think people's work comes under attack or highly scrutinized when political moments just call for different work? How do you personally chart an intellectual journey with your own scholarship?

J. C. N.: That's such a great question. My work is an index of my preoccupations in a particular moment. I've come to particular projects in certain moments in my life that in earlier moments would have been inconceivable to me, so like I never would have written about Black motherhood or been like, "Motherhood: nothing is more boring." (Laughs) and then I had a child and I was like "I'm writing about motherhood." (Laughs). So, it's interesting for me to sort of like reflect on how my preoccupations—my work—reflects my preoccupations. My second book on intersectionality, much of that came out of my own, sort of, conscription into university service. I found myself directing the women's studies program at George Washington University and having to say things like, we're a transnational, intersectional program that trains students to be global citizens and also being like "Ugh, why am I saying this?" But I'm saying it because I want resources (laughs). I was trying to make sense of that dance and trying to make sense of how I thought so many of my Black female colleagues engaged in that same kind of dance, like talking out of both sides of our mouths because we wanted resources for the things we love and believe in, even as we critiqued the language we had to use to garner resources. So, there's that. And then I think, you know, my second project on intersectionality I started long before Trump was elected and it was entirely a book about the university; and then he was elected and I remember when I got my first reader's report: one of the readers basically was like you can't write this book and not write about Trump and the women's march and the "pussy hats," and I thought, that's a different book. And there was a way in which intersectionality was suddenly on this national and global stage that I'd never anticipated. That would require a different project. And so I ended up sort of gesturing to some of it in the conclusion but also realizing I couldn't do justice to it in sort of the framework that I had setup. And so it would have been interesting to see how the book . . . it's impossible to read the book without reflecting on the ongoing fights in popular feminism about what is white feminism, and is intersectionality the opposite of white feminism?

***

Finally, our conversation concludes with a discussion of Dr. Nash's most recent work on Black motherhood and Black feminism's response to our current political climate surrounding the Movement for Black Lives.

M. C.: When I hear a comment like that from a reader, the questions I'm always returning to is, "Can we not talk about Black feminism for one second?" and "Why do we have to bring in these broader, more topical issues to assume that Black women are under a particular microscope in a Trump presidency, rather than a Reagan or Bush presidency?" It's almost an assumption about, and with that, an erasure of, the plight of Black women. There is some social and political assumption there. I'm reading Barbara Omolade's work about her persistent critique of sociologists working with teen mothers. She demands of readers that one can't talk about Black mothers over the age of 21 the way that we're talking about teen mothers and the vilification of Black mothers, Black teen mothers.[13] I'm curious to know your take on how we can still fight against singular forms of study when it comes to understanding Black women's experiences. Do you think Black women sociologists have manifested a singular formation of Black Motherhood Studies? How do you think Black motherhood studies is coming into this political moment as something different or requiring new language or tools or methods needed?

J. C. N.: Part of what I'm trying to think about in my book is a set of public health conversations and aesthetic conversations that unfold around Black Lives Matter. And trying to think about how, in my mind, Black mothers have become a kind of icon of Black Lives Matter. What I'm trying to think through in my project is how Black Lives Matter came to position Black motherhood as in crisis and how Black mothers have both strategically deployed the idea of crisis to garner resources, to make visible Black infant mortality, Black maternal mortality, obstetric violence, and also how disrupted this idea [is] that Black maternal bodies are in crisis. So that's sort of the frame. I'm really interested in the kind of the romantics around Black motherhood, and I'm interested in Black feminism—the moments in Black feminism that speak in a romantic register about Black motherhood—and we know how to do that because we have tools like, other mothering, and community mothering, and even some of what Dani McClain is up to in this idea of like "we live for the we" and Black motherhood is this kind of collective—a collective endeavor—to safeguard Black life. We also have this other tradition in Black feminist studies which is like deep ambivalence about Black mothering. I think of Alice Walker in "In Search of Our Mothers Gardens," her essay on having one child and where she talks about her tremendous ambivalence about having Rebecca, her sense of her life as an artist would be destroyed, and I find that really fascinating because it's an essay that doesn't get assigned, canonized, talked about much, although people do know about Alice and Rebecca and their kind of ongoing public feud, but it's like what do we Black feminists do with a piece like Alice Walker's essay about a kind of radical disavowal of motherhood and a refusal of certain aspects of motherhood in a moment when we're sort of hailing motherhood defined capaciously?[14] I think Black feminists are defining motherhood capaciously but when we think of Black motherhood as sort of the radical political act. So, I'm trying to think through those questions, and coming off the second book, I'm really interested in how Black feminist ideas and ideologies and tools get institutionalized, and I think some of that institutionalization is institutions taking up Black feminist logic. Some of it is Black feminists' own ongoing attachment to institutions, and reasonably so because it's institutions that often are imagined as places that have the resources that we need to live. So I'm trying to think about . . . I have a chapter that I've written on doulas based on some interviewing I did with doulas, and I'm trying to think through like how do we get to a moment where there's this all this attention around Black infant mortality and Black maternal mortality and obstetric violence and really what the state has given us is like offering marginal, almost no funding, to Black women to get trained as Black doulas and essentially said, "Save yourself." That's a super fascinating moment. [What] I find myself thinking through again and again is when did we come to think of motherhood as the quintessential political act. And why is it that a set of voices in the last five years have coalesced around a kind of celebration of motherhood in precisely the same moment that we get like another feminist conversation happening that's about sort of— or a non-Black feminist conversation happening—that's about disavowal of motherhood, rejection of motherhood, ambivalence, so that's sort of what I'm trying to think through. I'm always interested in a Black feminist project that's capacious enough to hold these subjects and analytics that seem, like, bad (laughs).

***

Dr. Nash's treatments of Black feminism are part of a larger Black feminist genealogy in contemporary scholarship. This genealogy breaks the institutional bounds of what constitutes "critical" scholarship in institutional settings, how disciplinary boundaries are formed and traversed, and the valuable intellectual labor of Black women both inside and outside these bounds. Barbara Omolade's (1995) proposed "language" through which this genealogy speaks is made possible through the ongoing disenfranchisement of Black women as subjects, scholars, and activists. This "language," or "the entire range of methods, theories, and tools used" when talking about black mothers has changed the field of sociology permanently and, working in tandem with Black feminist creative thinkers, has broken barriers and prevailing protocols of white, patriarchal modes of knowledge production in all intersecting fields.

Notes

1. Rose M. Brewer. 1989. "Black Women and Feminist Sociology: The Emerging Perspective." *American Sociologist* 20(1): 57–70.
2. B. Judd. 2019. "Sapphire as Praxis: Toward a Methodology of Anger." *Feminist Studies* 45(1): 178–208.
3. Rhaisa Kameela Williams. 2016. "Toward a Theorization of Black Maternal Grief as Analytic." *TRAA Transforming Anthropology* 24(1): 17–30.
4. Jennifer C. Nash. 2019. *Black Feminism Reimagined: After Intersectionality.* Next Wave: New Directions in Women's Studies. Durham, NC: Duke University Press.
5. Patricia Hill Collins. 2000. *Black Feminist Thought: Knowledge, Consciousness, and the Politics of Empowerment.* London: Routledge.
6. D. McClain. 2019. *We Live for the We: The Political Power of Black Motherhood.* New York: Bold Type Books.
7. For more on this see, Patrisse Cullors. 2019. "Fuck White Supremacy, Let's Get Free." *Performance at Frieze LA*, 16 June 2020.
8. S. Strings. 2019. *Fearing the Black Body: The Racial Origins of Fat Phobia.* New York: New York University Press.
9. Judd 2019.
10. A. duCille. 1994. "The Occult of True Black Womanhood: Critical Demeanor and Black Feminist Studies." *Signs* 19(3): 591–629.
11. Saidiya V. Hartman. 2019. *Wayward Lives, Beautiful Experiments: Intimate Histories of Social Upheaval.* New York and London: W.W. Norton & Company.
12. For more, see Ariane Cruz. 2016. *The Color of Kink: Black Women, BDSM, and Pornography.* New York: New York University Press; LaMonda Horton-Stallings. 2015. *Funk the Erotic: Transaesthetics and Black Sexual Cultures.* Urbana: University of Illinois Press; Rosamond S. King. 2014. *Island Bodies: Transgressive Sexualities in the Caribbean Imagination.* Gainesville: University Press of Florida; Mireille Miller-Young. 2014. *A Taste for Brown Sugar: Black Women in Pornography.* Durham, NC: Duke University Press.
13. Barbara Omolade. 1995. "'Making Sense': Notes for Studying Black Teen Mothers." In *Mothers in Law: Feminist Theory and the Legal Regulation of Motherhood*, edited

by Martha Albertson Fineman and Isabel Karpin, 270–288. New York: Columbia University Press.

14. A. Walker. 1983. *In Search of Our Mothers' Gardens: Womanist Prose*. San Diego, CA: Harcourt Brace Jovanovich.

References

Brewer, Rose M. 1989. "Black Women and Feminist Sociology: The Emerging Perspective." *The American Sociologist* 20(1): 57–70.

Collins Hill, Patricia. 2000. *Black Feminist Thought: Knowledge, Consciousness, and the Politics of Empowerment*. New York: Routledge.

Cruz, Ariane. 2016. *The Color of Kink: Black Women, BDSM, and Pornography*. New York: New York University Press.

Cullors, Patrisse. 2019. "Fuck White Supremacy, Let's Get Free." *Performance at Frieze LA*, June 16, 2020.

duCille, A. 1994. "The Occult of True Black Womanhood: Critical Demeanor and Black Feminist Studies." *Signs* 19(3): 591–629.

Hartman, Saidiya V. 2019. *Wayward Lives, Beautiful Experiments: Intimate Histories of Social Upheaval*. New York: W.W. Norton & Company.

Horton-Stallings, LaMonda. 2015. *Funk the Erotic: Transaesthetics and Black Sexual Cultures*. Urbana: University of Illinois Press.

Judd, B. 2019. "Sapphire as Praxis: Toward a Methodology of Anger." *Feminist Studies* 45(1): 178–208.

King, Rosamond S. 2014. *Island Bodies: Transgressive Sexualities in the Caribbean Imagination*. Gainesville: University Press of Florida.

McClain, D. 2019. *We Live for the We: The Political Power of Black Motherhood*. New York: Bold Type Books.

Miller-Young, Mireille. 2014. *A Taste for Brown Sugar: Black Women in Pornography*. Durham, NC: Duke University Press.

Nash, Jennifer C. 2019. *Black Feminism Reimagined: After Intersectionality*. Durham, NC: Duke University Press.

Omolade, Barbara. 1995. " 'Making Sense': Notes for Studying Black Teen Mothers." In *Mothers in Law: Feminist Theory and the Legal Regulation of Motherhood*, edited by Martha Albertson Fineman and Isabel Karpin. New York: Columbia University Press.

Strings, S. 2019. *Fearing the Black Body: The Racial Origins of Fat Phobia*. New York: New York University Press.

Walker, A. 1983. *In Search of Our Mothers' Gardens: Womanist Prose*. San Diego, CA: Harcourt Brace Jovanovich.

Williams, Rhaisa Kameela. 2016. "Toward a Theorization of Black Maternal Grief as Analytic." *TRAA Transforming Anthropology* 24(1): 17–30.

Part 2

Black Feminist Sociological Communities and How They Speak to Us

Chapter 5

Reflections on Re-Creating Biological Race and the Entrapment of Black People

Dorothy Roberts

On *Killing the Black Body*

I want to start this talk by reflecting on conversations I had with my editor about the title of my book, *Killing the Black Body*, because, I admit, I was concerned that "killing" might be too extreme a word to use.[1] I wanted to emphasize the racist and sexist ideologies that devalue Black women's bodies, and that are a way of propping up an entire racist regime in the United States and around the world. That's the function that I wanted to emphasize, but I was a little bit reluctant about whether it was a good idea to call it *Killing the Black Body*. In the end I stuck with "killing" as a kind of metaphor to describe the disrespect that this nation has had for Black women's bodies and the way it has treated Black people as less than human. That's what I meant by killing, but I have to say today, I no longer have any qualms about using "killing" as a literal meaning of what we need to address.

One thing that I've been told I have a talent for is connecting all the dots and helping to predict the path we have ahead of us—ringing the alarm! Helping to envision what would be another way of thinking about this world we live in, one that is not a death machine, that is not dehumanizing, that is not killing Black people's bodies. So yes, yes, 20 years later I can say that *Killing the Black Body* describes precisely, precisely the aim of these US government policies and practices.

Killing the Black Body—Black Maternal Health Today

The US white supremacist regime is a machine of death and destruction and that's intensified under the current administration. The maternal mortality rate, that's the rate of deaths from pregnancy-related causes, is actually going up in the United States, which is unlike any other so-called advanced developed nation in the world. In just about every other place in the world, the maternal mortality rate is going down. So, the US stands

DOI: 10.4324/9781003199113-8

out for the deaths of people from pregnancy-related causes and Black women's death rate is higher than any other group—four times higher than white women's death rate. It is actually safer for Black women to be pregnant in Rwanda or Kenya than in the Mississippi Delta. This ongoing assault on reproductive justice would only be exacerbated if *Roe* v. *Wade* is overturned because it puts all pregnant people, especially Black women, at risk of state control and death because they're pregnant. That's why my very first work was about how Black women were being prosecuted for drug use during pregnancy and how that punishment of their giving birth has expanded into policies that today have led to over a thousand women confined, jailed, strapped down in hospital wards and forced to undergo all sorts of procedures—even procedures that have killed them—just because they were pregnant.

Killing the Black Body—Police Violence

Police killing unarmed Black women, men, and children with impunity is probably the most striking aspect of the state's lethal apparatus but these brutal deaths are only a fragment of Black people's lives cut short by the gigantic US prison system that locks up more people than anywhere in the world, than ever in US history. It cages Black people at rates that are only characteristic of a totalitarian police state, and we've only begun to fathom the death toll from that. It is incredible to me that people would look to Black people's supposedly peculiar genes to try and figure out why Black people have higher rates of death, when they haven't even looked at the impact of the prison system on Black people's health. It's absurd, right?

Torture and Loss of Black and Brown Lives

The *New York Times* reported last week that migrant teenagers are being tortured in detention centers by guards who strap them in their underwear with bags over their heads.[2] When the *New York Times* reported it, it was almost like they were saying these techniques were developed for migrant children who were separated from their parents at the border, but there's nothing new about torturing even children—mostly Black children—in US juvenile detention centers and prisons. Sometimes that torture kills them, like it did to Kalief Browder, who took his own life after being starved and put in solitary confinement for three years in Rikers Island for allegedly taking a backpack. In my article "Torture and the Biopolitics of Race," I tied torture lynching to torture in Vietnam and to torture of Black suspects in the Chicago police department after Jon Burge returned from Vietnam and actually used the same torture devices on them.[3] I also wrote about the widely distributed torture scenes from Abu Ghraib because I was writing about it during the US war in Iraq. The assault on Iraq and videos and photos from Abu Ghraib and the torture of enemy combatants were mirrored in the chilling footage of guards in a Panama, Florida, bootcamp tormenting 14-year-old Martin Lee Anderson to death in January 2006. One video shows a nurse standing by deliberately watching the entire ordeal as if giving medical sanction to the guards' deadly brutality. This scene ties the legacy of lynching to the present day and situates it at the police station and prison cell.

The Carceral State

The first development I want to talk about is the expanding carceral state. The relationship between Black communities and law enforcement is better characterized as a system of mass control than any kind of system of protection. Incarceration doesn't even have to do with guilt or innocence. Black people are locked up, most of them in jails, without any adjudication and are forced to plead guilty, just to get out of jail. So it's not about adjudicating their moral culpability.

Mass incarceration is just one part of an expanding carceral regime that governs every single institution in this country and touches every aspect of Black people's lives. Sitting on the stoop, talking, playing music, barbequing, just leading ordinary lives put Black people at risk of death and imprisonment. In 1998, Angela Davis observed the far reach of prisons when she wrote: "corporations that appear to be far removed from the business of punishment, are intimately involved in the expansion of the prison industrial complex."[4]

Police as First Responders for White people

Debanjan Roychoundhury [a student attending the conference] and I were talking about how the police operate in all these multiple systems and Debanjan said "Yeah they're the first responders." Police as first responders includes the new trend recorded on video of white people calling 911 like the police are their personal service to put Black people in their place. They know what they're threatening: "If you, Black little boy and girl or woman and man, don't do what I say, if you don't move fast enough, I'm going to call the police—who might kill you." This has nothing to do with white people being afraid. They're not afraid; they're bold. They're saying, "Put out that barbecue," right? [Collective laughter] "Stop selling that water, what are you doing in my neighborhood?" "Get out!"[5]

Once I was in Penn Station in a big crowd of people merging into each other to line up for the train. I'm not sure who bumped into whom, but a white lady and Black lady start arguing with each other. Well as soon as the Black lady raised her voice one decibel, the white lady shouts, "Police! Police!" I was shocked she did it so automatically. I thought, "How did she know to do that?" She just knew that the police would come at her behest, and they did! They were dressed in military uniforms and they had a dog with them. They didn't even ask what's going on. They didn't even look to see if the white woman had done something wrong. They simply pulled the Black woman out of the line just like that [snaps]. To me, the white woman had been trained: "If a Black person messes with you, call or shout 'Police,' and they will come."

Police and Prisons as Killing Black Bodies and Harming Black Women

The US is involved in perpetuating the prison industrial complex and funding it and fueling it. Focusing on the multiple ways the state regulates Black women's bodies, in particular, reveals how far the carceral state extends. It reaches beyond prison to healthcare to schools, welfare, foster care, immigration—even systems that are supposed to protect us, like the police. Foster care is supposed to protect children, right? Healthcare is supposed to provide you with well-being. Those systems that are supposed to protect people are the very systems that are monitoring and assaulting Black women. And treating us as dangerous reproducers in need of control. In fact, I think it is now impossible to disentangle the intersecting tentacles of the carceral state. Little Black kids in elementary school are violently restrained, put in handcuffs that can't even hold their tiny wrists. Incarcerated mothers are prevented from seeing their children and many of those children are put in foster care. And then the mother's rights can be terminated so they have no legal relationship and most likely will never see their children again because they allegedly didn't maintain a bond with them. Black women who desperately demand medical care have been dragged out of hospitals by guards and left on the street or put in jail, simply for speaking up and saying, "I need medical help."

You may recall Barbara Dawson in Florida who was killed when she was in a waiting room saying, "I can't breathe. I can't breathe, I need help." Instead of giving her help, they called the police on her. The police officer tried to drag her into the police car after she collapsed on the ground. Finally, the police and hospital staff bring her back in the hospital, and within a few hours she had died from a blood clot in her lungs. On the tape of the police encounter, one of the statements that stands out to me is the police officer saying to her, "No matter what you do, you're going to jail." No matter what you do, you're going to jail.

Black people who can't afford parking tickets are cycled in and out of jail. And some die there, too. People who live in public housing are targeted for surveillance and arrested for trespassing outside their very homes. Trump is now threatening to deport people who have immigrated here legally but have used public assistance. Hungry children forced to snatch food from a grocery store are tased by police. Just this week, a Cincinnati off-duty police officer working as a security guard stunned an 11-year-old Black girl who was suspected of shoplifting food. According to the Cincinnati police department's manual, officers may use tasers on children as young as seven but must consider the severity of the crime and the risk of danger to others if the person is not quickly apprehended. But they apply this under racist ideology that even little Black kids are criminals and dangerous—Tamir Rice is an example. The police department's excuse is that the officer was Black and therefore race had nothing to do with it. Ask that Black officer if he would tase an 11-year-old white girl in the Kroger grocery store.

You see the dots that I am trying to connect here? The US treats police and prison as the ultimate solution to every social problem, and every social solution, regardless of the institution, looks like or leads to prison. Police are the first responders, the first way to address this. And locking people up is supposedly the answer. In all these institutions—schools, foster care, welfare, healthcare—the answer to the massive deprivation, disenfranchisement, and suffering caused by the current regime is to punish people. In fact, it punishes the people who are suffering the most from it. Those of you who were here for Sonia Sanchez's remarks will remember that she quoted Dr. King saying, "an edifice that produces beggars needs to be restructured." Well, the carceral state's logic is that the edifice should be protected by locking up beggars, or little 11-year-old girls who are looking for food because they are hungry.

Punishing Black Mothers

Punishing Black mothers has been essential to this conglomeration and entanglement of all these aspects of the carceral state. As Patricia Hill Collins said, Black women are perpetually under surveillance in academia but also in our everyday lives. Based on the images of Black welfare queens, welfare was abolished as an entitlement and is now a behavior modification program to control the sexual and childbearing decisions of cash-poor mothers. That is all it is for: to regulate them by coercing them to get married, have fewer babies, and take low-wage jobs. The multi-billion-dollar foster care apparatus is a critical part of the carceral regime that operates in tandem with prisons and welfare. Black mothers experience the child welfare system surveillance and family disruption as a form of Jane Crow.[6] Malcolm X called it modern-day slavery in his autobiography, where he describes how the welfare system came in and took him and his siblings from his mother and put them in foster care. It is based on the belief that Black children need to be away from their mothers and their communities and adopted preferably by white families. It is the idea that Black children are not harmed when the state takes them away from their families. It does not come up explicitly in many policy discussions, but the question is, how do we "free" them from their mothers?

New Racist Science

The second trend I want to bring to the attention of Black sociologists is the emergence of a new racist science. Racist science may seem disconnected from the expansion of the carceral state, but I see it as related because it promotes biological explanations for what are actually white supremacist structural inequities. I first focused on how policy makers justify policing Black women's bodies by blaming them for social problems. Now, that same idea is being put into a new racist science.[7]

For more than half a century, most scientists and scholars have taken it as common knowledge that race is a social construction with no biological validity. Eugenics was mainstream science in the United States from the turn of the 20th century until the Nazis borrowed it from US science and ended up exterminating millions of Jews and other marginalized people. After World War II, US scientists formally disavowed eugenics. And in the decades that followed prominent evolutionary biologists disproved the biological basis of race and sociologists showed the socially contingent nature of race as a social-political grouping. The Human Genome Project confirmed race isn't genetic.[8]

But what has emerged since the mapping of the human genome is a spike in research looking for race-based genetic difference and using that to explain all sorts of social inequalities. A branch of population genomics began to define race as a statistical grouping based on genetic similarity. Biomedical research, medical practice, and drug development, like race-specific medicines, are incorporating this reinvented concept of race as a genetic group. Instead of abandoning the concept of biological race altogether, these scientists are distinguishing their research from what they call ideological uses of race by white supremacists and eugenicists for repressive purposes. That's what they call scientific racism. But we have a lot of work to do to challenge the core of Western scientific thinking, which incorporates racism.

Unfortunately, some sociologists are joining the racial genomics bandwagon. Some of them are helping to develop a field known as social genomics, or socio-genomics, which investigates the genetic contributions to behaviors that sociologists used to attribute to social forces. One of my "favorites" is a study a few years ago that turned Elijah Anderson's *Code of the Street* into a genetic code by testing Black people for their genetic predisposition to have various street behaviors. In 2012, sociologists wrote an article that synthesized genomic and sociological approaches to race that accepted the claim that races are clusters of genetic similarity. What they're saying is that the social construction of race means the social construction of race as a biological category: race is biologically real and then it gets constructed in society. Then the genomic scientists respond, "Yeah, race is biologically real and only constructed by society, so what's really important are the innate qualities."

Socio-Genomics and "Educational Achievement"

Socio-genomic researchers are increasingly investigating gaps in innate cognitive ability by attributing "educational achievement" to genes. In 2016, in *Molecular Psychiatry*, a study claimed that its findings marked a turning point in the social and behavioral sciences because it may be possible to predict educational achievement directly from DNA.[9] And they propose that polygenic scores may soon become a useful tool for early prediction and prevention of educational problems. Some socio-genomic scientists claim that this knowledge is going to help Black children because DNA testing to identify which ones are the most predisposed to do poorly in school will allow us to devise special interventions for them. Now you heard what I said about how Black children are treated as innately dangerous; do you want special interventions for Black children who are identified supposedly to be genetically less likely to achieve in school?

Just a couple weeks ago, there was yet another *New York Times* headline: "Years of Education Influenced by Genetic Makeup, Enormous Study Finds."[10] The researchers had a huge DNA database, and they were looking to see if they could figure out which genes predisposed people to have more or less educational attainment. Then the next day, Kathryn Paige Harden, a psychologist who studies how genetic factors shape adolescent development, published an op-ed in the *New York Times*: "Why Progressives Should Embrace the Genetics of Education."[11] Harden writes, "Progressives should embrace the genetics of education," and she says there is a battle between people who are willing to embrace this biological determinism and people who contest it, who are anti-science, or they don't understand science, or they're letting their ideology get in the way, or they don't understand how genetics can actually help improve the lives of Black children. She says the history of eugenics has led people who value social justice to argue that when it comes to issues like education, genetic research should simply not be conducted. She referred specifically to an article I wrote arguing that this kind of research cannot possibly be socially neutral and in fact will intensify social inequities. I'm glad she linked to a paper where I said that! I did not say all of this research is racist, but at least you have to admit, it's not socially neutral.

Harden continues her criticism of me: "She joins a long tradition of left-wing thinkers who consider biological research inimical to the goal of social equality." Did I say all biological research is inimical to social equality—no! I said testing children for their genetic predisposition to intelligence is inimical to social justice. She concludes, "This is a mistake. Those of us who value social justice should instead be thinking, 'How could the power of the genetic revolution, be harnessed to create a more equal society?' Discovering specific DNA variants that are correlated with education will help." Instead of saying, "Maybe the reason why Black people have a lower level of educational attainment, on average, is not because of their genes, it's because of the racist educational system," they say, "We now need a new study of Black people's genes to figure out how genetics predisposes certain Black children to lower educational attainment than other Black children to give them extra help." We live in a society where Black children are subjected to inferior education already. So how is testing them genetically going to help?

Biosocial Science

Now I want to talk about another type of sociobiology, or biosocial science, that is different from the socio-genomics I've been talking about. W. E. B. Du Bois was in fact the first sociologist to synthesize biological and social science knowledge and research about the biological fallout of racism, both during slavery and after emancipation, on Black people's bodies. He conducted that research at University of Pennsylvania, and in the *Philadelphia Negro*, published in 1899, he wrote that "particularly with regard to consumption, it must be remembered that Negros are not the first people that have been claimed as its particular victims." You have to understand at the time, all the white scientists were saying the reason why Black people were suffering from higher rates of illnesses like tuberculosis was because their bodies weren't suited for freedom. They were saying the reason why Black people have such poor health is because their bodies innately are rejecting freedom. Du Bois was writing in the midst of that, and he points out that Irish people were once thought to be the peculiar victims of these diseases. And then he adds, "But that was when Irishmen were unpopular." He's saying this isn't about groups' innate predispositions; this is about groups' political position in society—that's what determines health and policy.

Du Bois was the first sociologist to engage in what is a growing branch of sociological research that investigates the biological impact of structural racism. For example, Black sociologist Abigail Sewell merged data from the 1994 Home Mortgage Disclosure Act with a project on human development in Chicago neighborhoods and, using her brilliant quantitative statistical skills, she found a connection between the dual mortgage map market, residential segregation, and childhood health inequalities.[12] Dr. Sewell's research question contrasts with the biosocial question, "How does the body's internal chemistry—its cells, epigenome, or brain, measured by biomarkers and brain scans—respond to the exposure of a harmful environmental signal?" By the time many researchers investigate that question, the racist social structure and practices that caused the biological impact in the first place are gone from their view. They're not looking at structural racism at all! They're looking entirely in the brains and the epigenomes and the cells of the people who are suffering from racism and asking, "What makes some of them able to cope and others not able to cope? How can we intervene in their bodies so they can cope better to these environmental exposures?" And their solutions are all about fixing the biology of these people!

Biosocial Science as Related to Black Women

A lot of the new biosocial research has to do with fixing Black mothers, based on the belief that Black mothers are transferring their negative environments for generations to come through epigenetic transmission or they're not helping their children cope with the damage to their brains from racism and poverty. Neuroscientists are now studying the impact of poverty on the gray matter of children's brains. And they're arguing that they can explain the academic achievement gap significantly by differences in brain functioning. Now, granted they say that these negative brain features stem from poverty, but they're attributing the educational disadvantages these children experience, again not to the structural impediments they're facing, but to defective brains. This model not only doesn't help to address what are actually the barriers to Black children having equal educational attainment, such as high rates of suspensions and expulsions and inferior school funding, but it also affirmatively hides those barriers. It therefore directs solutions to the brains of these children, instead of dealing with ending the structures that are causing the problem.

What Can We Do?

My goal is to close this amazing meeting with some thoughts about how the new Black sociologists can continue the legacy of building a better world. The racist function of carceral institutions suggests that a reformist approach isn't adequate. Improving the procedures with which these systems are designed to exclude and kill us can actually hide their oppressive aspects, or even make killing Black people more efficient. It just doesn't make sense to say that these systems will be fixed by ensuring greater obedience by people that the systems are designed to oppress and subjugate and subordinate. That means that the new Black sociologists have to be abolitionists—of prison, foster care, the whole nine yards. An abolitionist sociology aims at releasing the stranglehold of law enforcement and these other carceral institutions on Black communities so they have more freedom to create their own egalitarian, democratic

Black loving ways of dealing with social problems and human needs that don't rely on police and jails.

Intersectionality

Here is a sentence from the Combahee River Collective: they wrote, "Black women have always embodied, if only in their physical manifestation, an adversary stance to white male rule."[13]

They're saying that Black women embody a political position. To the Collective, embodiment is not just a physical state. It's a political state. It entails not only being exposed to adverse social conditions and experiencing biological outcomes to be studied, but also, more importantly, being bodily positioned in relation to unjust power relationships.

Black feminists have begun to think about and work toward what abolition would mean, especially in the context of anti-carceral approaches to domestic violence. We start from the premise that policies that protect Black women must prevent intimate and institutional violence simultaneously; they're connected dots. We recognize that when a Black woman calls the police in a domestic violence situation, she is likely to be arrested, beat up, or even killed. Many of the cases of Black women being killed by the police are cases where they called the police or their families called the police to help them, and instead they ended up with their heads bashed against the sidewalk, shot to death, beat up. As the Combahee River Collective instructs, we are forced to think of other ways of dealing with violence. We, Black women, are forced like no other group to figure out how can we be safe, how can we ensure well-being, how can we meet people's material needs without relying on calling the police and locking people up? So I think the work of Black feminists suggests that we can abolish these systems. And we can, still, and even more so, be safe and healthy and whole and living in peace.

New Black Sociologists: Visions for the Future

The final point I want to make is that the new Black sociologists are absolutely essential to resisting the new racist science and to revolutionizing the scientific study of the relationship between biology and society and what it means to be human. As I've said, what's going on now just repeats in new form the same old ideas that focus on biological deficits of the people who have been harmed and killed by a racist system instead of ending the racist system. There's nothing wrong with Black people! There's nothing wrong with us!

Moving forward, I firmly believe we have to collaborate intellectually and politically with critical humanities scholars: feminists, intersectionality, race, queer, disability, and fat studies scholars, all of these theorists who are critically examining outside of sociology and biology these questions of the relationship between biology and society. It's so cool that Sonia Sanchez opened up the meeting with poetry and with activism. I think that looking at how Black feminist science fiction writers envision a different world that doesn't rely on Black pathology as explaining everything but instead loves Black people. It has made me think about the work of the great science fiction author Octavia Butler, who wrote, "There's nothing new under the sun, but there are new suns."[14] We can envision a completely different universe.

Marcus Hunter's words, I thought, were challenging us to break out and envision something completely new. Zandria Robinson called up in her talk on Lorraine Hansberry, who in addressing the nature of racism of America, didn't say, "What's a way to reform the criminal justice system? What's a fairer way of punishing the crimes of Black people?" She said the "paramount crime in the United States" was "the refusal of its ruling classes to admit or acknowledge in any way the real scope and scale and character of their oppression of Negroes." So the crime, the problem, is not us.

The new Black abolitionist sociologists can expose the crimes the carceral state continues to perpetuate in new guises, new technologies, new theories against Black people every day. And we can work with Black communities to envision and create anti-racist, loving ways to meet social needs and address social harms—not only for ourselves, but for this corrupt nation, and for the entire world. Thank you.

Notes

1. This chapter draws on Roberts' transcribed talk from the Association of Black Sociologists 2018 meeting. Dorothy E. Roberts. 1999. *Killing the Black Body: Race, Reproduction, and the Meaning of Liberty*. New York: Vintage Books.
2. Jess Bidgood, Manny Fernandez, and Richard Fausset. 2018. "Restraint Chairs and Spit Masks: Migrant Detainees Claim Abuse at Detention Centers." *New York Times*, August 4, 2018. www.nytimes.com/2018/08/04/us/migrant-children-detention-centers.html.
3. Dorothy Roberts. 2007. "Torture and the Biopolitics of Race." *University of Miami Law Review* 62: 229.
4. Angela Davis. 1998. "Masked Racism: Reflections on the Prison Industrial Complex." *Colorlines*, September 10. www.colorlines.com/articles/masked-racism-reflections-prison-industrial-complex.
5. See Jessica Guynn. 2018. "BBQ Becky, Permit Patty and Why the Internet Is Shaming White People Who Police People 'Simply for Being Black.'" *USA TODAY* (blog), July 18, 2018. www.usatoday.com/story/tech/2018/07/18/bbq-becky-permit-patty-and-why-internet-shaming-white-people-who-police-black-people/793574002/.
6. Dorothy Roberts. 2009. *Shattered Bonds: The Color of Child Welfare*. New York: Basic Books.
7. Dorothy Roberts. 2011. *Fatal Invention: How Science, Politics, and Big Business Re-Create Race in the Twenty-First Century*. New York: New Press/ORIM.
8. National Human Genome Research Institute. N.d. "Race." www.genome.gov/genetics-glossary/Race. Accessed November 18, 2020.

9. S. Selzam, E. Krapohl, S. von Stumm, P. F. O'Reilly, K. Rimfeld, Y. Kovas, P. S. Dale, J. J. Lee, and R. Plomin. 2017. "Predicting Educational Achievement from DNA." *Molecular Psychiatry* 22(2): 267–272. https://doi.org/10.1038/mp.2016.107.
10. Carl Zimmer. 2018. "Years of Education Influenced by Genetic Makeup, Enormous Study Finds." *New York Times*, July 23, 2018. www.nytimes.com/2018/07/23/science/genes-education.html.
11. Kathryn Paige Harden. 2018. "Why Progressives Should Embrace the Genetics of Education." *New York Times*, July 24, 2018. www.nytimes.com/2018/07/24/opinion/dna-nature-genetics-education.html.
12. Abigail A Sewell. 2016. "The Racism-Race Reification Process: A Mesolevel Political Economic Framework for Understanding Racial Health Disparities." *Sociology of Race and Ethnicity* 2(4): 402–432. https://doi.org/10.1177/2332649215626936.
13. Combahee River Collective. 1977. "Combahee River Collective Statement." *History Is a Weapon*, February 18, 2012. http://historyisaweapon.com/defcon1/combrivercoll.html.
14. https://www.facebook.com/octaviasbrood/posts/theres-nothing-new-under-the-sun-but-there-are-new-suns-octavia-butler-unpublish/257110384474951/.

References

Bidgood, Jess, Manny Fernandez, and Richard Fausset. 2018. "Restraint Chairs and Spit Masks: Migrant Detainees Claim Abuse at Detention Centers." *New York Times*. August 4, 2018. www.nytimes.com/2018/08/04/us/migrant-children-detention-centers.html.
Combahee River Collective. 1977. "Combahee River Collective Statement." *History Is a Weapon*. February 18, 2012. http://historyisaweapon.com/defcon1/combrivercoll.html.
Davis, Angela. 1998. "Masked Racism: Reflections on the Prison Industrial Complex." *Colorlines*. September 10, 1998. www.colorlines.com/articles/masked-racism-reflections-prison-industrial-complex.
Guynn, Jessica. 2018. "BBQ Becky, Permit Patty and Why the Internet Is Shaming White People Who Police People 'Simply for Being Black.'" *USA TODAY* (blog). July 18, 2018. www.usatoday.com/story/tech/2018/07/18/bbq-becky-permit-patty-and-why-internet-shaming-white-people-who-police-black-people/793574002/.
Harden, Kathryn Paige. 2018. "Why Progressives Should Embrace the Genetics of Education." *New York Times*. July 24, 2018. www.nytimes.com/2018/07/24/opinion/dna-nature-genetics-education.html.
National Human Genome Research Institute. n.d. "Race." www.genome.gov/genetics-glossary/Race. Accessed November 18, 2020.
Roberts, Dorothy E. 1999. *Killing the Black Body: Race, Reproduction, and the Meaning of Liberty*. New York: Vintage Books.
Roberts, Dorothy E. 2007. "Torture and the Biopolitics of Race." *University of Miami Law Review* 62: 229.
Roberts, Dorothy E. 2009. *Shattered Bonds: The Color of Child Welfare*. New York: Basic Books.
Roberts, Dorothy E. 2011. *Fatal Invention: How Science, Politics, and Big Business Re-Create Race in the Twenty-First Century*. New York: New Press and ORIM.
Selzam, S., E. Krapohl, S. von Stumm, P. F. O'Reilly, K. Rimfeld, Y. Kovas, P. S. Dale, J. J. Lee, and R. Plomin. 2017. "Predicting Educational Achievement from DNA." *Molecular Psychiatry* 22(2): 267–272. https://doi.org/10.1038/mp.2016.107

Sewell, Abigail A. 2016. "The Racism-Race Reification Process: A Mesolevel Political Economic Framework for Understanding Racial Health Disparities." *Sociology of Race and Ethnicity* 2(4): 402–432. https://doi.org/10.1177/2332649215626936.

Zimmer, Carl. 2018. "Years of Education Influenced by Genetic Makeup, Enormous Study Finds." *New York Times*. July 23, 2018. www.nytimes.com/2018/07/23/science/genes-education.html

Chapter 6

Centering Us
What Doing Black Feminist Sociology Really Looks Like

Lori Latrice Martin

For centuries, Black women have asked and answered important questions about how the world works and their place in it. Black women in America have understood that their experiences were in many ways similar to those of Black men during the institution of slavery but different in other ways. Black women have also understood that gender simply did not have the same meaning for Black people as it did for white people. Sojourner Truth famously made this point clear in her address to a predominantly white audience in Ohio in the early 1850s. In the address, published by the National Park Service, Truth stated,

> That man over there says that women need to be helped into carriages, and lifted over ditches, and to have the best places everywhere. Nobody ever helps me into carriages or over mud-puddles or gives me any best place! And ain't I a woman? Look at me! Look at my arm! I have ploughed and planted, and gathered into barns, and no man could head me! And ain't I a woman? I could work as much and eat as much as a man—when I can get—and bear the lash as well! And ain't I a woman? I have borne thirteen children, and seen most all sold off to slavery, and when I cried out with my mother's grief, none but Jesus heard me! Ain't I a woman?[1]

Truth articulated the fact that Black men and Black women performed the same types of labor, endured various forms of brutality, including assaults on their physical bodies, and separation from their biological offspring at birth and over the life course. At the same time, Truth also understood that the benefits of whiteness extended to white women who were considered by virtue of their birth worthy of protection, especially from Black men. Black men in the white imagination were nonhuman predators. Black women, like Truth, also knew their place in the American social structure was far below those of both white women and white men. Truth's observations about and investigation into the unique position of Black women in American society and how that position was shaped by,

DOI: 10.4324/9781003199113-9

and shaped, American society is part of the genealogy of Black feminist sociology. She demonstrated awareness about Black women's orientation and the myriad ways their orientation and marginalization are impacted by what Patricia Hill Collins[2] described a complex system of oppression.

Black feminist sociologists today carry with them this tradition of examining Black women's place in the world as they deploy a variety of sociological, theoretical, and methodological approaches. Like Truth, Black feminist sociologists today also demonstrate a commitment to addressing social justice issues. Contemporary Black feminist sociologists seek to challenge society as well as their discipline. In the hearts and minds of Black women, both past and present, the boundaries between theory, methods, and activism are not only fluid, they also place Black women and the experiences of Black women at the center. Examining Black women's place in the world through the use of existing and emerging sociological theories and methodological approaches that aim to address the multiple sources of oppression that inform the experiences of Black women is a signature of Black feminist sociology.

The growth in scholarly and popular interest in Black feminist sociology since about the early 1990s is exciting. To maintain interest, excitement, relevance, and the scholarly impact of Black feminist sociology, I propose that Black feminist sociology must reflect the following principles: (1) recognize that doing gender is not the same for Black and white women, (2) recognize that doing race is not the same for Black men and Black women, (3) recognize that scholarship conducted by Black women for Black women has value, (4) draw scholarship from a number of areas of study, (5) demonstrate respect for various theoretical and methodological approaches, (6) challenge stereotypes and myths about Black women, (7) address social justice issues and (8) challenge oppression from multiple sources. In this chapter I expand upon each principle, and also address the fact that doing Black feminist sociology is not without risks. Before discussing the principles of Black feminist sociology, I share some experiences from my academic journey.

In Search of Black Women in Sociology: My Academic Journey

When I began my journey in a doctoral program in the late 1990s, I was not introduced to scholarship that I would consider representative of doing Black feminist sociology in any of the required courses, nor in many of the electives offered. It was not until well into my studies that I was introduced to the works of people such as Dorothy Roberts. Her book, *Killing the Black Body*, was written by a Black woman scholar about Black women from sociological, historical, and demographic perspectives, all of which were of interest to me. Black women's scholarship does not regularly appear on syllabi for required sociological courses, many of which are taught by white men and/or by sociologists who only find value in the sociological canon, which features white men like Karl Marx, Emile Durkheim and Max Weber. I was interested in understanding housing tenure but only came across literature about differences between men and women, while ignoring within-group differences. I made it part of my mission as a scholar to include Black women in my research in meaningful ways. This allowed me to address gaps in the literature on race and gender. I published a study examining variations in the likelihood of home ownership for non-married Black women and non-married white women. I drew attention to the impact of Black women's dual minority status as an important predictor of attaining one of the most powerful symbols of the American Dream.[3] Over the course of my academic journey, I read books and scholarly articles within and beyond my discipline, which enhanced my ability to not only think critically about the world, about American society, but also to think about my place in it as a Black woman scholar. As I read about the theories and methodological approaches used in disciplines other than sociology, as well as reading critical sociological perspectives, I was able to more critically analyze sociology as a discipline and the many ways it marginalizes people, ideas, theories, methodologies, experiences, and scholar activism. It became clear to me that sociology centers whiteness and views whiteness as normative. I saw in works by people like Patricia Hill Collins, W. E. B. Du Bois, Toni Morrison, Dorothy Roberts and others the significance of understanding whiteness. I embraced the need to do my part to decentral-ize whiteness[4] and join others in their efforts to decolonize the discipline.

Consequently, my teaching and my scholarship in more recent years reflect what I consider examples of doing Black feminist sociology. This is due in part to a number of factors, including my experiences as a Black woman, as a Black mother, as a Black scholar at a predominately white institution, and as someone who is committed to using my skills to serve as a catalyst for positive social changes. For example, I recently developed and taught a graduate course about African Americans in sociology, which included *Black Feminist Thought* and Audre Lorde's *Sister Outsider*, among other texts.[5]

I drew inspiration from Black women intellectual thinkers in the development of the graduate course and in my own research. For one of my most recent books, *Black Community Uplift and the Myth of the American Dream*, I was motivated to build upon Evelyn Brooks Higginbotham's study of Black women during the latter part of the 19th century and the early part of the 20th century in *Righteous Discontent*. I wanted to show that understanding how Black Baptist women tried to control their self-images and control their own destinies, while fighting for social justice, was significant. The latter point is often missed through misunderstandings about the distinctions between the *politics of respectability* and *respectability politics.* I argued that the politics of respectability provides a powerful framework for understanding the experiences of Black women, both then and up to the present day.

My teaching, scholarship, service, and activism derive strength from others doing what we could consider in the tradition of Black feminist sociology. Ida B. Wells and her efforts to define, quantify, and problematize lynching in America is a good example. Dr. Shaonta' E. Allen details the life and legacy of Wells in her chapter in this book, "Crusading for Justice Through Black Feminist Scholar-Activism." Wells also mobilized others to tackle the tough challenge to bring an end to the brutal, often state-sanctioned Black deaths. Indeed, W. E. B. Du Bois listed Wells as among the prominent Black women in the early 1900s.[6] bell hooks, Angela Davis, and Toni Morrison are among the many other brilliant minds that have done and are doing Black feminist sociology.[7]

In their works and public engagements, each scholar refused or refuses to concede the marginalization of Black women as necessary and expected. Moreover, each woman regularly debunked or continues to debunk the myth of the pathology of Black womanhood. While these scholars may come from different disciplines they clearly share some very important features. Many of the scholars I have identified here may not identify as either a Black feminist or a sociologist. However, many scholars considered founders of a host of disciplines were not specifically trained in the discipline. Karl Marx, for example, is considered a founder of sociology. He was not a sociologist, but his influence on the discipline is undeniable. Similarly, the works of many of the scholars mentioned in this chapter are important to understanding Black feminist sociology, and are illustrative of what doing Black feminist sociology looks like.

Can We Talk? Black Feminist Thought, Meet Black Sociology

As we contemplate what doing Black feminist sociology looks like, I argue that this requires placing two important bodies of thought in conversation with each other, namely Black feminist thought and Black sociology.[8] Placing the two in conversation with one another points us in the direction of the principles for doing Black feminist sociology. This is imperative because doing Black feminist sociology is critical to understanding the experiences of Black women, as well as other historically disadvantaged groups. A close and careful reading of both Black feminist thought and Black sociology makes it clear that Black feminist sociology is not and cannot be about Black scholars merely engaged in feminist sociology, because doing so ignores the significance and centrality of race. Likewise, Black feminist sociology is not feminist sociology concerned with issues impacting Black people, because doing so ignores the interaction effects of race and gender. Feminist sociology prioritizes gender over race. Feminist sociologists conducting studies on Black people tend to maintain and not challenge the status quo, as feminist sociology is dominated by white women and white women remain some of the greatest beneficiaries of the wages of whiteness.

Black feminist sociology has implications for many areas of society. Black feminist sociology has the potential to enhance society's understanding of the experiences of Black women in the US, and Black feminist sociology also has the potential to provide the exploratory, explanatory, and predictive power for understanding a number of critical social issues, including responses to sexual violence against Black women, state-sponsored killings of unarmed citizens, and persistent racial wealth inequality, among others. What is needed is more clarity around what doing Black feminist sociology looks like. The absence of a shared vision impedes the ability of Black feminist sociology, and Black feminist sociologists, to add to relevant bodies of literature, including their own. The absence of a clear understanding of what doing Black feminist sociology looks like also limits the ability of Black feminist sociology and Black feminist sociologists to provide a grammar for articulating Black women's experiences in the past and in contemporary times, which can contribute to various ongoing struggles for liberation.[9]

Eight Principles for Doing Black Feminist Sociology

I argue there are several core principles for understanding what constitutes doing Black feminist sociology.

1. *Black feminist sociology recognizes that doing gender is not the same for Black and white women.* While notable feminist sociologists have debated about whether gender is best understood as an "emergent feature of social institutions"[10] or as a social institution,[11] what is clear is that gender, however it is defined, is not the same for Black and white women.[12] As much as there are calls for bridge-building and creating collaborations between Black women and white women, both in the academy and in the broader society, the fact still remains that the differences between these two groups are great and must continually be acknowledged. Black women in the tradition of Black feminist sociology dating back hundreds of years have testified about white women's inability and/or unwillingness to not only treat Black women as equals, but also to neglect to see their husbands, sons, uncles, and brothers, as humans also. In the academy, when Black women scholars—many of whom have been Black women sociologists, including Zandria Robinson and Saida Grundy—find themselves attacked by

virtual mobs for merely doing their jobs and challenging assumptions about whiteness, their white women colleagues remain silent. That silence speaks volumes.[13] The use of the term *woman* in America, including in sociology, means white women and their experiences are still considered universal and representative of the experiences of all women. Race is gendered and gender is raced; doing gender must be racialized.

2. *Black feminist sociology recognizes that doing race is not the same for Black men and Black women.*[14] Although whiteness is in many ways totaling it does not impact Black men and Black women in the same way at the same time. While Black men and Black women performed the same types of labor during slavery, for example, and both experienced sexual violence, their experiences were also very different. The varying experiences of Black men and Black women do not end there. While research shows that Black people tend to lag behind white people on many sociological outcomes there are variations between Black men and Black women.[15] Black feminist sociologists should not reify dominant narratives about either Black men or Black women. Black feminist sociology must consider the ways in which race and gender and other characteristics interact to further subjugate Black women and Black men in complex, multilevel, and multidimensional ways.

3. *Black feminist sociology recognizes value in work conducted by Black women for Black women.* Patricia Hill Collins has addressed the need for authenticating the work of Black feminist sociologists. In *Black Feminist Thought* she identified three competing groups that Black feminist sociologists have to consider as they do their work, and the first group is ordinary Black women. Black feminist sociologists have the benefit of their lived experiences and could further enhance their credibility and authenticity by increasing their engagement with the communities where they live and work.

The work of Black feminist sociology must center the experiences of Black women and centered them in a way that does not attempt to mimic the centering of whiteness and the continued marginalization of other groups, such as Black men and other people of color. Black feminist sociology reflects the fact that Black women's lives matter and they matter in positive ways.

The second group Collins says Black feminist sociologists need to keep in mind as they do the hard work of challenging the social structure as it relates to Black women are other Black feminist sociologists. Thankfully, efforts are ongoing to develop and further expand networks of Black feminist scholars and Black feminist sociologists to vet, share, and review research and activist projects at every stage of development. This includes Black feminist sociologist writing groups, presentations at professional meetings, and networking on a variety of social media platforms. It also includes reading and reviewing one another's work and citing each other when appropriate.

The third group signaled in *Black Feminist Thought* that Black feminist sociologists have to contend with is white men in the academy. White men in the academy still hold on to the idea that Black feminist sociologists, like other Black scholars, should simply be grateful for their positions and that the mere act of hiring Black women in their respective departments is evidence that they are not racist or anti-Black.[16]

4. *Black feminist sociology must engage with a number of areas of study.* Undoubtedly, Black women scholars identifying as Black feminist sociologists are likely to also identify with women's studies, Black studies, Black women's studies, or women's and gender studies, for examples. Black feminist sociology should not only be in conversation with these areas of studies but also with many others. Black feminist sociology must be in conversation with, and not in opposition to, other areas, such as Black masculinities studies, Africana philosophy, African American religion, Afrofuturism, and Afro-pessimism, which helps us to think about the nature of knowledge, reality, existence, and orientations in ways that place the experiences of Black people as the focal point.[17] Historically, Black scholars, and Black people more broadly, have drawn from a variety of traditions and sources to do the work necessary in the liberation struggle. Engagement across fields of study will help to ensure that Black feminist sociology remains innovative and cutting-edge.

5. *Debates about whether quantitative or qualitative research is best must not consume Black feminist sociology.* Historically, top-tier journals are considered the gold standard in sociology. Quantitative research is overrepresented in such publishing outlets. Within the broader discipline of sociology there is a bias in favor of quantitative research. Such debates cannot befall Black feminist sociology. Research questions determine the theoretical and methodological approaches that are most appropriate for a given study. Black feminist sociology demonstrates a respect for various theoretical and methodological approaches, which could include innovations and new grammars.[18] The time has long since passed for simply adding the term "Black" in front of a sociological term, concept, or social institution and concerning one's work simply with the extent to which Black women, and Black people as a whole, are similar to, or different from, white people. Eduardo Bonilla Silva and Tukufu Zuberi took on this issue in their edited volume *White Logic, White Methods.*[19]

6. *Black feminist sociology must challenge stereotypes and myths about Black women.* Stereotypes and myths about Black women may be overt or

covert, or a combination of the two.[20] They may find expressions in mass media, social media, popular culture, sociology, and throughout the academy. Misrepresentations about Black feminist sociologists and their work and misrepresentations about Black women, and the Black community, as a whole cannot go unchecked. Black feminist sociologists are well positioned to debunk such myths given their individual and collective experiences and expertise.

7. *Out of a great deal of appreciation and respect for the communities from which many Black feminist sociologists come, their work must address social justice issues.* The stakes are too high. Black feminist sociologists do not have the luxury of ignoring social justice issues. Debates about living wages, minimum wage, reproductive freedom, health care, sexual violence, wealth inequality, marriage, families, sports, asset poverty, immigration, police brutality, mass incarceration, and the school-to-prison pipeline all impact the lives of Black female sociologists and the people they love and it is imperative that Black feminist sociologists use their available resources to address these social issues, and others. It is important to note that the likelihood of seeing meaningful change within our lifetime is not great. It is also important to know that there is value in the struggle.

8. *Black feminist sociology challenges oppression from multiple sources.* Black feminist sociologists do not have to choose whether their race, gender, class, sexuality, or any other characteristic matters more.

Conclusion

Doing Black feminist sociology is critical to understanding the experiences of Black women. Black feminist sociology has the potential to enhance society's understanding of the experiences of Black women in the US, and Black feminist sociology has the potential to enhance our understanding of critical social issues. Clarifying what doing Black feminist sociology looks like strengthens the ability of Black feminist sociology and Black feminist sociologists to provide a grammar for articulating Black women's experiences in the past and in contemporary times, which can contribute to various ongoing struggles aimed at creating a more fair, equitable, and just society.

Black feminist sociologists do not need to cut ties with the fields with which they are affiliated, but they should be confident in living and working as Black feminist sociologists with the knowledge that the number of such scholars is growing. Black feminist sociologists can boldly and unapologetically find a home in an area of study that understands the many sources of oppression they face and combat each through their work.

Notes

1. National Parks Service. "Sojourner Truth: Ain't I a Woman? Women's Rights National Historical Park. www.nps.gov/articles/sojourner-truth.htm
2. Patricia Hill Collins. 1990. *Black Feminist Thought*. New York: Routledge.
3. L. L. (Martin) Sykes. 2005. "A Home of Her Own: An Analysis of Asset Ownership for Non-married Black and White Women." *The Social Science Journal* 42(2): 273–284. https://doi.org/10.1016/j.soscij.2005.03.010
4. W. E. B. Du Bois. 1920. *Darkwater: Voices from within the Veil*. San Diego, CA: Harcourt, Brace; David S. Owen. 2007. "Whiteness in Du Bois's *The Souls of Black Folk*." *Philosophia Africana* 10: 107–126. https://doi.org/10.5840/philafricana20071022; James Perkinson. 2014. "The Ghost in the Global Machine." *Cross Currents* 64: 59–72. https://doi.org/10.1111/cros.12058; George Yancy. 2000. "Feminism and the Subtext of Whiteness: Black Women's Experiences as a Site of Identity Formation and Contestation of Whiteness." *The Western Journal of Black Studies* 24: 156–166.
5. Lorde Audre. 1984. *Sister Outsider*. New York: Crossing Press.
6. W. E. B. Du Bois. 1900. "Letter from W. E. B. Du Bois to Bertha Knobe." W. E. B. Du Bois Papers (MS 312) Special Collections and University Archives, University of Massachusetts Amherst Libraries.
7. Bell hooks. 1981. *Ain't I a Woman: Black Women and Feminism*. Cambridge, MA: South End Press; bell hooks. 1989. *Talking Back*. Boston, MA: South End Press; bell hooks. 2000. *Feminism is for Everybody: Passionate Politics*. Cambridge, MA: South End Press; bell hooks. 2006. *Outlaw Culture*. New York: Routledge; bell hooks. 2010. *Feminist Theory: From Margin to Center*. Cambridge, MA: South End Press; Angela Davis. 1981. *Women, Race, and Class*. New York: Penguin Random House; Toni Morrison. 2019. *The Source of Self-Regard: Selected Essays, Speeches, and Meditations*. New York: Alfred A. Knopf.
8. Collins 1990. Earl Wright and Edward Wallace. 2015. "Black Sociology: Continuing the Agenda." In *The Ashgate Research Companion to Black Sociology*, edited by E. Wright II and E. Wallace, 3–14. Burlington, VT: Ashgate.
9. Hortense J. Spillers. 1987. "Mama's Baby, Papa's Maybe: An American Grammar Book." *Diacritics: A Review of Contemporary Criticism* 17: 65–81. https://doi.org/10.2307/464747
10. Candace West and Don Zimmerman. "Doing Gender." *Gender and Society* 1: 125–151, 127. https://doi.org/10.1177/0891243287001002002
11. Patricia Yancey Martin. 2003. "'Said and Done' Versus 'Saying and Doing': Gendering Practices, Practicing Gender at Work." *Gender and Society* 17: 342–366. https://doi.org/10.1177/0891243203017003002
12. Collins 1990.
13. Stephen Finley, Biko Gray, and Lori Latrice Martin. 2018. "Affirming Our Values: African American Scholars, White Virtual Mobs, and the Complicity of White University Administrators." *Journal of Academic Freedom* 9: 1–20.
14. Hazel Rose Markus and Paula Moya. 2010. *Doing Race*. New York: W.W. Norton & Company.
15. Lori Latrice Martin. 2018. *Black Community Uplift and the Myth of the American Dream*. Lanham, MD: Lexington Books.
16. Sara Ahmed. 2007. "A Phenomenology of Whiteness." *Feminist Theory* 8: 149–168. https://doi.org/10.1177/1464700107078139
17. Charles Long. 1995. *Significations: Signs, Symbols, and Images in the Interpretation of Religion*. Aurora, IL: The Davies Group.
18. Spillers 1987.
19. Eduardo Bonilla-Silva and Tukufu Zuberi. 2008. *White Logic, White Methods*. Lanham, MD: Rowman & Littlefield.

20. Collins 1990. Melissa Harris-Perry. 2011. *Sister Citizen: Shame, Stereotypes, and Black Women in America*. New Haven, CT: Yale University Press.

References

Ahmed, Sara. 2007. "A Phenomenology of Whiteness." *Feminist Theory* 8: 149–168. https://doi.org/10.1177/1464700107078139

Bonilla Silva, Eduardo, and Tukufu Zuberi. 2008. *White Logic, White Methods*. Lanham, MD: Rowman & Littlefield.

Collins, Patricia Hill. 1990. *Black Feminist Thought*. New York: Routledge.

Davis, Angela. 1981. *Women, Race, and Class*. New York: Penguin Random House.

Du Bois, W. E. B. 1900. "Letter from W. E. B. Du Bois to Bertha Knobe." W. E. B. Du Bois Papers (MS 312) Special Collections and University Archives, University of Massachusetts Amherst Libraries.

Du Bois, W. E. B. 1920. *Darkwater: Voices from within the Veil*. San Diego, CA: Harcourt, Brace.

Finley, Stephen, Biko Gray, and Lori Latrice Martin. 2018. "Affirming Our Values: African American Scholars, White Virtual Mobs, and the Complicity of White University Administrators." *Journal of Academic Freedom* 9: 1–20.

Harris-Perry, Melissa. 2011. *Sister Citizen: Shame, Stereotypes, and Black Women in America*. New Haven, CT: Yale University Press.

hooks, bell. 1981. *Ain't I a Woman: Black Women and Feminism*. Cambridge, MA: South End Press.

hooks, bell. 1989. *Talking Back*. Cambridge, MA: South End Press.

hooks, bell. 2000. *Feminism is for Everybody: Passionate Politics*. Cambridge, MA: South End Press.

hooks, bell. 2006. *Outlaw Culture*. New York: Routledge.

hooks, bell. 2010. *Feminist Theory: From Margin to Center*. Cambridge, MA: South End Press.

Long, Charles. 1995. *Significations: Signs, Symbols, and Images in the Interpretation of Religion*. Aurora, IL: The Davies Group.

Markus, Hazel Rose, and Paula Moya. 2010. *Doing Race*. New York: W.W. Norton & Company.

Martin, Lori Latrice. 2018. *Black Community Uplift and the Myth of the American Dream*. Lanham, MD: Lexington Books.

(Martin) Sykes, L. L. 2005. "A Home of Her Own: An Analysis of Asset Ownership for Non-married Black and White Women." *The Social Science Journal* 42(2): 273–284. https://doi.org/10.1016/j.soscij.2005.03.010

Morrison, Toni. 2019. *The Source of Self-Regard: Selected Essays, Speeches, and Meditations*. New York: Alfred A. Knopf.

National Parks Service. "Sojourner Truth: Ain't I a Woman? Women's Rights National Historical Park." www.nps.gov/articles/sojourner-truth.htm

Owen, David S. 2007. "Whiteness in Du Bois's *the Souls of Black Folk*." *Philosophia Africana* 10: 107–126. https://doi.org/10.5840/philafricana20071022

Perkinson, James. 2014. "The Ghost in the Global Machine." *Cross Currents* 64: 59–72. https://doi.org/10.1111/cros.12058

Spillers, Hortense J. 1987. "Mama's Baby, Papa's Maybe: An American Grammar Book." *Diacritics: A Review of Contemporary Criticism* 17: 65–81. https://doi.org/10.2307/464747

West, Candace, and Don Zimmerman. "Doing Gender." *Gender and Society* 1: 125–151. https://doi.org/10.1177/0891243287001002002

Wright, Earl, and Edward Wallace. 2015. "Black Sociology: Continuing the Agenda." In *The Ashgate Research Companion to Black Sociology*, edited by E. Wright II and E. Wallace, 3–14. Burlington, VT: Ashgate.

Yancey Martin, Patricia. 2003. " 'Said and Done' Versus 'Saying and Doing': Gendering Practices, Practicing Gender at Work." *Gender and Society* 17: 342–366. https://doi.org/10.1177/0891243203017003002

Yancy, George. 2000. "Feminism and the Subtext of Whiteness: Black Women's Experiences as a Site of Identity Formation and Contestation of Whiteness." *The Western Journal of Black Studies* 24: 156–166.

Chapter 7

Nothing About Us, Without Us

Reinscribing Black Feminism in Sociology

*Endia Louise Hayes, Ashley E. Hollingshead,
Jomaira Salas Pujols and Brooklynn K. Hitchens*

Round tables, eight women, dinners for the good of the soul. Semester gatherings have been our offering in our desire to survive. In reverence, we eat, laugh and encourage crafting another space of community and sisterhood. We muse over the last semester and summer shenanigans while grooving to the Black restaurant's soft background music of H.E.R. and SZA. Around that table, we all come in need of restoration and a sharing of joy. This joy, for us, Audre Lorde terms as the erotic.[1] Around that table, it is tradition the wisest among us asks "What are your plans for this upcoming year?" making space for "*that creative energy empowered.*" It is tradition to share one another's advice for forming committees and paper ideas knowing "*we are now reclaiming in our language, our history . . . our work.*" We gather to ready ourselves for an uncertain but exciting future through a "*sharing of joy, whether physical, emotional, psychic, or intellectual, form[ing] a bridge.*" There is care in the bridge we make with one another around that table of oxtails, blackened salmon, cornbread muffins, and martinis. Yet, this bridge is deeply foundational to our varied approaches to nuanced perspectives in sociology. It is an *offering*—our declarations of "readiness"—embracing the "open and fearless" power of Black Feminist fervor for both the work and the gathering.[2]

Our collaborative chapter centers how we intentionally draw on and create a Black feminist praxis through our engagements with Black feminist sociology in our departments, research methods, and relationships with each other. We begin by acknowledging the legacies of early Black feminist theorists to sociological thought and practice. Next, we illuminate Black feminist sociologists' significant contributions to the discipline, underscoring that our experiences as Black women graduate students have been buffered by the empirical grounding and theoretical critique of Black feminists. As we anchor our contemporary experiences within the theoretical and methodological foundations they have built, we are able to frame our current strategies for surviving academia within a long history of Black Feminist resistance in sociology.

DOI: 10.4324/9781003199113-10

We then explore how we build methodologically on these legacies as practitioners of Black feminist sociology. Specifically, we show how our methods build not only on the Black women scholars before us, but more so, the Black women with whom we study and engage. We argue that the use of methods such as archival analysis, participatory action research (PAR), and ethnography conceptualize Black women's worldviews within a framework of *participation, action, power,* and *lived experience,* allowing us to situate these women as agents in our fight toward a Black feminist epistemological shift in the discipline of sociology. Our examination of the historical narratives of formerly enslaved women to contemporary experiences of young Black female graduate students underscores that Black women provide the answer to that which has been, and continues to be, neglected in sociology. We conclude this chapter by sharing how our collaboration as four Black female graduate students is an embodiment of the Black feminist sociological praxis. We assert that our engagement with the organic intellectualism of Black women not only provides us with opportunities to contribute to the discipline but also the tools to survive and thrive as graduate students in predominantly white departments and research-one institutions. Our strategies for navigating academia through a Black feminist sociological praxis require that we pour into each other as scholars, providing the space to write, learn, and theorize ourselves in tangent with other sister-scholars. These strategies are not only for the academy but for our lives. Exploring these life-giving practices centers Black women's care for one another as integral to Black feminisms and its *"deepest meanings."* This chapter is a celebration of the legacy of Black feminist sociology and its impact on the next generation of scholars.

Pedagogy of (Just a Few) Black Feminist Legacies

Black feminism is one theoretical framework that fully encompasses the complexity of Black womanhood and the dynamic dimensions of her intellectual contributions. Seven years before Du Bois's *Philadelphia Negro,* Anna Julia Cooper's *A Voice from the South* contested the struggles of Black women in the US South as not merely a race problem but also a question of womanhood.[3] Cooper's seminal text articulated the sociocultural strategies that Black Southern women could use to grapple with their raced and gendered identities in the context of structural oppression. Cooper believed that once they recognized the agency of their social location, *only* Black women possessed the power to shift the trajectory of the entire Black race into one of success, progress, and formidability. Ida B. Wells followed in Cooper's intellectual legacy of scholar activism through the creation of the public intellectual. Her writings on the "horrors" of the American South were published in newspaper columns and were digested by the "most vulnerable"—poor, Black folks who were most at risk to racialized violence and terror. Using her empirical analysis on the "728 lynchings that had taken place,"[4] Wells sought to ignite a critical consciousness in the minds of poor Black southerners about the value of Black life and economic progress. Her commitment to using rigorous research methods to illuminate the horrors of lynchings supplies a blueprint for how Black feminist sociologists can leverage social science for social justice. Yet, everyday Black women were integral to the success of Wells's *Southern Horrors* as the booklet was only published with the assistance of 250 Black women who collectively raised $500 and held a testimonial event in support of Wells. Their support further demonstrates how collaboration among Black women, in celebration of Wells's and Cooper's pursuit of the whole race, has always been foundational to our research and social justice agenda. In a field that too often promotes "objectivity" and competitive division, Cooper and Wells remind us that we should be, and never are, alone in our pursuit of liberation.

Black feminists build on the intellectual traditions of one other. Black feminism's greatest theorizations have often stemmed from our time and observations with each other, concluding that the domination and marginalization Black women face does not exist in a vacuum. As Deborah King's theory on "multiple jeopardy" suggests, Black women experience various forms of subjugation simultaneously.[5] The multiplicity of these oppressions contributes to the unique social location of the Black woman who often cannot rely on her race, gender, or class to neutralize the inequities she experiences.[6] King's "multiple jeopardy" grew as a theoretical expansion to Frances Beale's "double jeopardy," which bridged Anna Julia Cooper's earlier call for the inclusion of race and gender in the early iterations of exclusionary white feminism. These concepts provided a foundation for Kimberlé Crenshaw's theorizing of "intersectionality," which argues that the intersectional identities of Black women often render them invisible in discussions on gender-related issues (e.g., domestic violence or rape) and race-related issues (e.g., police violence or mass incarceration).[7] In this communion, we can draw on Black Feminist sociologists like Patricia Hill Collins who remind us that Black feminist thought is a social theory that is critical in how we understand the complex social issues facing Black women across diverse strata, particularly the marginalization of Black womanhood and the dehumanization of Black bodies. Like in the work of Black feminists before her, Collins's *Black Feminist Thought* emphasizes the necessity for Black women, like ourselves, to define and produce knowledge of our unique experiences with power and resistance, inciting thorough and nuanced understandings of Black womanhood.[8] In a Black Feminist tradition, theories of Black women should continue to build and affirm our womanisms inside and outside of academia.

Critical Mappings of Black Feminist Methodologies When the Academy Isn't Enuf

Black Feminists legacies ask that we continue to build and revise our approaches to Black womanhood. Researching Black women requires that we see our participants as possessing intellectual knowledge to be shared and engaged with. While leaning on the language of Black feminisms, we use the following methods to demonstrate how we center the daily pedagogies of Black girls and women. These methods show us how to actively listen to us, engage us, and honor our lives. In this section, drawing from the prompt of Ntozake Shange, we describe how we locate Black women's words, labor, and knowledge through the use of archival analysis, participatory action research, and ethnographic methods.

The Bellies of Our Ghosts

As Black Feminist writers, we often use reflections of the past to better situate the historical context of our present. Our attentiveness to the past echoes sociologist Avery Gordon's call to attend to the ghosts that haunt sociology—in other words, the present and inevitable futures of Black life studied through a sociological lens must first focus on the impact of slavery's afterlife still found at the core of the discipline.[9] A repeated drawing from the past by Black feminist scholars remind us that the depths of a harrowing U.S. history remains unacknowledged. Yet, Black folks still speak in those historical erasures. For one of our authors, she centers her work on the following questions: (1) What would it look like to investigate formerly enslaved women as critical social theorists? (2) How are enslaved folks pushing the definitions of a critical sociological text crafting knowledge through the flesh—*hands* holding both white and Black children, *feet* that walked across states in chains and *backs* bent in plantation fields, over stoves and spinning looms? Their language of labor, along with their languages and expressions of pain, desire, and pride—their appetites, *bellies*— reflect the enslaved Black woman's physical, spiritual, and psychological intellectualism forged alongside violent encounters. Archival analysis, through a Black Feminist sociological praxis, demands that we can intentionally teeter the temporality of linear Western thought and the imaginative transcendence of Blackness. Here, she draws again on Collins to argue that in making visible the theoretical contributions of Black women in and outside of academia, here on plantations, we shift our approach to archival research by implementing a radical practice of centering enslaved women as early enactors of social praxes and Black Feminist pedagogy.[10]

The archives give us additional ways to think and articulate beyond Western forms of logic and reason. For example, archives preserved from the *Born in Slavery: Slave Narratives from the Federal Writers'*

Project, 1936–1938 through the Library of Congress's Works Progress Administration (WPA) are perhaps the foremost and premier collection of enslaved words found in the United States. Recorded in the 1930s, enslaved folks shared their stories with mostly *white* interviewers interested in recording their experiences as former slaves. Although "me-search" and subjectivity are too often vilified and devalued in our discipline of sociology, the work of Black feminist scholars like Saidiya Hartman,[11] Deborah Gray-White,[12] and Marisa Fuentes[13] discuss a framework of violence that marks the archival condition. This is particularly salient in the WPA narratives. Hartman warns of this violence that cannot fully account for enslaved life as she thought through and against these WPA narratives in her first text *Scenes of Subjection*. She warns of "the imperative to construct a usable and palatable national past [that] certainly determined the picture of slavery drawn in the testimonies gather ed by the Works Progress Administration."[14] Hartman proposes alternative methods, such as critical fabulation and speculation, where one can imagine alongside the lives of other Black folks. Bringing a method like fabulation or imagination into readings of US enslavement critically remaps and represents Black life. Black feminism unearths epistemological contributions not located in white frameworks of understanding (i.e., the WPA), but finds a greater onus and interest imagining beyond testimonies and shared silences.

Archival excavation of Black life is never done. Entire social worlds built by the enslaved while crafting knowledge using food or moving in and out of the plantation bounds have yet to be touched, but they are a part of our methodological bridge to expanding Black feminism's place in sociological practice. Our tasks as Black feminist sociologists are to honor their words using their testimonies to uncovering a past that has neglected them and the violence they may not have been comfortable discussing. Similarly, if we take the words and labor of enslaved women and folks seriously, they could assist in reimagining a history foundational to Black feminist sociology in the US. This means we focus on the enslaved as exploring the sociological using embodied discourse, Black knowledge curated through engagements of Black flesh described by Katherine McKittrick as "Black women's histories, lives and spaces must be understood as enmeshing with traditional geographic arrangement in order to identify a different way of knowing and writing the social world."[15] Archival analysis describes how enslaved understandings and makings within the colonial nation-state were forged by folks at the frontlines of cultural convergence intermingling with the French, Mexican, British, Indigenous, German and many others. Black enslaved flesh provides Black feminist sociological scholarship a past with which to frame the present, but it is my practice to excavate their wisdom that has been passed to Black feminists before us and incorporate it into our developing scholarship.

Black Voices, Black Movement, Black Life

We also believe that ethnographic and participatory action research (PAR) methods can utilize a Black feminist framework to leverage sociology toward social justice. Black women have long contributed to the literature on feminist ethnography with Dána-Ain Davis defining *feminist activist ethnography* "as drawing on methodological strategies that embrace the everyday experiences of people—especially those forced to live on the margins—as epistemologically valid."[16] Similarly, participatory action research has a reflexive, action-based orientation that privileges the lived experiences of marginalized groups and equips researchers to collaborate with these groups to develop research questions, methodologies, and analyses that empower and liberate communities.[17] One of the authors uses PAR methodology and Black feminism in her work on the lived experiences of street-identified Black women and girls with violent crime, and this work actively includes these women in the research process.[18] This methodology calls for an epistemological shift in the "location of power in the research process"[19] recognizing that marginalized communities hold the intellectual keys to freedom and social change.[20]

Through ethnography and PAR, we follow a long lineage of Black feminists such as Ida B. Wells, Joyce Ladner, Zora Neale Hurston and Dána-Ain Davis who reject objectivity, and instead embrace the wisdom and knowledge to be gained from the perspective of the Black subjective. Our work for social change in Black feminist sociology frames our desires, and appetites, to condemn oppression and systems that bind our communities.

When Joyce Ladner began conducting research for her groundbreaking book *Tomorrow's Tomorrow*, she engaged a deeply affective connection to her subject: Black girlhood. Ladner writes that her pursuit of this study stemmed from a deep unease with the dominant narrative about Black girls. Instead, she reshaped traditional ethnographic methods to move from a distant observer to an accountable community member—a distinction also made with Hurston's ethnographic works.[21] When pursuing our own ethnographies, we have come to a similar self-realization. Like Ladner, our Black feminist ethnography is built on an intense desire to expose the consequence of centuries of neglect, abuse, and oppression, but also to shine light on the indelible ability that our communities have to resist such systemic treatment. A Black feminist ethnography then not only rejects objectivity, but purposely asks: what becomes visible when we take Black people's beliefs, values, and behaviors seriously? What shifts become necessary when these injustices are exposed? And how do we actively pursue research that condemns the institutions and policies that harm and oppress our communities?

Black Feminist sociologists conducting ethnographic methods lie at an important nexus in the academy. We envelope Black women's knowledge both in and out of the academy to reorient how Black life is discussed and examined in sociology. Both PAR and ethnography involve redefining what sociology is understood to be, what questions are most insightful, and what actions must follow research findings. This is not a sociology for knowledge's sake, but one that demands more just practices, more equitable institutions, and more reparative policies. For example, if we take up Collins's assertion that Black communities do hold knowledge outside the academy, then PAR becomes increasingly necessary as it requires that we work with community members to craft research questions that are responsive to what they need and desire. We also recognize that Black feminist influences reach beyond PAR by showing us how to leverage not only our institutional resources in benefit of our communities[22] but these resources can aid in our, and communities, condemnation of systematic oppression.[23] In our own work, we have used ethnography to collaborate with small community nonprofits on pilot studies that are reflective of our research interests but also of the community's needs. These nonprofits can leverage our findings to pursue funding, recruit participants, and advocate for policy shifts. Similarly, through the use of PAR, we have trained and employed community members on research methods and been intentional about how we write and disseminate our findings to ensure that our research is supporting, rather than harming, our research communities. Our methodological approaches redefine traditional ethnographic methods as they demand that the needs of Black communities be placed at the center, not behind, the requirements of academia. Whether through ethnography or through PAR, we see a radical positioning of Black women in sociology's imaginary where all Black women possess a sociological imagination to observe and speak on their social world.

Black feminist sociology centers Black womanhood by offering systems of worth to Black women that exist and are engaged both in and outside the academy. The course for liberation from dominant sociology belongs with those who use knowledge as an avenue to improve Black life. What can we learn about the "method" of navigating academia from a Black feminist praxis? A Black feminist approach to PAR and ethnography reminds us that we *can* leverage our institutional privilege (despite our marginalization within the institution) to help transform the conditions of our communities. We argue then, that we cannot be Black feminists without practicing Black feminist solidarity with each other. In other words, in a discipline that values competition, we must extend the same care that we extend to Black communities we study to each other.

Lifting as We Climb: For Us, by Us

Black feminist sociologists have created a blueprint that help us sharpen our approaches to navigating the academy. They have given us a frame through which to love and care for each other by demonstrating that if we can care for research participants then we may fight for that very same care for each other. Our scholarly knowledge is not the only way we incorporate our social interactions and observations. We utilize our knowledge of each other and for each other's success inside and outside the academy. In the following, we share our personal commitments to Black Feminist sociology as a lifestyle.

Black feminism is *care and support*. Sharpe reminds us that we can "reimagine and transform spaces for and in practice an ethics of care (as in repair, maintenance, attention), an ethics of seeing, and of *being* . . . as consciousness."[24] Much like Well's homegirls who came together to ensure the successful publication of *Southern Horrors*, we have also poured onto each other so that we may join the legacy and growing numbers of Black women in academia. While the first day of classes are a mix of nerves and fear, we built our own networks of support outside of the academic structure. This web of support first began with holding dinners. This grew into the fall semesters becoming an opportunity for incoming Black female doctoral students to meet, learn from, and bond with Black women in advanced cohorts. We shared lessons of academia's hidden curriculum and white/male centered networks that leave us without certain knowledges to successfully navigate our programs. We decided to be intentional about passing down knowledge through oration, as Black women have long done through stories, tips, and cautionary tales. The knowledge we have shared has been central to our ability to access institutional resources, circumvent disciplinary conventions, and assuage the painful wounds of moving against the grain. We throw money at countless happy hours and brunches needed to vent about a stall in our process, bumps in the road and bullshit. We laugh at obscene suggestions that dismiss Black feminisms or relegate them to one reading at the end of the semester by offering each other articles and book suggestions that help us cite and center Black women's thoughts in our work.

We reject the convention that there is only space for one of us. Instead, we share successful grant applications, celebrate dissertation defenses with family, pick up free copies of *When and Where I Enter* for one another, read drafts for competitive applications and sleep on each other's couches when we live too far away to make early classes the next morning. We do not just read about ethics of care, we practice it and continue to initiate new practices of self and communal support. For summers, we travel with friends and families. We travel to homecomings in the South. We travel as an ode to our roots and, possibly, to enhance our scholarship. Support finds ways we can carry each other, our participants, and our foremothers. Support is necessary for our lives in sustenance for one another and our desire to further Black feminist sociology. We mirror Black feminist acts of Bethune's National Council of Negro Women's mission to lift as we climb, creating community to liberate ourselves from competing against the few folks who look like us. In this praxis, we celebrate the legacy of Black feminists that have shown us how to care for our communities and each other. We search, engage and honor the pathway that they have cleared. The wounds, though still present, are tended through our recognition that we are not the only ones, that others have done it before us, and that others will come after.

Black Feminism for us is *liberatory*. In a discipline that often deems Black feminism as illegitimate, our work opens up doors for young, Black girls whose bodies and lives matter. Reading the writings of Toni Morrison, bell hooks, Angela Davis, Denise Ferreira da Silva, June Jordan, Sarah Haley, and Nell Painter opens new Black worlds full of the songs of blues women, memories, revolutions, and fictive lives of the enslaved. Liberation is inscribed on our happy faces that light up when another Black woman enters the room. Liberation intentionally revisits what social change looks like for the women we study and for us in our engagements in graduate school. Its praxis includes demystifying the graduate process that leaves many of us without certain knowledge and opportunities, and making decisions regarding advisors, networking, and personal branding. Liberation makes space for our individual journeys to develop naturally, yet strategically, as we make known our success with one another and our community.

Black Feminism for us is a *healing praxis*. Healing encompasses a process of making well again, mending, and overcoming. A healing praxis becomes a process of becoming or restoring. Though within Black feminism, Blackness has nothing to restore, in its essence, rather, its healing praxis highlights the magnificence that has always existed—this also centers the magic we continue to make. We self-reflect on our positionalities to better interact with various communities, often a curiosity not extended to us. We confront our fears of not being heard by making space with each other, sharing resources on how to take care of ourselves as people, researchers and marginalized students in and outside of the department. We plant ourselves intentionally in this circle of Black Feminist love that leads to collaborations like this one. We check and recheck on each other to pour life as we grow. Embodying a Black Feminist healing praxis leaves space for our individual growth while remaining in tune with other Black women in holistic and medicinal ways. Celebrating our small and large victories are sites of joy, and we reap what we have sown after giving so much of our tears, time, bodies and minds.

Conclusion

Our Black feminist sociological pedagogy asks that we attend to the influence Black women have on one another—influence we may not be able to put in name but is certainly offered to us through the bridges we form. We are fortunate to enter the academy after the likes of Cooper, Wells, Ladner, Collins, and countless others. These women have made this path a little more bearable, a little more doable, a little more joyful. Their lessons not only impact our sociological methods, but our methods for navigating the academy emerged in "our desire to find in Black feminist theoretical history a new roadmap, and new methods, that can point to more just futures for Black women and girls," and ourselves.[25] Within our Black Feminist social reality, we validate one another in and out of academic spaces. We cannot separate our bodies from our scholarship, from our experiences as Black female graduate students, nor from the Black female bodies that form some of the beginnings of American sociology. Instead, by leaning into the legacy of Black feminists, we center ourselves and the Black women we carry with us as knowledge producers.[26] Such recentering shifts the discipline from merely "valuing our knowledge" to recognizing it as indispensable to the canon. Grounding this chapter in our contemporary challenges and successes as young doctoral students, we resurface the ties to Black feminism as foundational to sociology and demonstrate how we navigate a deeply hostile academy. It is our experiences as Black women studying Black feminism's ancestors and living legends, alongside our Black women participants and magic of our Blackness, that we center Black feminist sociology as an important addition within Black feminism's power.

Notes

1. Audre Lorde. 2019. "Uses of the Erotic." In *Annotated in Pleasure Activism: The Politics of Feeling Good*, edited by Adrienne Maree Brown, 27–35. Chico: AK Press.
2. "Offer | Definition of Offer." *Merriam Webster*. www.merriam-webster.com/dictionary/offer.
3. Anna Julia Cooper. 1892. *A Voice from The South*. New York: Dover Publications.
4. Paula Giddings. 1984, 1996. *When and Where I Enter: The Impact of Black Women on Race and Sex in America*, 28. New York: W. Morrow.
5. Hillary Potter. 2013. "Intersectional Criminology: Interrogating Identity and Power in Criminological Research and Theory." *Critical Criminology* 21: 305–318. Deborah K. King. 1988. "Multiple Jeopardy, Multiple Consciousness: The Context of a Black Feminist Ideology." *Signs: Journal of Women in Culture and Society* 14(1): 42–72.
6. Patricia Hill Collins. 1990, 2000, 2009. *Black Feminist Thought: Knowledge, Consciousness, and the Politics of Empowerment*, 519. New York: Routledge.
7. Kimberlé Crenshaw. 1991. "Mapping the Margins: Intersectionality, Identity Politics, and Violence against Women of Color." *Stanford Law Review* 43(6): 1241–1249.
8. Collins 1990, 2000, 2009.
9. Avery Gordon. 1997, 2008. *Ghostly Matters: Haunting and the Sociological Imagination*. Minneapolis: University of Minnesota Press.
10. Patricia Hill Collins. 1986. "Learning from the Outsider Within: The Sociological Significance of Black Feminist Thought." *Social Problems* 33(6): 14–32. Collins 1990, 2000, 2009.

11. Saidiya Hartman. 2008. "Venus in Two Acts." *Small Axe: A Caribbean Journal of Criticism.* 12(2): 1–14; Saidiya Hartman. 1997. *Scenes of Subjection: Terror, Slavery, and Self-Making in the Nineteenth Century.* New York: Oxford University Press.
12. Deborah Gray White. 1985. *Ar'n't I a Woman? Female Slaves in the Plantation South.* New York: W. W. Norton & Company, Inc.; Deborah Gray White. 1987. "Mining the Forgotten: Manuscript Sources for Black Women's History." *Journal of American History* 74(1): 237–242.
13. Marisa Fuentes. 2018. *Dispossessed Lives: Enslaved Women, Violence and the Archive.* Philadelphia, PA: University of Pennsylvania Press.
14. Hartman 1997, 10.
15. Katherine McKittrick. 2006. *Demonic Grounds: Black Women and the Cartographies of Struggle,* xiv. Minneapolis: University of Minnesota Press.
16. Dána-Ain Davis. 2014. "Border Crossings: Intimacy and Feminist Activist Ethnography in the Age of Liberalism." In *Feminist Activist Ethnography: Counterpoints to Neoliberalism in North America,* edited by C. Craven and D. A. Davis, 23–38, 27. Lanham, MD: Lexington Books.
17. Yasser Arafat Payne. 2017a. "Participatory Action Research." In *The Wiley Blackwell Encyclopedia of Social Theory,* edited by B. S. Turner, C. Kyung-Sup, C. F. Epstein, P. Kivisto, W. Outhwaite, and J. M. Ryan, 1–15. Hoboken, NJ: Wiley-Blackwell.
18. Brooklynn K. Hitchens and Yasser A. Payne. 2017. "Brenda's Got a Baby: Black Single Motherhood and Street Life as a Site of Resilience in Wilmington, Delaware." *Journal of Black Psychology* 43(1): 50–76; Brooklynn K. Hitchens. Forthcoming. "Revisiting Brenda's Got a Baby: Black Motherhood, Families, and Structural Violence in the Streets." *Afrikan American Women: Living at the Crossroads of Race, Gender, Class, and Culture,* edited by H. Jackson-Lowman. 2nd ed. San Diego, CA: Cognella Academic Publishing.
19. Andrea Cornwall and Rachel Jewkes. 1995. "What Is Participatory Research?" *Social Science & Medicine* 41(12): 1667–1676, 1687.
20. Yasser Arafat Payne. 2017b. "Participatory Action Research and Social Justice: Keys to Freedom for Street Life-Oriented Black Men." In *Free at Last? Black America in the Twenty-First Century,* edited by J. Battle, M. Bennett, and A. J. Lemelle, 265–280. New York: Routledge.
21. Joyce A. Ladner. 1971. *Tomorrow's Tomorrow: The Black Woman,* xix–xxviii. Garden City, NY: Doubleday.
22. Davis 2014; Zora Neale Hurston. 1935. *Mules and Men.* Philadelphia, PA: J. B. Lippincott Co.
23. Hurston 1935.
24. Christina Sharpe. 2016. *In the Wake: On Blackness and Being,* 131. Durham, NC: Duke University Press.
25. Samantha Pinto. 2017. "Black Feminist Literacies: Ungendering, Flesh, and Post-Spillers Epistemologies of Embodied and Emotional Justice." *Journal of Black Sexuality and Relationships* 4(1): 25–45, 28.
26. Collins 1990, 2000, 2009.

References

Collins, Patricia Hill. 1986. "Learning from the Outsider Within: The Sociological Significance of Black Feminist Thought." *Social Problems* 33(6): 14–32.
Collins, Patricia Hill. 1990, 2000, 2009. *Black Feminist Thought: Knowledge, Consciousness, and the Politics of Empowerment.* New York: Routledge.
Cooper, Anna Julia. 1892. *A Voice from The South.* New York: Dover Publications.

Cornwall, Andrea, and Rachel Jewkes. 1995. "What Is Participatory Research?" *Social Science & Medicine* 41(12): 1667–1676.

Crenshaw, Kimberlé. 1991. "Mapping the Margins: Intersectionality, Identity Politics, and Violence against Women of Color." *Stanford Law Review* 43(6): 1241–1249.

Davis, Dána-Ain. 2014. "Border Crossings: Intimacy and Feminist Activist Ethnography in the Age of Liberalism." In *Feminist Activist Ethnography: Counterpoints to Neoliberalism in North America*, edited by C. Craven and D. A. Davis, 23–38. Lanham, MD: Lexington Books.

Fuentes, Marisa. 2018. *Dispossessed Lives: Enslaved Women, Violence and the Archive*. Philadelphia, PA: University of Pennsylvania Press.

Giddings, Paula. 1984, 1996. *When and Where I Enter: The Impact of Black Women on Race and Sex in America*. New York: W. Morrow.

Gordon, Avery. 1997, 2008. *Ghostly Matters: Haunting and the Sociological Imagination*. Minneapolis: University of Minnesota Press.

Hartman, Saidiya. 1997. *Scenes of Subjection: Terror, Slavery, and Self-Making in the Nineteenth Century*. New York: Oxford University Press.

Hartman, Saidiya. 2008. "Venus in Two Acts." *Small Axe: A Caribbean Journal of Criticism* 12(2): 1–14.

Hitchens, Brooklynn K. Forthcoming. "Revisiting Brenda's Got a Baby: Black Motherhood, Families, and Structural Violence in the Streets." In *African American Women: Living at the Crossroads of Race, Gender, Class, and Culture*, edited by H. Jackson-Lowman. 2nd ed. San Diego, CA: Cognella Academic Publishing.

Hitchens, Brooklynn K., and Yasser A. Payne. 2017. "Brenda's Got a Baby: Black Single Motherhood and Street Life as a Site of Resilience in Wilmington, Delaware." *Journal of Black Psychology* 43(1): 50–76.

Hurston, Zora Neale. 1935. *Mules and Men*. Philadelphia, PA: J. B. Lippincott Co.

King, Deborah K. 1988. "Multiple Jeopardy, Multiple Consciousness: The Context of a Black Feminist Ideology." *Signs: Journal of Women in Culture and Society* 14(1): 42–72.

Ladner, Joyce A. 1971. *Tomorrow's Tomorrow: The Black Woman*. Garden City, NY: Doubleday.

Lorde, Audre. 2019. "Uses of the Erotic." Annotated in *Pleasure Activism: The Politics of Feeling Good*, edited by Adrienne Maree Brown, 27–35. Chico: AK Press.

McKittrick, Katherine. 2006. *Demonic Grounds: Black Women and the Cartographies of Struggle*. Minneapolis: University of Minnesota Press.

"Offer | Definition of Offer." Merriam Webster. www.merriam-webster.com/dictionary/offer.

Payne, Yasser Arafat. 2017a. "Participatory Action Research." In *The Wiley Blackwell Encyclopedia of Social Theory*, edited by B. S. Turner, C. Kyung-Sup, C. F. Epstein, P. Kivisto, W. Outhwaite, and J. M. Ryan, 1–15. Hoboken, NJ: Wiley-Blackwell.

Payne, Yasser Arafat. 2017b. "Participatory Action Research and Social Justice: Keys to Freedom for Street Life-Oriented Black Men." In *Free at Last? Black America in the Twenty-First Century*, edited by J. Battle, M. Bennett, and A. J. Lemelle, 265–280. New York: Routledge.

Pinto, Samantha. 2017. "Black Feminist Literacies: Ungendering, Flesh, and Post-Spillers Epistemologies of Embodied and Emotional Justice." *Journal of Black Sexuality and Relationships* 4(1): 25–45.

Potter, Hillary. 2013. "Intersectional Criminology: Interrogating Identity and Power in Criminological Research and Theory." *Critical Criminology* 21: 305–318.

Sharpe, Christina. 2016. *In the Wake: On Blackness and Being.* Durham, DC and London: Duke University Press.

White, Deborah Gray. 1985. *Ar'n't I a Woman? Female Slaves in the Plantation South.* New York: W.W. Norton & Company, Inc.

White, Deborah Gray. 1987. "Mining the Forgotten: Manuscript Sources for Black Women's History." *Journal of American History* 74(1): 237–242.

Chapter 8

#BlackGirlMagic and Its Complexities

Maria S. Johnson

You just searched online for the phrase #BlackGirlMagic—what might you find? The results may vary daily, but at the time of this writing, you'd likely find tweets, blog posts, Instagram posts, media articles, and merchandise. You'd also find different messages about #BlackGirlMagic, from celebratory to critical. In this chapter, I explore "#BlackGirlMagic" (hereafter #BGM), which emerged in its current form on social media in 2013 and has since become enormously popular.[1] #BGM celebrates the existence and actions of Black women and girls by highlighting their emotions, stylings, accomplishments, and their efforts to supersede societal limitations.

As a Black feminist sociologist, I was intrigued when I first encountered #BGM online. Working within a predominantly white field, often teaching about racism and sexism, I found myself looking at content online related to #BGM. I felt a sense of kinship and community with friends who shared the posts and people who created the initial social media content. I was particularly interested in how Black women and girls[2] used #BGM, which later led to a formal research project.

In the following sections, I use my research to detail how despite people's intentions regarding inclusivity and diversity, the most frequent and popular proclamations of #BGM during the time period I studied were of academic and professional achievements and mainstream and colorist notions of Black beauty and ability. I found that although #BGM was widely understood as a positive term, it was also a contested idea that could be used to promote limited ideas about Black women and girls. However, this finding is not straightforwardly "positive" or "negative." It raises important questions about how we study social media phenomenon like #BGM. Rather than prescribing if or when the expression should be used, I explore some of the paradoxes of its use. As a reader, you may see yourself in the quotes or arguments presented or you may recoil at the expression and its use. I invite you to not ask whether it's "right" or "wrong" to use #BGM but to sit with the contradictions and complexities that emerge.

DOI: 10.4324/9781003199113-11

Background: Making #BGM

Popularly understood as a phrase intended to empower and praise Black women and girls, #BGM is commonly attributed to CaShawn Thompson, a social media figure who tweets under the name @thepbg. In a 2015 *Los Angeles Times* interview, CaShawn Thompson described #BGM in the following manner, "I say 'magic' because it's something that people don't always understand. Sometimes our accomplishments might seem to come out of thin air, because a lot of times, the only people supporting us are other Black women."[3] Thompson sought to expose Black women's hard work that could be chalked up to luck or natural ability.

However, Thompson was not the first to use the expression as a hashtag or to ascribe magical qualities to Black women and girls. For instance, in 2011, a South African artist with the twitter handle @desiremarea tweeted, "@mzeezolyt_e I'm loving your talk show mindset! Mwah! Hamba #blackgirlmagic." Additionally, writers, like Joan Morgan and Alice Walker, using other platforms and formats, like literature, have referred to the "magic" of Black women prior to Thompson's use of #BGM.[4]

Nonetheless, Thompson's use of #BGM as a form of empowerment and self-affirmation for Black women and girls has gained the most traction and popularity. Thompson first used the terms "BlackGirlMagic" and "Black Girls are Magic" in 2013. In February 2013, she raved about the work of Ntozake Shange and called it "Black Girl Magic" without a hashtag. In June 2013, she used a hashtag, posting "Oh, but we are. We are definitely the Force #BlackGirlMagic." A Twitter user with the handle @lifeofaladybug responded with, "That is now my new favorite hashtag." Thompson started selling sweatshirts with the phrase "Black Girls are Magic" in January 2014. Since its creation, #BGM has been used on various social media outlets, like Twitter, millions of times.

As with anything that becomes widespread, #BGM has diverse meanings. Although #BGM includes the word "girl," the hashtag has arguably been applied more to Black women given the colloquial way in which "girl" is used as a term of affection. There have also been disagreements over who "owns" the phrase, with various people (like CaShawn Thompson and Beverly Bond, a business woman and founder of Black Girls Rock!) and entities (like Essence Communications, Inc.) trademarking variations of "Black Girl Magic."[5] Additionally, #BGM has influenced research topics and analysis. Search results of "Black Girl Magic" on research databases, like Google Scholar, include research papers that explore topics like Black women's work experiences or their mental health. #BGM doesn't just have a meaningful presence on social media. It now exists in the virtual and physical worlds, influences social and professional spaces, and has sparked research and commercial enterprise.

In early 2016, the debate around #BGM became particularly pronounced. In January, *Essence* magazine released its February 2016 Black History Month issue with a cover story titled "Black Girl Magic Class of 2016." The issue profiled actresses Teyonah Parris and Yara Shahidi and activist Johnetta Elzie as emerging Black cultural leaders and proclaimed them as exemplars of #BGM. Within days, Professor Linda Chavers responded to the *Essence* article with a piece titled "Here's My Problem with #BlackGirlMagic" on *Elle* magazine's website. Chavers argued that #BGM fits into a longstanding expectation that Black women and girls be exceptional and resist pain and vulnerability. Although she acknowledged the positivity of celebrating Black women and girls, she noted the phrase's potential to demand superhuman strength from Black women and girls. As a Black feminist scholar with a disability, Chavers felt, both personally and politically, that such a focus on strength could be harmful.

Journalists, bloggers, and social media communicators responded swiftly to Chavers's piece.[6] *Essence* published a rejoinder essay by journalist Bené Viera, titled "#BlackGirlMagic: Why Black Women Have 'That Thing' And You Don't Have to Understand It." In a subsequent interview with Kimberly Foster, the editor-in-chief of *For Harriet* (an online community for Black women), Chavers clarified that her critique came from a place of love and concern for the health and well-being of Black women and girls. It was clearly a moment of clarification and contestation for #BGM as a broader social and cultural phenomenon.

Responding to various critiques of the use of #BGM, Thompson has sought to clarify her original intent. She is quoted with saying, "I started #blackgirlsaremagic to honor the Black women in my family and all around me that I saw doing incredible things, so much so that they appeared to be magical to me."[7] In 2017, Thompson emphasized the phrase's positive effects: "The hashtag has been one of love and community-building for Black women online."[8] She also insisted that #BGM was an inclusive term:

> Hood Black girls got magic too! So do Black girls that do hair in their kitchen, disabled Black girls, lesbian Black girls, fat Black girls, poor Black girls, Black girls with relaxers and weave, Black girls that are single moms, Black girls that haven't figured out how to blend their make-up, Black girls that are incarcerated, trans-Black girls, teenage Black girls, uneducated/undereducated Black girls, Black girls that work low paying jobs, Black girls that present as masculine, etc. Ya dig?[9]

Thompson's description of #BGM reads as a manifesto of sorts, proclaiming a safe space for an array of Black women and girls.

Representing Black Women and Girls: Then and Now

There is a well-established body of scholarship that examines how Black women and girls have been and are represented in the media. Black feminist sociologists have been at the forefront of this work with key figures such as Patricia Hill Collins and others providing critical analyses of racial and gender stereotypes or "controlling images."[10] From representations of "angry Black women" to sexually promiscuous "jezebels," there has been no shortage of negative imagery. Whereas much research in this field examines traditional forms of media and representation, more recent work tackles social media.

Social media is an important social world for the daily lives of Black women and girls. Media studies scholar Meredith Clark has argued that Black people created an online Twitter community, commonly called "Black Twitter,"[11] a virtual space through which "to coalesce around an issue, to speak back to depictions and to really offer an alternative way of seeing black lived experiences."[12] Further, Black feminist sociologist Melissa Brown has argued that social media fosters Black people's empowerment, activism, and community-building through collective action in movements like Black Lives Matter.[13] Nevertheless, the internet can also circulate harmful notions of race and gender both within and outside of Black online communities.

Fortunately, a growing number of scholars are asking questions about the views of Black girls. Researcher and girl empowerment expert Carla Stokes reported that Black teen girls have diverse expressions of their sexuality on the internet. Black feminist political scientist Ruth Nicole Brown's and Black feminist anthropologist Aimee Cox's work pushes us to explore Black girls' identity-making and creativity through performance and music. And Black feminist sociologist Nikki Jones has explored the role of race and urban space in shaping the behaviors, attitudes, and views of Black teen girls. However, more research examining the specific dynamics of social media in which the inequalities of the "real" world are disrupted and reproduced by Black girls and women is needed.

Researching #BGM

This chapter focuses on content produced in January 2016, a time when debates abounded in large media outlets and social media about the definition and merits of #BGM. To this end, I, along with a graduate student research assistant, D'Janna Hamilton, looked at magazine articles,[14] blog posts, and Twitter posts (also referred to as tweets) that used some variation of #BGM. We coded the articles and posts by identifying broad and specific themes. We then used the codes that emerged to analyze tweets. I used Sifter and DiscoverText, social media analysis programs, to gather and analyze English-language tweets posted January 5, 2016, to January 22, 2016,[15] with the hashtags "blackgirlmagic" or "blackgirlsaremagic"—a total of 81,672 tweets. I focused on Twitter posts because of the Black Twitter community and *Essence* advertised its #BGM issue on Twitter. Although most posts were written using "we/us/I" voice, Black women and girls were not the only ones who used #BGM. I did not filter tweets based on race of poster, which could be difficult to ascertain without direct contact, which I did not have with any of the Twitter posters. Using themes identified from media materials and tweets, I analyzed topics of popular posts that acquired more than 100 retweets or likes.

Who and What Gets to be "Magical"?

Essence magazine author Bené Viera proclaimed, "Our very existence is magic, and that's worthy of celebration." Who would not want to exalt and affirm Black women and girls, especially considering the oppressive social spaces that shape so much of our existence? #BGM causes us to ask, whose existence is exalted as magical and worth celebrating?

During the time period I examined, the five most popular #BGM topics were: (1) a *Teen Vogue* article and video series about #BGM featuring actress Amandla Sternberg; (2) the 2016 *Essence* article on #BGM featuring activist Johnetta Elzie and actresses Teyonah Parris and Yara Shahidi, and posts related to the article; (3) a photograph of the women's swim team at North Carolina Agricultural and Technical State University, a historically Black college/university (HBCU), celebrating Black women's participation in a sport with which Black people are not typically associated; (4) the *Elle* magazine article by Linda Chavers on #BGM, described earlier; and (5) another article published in *Elle*, this time by Ashley Ford, titled "There Is Nothing Wrong With Black Girl Magic," in response to Chavers's article. Moreover, Black women and girl celebrities were topics of tweets and #BGM influencers (meaning their posts were often retweeted, commented on, and liked). In addition to the debate about the definition of #BGM, the most common topics were about beauty and appearance, and educational and professional accomplishments.

Beauty and Appearance

Black women and girls' beauty and style represent a major aspect of #BGM. Most #BGM images represented a range of skin tones and facial features, yet they presented more traditionally feminine depictions. Many images of Black women and girls with medium to dark brown complexions were of women with long hair, both straight and curly, and sometimes blonde.

For instance, one of the more popular images was of a dark-skinned Sudanese woman wearing a blonde wig. The prevalence of made-up appearances paired with phenotypes associated with light skin tones and looser curled hair is not inclusive of all Black women and girls and can be an indication of colorism, a racial/ethnic group hierarchy based on skin color that privileges people with lighter skin tones.[16] This is not to minimize the experiences of Black women and girls with light brown skin tones or curly hair or infer they should not be celebrated. Instead, there should be recognition that #BGM can reflect our limitations as a community, which in this instance would be colorism.

Some tweets celebrated Black women and girls' hair and complexions that were unaltered by chemicals or products. Society should appreciate these images of beauty, but I caution against looking down upon enhanced feminine appearances. As race and sexuality scholar Kaila Story argues, ultra-feminine appearance can be an act of resistance, particularly for those who are not traditionally included in dominant ideas of femininity. The magic that is celebrated in those instances is sometimes the ingenuity of Black women and girls to use their bodies as canvases for makeup and fashion to express their creativity or establish trends.

Accomplishments

Educational and professional accomplishments about school graduations, entrepreneurship, job promotions, and progress within spaces overrepresented by white people were commonly identified as #BGM. Accomplishment-related retweets focused on images such as a picture of four Rwandan ballerinas wearing pink leotards with their hair styled in plaits and braids. As prominent Black ballerina Misty Copeland shared in an interview aired by National Public Radio, ballet has a long history of limited opportunities for Black women and girls and bias against some Black women and girls' appearances.

However, there weren't many representations of women working low-status jobs or everyday achievements like getting out of bed during a depressive episode or making enough money to cover expenses. Some Twitter users wrote that "hood" Black girls were excluded from #BGM, despite having lives worth celebrating. #BGM posts rarely exposed failure, vulnerability, or mistakes, which isn't surprising since people often present their best selves on social media. However, it can be problematic when whole groups of people are not celebrated.

Humanizing Black Women and Girls

Some tweets during the time period I explored were written in response to Chavers's critique of #BGM as promoting harmful notions of Black women as strong or supernatural. I did not find any tweets that agreed with Chavers's critiques of #BGM that received over 100 likes, which may indicate that Chavers's criticism failed to resonate with as many people as statements in support of #BGM.[17] Instead, many Twitter users explained that they embraced #BGM to humanize Black women and girls. As @KarenAttiah put it, "For me, the 'magic' in #blackgirlmagic is about sharing + celebrating the beauty and the humanity of black women + girls, not superhumanity." Some, like Morgan DeBaun (founder of Blavity, a technical company targeting Black millennials) endorsed the idea of "magical" Black women as a form of empowerment. DeBaun tweeted, "For the record I actually do think I have magical powers. #blackgirlmagic." These posts show that for many, using #BGM represents an opportunity to disrupt negative assumptions regarding Black femininity, rather than a thoughtless application of a trendy term.

Limited Representations of Sexualities

Popular posts lacked explicit statements about sexuality, sexual identity, or LGBTQIA+ issues. Most posts revealed traditionally feminine aesthetics and highlighted cisgender women, like Michelle Obama, many of whom are known for their relationships with cisgender men. A notable exception is a video from Amandla Sternberg's #BGM *Teen Vogue* series in which she identified as bisexual and wore a "Black Girls are Magic" sweatshirt sold to her by CaShawn Thompson. Sternberg stated that talking about her sexuality, along with her racial and gender identity, required vulnerability and commitment to be her true self. Nevertheless, most #BGM Twitter posts I analyzed didn't explicitly discuss diverse sexualities or gender expressions such as masculine Black women.

Issues for Black Feminist Sociologists to Explore

Black feminist sociologists face some challenges when coding and analyzing social media data like #BGM. One, how do they accurately identify the emotions and ideas of the posts? Critical race theorist and feminist ethnographer, France Winddance Twine, has argued many experiences with race and racism are expressed through visual mediums, and sociologists must analyze visual culture (e.g. videos, film, photographs) to better understand race and racism. This is particularly true for #BGM images posted online. In my exploration of #BGM media articles and Twitter text and photographs, there were several instances in which communicators expected that people would understand the meaning of their posts, due to a shared culture and use of language. For instance, in January 2016, *Essence* author Bené Viera wrote, "We intuitively understand the difference between a 'girl' and a 'girrrrrrl' response." There are colloquial phrases that Black women and girls use to communicate and express affection. Researchers must capture communicators' intended meanings of words like "girl" or "girrrrrrl" or even a southern variant like "gurl," which are often expressed with various intonations to convey different meanings.

Black feminist sociologists must not assume to know meanings simply from our experiences. For example, on January 6, 2016, Johnetta Elzie shared a photograph on Twitter from *Essence*'s February 2016 special issue. In the photo, Elzie wore a red jacket and a red dress with a fringed hem and stood with her hips tilted to the side, eyes closed. People retweeted the photo with comments such as a Black queen emoji, "WERK!!!" "slay," and "you are the epitome of #BlackGirlMagic." Analysis of these types of photos requires that Black feminist sociologists understand not only visual elements of pictures but also slang, colloquial phrases, and other dynamics of intragroup communication among Black women and girls and the broader Black community.

The second challenge is how, methodologically and theoretically, do Black feminist sociologists study posts that we can't see but are visible to others? Black feminists consider both the public and private to be political. In the case of social media posts, there are posts that are actually private, which can make it difficult to study or understand the internal lives and intentions behind posts. Nevertheless, public posts are what people want to share with the world and provide us insight into messages Black women and girls publicly communicate.

Third, how do we discuss the thoughts of Black women and girls on social media when it is difficult to know that users identify in-person as they present themselves online? Someone could post as a Black woman or girl and not identify as one in their daily face-to-face lives. Thus, it is important to provide strong context for our findings and analysis, and not to assume that every post presented as being by a Black woman or girl is one. Further, people who do not identify as Black women and girls actively use #BGM. For instance, some popular tweets about Black girls were posted by fathers proudly announcing their daughters' achievements. Thus, part of the analytical and theoretical work of exploring #BGM also involves understanding how people of various racial or gender identities use or even reject the expression.

Lastly, how should we code for colorist, classist, and heterosexist images? As I discussed earlier, many of the popular #BGM posts focus on celebrities and people whose appearances are aligned with mainstream notions of gender, sexuality, or beauty or represent colorist notions of Black beauty. Sociologists Angela Dixon and Edward Telles have argued that social scientists need multifaceted approaches to collecting and examining data about skin tone and colorism. Yet, it can be challenging examining aspects of appearance like complexion or shapes and facial features without harkening to archaic notions of race and gender or dangerous pseudoscientific approaches to studying race, gender, and appearance.

Additionally, studying physical appearance can reveal researchers' biases as much as the biases of the people who create the original content. For instance, early in the data analysis process, my graduate assistant and I discussed #BGM photos and colorism. She said she would consider me "light skin"; however, I consider myself as more medium brown, though admittingly a lighter, medium brown. To her, Whitney Houston was the quintessential medium brown and I am lighter, thus a light skin complexion. So, how do we code and write about colorism? Do we use charts of skin color gradients? Or do we use scales with words like "medium brown" and hope most can agree on what that complexion looks like? What do these various measures mean for our assertions about colorism and appearance in the pictures we analyze?

Toward Multiple Magics

The findings I present do not neatly fall into positive or negative categories. On one hand, there's much positive to be said about lauding Black women's and girls' success and beauty. On the other hand, there's also the danger of reinforcing narrow definitions of success and beauty. Even if less popular hashtags like #freeblackgirls gained the popularity of #BGM, how could we ensure the hashtags wouldn't become mired by limited notions of success and beauty that plague many #BGM posts (if they are not already)? So, it's less about looking at any one image or comment and saying, "this is positive" or "this is negative." The key is looking at patterns and asking how or why images of some groups bear this burden while others don't and pushing for expanded ideas of self-definition and empowerment.

One example of expanded definitions is promoting multiple magics. There is more than one way to be magical. It is important to separate outcomes/products from process. This is especially important since many oft-exalted achievements are in spaces with long histories of limiting opportunities for Black women and girls. Instead, the magic is in the processes or acts of living that Black women and girls perform daily to survive and thrive in environments that are not necessarily meant for them to flourish. People are magical as they fail, get fired, and live their truths in diverse experiences and identities. There is magic in the successes but also the vulnerabilities, failures, difficulties, and lessons.

"Melanin," by Ciara Featuring LaLa, City Girls, Ester Dean & Lupita Nyong'o, https://ciara.ffm.to/melanin

Notes

1. For this chapter, #BGM encompasses the hashtag, phrase, and general idea.
2. My use of "women and girls" is inclusive of cisgender women, cisgender girls, transgender women, transgender girls, and femmes. Nevertheless, debate about expansive

understandings of gender identities and the centering of the voices of transgender girls and transgender women within Black spaces continues. For instance, during *Essence's* Survivor's Agenda Femme Townhall, actress and transgender rights advocate Angelica Ross criticized *Essence* for failing to highlight transgender women on its magazine covers and in high profile events like the *Essence* Festival.

3. Dexter Thomas. 2015. "Why Everyone's Saying 'Black Girls are Magic'." *Los Angeles Times*, September 9. www.latimes.com/nation/nationnow/la-na-nn-everyones-saying-black-girls-are-magic-20150909-htmlstory.html

4. Each wrote about Black women's magical qualities, Alice Walker in *In Search of Our Mother's Gardens* and Joan Morgan in *When Chickenheads Come Home to Roost: A Hip-Hop Feminist Breaks It Down.*

5. For the history and status of trademark efforts, search "Black Girl Magic," "CaShawn Thompson," "Beverly Bond," or "Essence Communications, Inc." in the United States Patent and Trademark Office's database at www.uspto.gov/trademarks-application-process/search-trademark-database. The commercialization of BGM is rapid and ever-changing with companies (many Black woman-owned) using the phrase to sell items like jewelry, wine (www.mcbridesisters.com/Black-Girl-Magic), and clothing.

6. Several sources have chronicled the disagreement. For instance, Akiba Solomon's piece at Colorlines.com titled "The Real Problem With the #BlackGirlMagic Backlash is That You're Missing the Point." Black Twitter started #ChaversNextArticle to joke about aspects of Black culture Chavers might critique. Additionally, in *Reclaiming Our Space: How Black Feminists are Changing the World from the Tweets to the Streets,* Feminista Jones wrote about CaShawn Thompson's reaction.

7. As quoted on the "about" page of Black Girl Magic Magazine. Quote retrieved July 15, 2021 (http://www.blackgirlmagicmag.com/about-1).

8. Thompson, CaShawn (Auntie Peebz). 2017. "Everyday Black Girl Magic." *Medium* (blog), January 17. https://medium.com/@thepbg/a-long-long-time-ago-on-a-blog-far-far-away-i-once-wrote-about-what-black-girl-magic-means-to-me-c4642e4f2f96.

9. Ibid.

10. Patricia Hill Collins. 2004. *Black Sexual Politics: African Americans, Gender, and the New Racism.* New York: Routledge.

11. Meredith Clark. 2018. "Black Twitter." In *How Black Twitter and Other Social Media Communities Interact with Mainstream News,* edited by Deen Freelon, Lori Lopez, Meredith D. Clark, and Sarah J. Jackson, 36–47. Miami, FL: John S. and James L. Knight Foundation. https://kf-site-production.s3.amazonaws.com/media_elements/files/000/000/136/original/TwitterMedia-final.pdf

12. Whitelaw Reid. 2018. "Black Twitter 101: What Is It? Where Did It Originate? Where Is It Headed?" November 28. https://news.virginia.edu/content/black-twitter-101-what-it-where-did-it-originate-where-it-headed

13. Melissa Brown, Rashawn Ray, Ed Summers, and Neil Fraistat. 2017. "#Sayhername: A Case Study of Intersectional Social Media Activism." *Ethnic and Racial Studies* 40(11): 1831–1846; also see Brown's chapter in this volume.

14. I selected the articles by searching "Black Girl Magic" in Google and in databases for newspapers and magazines like LexisNexis. I focused on articles that were published by print and online media outlets that were well established or who marketed to Black people.

15. I chose dates to capture comments immediately before, during, and after the release of the *Essence* article and response pieces, which allowed me to explore what people talked about before, during, and after the controversy.

16. See Angela R. Dixon and Edward E. Telles. 2017. "Skin Color and Colorism: Global Research, Concepts, and Measurement." *Annual Review of Sociology* 43(1): 405–424 for more details regarding colorism.

17. Debate regarding whether BGM is a helpful or harmful term continues. For instance, during a 2020 episode of her podcast show titled "Under the Blacklight," renowned

Black feminist Kimberlé Crenshaw stated that while she advocated for Black women and girls' lives, she questioned society's emphasis on Black women and girls having to be "magical" in order to be valued.

References

Brown, Melissa, Rashawn Ray, Ed Summers, and Neil Fraistat. 2017. "#Sayhername: A Case Study of Intersectional Social Media Activism." *Ethnic and Racial Studies* 40(11): 1831–1846.

Chavers, Linda. 2016. "Here's My Problem with #BlackGirlMagic." *Elle*. January 13. Retrieved February 2, 2020 (www.elle.com/life-love/a33180/why-i-dont-love-blackgirlmagic).

Clark, Meredith. 2018. "Black Twitter." In *How Black Twitter and other Social Media Communities Interact with Mainstream News*, edited by Deen Freelon, Lori Lopez, Meredith D. Clark, and Sarah J. Jackson, 36–47. Miami, FL: John S. and James L. Knight Foundation. Retrieved February 2, 2020 (https://kf-site-production.s3.amazonaws.com/media_elements/files/000/000/136/original/TwitterMedia-final.pdf).

Collins, Patricia Hill. 2004. *Black Sexual Politics: African Americans, Gender, and the New Racism*. New York: Routledge.

Crenshaw, Kimberlé. 2020. "Under the Blacklight: Politics Power, & the Struggle against Black Precarity." September 14. Retrieved September 21, 2020 (www.youtube.com/watch?v=iGy-ISlvlLo&ab_channel=AfricanAmericanPolicyForum).

Dixon, Angela R., and Edward E. Telles. 2017. "Skin Color and Colorism: Global Research, Concepts, and Measurement." *Annual Review of Sociology* 43(1): 405–424.

Essence. 2016. "ESSENCE Celebrates #BlackGirlMagic Class of 2016 on February Cover." *Essence*. January 6. Retrieved February 2, 2020 (www.essence.com/celebrity/essence-celebrates-blackgirlmagic-class-2016-february-cover/).

Essence. 2020. "Survivor's Agenda Femme Townhall." September 2020. Retrieved July 15, 2021 (https://fb.watch/6M1mWMKPdQ/).

Ford, Ashley. 2016. "There Is Nothing Wrong with Black Girl Magic." *Elle*. January 14. Retrieved February 2, 2020 (www.elle.com/life-love/a33251/there-is-nothing-wrong-with-black-girl-magic/).

Reid, Whitelaw. 2018. "Black Twitter 101: What Is It? Where Did It Originate? Where Is It Headed?" November 28. Retrieved February 2, 2020 (https://news.virginia.edu/content/black-twitter-101-what-it-where-did-it-originate-where-it-headed).

Thomas, Dexter. 2015. "Why Everyone's Saying 'Black Girls are Magic.'" *Los Angeles Times*. September 9. Retrieved February 2, 2020 (www.latimes.com/nation/nationnow/la-na-nn-everyones-saying-black-girls-are-magic-20150909-htmlstory.html).

Thompson, CaShawn (Auntie Peebz). 2017. "Everyday Black Girl Magic." *Medium* (blog). January 17. Retrieved November 19, 2017 (https://medium.com/@thepbg/a-long-long-time-ago-on-a-blog-far-far-away-i-once-wrote-about-what-black-girl-magic-means-to-me-c4642e4f2f96).

Viera, Bené. 2016. "#BlackGirlMagic: Why Black Women Have 'That Thing' and You Don't Have to Understand It." *Essence*. January 14. Retrieved February 2, 2020 (www.essence.com/lifestyle/black-girl-magic-bene-viera-february-cover-story/).

Chapter 9

Learning, Teaching, Re-Membering and Enacting Black Feminist Sociology at a Black Women's College

Love Letters to One Another

Spelmanites: LeConté J. Dill, Mercedez Dunn, Mona Taylor Phillips, Nzali Scales and Cynthia Neal Spence

These letters narrate how the Spelman College Department of Sociology and Anthropology is an embodiment of Black feminist sociology theory, pedagogy, and praxis. We situate the importance of a sociology department housed within a Black women's college. Our chapter is co-written by a group of Black feminist sociologists who all have relationships with each other and with the Department of Sociology and Anthropology at Spelman in a direct scholarly lineage that spans over 45 years. As coauthors, we are all alumnae of Spelman, we were all sociology majors at Spelman and two of us are currently professors in the Department of Sociology and Anthropology at Spelman. As coauthors, we experience and engage in bidirectional mentorship. We reflect on the Department of Sociology and Anthropology's commitment to lifelong mentoring, and further unpack being mentored by and mentoring Black feminist sociologists. Importantly, our manuscript is written in the creative format of letters and poems, where we are in conversation with one another, with our disciplinary ancestors, and with future Black feminist sociologists. In these letters and poems, we talk with one another as Sista-Scholars. These letters and poems enact a pedagogy and praxis of love. We share how we found our way to the Department of Sociology and Anthropology initially, and how we continue to find our way back to it and to one another. We reflect upon whom we learn(ed) from in the Department of Sociology and Anthropology at Spelman and in the broader Black feminist sociological canon. We excavate how the Department of Sociology and Anthropology at Spelman enacts Black feminist sociology and how it does not. We talk about our community building with other Spelman sociology professors, students, alumnae and community partners. We offer some musings on how the Department of Sociology and Anthropology at Spelman will continue to shape Black feminist sociology and the discipline of sociology in the 21st century and beyond.

DOI: 10.4324/9781003199113-12

A Letter to My Young Sister Scholars,

Several years ago, Frances Maher and Mary Kay Thompson published *The Feminist Classroom: Dynamics of Gender, Race, Class and Privilege*.[1] My dear colleague Mona Taylor Phillips contributed to their research and analysis, and I used the text in a publication when I was addressing the special environments that can be created within single-sex institutions. The significance of this text to this communication to you is that first and foremost, we must know where we are when we enter the spaces we occupy as teachers, scholars, and mentors. How do we as Black professors, mentors, and scholars give meaning to the culture of the institution? How does our work inform the ways our students see and know themselves within the larger institutional structure and within the special place of the classroom? These are questions that must be asked.

Diana Danner was the first person whose gender politics as a white woman helped me to understand the complexities of being forced to perform a gender identity in a space that encourages the uplift of women but does not condone or embrace gender role nonconformity. Dr. Danner did not engage Black feminist analysis, but her commitment to feminist analysis was clear from not just the content of the courses she so eloquently and patiently taught to me and others, but in her day-to-day engagement with students. Her understanding of theory informed her praxis.

A few years after I returned to teach at Spelman College, Diana came out as lesbian. While I was clear that her previous marriage did not assume a heterosexual identity, my assessment of Diana did not suggest to me that she was same-gender loving. I certainly did not have this language at the time. Terminology like this and gender fluidity were not introduced in the courses I enrolled in at Spelman College. Diana became a model for me as I reflected on my role in the teaching and learning space. Her commitment to the development of every student she taught, regardless of varied levels of preparation, instilled in me the responsibility we all hold when young Black girls, like me, enter Spelman College. Her ability to navigate what she perhaps considered a hostile environment for the good of her students will always be ingrained in my teaching, mentoring, and administration. We must seek to make sure that we do not become accomplices in creating narrow and suffocating spaces for the growth and development of our students and colleagues.

Seeing a young, "Angela Davis afro wearing," full professor, like Anne Washington, teach criminology and criminal justice courses was my true awakening to the fact that Black women scholars have a particular analytical framework when they enter the classroom. At the time, the phrase "Black Lives Matter" was not in existence, but Anne, in her course *Blacks and the Criminal Justice System*, asserted this reframing in the varied ways she introduced her class to the inner workings of police, courts, and corrections. Her commitment to unveiling the discriminatory practices of the criminal justice system expanded my analysis and forced me to confront what C. Wright Mills asserts: the sociological imagination must prepare us to ask questions about the relationship between larger social structural issues and individual behaviors and the choices individuals make.

I don't remember Anne engaging a specifically Black feminist theoretical analysis, but something about her presentation and intellectual engagement represented the embodiment of a Black woman who embraced feminist thought and saw herself as an equal contributor to sociological and criminological thought and criticism. As we listened and took notes from this very young jeans-and-bell-bottoms-wearing sister with the big afro, I was able to imagine how young Black women scholars enter the space of the academy with the fullness of themselves. She was a novelty for me in the department of sociology.

My teaching and service life at Spelman College have been multi-faceted. Most significant is my work with Dr. Beverly Guy-Sheftall, another Black feminist scholar and Spelman alumna whose work and practice have pushed me further than anyone to live and breathe Black feminist practice. Her foundational text *Words of Fire: An Anthology of African-American Feminist Thought*[2] serves as a launching point for all classes I teach. The book she co-edited with my dear friend, the late Dr. Rudolph Byrd, *Traps: African American Men on Gender and Sexuality*,[3] helped me to begin to see the lives of Black male scholars like W. E. B. Du Bois in ways that my early introduction to these thinkers did not address. Rudolph and Beverly helped to expand and complicate my gendered analyses of scholars and texts. Working with Beverly and other young scholars whose work focuses on LGBTQ scholarship has been extremely impactful as I use Black feminist scholarship as a framework to enter those areas of scholarship that were not known to me. Young scholars must reach beyond their departments and disciplines to engage and embrace the perspectives of others, even when different perspectives and experiences may initially challenge the way you see and know your world.

Love, Cynthia

Hello Good People:
I am greedy.
I want so much.
I want to be greedy enough to think about and read everything.
I want to ask questions for which I honestly have no answers.
I want us to be generous and greedy and read everything and ask questions impossible to answer . . .
I want us to elevate listening/hearing to a high art.

I have come from a long line of greedy and generous women:
Johnnie Mae, who along with my father raised me and my brothers and sister in Chattanooga, Tennessee.

Her brother, our Uncle Freddy, told us that she always "had her head in a book" when they were children.
Johnnie Mae filled our home with Dr. Seuss, *Lady Chatterley's Lover*, romance novels, comic books . . .
And we read them all.

In August of 1972, Johnnie Mae and my family drove me to Spelman College.
She sprayed down my dormitory mattress, looked at my roommate with some suspicion
And left me in the care of other generously greedy women she would never meet:

Diana Danner, a white woman, dressed in bell-bottoms and boots, taught the power of statistics for story-telling.
She moved quickly and talked fast, and taught statistics facing us . . .
Using the board to show us the tools that might be useful for the questions we wanted to ask.
I think for Diana the *question* was the thing, but how could we form questions without seeing her face?

Johnnie Mae left me in the care of Claudia Jones—a short and greedy and generous Black woman with an afro.
Her praxis was animated by the 1960s and 1970s Black Arts and Black Studies movements.
We read E. Franklin Frazier and Joyce Ladner and W. E. B. Du Bois.
She moved quickly and talked fast
hands always in motion as she taught us how to write.
Facing us—sometimes looking up to us to meet our eyes when we were standing so we could understand why Du Bois and Angela Davis were so important for us to know in 1974.

When I returned to Spelman in 1983 I was assigned Diana's old office.
She had left her books behind:
Man Alone: Alienation in Modern Society
The Black Woman: An Anthology
Who Needs the Negro?
I read them all.

I think about these women as I have gotten older and a little worn.
I have questions:
Was Spelman a good fit for their greed, generosity, and desire?
Or was the classroom—with us—the safest space to hone the skills necessary

For bearing witness?

Did they have a community of greedy and generous women?

(I do)

Did they have a community where they plotted and planned curriculum and courses and syllabi for us?

(I do)

How did the very complex world of the 1970s bear down on the classroom?

How did they know when to open the door and let that world inside?

How did they know when to close the door so we could all breathe and read and think and write for the pure joy of it?

I would ask these questions because I know the tensions that can exist between a college's story of itself and the stories we live inside of it.

I now know how important it is to have a community that fills the void between the college's story of itself and our dreams.

I lived the tension between institutional story and my own desires while a student . . .

And I live it now as a professor

I sent an apology email to students this past semester:

As my mother would sometimes tell me

My/your eyes were too big for my stomach.

I had assigned too much.

We have to adjust.

But the students must take responsibility:

They had sent me titles of books, specials, and documentaries that I had to include as required material.

They had written examinations that forced me to type:

Amen.

Amen.

Once there was a restlessness in the class when I walked in:

We need to discuss something more important than anything you (me!) are talking about today.

Well, the students were not wrong—nor were they completely right.

But the world had crashed into the classroom and could not remain subtext.

Or elegantly woven into whatever theories we were discussing that day.

And so the syllabus was thrown into disarray yet again.

I am grateful for this letter in this particular moment when the sociological imagination is painful When no one knows if the center will hold

When I do not care if students "choose to change the world"
But do care that students leave us with a generosity that listens and
   speaks.

Facing us: I have only become aware of how important it is for us to see
   each other in the classroom. My only memory of my graduate school
   statistics professor is of his back . . . and endless storyless symbols on
   the board. My memory of my women Spelman sociology professors
   are of their faces.

I must thank them for forcing me to see beyond my own memories and
   really
See them as we face one another.

I must thank them for their patience as I am pondering what is necessary to be both greedy and generous

Know a discipline without being disciplined by it:
Connect Du Bois to Anna J. to Hellman to Rankine to Mead and
   Cooley to Cottom to
Baldwin to Foucault to Said to Anzaldúa to R. Ferguson to Roy to
   Ladner to Cox . . .
Call on Hofstadter and Arendt and Gessen and Ida B. and Angela Davis
   so that we can know when we have been here before and how this
   time is different . . .
We must center/energize our classrooms with the ideas and research of
   our 21st-century Black feminist intellectuals . . .
As we recreate the discipline in our own images.

Johnnie Mae, LeConté, Tara, Mercedez, Claudia, Diana, Cynthia,
   Nzali—all of you . . .
Are in the classroom with me.
Sometimes the room is not large enough for everyone and all the his-
   tory and
Stress and strain and disappointment and weariness and anger and
   worry . . .
We are an imperfect and generous and greedy community.
We will be alright.

Love, Mona

Maybe I was a Sociologist all along
Maybe I was a Sociologist in South Central
Maybe I was a Sociologist in my mom's Oldsmobile

Staring out the window, looking at street signs, blocks, alleys, buildings,
   people, neighborhoods
Always with a something to read, a notebook to write in, a tape
   recorder
I didn't know nothin bout Sociology back then
or didn't think I did
But I did know bout Spelman

By the time I finally got to Spelman
Spent most of my time dashing in between the Science building and the
   English building
Spent most of my time explaining to my Biochemistry classmates why
   I was a Creative Writing minor
Spent most of my time explaining to my Creative Writing classmates
   why I had to go to the lab
But isn't that dashing the joy of the Liberal Arts
and what makes one Interdisciplinary?
But soon I grew tired of the lab, the pipette, and the microscope
Had questions about this city, this country, this world and its ways, our
   ways
Some of those same questions that were swirling in my head in my
   Mom's Oldsmobile
Now, I heard it was okay for this Imagination of mine to be Radical
In Giles Hall, I learned that Sociology is Black
is Feminist
is Black Feminist
is on the page and is in the community
is professors that practice a deep care –

Dr. Cynthia Neal Spence was and will forever be known as "Dean"
I didn't exactly know what a Dean was, but she encouraged us to go see
   some world outside of Spelman
That Spelman would still be here for us with open arms
That I could thrive in the Ivy League for a semester on exchange
That I could exchange some ideas with some Ivy Leaguers
who actually coveted Spelman
That I could come back home still thriving

In Giles Hall, I found the only Medical Sociologist in the building, and
   asked him if he could be my "Advisor"
Found him behind a pile of books and papers and glasses and a warm
   smile
Maybe Dr. Bruce Wade could be my guide

in this new building
in this new Major
in this new, but old, Radical Sociological Imagination of mine
in this growing Public Health Imagination of mine
I don't know if we knew we were becoming #DrWadesBrigade
I don't know if we knew we would become some of *your* favorite scholars, educators, policymakers, and practitioners:
Mina Schoffner-Green, Esq., Alisha Thomas Morgan, Marcia Olivia Payne, Dr. Ruha Benjamin, Dr. Maranda Ward, Dr. Dara Mendez, Dr. Dione King, Taneya Gethers-Muhammad (RIP), Dr. LeConté Dill . . .

People were scared of the Contemporary Social Theory course
People dropped the Contemporary Social Theory course
Dr. Mona Taylor Phillips asked us to read
a lot
Invited us to think
Critically
Reminded us that "Theory" is not a bad word
is not a white word
is not a word for only old, dead, white guys
That 21-year-old Blackgirls are theorists, too
I named and claimed myself as an "Ethnographer"
Dr. Phillips said "Amen!"
Dr. Phillips reminded me that I could bring my poetry outside of the English building
In class, in office hours, on assignments, in internships, and through my Bachelor's thesis,
I began to craft LeConté's Radical Sociological Imagination: I could be in conversation with
sociologists, characters from novels, artists, therapists, health educators, entertainers, and my own journal entries and poems

Spelman's Sociology Professors are lifelong mentors
They dole out hugs, nudges, letters of recommendation, emails, and texts
Drinking tea and spilling the tea
Reminding us that we have a home
again and again

Through Dr. Spence, I met Mercedez
Ending her Junior year, and my junior in age, but my Co-Scholar from the start
It's the Spelman way

She be "Fellow" and I be "Mentor"
Yes, me as guide, but we would write and read and question and research
and publish TOGETHER

Through Dr. Phillips, many of us would re-interrogate *Beloved*
We be interdisciplinary
We love Morrison   Asé!
And her words, and numbers, and phrases, and puzzles, and theories,
and stories, and histories, and futures
It is here where I began to practice how I would use literature to under-
stand health concepts and to plan health interventions together with
my own students in my own classroom

Through Dr. Wade, I was invited to department meetings, behind academia's veil
Where syllabi and study abroad trips and office hours and journal articles get crafted
He is an Ancestor now   Asé!
But our conversations and our meeting notes are still maps for me
My Sociology is Black
is Feminist
is Black Feminist
is Radical
is Public Health
is healing
always
is you good, Sis?
is Nzali –
We just met
here on this page
but we be Tribe
we be cracked open in Giles Hall
radiating our Radical Sociological Imagination
for Spelmanites for years to come

                                        In Sisterhood, LeConté

My momma, Deborah, loved to dance. Her hips swayed side to side, her
head in the air, every floor was hers. She made space for herself if she had
to, but neither feet nor hips stopped moving to the beat, her beat. That's
just how she paced hospital floors, prison clinics, nursing homes, community health screenings, in her Nikes and scrubs. She'd read medical terminology books every day and ask patients again and again if they got it,
if they were alright. Because doctors never broke it down in our language,
she said. Because she had to help our folks be well.

She wanted me to go to Spelman—it would help me become "more me." In Giles Hall, I devoured the words of Anna Julia Cooper, Ida Wells-Barnett, Patricia Hill Collins, Audre Lorde, W. E. B. Du Bois, and yours. They were a balm and a match. These texts spoke to my soul and ignited me to do something about the things that kept me up at night and create more of the things that brought me joy. Nestled in between pages of Zora Neale Hurston, bell hooks and Beverly Guy-Sheftall, I saw Dorothy, Tina, Willie Mae, Elaine, Brenda and Deborah—the community of six sisters I had been birthed into—who raised our family like a village and dubbed it "Dunnville." Resilient, joyful and unapologetic.

Your classrooms encouraged me to engage further than the words on the page but remember that Black feminist sociology exists in the rest of the world. To imagine, and to theorize, to reflect, to struggle with ideas, and be in conversation with these scholars because I, too, was *already* a scholar but not just a scholar. You ensured me that somebody, somewhere needs some of what I have, too.

In your classrooms, my voice counted, I mattered. Alabama born, too Black but not "Black enough," body taking up too much space and thoughts too loud, "tenderhearted" in a world that has been unkind to too many of us. All of that could come, in fact all of it had to. You required my engagement, there was nowhere to hide but everywhere was safe.

Because of this, my sociology siblings see each other as a sanctuary. I am forever grateful for this homeplace, for letting me know that you expected excellence because that's what we all are. And for Dr. Wade, too. Who let me know that I didn't have to choose between public health and sociology. And Dr. Dill, who concurred. For Alesha and Camesha and LaToya. For Nzali and Deborwah. Who all flourished because of that and because of you.

These communities inspire my audacity to *be*. As I witness the ways you engage academic arenas and your everyday lives, you challenge me to not merely produce or teach, but to acknowledge the significance of the hows and whys of our pedagogy, scholarship, praxis, and service. As we enter classrooms, boardrooms, stores, and dinner tables, we must remember that how we show up and hold space for people matters.

Deb and Dr. Dill taught me that wellness is Black feminist praxis. As an instructor, this lesson has been reinforced. Being is critical to personal and community wellness. I have learned in my classroom, co-learners need to be seen, to be heard, to take up space above all else. As we face mass shootings, deportations, sexual violence, and hostile racial campus climates, Black feminist sociology and praxis is critical to consider how factors at multiple levels impact our wellness. We take a line from our sheroes. We engage the transformative potential of love, how they've taught and shown it can heal us, make us well. We use our voices to center wellness with self-love as the catalyst, telling our stories of how we love and honor ourselves. How critical this is for *how* we show up in the world and the impact of this for our well-being and our communities and our world.

As I watched students shut down the major transit hubs, get a eugenicist's name removed from a building, protest outside the president's house, it is clear that students are not just studying sociology but they are putting sociology into action. With signs, they declared "Black Lives Matter." They informed "We'll Keep Comin' Back' Til We're Heard." And come back they would, to reveal the university's legacy of honoring racists, to hold administration accountable for injustices on campus, and to provide momentum for future students to work towards equity, inclusion, and justice.

This is what has been done and will continue to be done through Black feminist sociology and pedagogy. From our syllabi to our office hours to linking arms with students chanting "No Justice, No Peace! Know Justice, Know Peace!" You all challenge me to reimagine the canon, to question the ways in which my academic training has taught me to privilege particular sources of knowledge, and how I need not forget that sociological imaginations exist outside of sociology and outside of the academy. That I need to remember to engage and allow space for others to engage lyrics, memes, tweets, and episodes of *Grown-ish* as sociological works.

I enter, in community, hips swaying, head in the air like my momma, to my own beat, with generations of Black women leaders, educators, advocates, public scholars, and change agents—who are seeking to thrive, are committed to liberation, and model authenticity. Black women who bring their entire selves to institutions of higher learning, so that I and others know that we can do the same. Black women who are fearless, and those of us who aren't yet rid of all of our reservations. Black women who see us, hear us, and who hold space, no matter how near or far away we may from the gates of 350 Spelman Lane. Because of them, and with them, we all will be transformed.

Sisterly, Mercedez

I thank my very first teachers
My parents:
Intentional HBCU graduates with a depth of perception
I am grateful for their lineages that taught them
to teach me
an awareness of their heritage: my heritage
A solid sense of belonging. Black excellence
that extends far beyond their libraries of Alice Walker, bell hooks, and
    W. E. B. Du Bois

louder than the shouts of their joy when reconnecting with a college
    friend during homecoming deeper than listening to Angelique Kidjo
    and Stevie Wonder throughout our College Park home
more complex than frequenting Greenbriar Mall's Medu Bookstore and
    the West End's Shrine of the Black Madonna
more colorful than my collection of Black dolls
This was all that my brother and I knew.
This, was home.

Black feminism is a way of seeing.
For Black girls and women to know that they, too, belong
Not just in the social world, but that of academia, too
That they do not have to look too far outside of themselves to inquire,
    "What about me?"
Black feminism is a theoretical home, a place of comfort and challenge,
    simultaneously

I was granted this vision in my College Park home
I learned how to call it out
How to name it for what *it* was, what *she* is and evolves to be,
    however
inside the gates of 350 Spelman Lane
. . . on the third floor of Giles Hall,
In the department of sociology/anthropology to be exact

If you asked me at the time why I chose soc, I could not give you a
    worthy response.
I did receive answers to this self-inflicted question the following semes-
    ter during my rites of passage, however.
A semester-long process of translation
To learn a new tongue,
to learn how to see the world with a deeper sense of clarity, if you
    will
Or what Mills would call a sociological imagination

There was something about Dr. Spence's warm and demanding pres-
    ence that kept me interested in defining different iterations of history
    + biography
Her passion motivated the classroom
Her love for her sister-scholars was empowering
And her knowledge inspired us, to say the least
It wasn't until Dr. Spence's 8am class
Introduction to the Sociological Imagination
that I felt seen

I, Nzali, wasn't just seen

I saw the class dynamics of my working-middle-class family in Karyn Lacy's ethnography *Blue Chip Black*

Du Bois's *double consciousness* gave me the terminology to reflect on the tokenism I experienced as one of the few Black faces at my all-girls boarding high school

My language advanced and so did my thoughts and interactions with my present and past sociological worlds

Social capital, intersectional identities, social institutions, marginalization, conflict theory, among other "academic jargon" were now in my vocabulary

Dr. Spence taught me to write and speak with precision.

I was becoming a Black feminist through and through.

These words of precision were uprooted from the narratives we shared amongst each other.

As sister-students, we spoke on moments that were defining for our race, our class, our gender.

We wrote critical reflections conceptualizing our identity politics.

I saw myself in my work: We saw ourselves in our work.

We were beginning to embody Black feminism.

Demanding space for our stories to be told for us, by us in academic spaces, in social spaces

We got personal.

And honey, the personal was political.

Dr. Phillips: seen as a producer of knowledge

There I was being mentored by my big sister and taught by my Spelman sister.

I was not used to that type of thinking . . . That intellectual love.

It was at this point that I felt like I belonged at Spelman.

I felt at home,

and my sisters to come, I hope you find your home . . .

                                                                        Love, Nzali

Notes

1. Francis Maher and Mary Kay Thompson. 2001. *The Feminist Classroom: Dynamics of Gender, Race, Class and Privilege.* Lanham, MD: Rowman & Littlefield.
2. Beverly Guy-Sheftall. 1995. *Words of Fire: An Anthology of African-American Feminist Thought.* New York: The New Press.
3. Beverly Guy-Sheftall and Rudolph Byrd. 2001. *Traps: African American Men on Gender and Sexuality.* Bloomington: Indiana University Press.

References

Barlow, Jameta N. 2016. "#WhenIFellInLoveWithMyself: Disrupting the Gaze and Loving Our Black Womanist Self as an Act of Political Warfare." *Meridians: Feminism, Race, Transnationalism* 15(1): 205–217. https://doi.org/10.2979/meridians.15.1.11

Barlow, Jameta N., and LeConté J. Dill. 2018. "Speaking for Ourselves: Reclaiming, Redesigning, and Reimagining Research on Black Women's Health." *Meridians: Feminism, Race, Transnationalism* 16(2): 219–229. https://doi.org/10.2979/meridians.16.2.03

Brakke, Karen, Michelle S. Hite, Azaria Mbughuni, Opal Moore, Bruce H. Wade, and Mona Taylor Phillips. 2014. "Our Beloved Journey: Using Storytelling to Foster Faculty Community." *Peer Review* 16(4/1): 7–9.

Byrd, Rudolph P., and Beverly Guy-Sheftall (eds.). 2001. *Traps: African American Men on Gender and Sexuality*. Bloomington: Indiana University Press.

Collins, Patricia Hill. 1990. *Black Feminist Thought: Knowledge, Consciousness, and the Politics of Empowerment*. New York: Routledge.

Cooper, Anna Julia. 1892. *A Voice from the South by a Black Woman of the South*. Xenia, OH: Aldine Printing House.

Cottom, Tressie McMillan. 2018. *Thick: And Other Essays*. New York: New Press.

Cox, Aimee Meredith. 2015. *Shapeshifters: Black Girls and the Choreography of Citizenship*. Durham, NC: Duke University Press.

Davis, Angela Y. 1981. *Women, Race and Class*. New York: Random House.

Dill, LeConté J., Orrianne Morrison, and Mercedez Dunn. 2016. "The Enduring Atlanta Compromise: Black Youth Contending with Home Foreclosures and School Closures in the 'New South.'" *Du Bois Review: Social Science Research on Race* 13(2): 365–377. https://doi.org/10.1017/S1742058X16000217

Du Bois, William Edward Burghardt. 1899. *The Philadelphia Negro: A Social Study*. Philadelphia, PA: University of Pennsylvania Press.

Du Bois, William Edward Burghardt. 1903. *The Souls of Black Folk*. Chicago, IL: A. C. McClurg & Co.

Frazier, E. Franklin. 1957. *The Negro in the United States*. New York: Palgrave Macmillan.

Guy-Sheftall, Beverly. 1995. *Words of Fire: An Anthology of African-American Feminist Thought*. New York: New Press.

hooks, bell. 1994. *Teaching to Transgress: Education as The Practice of Freedom*. New York: Routledge.

Hull, Gloria T., and Patricia Bell (eds.). 1982. *All the Women Are White, All the Blacks Are Men, But Some of Us Are Brave: Black Women's Studies*. Old Westbury, NY: Feminist Press.

Hurston, Zora Neale. 1984 [1942]. *Dust Tracks on a Road: An Autobiography*. 2nd ed. Urbana, IL: University of Illinois Press.

Jackson, Fleda Mask, and Mona Taylor Phillips. 2003. "Collaborative Research and Reproductive Health Outcomes among African American Women." *American Journal of Health Studies* 18(4): 1978–1987.

Jackson, Fleda Mask, Mona Taylor Phillips, Carol J. Rowland Hogue, and Tracy Y. Curry-Owens. 2001. "Examining the Burdens of Gendered Racism: Implications for Pregnancy Outcomes among College-educated African American Women." *Maternal and Child Health Journal* 5(2): 95–107. https://doi.org/10.1023/A:1011349115711

Josephson, Eric, and Mary Josephson (eds.). 1962. *Man Alone: Alienation in Modern Society*. New York: Dell.

Kelley, Robin D. G. 2002. *Freedom Dreams: The Black Radical Imagination.* Boston, MA: Beacon Press.

Ladner, Joyce. 1971. *Tomorrow's Tomorrow: The Black Woman.* Garden City, NY: Anchor.

Lorde, Audre. 1981. "The Uses of Anger." *Women's Studies Quarterly* 9(3): 7.

Lorde, Audre. 1984. *Sister Outsider.* Trumansberg, NY: Crossing.

Maher, Frances A., and Mary Kay Thompson Tetreault. 2001. *The Feminist Classroom: Dynamics of Gender, Race, and Privilege.* Lanham, MD: Rowman & Littlefield.

Mills, C. Wright. 1959. *The Sociological Imagination.* New York: Oxford University Press.

Phillips, Mona Taylor. 2000. "A Case Study of Theory, Voice, Pedagogy, and Joy." In *Opening Lines: Approaches to the Scholarship of Teaching and Learning,* edited by Pat Hutchings, 73–79. Menlo Park, CA: The Carnegie Foundation for the Advancement of Teaching.

Phillips, Mona Taylor. 2016. "Spirit, Truth and The Bright Colors of Books: Institutional Well-Being and Productive Disorder at a Black Women's College." In *Well-Being and Higher Education: A Strategy for Change and the Realization of Education's Greater Purposes,* edited by Donald W. Harward, 185–190. Washington, DC: Bringing Theory to Practice.

Wade, Bruce H., and Jack H. Stone. 2010. "Overcoming Disciplinary and Institutional Barriers: An Interdisciplinary Course in Economic and Sociological Perspectives on Health Issues." *Journal of Economic Education* 41(1): 71–84. https://doi.org/10.1080/00220480903382198

Wells-Barnett, Ida B. 1970. *Crusade for Justice: The Autobiography of Ida B. Wells.* Chicago, IL: University of Chicago Press.

Wilhelm, Sidney M., and Elwin H. Powell. 1964. "Who Needs the Negro?" *Trans-action* 6: 3–6. https://doi.org/10.1007/BF03182279

Part 3

Black Feminist Sociology Epistemologies and What They Reveal to Us

Chapter 10

Black Feminist Sociology and the Politics of *Space* and *Place* at the Intersection of Race, Class, Gender and Sexuality

Carolette Norwood

Introduction

Although space and place have largely been absent in sociological inquiry,[1] they are central to sociology. *Space* is where things are and where they happen; it is the location of "social facts" and the site of social interactions; space is often transformed and utilized for social, economic, and other processes.[2] Space and place, according to Thomas Gieryn, are geographically circumscribed sites where social communities emerge alongside collective political action. As such, space and place are political and personal, as well as material and poetic, and they also can be conceptualized as the mediator between structure and the individual (e.g., a byproduct of social policy).[3]

Black feminist social scientists center the experiences of Black women and analyze the role of structural inequalities in shaping Black women's lived experiences, with the understanding that Black women are not an essentialized, undifferentiated unit of analysis; rather, Black women represent an intersectional reality of social identities and staggered positionality within these identities. Black feminists insist that "Black" + "woman" as a statistical interaction is a problematic additive[4] and that as Black women, according to Adichie, we are complicated embodiments of more than a "single story." And though space and place are an essential feature of Black feminist thought, they have not always been explicitly taken up and conceptualized within frameworks of power and identity as expressed through intersectionality. In this chapter, I discuss new directions for Black feminist sociology as a spatial project.

Theorizing Space and Place

In sociology, space has been conceptualized from two different viewpoints: the *Absolutist (dualist division)* view, which sees space and body as independent of each other, and the *Relativist (monist)* view, which regards space

DOI: 10.4324/9781003199113-14

as deriving from the relationship between the bodies and space, where bodies are always in motion. According to Löw, the former maintains that space exists independent of action and that bodies rest within space; the latter argues that space is derived from an arrangement of bodies that are always in motion, which means that space is always changing. Space and place are both temporal and scaled, according to Wendy Cheng and Rashad Shabazz, and because "space is negotiated in tandem with other people,"[5] space and place are often sites of domination and contestation, according to Katherine McKittrick.

Black and critical feminist geographers are readily taking up "intersectional spatialities" as a way of "placing, unsettling and decentering whiteness (as a hegemonic power formation), interrogating how norms of racial privilege rely on and are spatially reproduced; and making visible multiple subjectivities and forms of power."[6] As Black feminist sociologists, however, we have not yet fully unraveled the ways spatialization informs life chances and life quality, and why spatiality is an important part of intersectional thinking, being and doing.

This is not to say that Black feminists do not routinely take up spatial complexities in their work (because they do) or that intersectionality as a theory isn't inherently spatial (because it is), as Kishi Ducre declares. In fact, "at its inception," as Mollett and Faria explain, intersectionality was "*already* a deeply spatial theoretical concept, process, and epistemology, particularly when read through careful and serious engagement with Black feminist thought. In short, the interlocking violence of racism, patriarchy, heteronormativity, and capitalism constitute a spatial formation."[7]

Intersectionality and Black feminism are often presented as mutually constitutive. It is important to recognize, however, as Sharlene Mollett and Caroline Faria do, that intersectionality is not Black feminism, per se; instead, it is a theoretical articulation of identity and oppression based on the lived experience of Black women. It is "a cohort of terms that black feminists created in order to analyze the interconnectedness of structures of domination."[8] This interconnectedness has a long history, grounded in anti-racist, feminist social justice advocacy, embodied in the activism of such brave Black women as Maria Stewart, Sojourner Truth, and Ida B. Wells, who engaged in their efforts long before the concept of intersectionality became part of the feminist vocabulary.

Jennifer C. Nash traces the disciplinary genealogies and migration of intersectionality and then asks a profound and necessary question: *What's beyond intersectionality for Black feminist theory?* Nash raises this question because the tendency to reduce Black feminism singularly to intersectionality is so pervasive and so intertwined that the uptake of intersectional theory by mainstream actors has led to "defensive" and proprietary responses by some Black feminists who are concerned with other disciplines appropriating the theory, making its roots in Black feminist activism and text invisible.

Over the years, intersectionality has pivoted its focus. For example, Nash notes the erasure of sexuality from intersectional theorizing during the "watershed years" (1987–90), which, she declares, "shifted the study of multiple marginalization from an investigation of race, class, gender and sexuality to a rigorous exploration of how race and gender collude to constrain black women's lives."[10] Since 1999 to present, however, third-wave hip-hop feminists and, more recently, Queer of Color scholars are boldly moving not only intersectionality forward but also Black feminist theorizing into the future by (re)taking up and advancing critical sexuality studies, according to Brittney Cooper. In addition to race, gender, class, and sexuality; space and place should be routinely centered in Black feminist sociological analysis.

Why Should Black Feminist Sociology Expressly Take Up Space and Place as Part of Our Analyses?

As noted previously, explicit attention to spatiality in sociology has been underwhelming. And although Black feminist epistemology (informed by literature, music, poetry, daily conversations, and everyday behavior, according to Patricia Hill Collins) is inherently inclusive of space, it is still worthwhile to ask: Why should Black feminist sociologists expressly take up *space and place* as part of our analyses?

Intersectionality is concerned with power and identity, but power and identity are inherently connected to space and place. Where people live shapes who they are and their access to resources and power. It also shapes life quality and life chances. For example, living in Flint, Michigan, in 2016 significantly raised the odds of being exposed to serious health problems. Anyone living in this city who used public water to drink, cook, bathe, clean, or for recreation was exposed to lead. As result, an estimated 30,000 school-age children in Flint were exposed to neurotoxin, which can impact brain development and the nervous system, according to Erica Green. While caution must be exercised to "avoid stigmatizing an entire city," it is important to understand that where people live, the spaces they navigate, shapes not only what they have access to; it also fundamentally shapes who they are.

In his now iconic article, "The Racialization of Space and the Spatialization of Race: Theorizing the Hidden Architecture of Landscape," George Lipsitz maintains "the lived experience of race has a spatial dimension and the lived experience of space has a racial dimension."[11] Race in the United States determines life quality, life chances, and ultimately, longevity. As such, not only is space racialized and race spatialized, but so too is opportunity both racialized and spatialized. Where you live, the schools you attend, the places where you travel, the venues where you shop, the networks to which you have access, and one's wellness and health all have spatial dimensions.

Since Black feminism is about theorizing the lived experiences of Black (diversely defined) women, spatial formations should be a manifest, not latent, object of focus. Likewise, since intersectionality theorizes identity and oppression, nuanced insights from analyses of space and place are fundamental for understanding diversely defined Black women. Not only does a spatial lens challenge homogenized presentations of Black women's lives, but it also situates these lives temporally and within and across specific contexts. Take, for example, Zora Neale Hurston's *Their Eyes Were Watching God*, which is set in the Black self-governing town of Eatonville. The main character, Janie Crawford, navigates life in what Dale Pattison describes as "subversive spaces," where she negotiates and resists spaces that challenge dominant narratives on race, gender, class, and sexuality. And though Hurston's work received very harsh critiques from some Harlem Renaissance writers who prioritize respectability politics, this work is now highly regarded for its authenticity and how it captures the esthetic of Black life and its dialect, thereby masterfully demonstrating the particularities of space and place of Eaton town.

The Politic, Identity, and Poetics of Space and Place

Black feminist sociologist Patricia Hill Collins offers an instructive articulation of space. In *Fighting Words: Black Women and the Search for Justice*, Collins introduces the concept of the *politics of containment*, which relates to citizenship, social mobility, segregation and surveillance, and knowing one's "place" in public and private spheres. This politics of containment erects spaces that are deliberately racialized, gendered, classed, and sexualized. It creates an assortment of what Cheng and Shabazz term *spatial typologies*, which range from ghettos, suburbs, barrios, and reservations to prisons and occupied territories to "children in cages." The politics of containment ultimately creates what France Twine and Bradley Gardener call a Geography of Privilege.

Jim Crow geographies, for example, are manifestations of structural violence from which geographies of privilege emerge, as I have noted in my earlier work. Jim Crow geographies, and the spaces and places embodied within them, are deliberate creations (Carolette Norwood, 2018). Such geographies are a consequence of regulating property through racial ordinances and restrictive covenants, redlining, racial steering, predatory lending practices, and gentrification. Therefore, these spaces and places are not absent of phenomena; rather, they are colonies of inhabitants. Further, under global capitalism, space is a commodity; its (land) use (determined by zoning regulations) and its (land) value (determined by market supply and demand) are largely outcomes of policy. Urban planners, for example, determine land use through zoning and the "development" of space within and around cities.

Before the profession of urban planning was solidified in the 20th century, city design and esthetics were mainly the domains of architects, while public health professionals and social welfare reformers took up functionality. As a newly constituted profession, urban planners were tasked with devising plans to improve the function and layout of cities. Cincinnati, Ohio, for example, was the first US city to unveil an official plan approved by the city council in 1922. The plan was completed in 1925. It determined what territorial spaces would be zoned for residential occupancy, parks and recreation, commerce and industry, and transport systems. And even though racial zoning ordinances were made unconstitutional by *Buchanan* v. *Warley* (1917), this prohibited neither the practice, nor the legality of such ordinances when they reemerged as "restrictive covenants."

Housing restrictive covenants were introduced in the 1920s to circumvent the 1917 federal ban of racial zoning. These restrictive covenants regulated the use and *users* of land. For example, restrictions were imposed on the raising of livestock within city boundaries, as it might compromise property market value. Not long after, however, covenants sought to regulate who could use the land and who could not. Property, for example, could not be sold to "undesirable users," such as "Negros" (and occasionally, depending on geographical area, Jews, Asians, and Mexicans) under the guise that the use or users of residential space would be "detrimental to the property values in a neighborhood."[12]

The politics of racialized confinement has a long and significant history in the United States. From the slave ships to plantation fields to prisons and urban ghettos, Black people in the United States have largely existed in highly surveilled, policed, and contained spaces. Jim Crow policies, erected in the 1880s in the post-reconstruction era, were originally formulated in Ohio as "Black Codes" in 1804. Ohio, a "free state" at inception, regulated Black mobility and sought to control where "free" Black people could and could not be in public space. In-migrating Blacks were made to register at a fee of $500, plus obtain sponsorship from a white resident willing to vouch for their good behavior. A politics of confinement is also illustrated in the Trail of Tears and the erection of Native reservation lands, China towns, and Japanese concentration camps in the 1940s; these are but a few examples of racialized space and spatialized race in the United States.

Space and place are not restricted to land; they can also be aquatic, as superbly demonstrated in Kevin Dawson's *Undercurrents of Power: Aquatic Culture in the African Diaspora*. In this text, Dawson masterfully shows how "Aquatics can leave ineffaceable impressions on cultures, on memories, and on one's sense of place and identity."[13]

The politics of containment also produces queer and other sexualized spaces. Until the early 1920s, many urban cities had sex districts, also named "red-light" districts. These were dedicated spaces where people could engage in vice. Often these districts were zoned in Black urban neighborhoods, in places like Chicago, Cincinnati, and New Orleans. In these spaces and places, night clubs hosted interracial patrons who were able to socialize, dance, and purchase sex, as long as these activities "did not transgress neighborhood boundaries."[14] Queer spaces are important sites for self-organizing, resisting hegemonic forces that stigmatize and criminalize the very being and doings of queer people. Club life and ballrooms provide the Black queer community a "house" or "safe" space to just be and to strategize against oppressive forces.[15] As Darius Bost demonstrates, however, club life also serves as a political terrain for mobilizing resistance and self-organizing to address the HIV epidemic in Washington, DC.

Space is also embodied. We not only live in space and place, but space and place live within us. Also, not only do we create space and place, but space and place create us. These points are well made in Aimee Cox's *Shapeshifters: Black Girls and the Choreography of Citizenship*. In this iconic book, Cox demonstrates how place—in this case, Detroit—and the spaces within the place—neighborhoods and communities—are manifestations of identity. Aimee Cox's use of "Detroitness" illustrates this point best. Here Cox maintains that "just as complicated and uncontainable as Blackness, Detroitness is an identity and a way of being in that has generated its own policed boundaries and criteria for inclusion."[16]

Finally, the spatial is both material and poetic. As Katherine McKittrick's work demonstrates, Black women and "space" (material and imagined) have always functioned together, and *place* is unquestionably linked to "body memory."[17] As sites of what McKittrick terms "embodied property," for example, Black enslaved women produced and reproduced capital that fueled what Philips calls "the plantation machine." *Material* geographies, such as the plantation fields, coexist with *poetic* geographies of imagination, dreams and memory.

Methodologies in the Black Feminist Sociology of Space and Place

Black feminist research is unapologetically concerned with issues of social justice; it actively and blazingly seeks to redress inequalities and by default, not only laments about what is but also resists and challenges the status quo; seeks to be visionary and reflective; and ultimately and with intention, strives to uncover what Collins refers to as *Oppositional Knowledge*. In addition, as Leith Mullings explains, the role of Black feminist research is: (1) "to create a distinct standpoint on the self, community, and society"; (2) "speak to the politics of race, class, and gender and address the dialectic struggle and community empowerment"; (3) "to excavate 'cultures of resistance'"; (4) to make sure that the voices of working-class and low-income Black women are represented and included in discussions of new constructions of gender; and (5) to gain insights from the everyday lives of African American women, but importantly to make sure *their* interpretations of *their* lives are represented. To do this, Mullings maintains, requires "conscious methodological approaches."[18]

Black Feminist urban ethnographies, such as sociologist Nikki Jones's *Between Good and Ghetto: African American Girls Inner City Violence*, illustrate how space and place can be cocentered alongside race, class and gender. In her illustrative work, Jones describes the quotidian violence present in the everyday lives of Black girls residing in a Philadelphia inner-city neighborhood. Jones contextualizes the space and place of these Philadelphia neighborhoods in the concentrated poverty of the 1980s and 1990s that resulted from deindustrialization and hypersegregation. Girls residing within these confines of a built environment, deliberately deprived of opportunity and access to decent-paying jobs, are often confronted with "unpredictable violence,"[19] which create a preoccupation with survival and presents "a uniquely gendered challenge for girls."[20]

Identifying patterns and generalizing findings about the social environments in which people live, work, and recreate are important features of sociological research. Black sociologists Marcus Hunter and Zandria Robinson, authors of *Chocolate Cities: The Black Map of American Life*, offer readers spatial insight into the political demographics of a Black cartography. The book opens with a famous quote by Malcolm X whereby he declares the "South" as any geographic area below Canada. Of course, implied here is that the "South" is not only a geographical reference of longitudinal and latitudinal coordinates of measurable distance but also about the politics regulating where Black people could be in public space, thus calling attention to the ubiquity of white racism and the exercise of Jim Crow.

Similarly, when Richard Rothstein wrote in *The Color of Law: A Forgotten History of How Our Government Segregated America*, "if in San Francisco then everywhere,"[21] he, too, was noting the widespread and uniform practice of spatial segregation of Blacks. If spatial segregation exists in the most liberal of cities, then this could happen anywhere. And while it is important to observe the white supremacy capitalist cisgender heteropatriarchy across and within geographical spaces in these United States (and beyond), as well as the formation of "chocolate cities" and an generalized map labeled "South" flanked by regional reference, it is equally important to emphasize nuanced areal differences so as not to conflate and reduce the racialized, gendered, and sexualized lived experiences within these spaces and places into a "singular" monolith. Black people in the US are *not* a singular people of a singular culture. Culture varies based on regionality as natural and built environment (space) shapes our diet, music, language, dress, etc. And yet, as Gupta and Ferguson explain, culture is neither "naturally" nor singularly linked to a discrete, bounded space and place.[22] Culture (in space and place) is also largely shaped by a diffusion of populations as a result of in- and out-migrations of peoples from "here" and "there." This diffusion blurs lines, marking culture as "deterritorialized."

Atlanta, New Orleans, Houston, Washington DC, Harlem, and Detroit may be characterized as "chocolate cities," but one chocolate city is not the same as another.

Mario Small makes a similar point when he writes "no two ghettos are alike."[23] In this thoughtful piece he advances the novel idea that so-called ghettos are not homogenous, instead they are very heterogeneous. In addition, he refutes the claim that what constitutes a ghetto is sparsely populated (high vacancy or low density) and uniformly deindustrialized spaces with scant organizational structure. Using empirical data, he demonstrates how this might have been true of William J. Wilson's Chicago but not true of Harlem. The tendency to generalize certain traits as being characteristic of all "ghettos" is problematic.

And while the feminist method rightfully advocates skepticism of empirical claims, there is value in this work, as Small demonstrates.[24] The goal of empirical research is to locate generalizable knowledge based on fabricated "categories" called variables, knowledge that can be replicated over large swaths of units of analysis (individuals, cities, countries, etc.). These data can help us glean important understandings that are unobtainable otherwise. Take, for example, my work on sexually transmitted infections (STIs) and HIV in Cincinnati. This work was initiated because of a newspaper article that declared some neighborhoods had "high" HIV prevalence, with no mention of the methods used to reach this conclusion. My qualitative work sought to understand how women residing in these neighborhoods navigated their day-to-day lives along race, gender, and sexuality within a spatial context of "risk." These data yield important findings on something I call "intersecting violence"; these data also couldn't confirm whether or not these were actually "high prevalent" neighborhoods. I needed to obtain quantifiable data on HIV status with spatial coordinates to determine both the spatial distribution and concentration of HIV and STI in the metropolitan area of Cincinnati (Norwood and Kim, publication forthcoming).[25] In doing so, I was able to establish and confirm a spatial dimension to sexual health disparities. And this is important, because the findings disrupt conventional narrative, which places blame of sexual health disparities on individuals' sexual proclivity.

Future methodological interventions that center spatiality should take into account not only patterns and distributions but also the particularities and nuances of locality and culture in shaping individuals, as well as how individuals shape locality and culture. As Black feminist researchers, it is important to unearth not only subjugated knowledge and individual sub-jectivities but also social patterns so long as it does not perpetuate essen-tialized categories, be they race, gender, sexuality, or space.

Conclusion

In this chapter, I make the case for why Black feminist sociologists should adopt a critical spatial lens in their work. Though space is diversely defined, issues of space and place are central to Black feminism and sociology alike. As Black feminists, we are tasked with understanding the lived experiences of Black women and to not only identify and lament, but also, as Col-lins pointed out, to resist, challenge, and produce oppositional knowledge. Race and gender are key ways Black women are identified and oppressed, but we must also include sexuality, social class, nation, immigration status, ableness and spatially. The spaces that we construct and that construct us (terrains of transgression and resistance) shape who we are and determine if and how we access resources and what knowledge is available to us. Sociologists need to follow the lead of Black feminists in recognizing the intersectional nature of spatiality.

Notes

1. Martina Löw. 2016. *The Sociology of Space: Materiality, Social Structures and Action.* New York: Palgrave Macmillan; John Urry. 2004. "The Sociology of Space and Place." In *The Blackwell Companion to Sociology*, edited by J. R. Blau, 3–15. Malden, MA: Blackwell Publishing, Ltd.
2. John Logan. 2012. "Making Place for Space: Spatial Thinking in Social Science." *Annual Review of Sociology* 38(10): 507–524; Hebert J. Gans. 2002. "The Sociology of Space: A Use-Centered View." *City & Community* 1(4): 329–339.
3. For the personal and political aspects, see H. Lefebvre. 1991. *The Production of Space.* Oxford and Cambridge, MA: Blackwell; George Lipsitz. 2007. "The Racialization of Space and the Spatialization of Race: Theorizing the Hidden Architecture of Land-scape." *Landscape Journal* 23: 10–23. For the material and poetic aspects, see Gaston Bachelard. 2014. *The Poetics of Space.* London: Penguin Classics; Katherine McK-ittrick. 2006. *Demonic Grounds: Black Women and the Cartographies of Struggle.* Min-neapolis: University of Minnesota Press; M. NourbeSe Philips. 1997. "Dis Place—The Space Between." In *A Genealogy of Resistance and Other Essays.* Toronto: Mercury Press. As a mediator of structure and the individual, see Lipsitz 2007; CaroletteNorwood. 2018. "Mapping Intersections of Violence on Black Women's Sexual Health within the Jim Crow Geographies of Cincinnati Neighborhoods." *Frontiers: A Journal of Women's Studies* 39(2): 97–135.
4. Bowleg Lisa. 2008. "When Black + Lesbian + Woman ≠ Black Lesbian Woman: The Methodological Challenges of Qualitative and Quantitative Intersectionality Research." *Sex Roles* 59: 312–325; Lisa Bowleg. 2013. "'Once You've Blended the Cake, You Can't Take the Parts Back to the Main Ingredients': Black Gay and Bisexual Men's Descriptions and Experiences of Intersectionality." *Sex Roles* 63: 754–767.
5. Yashminah Beebeejaun. 2017. "Gender, Urban Space and the Right to Everyday Life." Journal of Urban Affairs 39(3): 324.

6. Sharlene Mollett and Caroline Faria. 2018. "The Spatialities of Intersectional Thinking: Fashioning Feminist Geographic Futures." *Gender, Place & Culture* 25(4): 566.
7. Ibid., 565.
8. Jennifer C. Nash. 2019. *Black Feminism Reimagined: After Intersectionality*. Durham, NC: Duke University Press.
9. Ibid.
10. Jennifer C. Nash. 2011. "'Home Truths' on Intersectionality." *Yale Journal of Law & Feminism* 23(2): 456.
11. Lipsitz 2006, 12.
12. Thomas Sugrue. 2009. *Sweet Land of Liberty: The Forgotten Struggle for Civil Rights in the North, 203*. New York: Random House.
13. Kevin Dawson. 2018. *Undercurrents of Power: Aquatic Culture in the African Diaspora*, 2. Philadelphia, PA: University of Pennsylvania Press.
14. Rashad Shabazz. 2015. *Spatializing Blackness: Architectures of Confinement and Black Masculinity in Chicago, 24*. Chicago, IL: University of Illinois Press.
15. For club life, see Darius Bost. 2015. "At the Club: Locating Early Black Gay AIDS Activism in Washington, DC." Occasion 8. https://arcade.stanford.edu/occasion/club-locating-early-black-gay-aids-activism-washington-dc. For ballrooms, see Marlon Bailey. 2013. Butch Queens Up in Pumps: Gender, Performance and Ballroom Culture in Detroit. Ann Arbor: University of Michigan Press.
16. Aimee M. Cox. 2015. *Shapeshifters: Black Girls and the Choreography of Citizenship*, 47. Durham, NC: Duke University Press.
17. McKittrick 2006, xxiv, 46.
18. Leith Mullings. 2000. "African-American Women Making Themselves: Notes on the Role of Black Feminist Research." *Souls* 2(4): 19–20.
19. Nikki Jones. 2009. *Between Good and Ghetto: African American Girls and Inner-City Violence*, 5. New Brunswick, NJ: Rutgers University Press.
20. Ibid., 7.
21. Richard Rothstein. 2017. *The Color of Law: A Forgotten History of How Our Government Segregated America*, 3. New York and London: Liveright Publishing Corporation.
22. Akhil Gupta and James Ferguson. 1992. "Beyond 'Culture': Space, Identity, and the Politics of Difference." *Cultural Anthropology* 7(1): 6–23.
23. Mario Small. 2014. "No Two Ghettos Are Alike." *Chronicle Review*, March 17, 1.
24. Mario Small. 2008. "Four Reasons to Abandon the Idea of 'The Ghetto.'" *City & Community* 7(4): 347–352.
25. Norwood, C. and Kim, C. J. In press. *Spatial & Statistical Analysis of STI and HIV/AIDS by Neighborhood Context*. New Orleans, LA: American Association of Geographers (AAG) annual conference, April 10–14, 2018.

References

Adichie, Chimamanda N. 2009. *The Danger of a Single Story*. Ted Talk. www.ted.com/talks/chimamanda_adichie_the_danger_of_a_single_story/transcript?language=en

Bachelard, Gaston. 2014. *The Poetics of Space*. London: Penguin Classics.

Bailey, Marlon. 2013. *Butch Queens Up in Pumps: Gender, Performance and Ballroom Culture in Detroit*. Ann Arbor: University of Michigan Press.

Beebeejaun, Yashminah. 2017. "Gender, Urban Space and the Right to Everyday Life." *Journal of Urban Affairs* 39(3): 323–334.

Bost, Darius. 2015. "At the Club: Locating Early Black Gay AIDS Activism in Washington, DC." *Occasion* 8. https://arcade.stanford.edu/occasion/club-locating-early-black-gay-aids-activism-washington-dc

Bowleg, Lisa. 2008. "When Black + Lesbian + Woman ≠ Black Lesbian Woman: The Methodological Challenges of Qualitative and Quantitative Intersectionality Research." *Sex Roles* 59: 312–325.

Bowleg, Lisa. 2013. "'Once You've Blended the Cake, You Can't Take the Parts Back to the Main Ingredients': Black Gay and Bisexual Men's Descriptions and Experiences of Intersectionality." *Sex Roles* 63: 754–767.

Cheng, Wendy, and Rashad Shabazz. 2015. "Introduction: Race, Space, and Scale in the Twenty-First Century." *Occasion* 8: 1–7.

Collins, Patricia H. 1998. *Fighting Words: Black Women and the Search for Social Justice*. Minneapolis: University of Minnesota Press.

Cox, Aimee M. 2015. *Shapeshifters: Black Girls and the Choreography of Citizenship*. Durham, NC: Duke University Press.

Dawson, Kevin. 2018. *Undercurrents of Power: Aquatic Culture in the African Diaspora*. Philadelphia, PA: University of Pennsylvania Press.

Ducre, Kishi A. 2018. "The Black Feminist Spatial Imagination and an Intersectional Environmental Justice." *Environmental Sociology* 4(1): 22–35.

Gans, Hebert J. 2002. "The Sociology of Space: A Use-Centered View." *City & Community* 1(4): 329–339.

Gieryn, Thomas F. 2000. "A Space for Place in Sociology." *Annual Review of Sociology* 26: 463–496.

Green, Erica L. 2019. "Flint's Children Suffer in Class after Years of Drinking Lead-Poisoned Water." *New York Times*. November 6. www.nytimes.com/2019/11/06/us/politics/flint-michigan-schools.html

Gupta, Akhil, and James Ferguson. 1992. "Beyond 'Culture': Space, Identity, and the Politics of Difference." *Cultural Anthropology* 7(1): 6–23.

Hunter, Marcus A., and Zandria F. Robinson. 2018. *Chocolate Cities: The Black Map of American Life*. Oakland: University of California Press.

Jones, Nikki. 2009. *Between Good and Ghetto: African American Girls and Inner-City Violence*. New Brunswick, NJ: Rutgers University Press.

Lefebvre, H. 1991. *The Production of Space*. Oxford and Cambridge, MA: Blackwell.

Lipsitz, George. 2007. "The Racialization of Space and the Spatialization of Race: Theorizing the Hidden Architecture of Landscape." *Landscape Journal* 23: 10–23.

Logan, John. 2012. "Making Place for Space: Spatial Thinking in Social Science." *Annual Review of Sociology* 38(10): 507–524.

Löw, Martina. 2016. *The Sociology of Space: Materiality, Social Structures and Action*. New York: Palgrave Macmillan.

McKittrick, Katherine. 2006. *Demonic Grounds: Black Women and the Cartographies of Struggle*. Minneapolis: University of Minnesota Press.

Mollett, Sharlene, and Caroline Faria. 2018. "The Spatialities of Intersectional Thinking: Fashioning Feminist Geographic Futures." *Gender, Place & Culture* 25(4): 565–577.

Mullings, Leith. 2000. "African-American Women Making Themselves: Notes on the Role of Black Feminist Research." *Souls* 2(4): 18–29.

Nash, Jennifer C. 2011. "'Home Truths' on Intersectionality." *Yale Journal of Law & Feminism* 23(2): 445–470.

Nash, Jennifer C. 2019. *Black Feminism Reimagined: After Intersectionality*. Durham, NC: Duke University Press.

Norwood, Carolette. 2018. "Mapping Intersections of Violence on Black Women's Sexual Health within the Jim Crow Geographies of Cincinnati Neighborhoods." *Frontiers: A Journal of Women's Studies* 39(2): 97–135.

Norwood, Carolette and Kim, C. J. In press. *Spatial & Statistical Analysis of STI and HIV/ AIDS by Neighborhood Context*. New Orleans, LA: American Association of Geographers (AAG) annual conference, April 10–14, 2018.

Pattison, Dale. 2013. "Sites of Resistance: The Subversive Spaces of *Their Eyes Were Watching God*." *Melus* 38(4): 9–31.

Philips, M. NourbeSe. 1997. "Dis Place—The Space Between." In *A Genealogy of Resistance and Other Essays*, 74–112. Toronto: Mercury Press.

Rothstein, Richard. 2017. *The Color of Law: A Forgotten History of How Our Government Segregated America*. New York and London: Liveright Publishing Corporation, a division of W.W. Norton & Company.

Shabazz, Rashad. 2015. *Spatializing Blackness: Architectures of Confinement and Black Masculinity in Chicago*. Champaign: University of Illinois Press.

Small, Mario. 2008. "Four Reasons to Abandon the Idea of 'The Ghetto.'" *City & Community* 7(4): 347–352.

Small, Mario. 2014. "No Two Ghettos Are Alike." *Chronicle Review*. March 17.

Sugrue, Thomas. 2009. *Sweet Land of Liberty: The Forgotten Struggle for Civil Rights in the North*. New York: Random House.

Twine, France W., and Bradley Gardener. 2013. *Geography of Privilege*. New York: Routledge.

Urry, John. 2004. "The Sociology of Space and Place." In *The Blackwell Companion to Sociology*, edited by J. R. Blau, 3–15. Malden, MA: Blackwell Publishing, Ltd.

Chapter 11

Global Health and BFS

Diasporic Research and
Interventions Rooted
in Advocacy

Alicia D. Bonaparte

Black mothers are and have been unnecessarily dying. When I see this phrase (or its ilk) as a researcher of Black maternal health disparities, it is not lost on me that the newfound attention in national and public health conversations is long overdue. I want to be clear that Black mothers deserve and want more than the shock and alarm that accompanies these news reports because #BlackMamasMatter.[1] In this chapter, I explore how and why global public health interventions that use Black women's voices and Black feminist scholarship demonstrate the utility of Black feminist sociology (BFS) to address sexual and reproductive health disparities for greater inclusivity of diasporic women.

As an advocate of Black maternal health, I found in my research that understanding the manifestation of health disparities is crucial. Feminist scholars Julia Chinyere Oparah and I along with health scholars David Williams and Jana Mossey note that these disparities include (but are not limited to): comparatively higher rates of maternal mortality; inadequate (or minimal) screening for illnesses such as various cancers, hypertension, and cardiovascular diseases; as well as limited pain management protocols.[2] These disparities lead to a listing of comorbidities (the presence of two or more chronic diseases in an individual), shorter life expectancy, and propensity for low birth weight babies and early onset of chronic degenerative diseases that lead to deleterious maternal and infant health outcomes in birthing settings.[3] These aforementioned birthing statistics and their various retellings inspired public health intervention on a global scale from groups such as the Gates Foundation, the World Health Organization, and Amnesty International, to name a few.[4]

I argue that the constant focus on numbers is a fear-mongering technique designed to catalyze action but really tells only part of the story. Such myopic vision lacks an investigation of the sociostructural factors that contribute to harmful clinical encounters and thus delimit successful intervention, especially for myself and other Black women. I counter this limitation by highlighting how and why global public health interventions

DOI: 10.4324/9781003199113-15

that use Black women's voices and Black feminist scholarship demonstrate the utility of BFS in addressing sexual and reproductive health disparities for greater inclusivity of diasporic women. As a Black feminist sociologist, I see that the writings of Black feminists and African feminists are reflective of one another. To illustrate, I detail how African feminism expands the current state of Black feminist sociological thought by its apolitical stance, centralization of women's freedom of choice to critique existing political systems, and embrace of communal responsibility. This vantage point is exciting for me because I believe this bridge of expansion can catalyze better global health initiatives for Black women. bell hooks's and Rose M. Brewers's articulations on what is Black feminism are my initial lens, while African feminist scholars Ampofo and colleagues, Jagire and Martin provide in their respective publications a deeper context for feminism enacted on the African continent.

In the following section, I outline the foreground of Black feminist and African feminist writing on reproductive health and wellness. Next, using examples of an intervention in the US and one in Africa, I provide a comprehensive discussion of how these interventions employ the lens of BFS. I conclude with suggestions for health advocates to consider the significance of what these interventions foretell for future successful Black sexual and maternal health interventions. As a reader, you may wrestle with how such progressive conversations can happen within the silos of public and global health, but I implore you to think about what will persist if such conversations don't occur.

Background and Context

BFS and Black Women's Health Interventions in the US

The scholarship of Black feminist and cultural critic bell hooks on Black women's health and wellness serves as my central starting point to locate Black women's experiences as the nexus of explication for health issues and directions for situationally based interventions in a diasporic context. In *Sisters of the Yam*, hooks identifies that healing requires "learning about the myriad ways racism, sexism, class exploitation, homophobia, and various other structures of domination operate in [Black women's] daily lives to undermine our capacity to be self-determining."[5] Lack of knowledge about these factors impedes the development of "meaningful strategies of personal and collective resistance."[6] Currently, the major reproductive health experiences of Black women in the US center around disproportionately high numbers of low birth weight babies, unnecessary cesarean sections, birth complications, premature births, and lack of prenatal screenings.[7] When researchers examine the reasons behind these most common outcomes for Black women, they locate that institutionalized racism, classism, heterosexism, as well as lack of cultural humility are responsible for inadequate, inconsistent, and dangerous healthcare.[8]

The Case for Community Health Workers in Black Birthing Enters

I champion reproductive health practitioners and interventions targeted toward Black women that acknowledge these aforementioned pervasive forces and engage Black female-identifying people in various ways that will mitigate these circumstances. Jennie Joseph, a midwife-activist, maternal health advocate, and contributor to *Birthing Justice*,[9] leads Commonsense Childbirth Inc. in Central Florida where she and her team empower and provide greater agency to Black birthing parents and their families using the JJWay© as the cornerstone of eradicating maternal and infant health disparities among marginalized populations across race and class lines. They achieve these goals by promoting the importance of "access to care, practitioners, support, education, and whatever else [is necessary to reach full term]," and ensuring partnerships between the birthing parent, their families, communities, and practitioners that are informational and educational for all those supporting the birthing parent.[10]

Community health workers (CHWs) undergird the JJWay© as integral members of healthcare that vitally assist vulnerable populations such as Black pregnant mothers. CHWs function as cultural brokers (often of the same racial, class, and gender backgrounds as the communities receiving health services) suitably placed to eradicate health disparities due to their shared backgrounds and roles as mediators between practitioners and patients within vulnerable populations.[11] Brewer outlines how BFS dictates that "race/gender/class situations reflect the inseparability of these forces for women of color, sociologically and practically";[12] consequently, programs employing Black women as CHWs like the JJWay© engage in like-minded conversations and resolutions to address reproductive health inequities by centering the voices of Black women and creating situation-specific interventions that engage self-valuation.

Additionally, Joseph's JJWay© invokes in me a deep commitment to reproductive justice and birth justice by encouraging health literacy. Health literacy is one's ability to navigate the healthcare system using acquired knowledge to enable clear and autonomous communication with healthcare providers, develop an understanding of clinician's advice and directions, and lastly, comprehend how health insurance works to engage in the best medical decision-making processes.[13] Education and nursing scholars Esther Prins and Angela Mooney locate marginalization and oppression vis-à-vis classism and racism oftentimes as drivers of low health literacy among Black women and other women of color.[14] Black feminist sociology as a lens articulates for me how these drivers function as axes of oppression while also cocreating negative social realities for Black women in the US and abroad, since access to educational and medical resources are two of the main sources of their health inequities. These drivers also function as axes upon which interventions such as the JJWay© can act.

An underlying aspect of Joseph's work is recognition that her childbirth center is nearby the tricounty area of Polk, Hardee and Highlands Counties, which is known as a clinician shortage area (CSA); consequently, women of color living within these counties suffer some of the worst infant and maternal outcomes. As she notes in our collaborative Black feminist chapter, her health activism not only dictates working in this area but also encouraging Black birthing parents to see the cultural significance of Black midwives in Florida.[15] Hence, nonprofit organizations including nongovernmental organizations (NGOs) provide a crucial access point for vulnerable Black women in bettering our understanding of how to engage in maternal health interventions for ourselves.

Phillips "recognizes women's NGOs as key players in emancipatory action for women."[16] As such, NGOs are an ideal pivot point for the engagement of feminist praxis as well as for catalyzing deeper analyses with both practical and theoretical implications since empowerment leads to gender equality within programming. Feminism is of high importance within gender equality programs because "[it] provokes complexity in debate and identity at both theoretical and practice levels. The data demonstrates [sic] that empowerment is a dominant framework in both specific gender equality programmes as well as in the thinking of feminist NGOs."[17]

Community health workers and the JJWay© illuminate key aspects of Black feminist sociology. As bell hooks notes, true healing for Black women necessitates addressing the sociostructural forces fomenting their oppression—namely, the removal of institutionalized racism, sexism, and classism within reproductive healthcare. Doing so allows for our liberation, that in truth, is an application of what Black feminist sociologist Rose M. Brewer calls for sociology as a discipline to do for Black women.

Black Mamas Matter Alliance and Black Feminist Praxis

Black Mamas Matter Alliance (BMMA) provides a clear example of an NGO engaged in Black feminist praxis operating as a pivot point for progressive shifts in maternal and sexual healthcare (blackmamasmatter.org). BMMA members advocate for a new type of relationship between Black birthing mothers and their practitioners: a relationship in which these women and their rights are respected via supportive prenatal and postnatal experiences. By enlisting the assistance of members of the American College of Gynecology (ACOG) toward affecting health and social policies geared toward protecting Black mothers, BMMA emulates what Black feminist writer Toni Cade Bambara states will lead to antisexist coalitions, "the fashioning of new relationships that . . . will obliterate the corrosive system of dominance, manipulation, exploitation."[18]

Black Women's Health Interventions in the African Diaspora and the BFS Lens

African feminist Jennifer Jagire provides an insightful application of Black feminist thought as a refutation against Eurocentric tyranny. Borrowing from Njoki Wane, she proposes that "placing Black women's ideas within the discourse of our own language" enables Black women's ability to center our experiences using theory as well as collective indigenous African knowledge.[19] Her work encouraged me to see distinctive parallels and nonparallels between African feminism and Black feminist thought. These parallels include valuing the knowledge borne from Black women's lived experiences, understanding the role white supremacy plays in the subjugation of Black women, as well as highlighting how history explains the perpetuation of power dynamics across race, class, and gender lines. African feminism's nonparallel extensions of Black feminism consider communities as a body of knowledge, its openness to an apolitical stance, a recognition of how bettering one woman's life offers communal benefits, and a focus on how colonialism, cosmology, and class conjointly influence the lives of African women.

Black people understand that education encompasses formal knowledge and informal knowledge acquired within communal networks both within North America and across the African diaspora. Jagire illustrates that African feminism's roots in oral cultures reflects these intergenerational transmissions of knowledge outside of a Eurocentric lens. We can see this implementation of African feminism within various African global health interventions who use "word of mouth" for health promotion and prevention efforts.[20]

Africana scholar Maria Martin identifies an apolitical stance as another aspect central to African feminism and uses the writings of Funmilayo Ransome-Kuti's articulations of a Pan-Africanist feminism as an exemplar.[21] This apolitical stance diverges from Collins's discussion of Black feminism as a political standpoint because an apolitical stance allows for "a place where women could speak their minds and discuss issues without fear of misrepresenting the ideologies of their affiliated party [and] the freedom of choice to champion certain issues and lead critiques of others."[22] Within her discussion of African feminist philosophy, Martin reveals how aligning Black feminist thought with African feminist thought allows for an extension of Black feminism while also acknowledging that African cosmology undergirds African feminism since all women are responsible for progressive change within communities.[23] This holistic perspective signifies that the betterment of our lives as Black women entails communal support, accountability, and recognition that improving one woman's life leads to collective progress for all community members.

Martin also offers that this extension of Black feminist thought requires a consideration of how culture, colonialism, and class intersect to shape African women's lives and highlight the cultural and historical realities of gendered expectations within an African context.[24]

Ampofo and colleagues' African feminist scholarship reveals prominent themes within the auspices of gender and women's studies, such as gender-based violence, sexual and reproductive health, and the roles of globalization and politics in African women's lives.[25] These scholars pinpoint some of the issues within scholarship on women's health in Africa—assumptions that modernization and democracy create trickle down impacts focused on mothering and being a wife rather than focusing on how cultural beliefs (e.g., traditional, hegemonic gender roles) and the aftereffects of colonial systems (such as dilapidated economic systems) predict maternal health concerns. Additionally, internationally funded programs have a problematic focus on overpopulation. I see that both issues faced by African women echo Black feminist Patricia Hill Collins argument that "there has also been a preoccupation with treating people of African descent as animals who had to be domesticated, managed and controlled."[26]

Black feminist scholarship highlights the importance of progressive community networks as a means of improving the well-being of Black women and children.[27] African feminism adds that the well-being of women and their communities relies on women's ability to "impact societal development through mothering, community building, balancing gender relations, contributing to the economy and infrastructure through entrepreneurship, and many other ways."[28] Jointly, these standpoints showcase why we must move beyond focusing on race, class, and gender to pinpoint how other sociostructural factors contribute to the inequities faced by Black women across the diaspora. Incorporating this understanding from African-based feminist scholars propels us to critique existing sexual and reproductive health interventions, and to require the presence of Black feminist sociology to address "what it means to exist between the lines [of various forms of oppression] as a black woman in this society."[29]

Ampofo and colleagues' work also shows that interventions directed toward increasing access to women's reproductive rights are rooted in access to job opportunities and education. Many African countries' reproductive healthcare interventions focus on a reduction of HIV rates among adults; but, some programs also examine sexual decision-making among teenage youth to address HIV contraction as well. SHAZ!, a Zimbabwean program designed to reduce HIV risk and promote better reproductive health outcomes for adolescent and teen girls, uses African feminism in its framework. A combination of theories of gender, power and female empowerment are the bastion of the intervention because participants have "[a] greater ability to negotiate safer sex for improved HIV and reproductive health outcomes" using various communication and financial strategies.[30] Knowing how financial hardship and traditional gender roles impact Zimbabwean women's ability to acquire resources pushed the program to increase access to information and healthcare, develop relationship communication skills, and guide participants with microgrants and vocational skills training.[31]

SHAZ!'s program exemplifies that newer approaches to addressing the healthcare needs of Black women must be more responsive to their social conditions—a nod to understanding the lived experiences of Black women in the diaspora. Designing these approaches requires identifying the complexities of shifting sociopolitical and economic contexts and addressing the needs of young Black women. Economic empowerment serves as an important vehicle for changing social realities and dismantling structural barriers impeding Black women's livelihoods and well-being. Moreover, it allows Black women to self-determine, as hooks contends, as well as engages why addressing economic contributions, social entrepreneurship, and more balanced gender relations lead to stronger communities that support Black women.[32]

Directions for Future Research

Praxis and Future Investigations of BFS's Utility in Maternal Healthcare

Highlighting the collaborative efforts of practitioners and social scientists who want to eliminate bad health outcomes mirrors what bell hooks calls collective resistance.[33] I argue that these interventions aid in Black women's progress across the diaspora. Yet, we need more quality improvements in global and public health interventions to go beyond a reduction in numbers. I call for a deeper integration of BFS in program development as an example of practical sociology. Looking at the work of Jennie Joseph and CHWs, the advocacy of BMMA with ACOG, and the work of SHAZ! demonstrates a true pivot toward the incorporation of both Black feminism and African feminism in order to truly center Black women's voices and autonomy, emphasize governmental accountability and engaging allyship, and focus on communal responsibility for the protection of all Black women.

For those of you who are public health advocates, burgeoning activists, or simply just want to support health promotion efforts, I suggest reading scholarship that engages indigenous African knowledge. This reading challenges all of us in health advocacy work to avoid operating from a "savior complex." Doing so is a reclamation of this ancient wisdom as we embrace the idea "helping one helps us all" to incite generational change for all

Black people. I created these other questions to continue exploring this need for a shift in interventionist work:

1. How could the incorporation of African feminist frameworks in US healthcare positively influence reproductive healthcare for Black women?
2. How could Black feminist scholars be invited into social and public policy conversations about reproductive healthcare for Black women across the diaspora with a deeper recognition of how Western frameworks are inadequate in applications of healthcare interventions?

I truly believe that resolving these questions will lead to a pronounced shift in international donors' and NGOs' approaches to maternal and sexual health inequity.

Conclusion

Black feminist sociology centers the lived experiences of Black women and encourages a recognition of how and why their social lives are impacted by various sociostructural factors beyond just race, class, and gender and also including culture, cosmology, and colonialism. Yet, its utility requires a deeper consideration of the lives of Black women in a diasporic context—BFS previously offered minimal attention to Black women on the African continent. Incorporating this population of women showcases that globally, Black women's health outcomes continue to reflect the pervasive impacts of institutionalized racism, heterosexism, classism, and ableism. I discussed these three health interventions utilizing tenets of Black feminist and African feminist thought to demonstrate the continued necessity of more holistic and communally oriented healthcare.

However, I acknowledge that some interventions with an African feminist orientation face challenges. Kululanga and colleagues[34] reveal how male involvement in Malawi's maternal health care is a useful tool for creating safer pregnancy spaces, especially when community leaders are engaged within public health interventions. These leaders are "custodians of culture"; as such, they function as agents of social and cultural changes.[35] Having chiefs and village headmen/women in this program generates increased participation by community members.[36]

The nexus of this study is recognition of traditional gender roles' influence on a limited embrace of this feminist approach to reproductive healthcare in the African country Malawi. These gender norms bar men from engaging in maternal health care, the perceived belief that men's involvement delimits women's agency in their birthing encounters, and, the utilization of traditional approaches that exclude men from participating in examining rooms as a means of relieving men "from a feminine environment" function as prohibitive factors.[37] Recommendations for the deeper utilization of a BFS lens entail educational programming by male- and female-identifying cultural health workers who are also community leaders to "engender" maternal healthcare in Malawi as well as other African nations.

Conversely, not only are Black women's lives influenced by gender norms but they also face the long-lasting issue of internalized sexism within the Black community. Black feminist Ula Taylor provides historiographic evidence of why antisexist coalitions are necessary by providing a historiography of how Black men have hurt Black women within different social contexts regarding activism. Taylor pulls from Toni Cade Bambara's admonition that "racism and chauvinism are anti-people. And a man cannot be politically correct and a chauvinist."[38]

I offer that the BFS lens within reproductive and sexual healthcare enables Black women facing maternal and sexual health decision-making the opportunity to do so in spaces alongside practitioners and family/community members who recognize how injustices are enacted and work to not reproduce those injustices during the vulnerable periods associated with clinical encounters. The narratives of women are crucial aspects of determining diagnoses and treatment options; such narratives enable practitioners to engage in narrative medicine and narrative humility to better patients' outcomes and increase patient satisfaction. As Richey outlines, when NGOs and other international aid donors are involved, their priorities are placed at the forefront, which leads to a "reproductive health agenda . . . implemented through what were previously donor, ministry, and local family planning institutions" with a primary focus on overpopulation rather than the reproductive healthcare rights and violations suffered by Black women living on the African continent in countries such as Uganda.[39]

BFS is vital today just as it was in the past when seeking to eradicate the health inequities faced by Black women across the diaspora. Black feminist sociologists are most equipped to engage in theorizing and creating viable solutions.

> The black feminist intelligentsia fill a vacuum by examining the complexities and complications of an inequality built on race, but also gender and class. As women of color, they argue for a revisioning of racial inequality as shaped by the sex/gender and class question.[40]

An expansive lens of BFS that employs both Black and African feminism may not only achieve Brewer's vision but also encourage other scholars to note the bridge between these forms of scholarship.

Notes

1. This hashtag started on Twitter and became a national campaign launched toward political advocacy, also resulting in the formation of the organization Black Mamas Matter: https://blackmamasmatter.org.
2. Jana M. Mossey. 2011. "Defining Racial and Ethnic Disparities in Pain Management." *Clinical Orthopedic Related Research* 469: 1859–1870.
3. David R. Williams, Selina A. Mohammed, Jacinta Leavell, and Chiquita Collins. 2010. "Race, Socioeconomic Status and Health: Complexities, Ongoing Challenges and Research Opportunities." *Annals of the New York Academy of Science* 1186: 69–101.
4. Adam Wagstaff and Mariam Claeson. 2004. *The Millennium Development Goals for Health: Rising to the Challenges*, xi. Washington, DC: World Bank.
5. bell hooks. 2015. *Sisters of the Yam*, 6–7. New York: Routledge.
6. Ibid.
7. Julia Chinyere Oparah and Alicia D. Bonaparte. 2015. *Birthing Justice: Black Women, Pregnancy, and Childbirth*, 1–4. New York: Routledge.
8. Julia Chinyere Oparah, Helen Artega, Dantia Hudson, Linda Jones, and Talita Osegura. 2018. *Battling Over Birth: Black Women and the Maternal Health Care Crisis*. Amarillo, TX: Praeclarus Press.
9. Oparah and Bonaparte 2015.
10. Alicia D. Bonaparte and Jennie Joseph. 2015. "Becoming an Outsider-Within: Jennie Joseph's Activism in Florida Midwifery." In *Birthing Justice: Black Women, Pregnancy, and Childbirth*, edited by Julia Chinyere Oparah and Alicia D. Bonaparte, 183. New York: Routledge.
11. Ted Lankester. 2009. *Setting Up Community Health Programmes: A Practical Manual for Use in Developing Countries*. Berkeley: Hesperian.
12. Rose M. Brewer. 1989. "Black Women and Feminist Sociology: An Emerging Perspective." *American Sociologist* 20(1): 67.
13. Don Nutbeam. 2000. "Health Literacy as a Public Health Goal: A Challenge for Contemporary Health Education and Communication Strategies into the 21st Century." *Health Promotion International* 15(3): 261.
14. Esther Prins and Angela Mooney. 2014. "Literacy and Health Disparities." *New Directions for Adult & Continuing Education* 2014(142): 25–35.
15. Bonaparte and Joseph 2015.
16. Ruth Phillips. 2016. "Challenging or Maintaining the Status Quo?" In *Women's Emancipation and Civil Society Organisations*, edited by Christina Schwabenland, Chris Lange, Jenny Onyx, and Sachiko Nakagawa, 21. Bristol: Bristol University Press and Policy Press.
17. Ibid., 39.
18. Toni Cade Bambara. 1970. *The Black Woman: An Anthology*, 164. New York: Signet.
19. Jennifer Jagire. 2013. "Indigenous African Knowledges and African Feminism: Resisting Eurocentric Ways of Knowing." In *Ruptures: Anti-colonial and Anti-racist Feminist Theorizing*, edited by Njoki Wane, Jennifer Jagire, and Zahra Murad, 83. Boston, MA: Sense Publishers.
20. Lucy I. Kululanga, Johanne Sundby, Address Malata, and Ellen Chirwa. 2012. "Male Involvement in Maternity Health Care in Malawi." *African Journal of Reproductive Health* 16(1): 145–157; Megan S. Dunbar and Imelda Mudekunye-Mahaka. 2017. "Empowering Adolescent Girls and Women for Improved Sexual Health in Zimbabwe: Lessons Learned from a Combined Livelihoods and Life Skills Intervention (SHAZ!)." In *Women's Empowerment and Global Health: A Twenty-First Century Agenda*, edited by Shari L. Dworkin, Monica Gandhi, and Paige Passano, 190–209. Stanford: University of California Press.

21. Maria Martin. 2016. "'More Power to Your Great Self': Nigerian Women's Activism and the Pan-African Transnationalist Construction of Black Feminism." *Phylon* 53(2): 54.
22. Ibid., 58.
23. Ibid., 55.
24. Ibid., 55–56.
25. Akosua Adomako Ampofo, Josephine Beoku-Betts, Wairimu Ngaruiya Njambi, and Mary Osirim. 2004. "Women's and Gender Studies in English-Speaking Sub-Saharan Africa: A Review of Research in the Social Sciences." *Gender & Society* 18(6): 687.
26. As quoted in Jagire 2013, 84.
27. Patricia Hill Collins. 2000. *Black Feminist Thought: Knowledge, Consciousness, and the Politics of Empowerment.* London: Routledge.
28. Martin 2016, 60.
29. Brewer 1989, 68.
30. Dunbar and Mudekunye-Mahaka 2017, 191.
31. Ibid.
32. Jagire 2013.
33. Hooks 2015.
34. Kululanga et al. 2012.
35. Ibid., 152–153.
36. Ibid., 153.
37. Ibid.
38. Ula Taylor. 1998. "The Historical Evolution of Black Feminist Theory and Praxis." *Journal of Black Studies* 29(2): 234–253.
39. Lisa Ann Richey. 2005. "Uganda: HIV/AIDS and Reproductive Health." In *Where Human Rights Begin*, edited by Wendy Chavkin and Ellen Chesler, 108. Newark, NJ: Rutgers University Press.
40. Rose M. Brewer. 1989. "Black Women and Feminist Sociology: An Emerging Perspective." *The American Sociologist* 20(1): 57–70.

References

Ampofo, Akosua Adomako, Josephine Beoku-Betts, Wairimu Ngaruiya Njambi, and Mary Osirim. 2004. "Women's and Gender Studies in English-Speaking Sub-Saharan Africa: A Review of Research in the Social Sciences." *Gender & Society* 18(6): 685–714.
Aoyama, Atsuko. 2001. *Reproductive Health in the Middle East and North Africa: Well-being for All.* Washington, DC: World Bank.
Bambara, Toni Cade. 1970. *The Black Woman: An Anthology*, 164. New York: Signet.
Bonaparte, Alicia D., and Jennie Joseph. 2015. "Becoming an Outsider-Within: Jennie Joseph's Activism in Florida Midwifery." In *Birthing Justice: Black Women, Pregnancy, and Childbirth*, edited by Julia Chinyere Oparah and Alicia D. Bonaparte, 176–186. New York: Routledge.
Brewer, Rose M.. 1989. "Black Women and Feminist Sociology: An Emerging Perspective." *The American Sociologist* 20(1): 57–70.
Collins, Patricia Hill. 2000. *Black Feminist Thought: Knowledge, Consciousness, and the Politics of Empowerment.* New York: Routledge.
Dunbar, Megan S., and Imelda Mudekunye-Mahaka. 2017. "Empowering Adolescent Girls and Women for Improved Sexual Health in Zimbabwe: Lessons Learned from a Combined Livelihoods and Life Skills Intervention (SHAZ!)." In *Women's Empowerment*

and Global Health: A Twenty-First Century Agenda, edited by Shari L. Dworkin, Monica Gandhi, and Paige Passano, 190–209. Stanford: University of California Press.

hooks, bell. 2000. *Feminism is for Everybody*. Boston, MA: New Press.

hooks, bell. 2015. *Sisters of the Yam*. New York: Routledge.

Jagire, Jennifer. 2013. "Indigenous African Knowledges and African Feminism: Resisting Eurocentric Ways of Knowing." In *Ruptures: Anti-colonial and Anti-racist Feminist Theorizing*, edited by Njoki Wane, Jennifer Jagire, and Zahra Murad, 77–89. Boston, MA: Sense Publishers.

Kululanga, Lucy I., Johanne Sundby, Address Malata, and Ellen Chirwa. 2012. "Male Involvement in Maternity Health Care in Malawi." *African Journal of Reproductive Health* 16(1): 145–157.

Lankester, Ted. 2009. *Setting Up Community Health Programmes: A Practical Manual for Use in Developing Countries*. Berkeley: Hesperian.

Martin, Maria. 2016. " 'More Power to Your Great Self': Nigerian Women's Activism and the Pan-African Transnationalist Construction of Black Feminism." *Phylon* 53(2): 54–78.

Mossey, Jana M. 2011. "Defining Racial and Ethnic Disparities in Pain Management." *Clinical Orthopedic Related Research* 469: 1859–1870.

Nutbeam, Don. 2000. "Health Literacy as a Public Health Goal: A Challenge for Contemporary Health Education and Communication Strategies into the 21st Century." *Health Promotion International* 15(3): 259–267.

Oparah, Julia Chinyere, Helen Artega, Dantia Hudson, Linda Jones, and Talita Osegura. 2018. *Battling Over Birth: Black Women and the Maternal Health Care Crisis*. London: Praeclarus Press.

Oparah, Julia Chinyere, and Alicia D. Bonaparte. 2015. *Birthing Justice: Black Women, Pregnancy, and Childbirth*. New York: Routledge.

Phillips, Ruth. 2016. "Challenging or Maintaining the Status Quo?" In *Women's Emancipation and Civil Society Organisations*, edited by Christina Schwabenland, Chris Lange, Jenny Onyx, and Sachiko Nakagawa. Bristol: Bristol University Press and Policy Press.

Prins, Esther, and Angela Mooney. 2014. "Literacy and Health Disparities," *New Directions for Adult & Continuing Education* 2014(142): 25–35.

Richey, Lisa Ann. 2005. "Uganda: HIV/AIDS and Reproductive Health." In *Where Human Rights Begin*, edited by Wendy Chavkin and Ellen Chesler, 95–126. Newark, NJ: Rutgers University Press.

Taylor, Ula. 1998. "The Historical Evolution of Black Feminist Theory and Praxis." *Journal of Black Studies* 29(2): 234–253.

Wagstaff, Adam, and Mariam Claeson. 2004. *The Millennium Development Goals for Health: Rising to the Challenges*. Washington, DC: World Bank.

Williams, David R., Selina A. Mohammed, Jacinta Leavell, and Chiquita Collins. 2010. "Race, Socioeconomic Status and Health: Complexities, Ongoing Challenges and Research Opportunities." *Annals of the New York Academy of Science* 1186: 69–101.

Chapter 12

Family Background and the Meanings of Economic Autonomy for Black Lesbian Women[1]

Mignon R. Moore

> I grew up watching the power dynamic between my parents, and my mom—I think a lot of the reason she stayed in the relationship so long was that she didn't have economic power at all, and it's hard to leave a situation like that. You think you may become homeless or you may become this or that. So I've always felt, even when I was dating guys, that I would have to have my own bank account. We could work out the expenses and all that other stuff but I've got to be self-sufficient. And I'm still like that. I've got to be self-sufficient.
>
> —Lynne Witherspoon,[2] attorney

> I love [my partner] to death and trust her more than any female I've ever known. [But] she ain't getting my check; you know what I'm sayin'? And I don't want her check. You work for your money. As long as you take care of responsibilities we got in the house, I don't care what you do with your money.
>
> —Carlie Lewis, croupier (casino card dealer) and hairstylist

In this work I examine the ways Black sexual minority women evaluate concepts of equality in their relationships. Past studies of lesbian households, drawing from feminist sociological theory, have emphasized the egalitarian nature of these couples *vis-a-vis* their division of family labor, which concerned chores such as cooking and cleaning, as well as care and supervision of children. But a Black feminist approach would necessarily analyze another aspect of egalitarianism: how lesbian couples distribute paid work, evaluate its importance in the relationship, and construct ideologies about self-sufficiency and autonomy. This is because regardless of sexuality, the home life of Black women has historically incorporated these behaviors and values into what it means to "take care of home." For example, Donna Franklin's 2015 book shows that throughout time, Black heterosexually married women have been particularly involved in the economic sphere of home life, offering greater financial contributions to their families relative to their white counterparts.[3] Looking at these dynamics from the perspective of Black women's histories and experiences brings

DOI: 10.4324/9781003199113-16

new ways for other family sociologists to understand household and marital relationships.

I have spent the better part of my career attempting to build a foundation of sociological research on the study of Black lesbian life and identity, with the intersection of race, gender, and class as the paradigmatic lens through which to analyze this population. That climb has come with certain risks that I have resolutely accepted because I believe that research on marginalized populations is essential to transform our discipline, and the best way to answer the research questions I have is through a Black feminist framework. In this chapter, I examine how family background influences the meanings of economic independence for Black sexual minority women. Collins' "power of self-definition"[4] is a neat scaffold for this work, uncovering the family as an institutional site where Black queer women employ self-definitions drawn from their structural locations and personal backgrounds to manage expectations in their unions. This course allows an expanded set of processes and interpretations about marital power to emerge, as I show in my 2008 paper on power in Black lesbian households.[5]

Black lesbians are an important population for studying family dynamics in same-sex relationships because historically they developed a sexual minority culture outside of lesbian-feminism. While white women largely came to understand their sexuality in the context of consciousness-raising meetings in the women's movement or gender studies classes on college campuses, racial segregation limited Black women's involvements in these groups. Instead, Black women were entering the lesbian world in predominantly Black social environments. Anita Cornwall's 1983 memoir and Abdulahad and colleagues' reflections on feminist organizing both reveal that these spaces were politically distant from lesbian-feminist ideals and influenced whether and in what form egalitarian ideologies would be expressed.[6] The analysis of household organization and feminist ideologies among Black women in same-sex unions allows for a study of these social processes through the lives of individuals who lie at the intersection of the single dimensions of race, gender, and sexuality. I would like others to see this work as part of a Black feminist corrective to academic scholarship.

Egalitarian Ideologies in Black Lesbian Marital Relationships

As part of my research, I conducted interviews and surveys with approximately 100 women who have formed families as lesbian, gay, bisexual, in the Life, or Women-Loving-Women.[7] The majority of my respondents professed views that are consistent with traditional measures of equality in relationships: 84 percent agreed that both mates should divide household tasks evenly, 89 percent agreed that both partners' career plans should be equally considered when making decisions about where to live, and

84 percent disagreed with the specialization model of one person taking on the major financial responsibility and the other person primarily caring for the home.

Despite their ideological support of these egalitarian principles, the data could suggest that respondents tend not to behave in egalitarian ways because in most households, one person spends much more time performing household chores. However, while this is sometimes a source of frustration for the partner who does more housework, it is not the primary source of conflict in their relationships, it is not the primary measure of whether respondents believe their relationships to be fair, and it is not related to the balance of power in the home. Instead, respondents place a premium on *economic independence* rather than the division of family labor as a value and behavior that is critical for marital satisfaction. This importance is expressed through the belief that each partner should contribute her own financial resources to the household.

In *Invisible Families: Gay Identities, Relationships and Motherhood among Black Women*, I argue that this aspect of egalitarianism is critical to the ways Black lesbians measure relationship satisfaction and is connected to Black feminist histories and ideologies.[8] But in this chapter, I look at differences in class backgrounds and experiences to explain why financial autonomy is so important for Black women. In my sample, one-third of the respondents grew up in poverty, a third were raised in working-class families, and a third lived in middle-class or upper-middle-class households in childhood. While almost everyone placed a high value on economic independence, I found important differences related to family socioeconomic status that explain why self-sufficiency is so highly valued in their intimate relationships.

Low-Income Family Background: Economic Independence Tied to Personal Survival and Ability to Move Out of Bad Relationships

Karen Jabar is a 42-year-old Black American woman and mother of three who left her Muslim husband of 21 years when she came out as gay. Karen is also a child of two alcoholic parents whose addictions resulted in traumatic consequences for everyone in the family. Under conditions of extreme poverty, homelessness, and instability, she and her ten brothers and sisters banded together in the neighborhood to protect one another from the taunting and bullying they received from other children. She states:

> My life was rough. We struggled. I would probably say that we were a poor family because I could remember eating sugar sandwiches, things like that. I remember mices and roaches being in the house, taking

care of my brothers and sisters, and not having electricity, or the fact that we would plug in the TV cord or the extension cord into the hallway socket to get light into your apartment; having the door cracked and not really knowing who is coming into the building.

When Karen was 13, her mother killed her father in self-defense during a fight that began after heavy drinking. After that incident, Karen and her siblings were separated from one another and she was sent to a group home for girls. She describes her teenage years as a life of loneliness, vulnerability, and uncertainty about her day-to-day future.

Despite the bleak circumstances of her childhood, Karen has been able to rise above some of the challenges she faced. After several starts and stops, she received a four-year college degree and provides for herself economically. Nevertheless, she says she does not maintain close relationships with her family members, battles depression and low self-esteem, and has a difficult time staying employed. She has held and lost positions in the U.S. Military, various private security firms, and several civil servant jobs.

While a snapshot at time of interview might have indicated a middle-class status (college education and a job as a supervisor for a city agency), I believe that Karen's family background of extreme poverty, her struggle to complete her education, and other factors in her personal life make her quite different from many of the middle-class lesbians usually studied by researchers. These background experiences have influenced many areas of her adult life, including the things she finds important in her intimate relationships. Economic independence, even through a succession of short-term jobs, allows her a measure of control over her own circumstances. Regardless of the financial stability of the women she dates, Karen says she always keeps a job so that she will be able to care for herself and have the resources to leave unhealthy relationships when she is ready to move on. While she has taken on more than her share of the financial expenses with past partners, she expects "equal sharing of all of the family responsibilities" in a serious relationship, and this includes paid work. For Karen, economic self-sufficiency rather than strict equality in the division of household chores carries the most weight in her satisfaction with a mate.

Working-Class Family Background: Economic Independence Tied to Childhood Experiences of Work in the Family

Roberta "Ro" Gaul is a 40-year-old licensed electrician born in Jamaica, West Indies. Throughout her adult life, her intimate relationships have only been with women. Ro and her siblings were raised with their mother, who was employed as a nurse's aide. Ro lives with her spouse Sifa Brody, and in separate interviews and surveys they both say that Sifa does the majority of the housework and that Ro does not do enough of it. However, they also both report being very satisfied with their union, and that they have equal power in the relationship.

Ro's feelings on the importance of financial independence stem from her own experiences with work as an adolescent. When asked about the qualities she looks for in a mate, she states:

> They have to be working because I'm extremely independent, and I believe [that] everybody should work. I grew up as a young child working, and I am still working, so I believe that you must have a job. If it means that the job is paying you enough for you to maintain yourself or your own independence, you have to be working.

While Ro links her opinions about work to her experiences in her family of origin and the necessity of each person's income to the well-being of the household, other working-class women draw on an ideology of independence as a protection against slipping into poverty.

Shelly Jackson is a 38-year-old bus driver. She was raised by her Black American parents, grandparents, and great-grandparents, who have all shared a two-family house since her parents married in 1962. She says her father took care of the family financially while her mother was "the homemaker." Prior to entering into a lesbian sexuality, Shelly had been married twice. At the time of interview, she was legally separated but not divorced from her second husband, and living with her children and her female partner Shaunte Austin. She is emphatic that regardless of sexuality, each partner should bring her own resources to a relationship, saying "I don't give a damn who you're with, you always need . . . to be independent and take care of yourself." She tells me she learned the importance of self-sufficiency by watching her father provide for the family:

> My father was always there to take care and provide for us, and that's what made me who I am today. 'Cause even when I was married, I always took that role of being the provider. I was always the one to go out there and work and pay the rent, and pay the bills, and do this and do that, and not look for him to take care of me. I've seen what my mother went through and that's not what I wanted to go through growing up, being an adult.

Interestingly, she defines a "provider" as someone who can take care of themselves without the help of others. Shelly's first marriage was tumultuous largely because of an abusive husband. After five years of kicking him out of the house and then letting him back in, she ended the relationship.

In Pepper Schwartz's 1994 study of egalitarian heterosexual marriages, she defines the provider role or provider complex as a combination of roles that gives one person the responsibility for financially supporting the family, and the other person responsibility for all of the auxiliary duties that allow the first person to devote themselves to their work.[9] Schwartz's definition is different from the way Shelly Jackson uses the term provider, and this becomes clear as Shelly describes the financial contributions she expects from her mate. On separate surveys, Shelly and Shaunte each report that Shaunte spends more time on household chores and takes on much of the childcare responsibilities. Shelly often works the night shift or double shifts, and relies on Shaunte to feed and bathe the children, help them with their homework, and keep the house tidy. However, when asked how happy she is with the way she and her mate divide household responsibilities, Shelly says she became much happier once Shaunte found a job:

> Don't get me wrong. She [Shaunte] has always been so good to me as far as helping me out with the kids, 'cause my hours [at work] is crazy and Shaunte is somebody I could depend on. But it was hard when she wasn't working. She wasn't having no income coming in, and I was like, "I'm not your sugar mama!"

Shelly's comment draws on negative images of a woman's dependence on a male "sugar daddy" and simultaneously emphasizes her expectation that her partner will contribute economically to the family. However, she has also prepared to provide for herself and her children in the event that her mate cannot or will not contribute her share, or if their relationship ends. For working-class lesbians raising families, economic independence provides a financial and psychological barrier against a step backward into poverty.

Middle-Class Family Background: Economic Independence Tied to Upward Mobility and Self-Actualization

Renee Martin is a physician. She grew up with her parents and younger sister in a middle-class neighborhood that bordered two racially segregated areas of a Southern city. One might characterize Renee's family background as upper-middle class. Her father was one of the first African Americans in their state to receive a doctorate in chemical engineering. After having two children, Renee's mother continued to work as a college professor until her retirement. Although her father earned more, Renee saw her mother thrive in a middle-class occupation that was personally fulfilling.

Renee owns her own home, has considerable authority at work, and is advancing steadily in her career. Renee's wife Naja Rhodes is ten years younger and holds a master's degree. They report spending similar amounts of time on household chores, though Renee tends to perform more of the stereotypically male tasks like yardwork, household repairs, and taking out the trash. Both say they are satisfied with the way they organize their household responsibilities and have equal power in the relationship. Renee's discussion of economic independence does not mention financial survival or a worry about being able to provide for herself in the absence of an employed partner. These issues are not part of her current life nor are they part of her past experiences. She could easily take on the traditional provider role in her relationship, relieving Naja from any obligation to contribute financially to the household.

Instead, Renee's discussion of marital equality involves ways of helping her spouse advance and find fulfillment in her own career. Renee encourages Naja to own her own property and has shown her how to build wealth. When talking about Naja, Renee makes reference to the independence her mother has always had from her father's income. She is proud of the fact that her mother has always maintained her own financial accounts and used her income to create a mutual interdependence in her marriage. In turn, Renee wants to help her own wife achieve these things.

The structure and functioning of Renee and Naja's relationship has its parallel in the way Renee's parents organized their marriage, and is described by Bart Landry in his historical research on Black working wives. Landry argues that for the Black middle class, women's paid work was not simply a response to economic circumstances but the fulfillment of women's rights to self-actualization.[10] His evidence lies in the existence of Black women throughout the 20th century who married men who could support them, yet continued to pursue careers throughout their marital lives. For couples like Renee and Naja, egalitarianism is expressed not merely through each person's ability to contribute economic resources, but in the desire of each person to pursue self-fulfillment in the economic sphere.

Katrice Webster is a 36-year-old attorney. She attended Ivy League institutions for college and law school and is employed at a corporate law firm. Katrice was born and raised in a small Midwestern city. Her parents divorced when she was six, and she and her siblings were raised by her mother, who worked her way up from administrative assistant to office manager at her place of employment. After the divorce, the children lived with their mother but spent holidays and vacations with their father who remained nearby. He was a business executive with a much higher income than what her mother earned and continued to contribute financially to their household throughout Katrice's childhood. An extensive extended family also lived in the area and served as an important source of support. Katrice describes her childhood as happy.

When asked about the qualities she looks for in a mate, she states, "They just have to have a drive and want to be successful at something. If they own their own house-cleaning business, they just have to run it well." Her partner Caroline Tate is a self-employed makeup artist. Caroline and Katrice each pay their own bills but Katrice pays for a greater portion of the family's expenses and is the sole owner of their co-op apartment. Caroline is the biological mother of their 17-year-old daughter, who was born in a prior heterosexual relationship. They pay for house-cleaning services, though Caroline still spends more time each week on other chores like cooking and laundry. They report some disagreement over parenting and discipline, but do not raise the issue of housework as a problem in the relationship. Katrice would like her partner to become more financially stable and learn about different methods of building assets. She says, "I try to encourage her to save because I always like to think everybody needs to have a nest egg for a rainy day." Promoting self-sufficiency in her partner will not improve Katrice's economic standing, but is a way to uplift her mate and help her become more stable for her own personal gain.

Among the Black women I study, it is uncommon to have parents whose lives represented the traditional patriarchal relationship that white feminist ideologies attempt to dismantle. Mothers and fathers tended to work (when they could find employment), and many households did not contain two married biological parents for a person's entire childhood. Just 36 percent of respondents were raised with two married biological parents, and very few reported having a stay-at-home mother. Forty-four percent grew up in single-mother households, and 42 percent of these single-parent families were multi-generational and included a grandparent or other adult female relative. Fourteen percent of women were not raised with any biological parents, and grew up in households with their grandparents or nonrelatives. These experiences suggest that the Black heterosexual family, in all of its varied forms, has been the dominant model for expectations African American lesbian women have in the creation of their own families.

Linking the Experiences of African American Women to Black Feminist Principles of Equality

Employing a Black feminist perspective to frame this research reveals that the ways Black lesbians think about partner responsibilities in their relationships are influenced by the social and economic conditions in which they were raised. Like lesbians in previous studies, the women here ideologically support the equal division of paid work and housework, but unlike in other work, they emphasize the importance of economic independence in their relationships. I tie this to how they understand their positions in families. They do not necessarily draw from lesbian feminist ideologies to organize their relationships, and insights from Black feminist thought can shed light on the reasons for this distance. Documents such as "A Black Feminist Statement," published by the Combahee River

Collective in 1983, or historical research on Black feminist ideology such as the important 1988 paper by Deborah King, reveal that the equal division of housework, childcare, and market labor in heterosexual relationships was never a dominant component of Black feminist frameworks.[11] This type of egalitarianism was important to Black feminists, but unlike white feminists who saw inequality as rooted in relationships between women and men in home life and in economic life, Black women concentrated their platform on how to reduce the gender inequality they believed was connected to other inequalities based on race and socioeconomic disadvantage.[12] They saw their own financial contributions as critical for their families to survive and thrive in a racially hostile world.

Applying a Black feminist lens to answer the research questions in this work reveals family background as an important pathway shaping the beliefs and experiences that Black women bring to their lesbian relationships. This work is an example of how an intersectional, Black feminist approach to theory, study design, and sociological analysis can offer greater complexity to our broader understandings of social life. Black feminist theory is not merely about "telling our truths" for their own sake. It can be used to shift the lens on what we study and how we study it; to produce new and more complete ways of understanding existing theories and processes; and to transform academic scholarship, which has always been a primary goal at the root of Black feminist thought.

Notes

1. Portions of this chapter were originally published in *Families as They Really Are*, edited by Barbara Risman. 2010. W. W. Norton.
2. All names are pseudonyms.
3. Donna Franklin. 2015. *Ensuring Inequality: The Structural Transformation of the African American Family*. New York: Oxford University Press.
4. Patricia Hill Collins. 1990. *Black Feminist Thought: Knowledge, Consciousness, and the Politics of Empowerment*. New York: HarperCollins.
5. Mignon R. Moore. 2008. "Gendered Power Relations among Women: A Study of Household Decision-Making in Black, Lesbian Stepfamilies." *American Sociological Review* 73: 335–356.
6. Tania Abdulahad, Gwendolyn Rogers, Barbara Smith, and Jameelah Waheed. 1983. "Black Lesbian/Feminist Organizing: A Conversation." In *Home Girls: A Black Feminist Anthology*, edited by B. Smith, 293–319. New York: Kitchen Table Press; Anita Cornwell. 1983. *The Black Lesbian in White America*. Tallahassee, FL: Naiad Press.
7. For details about the framework and sample for the larger study, see Mignon R. Moore. 2011. *Invisible Families: Gay Identities, Relationships and Motherhood among Black Women*. Berkeley: University of California Press.
8. Moore 2011.
9. Pepper Schwartz. 1994. *Peer Marriages: How Love Between Equals Really Works*. New York: Free Press.
10. Bart Landry. 2000. *Black Working Wives: Pioneers of the American Family Revolution*. Berkeley: University of California Press.

11. Combahee River Collective. 1983. "A Black Feminist Statement." In *Words of Fire: An Anthology of African-American Feminist Thought*, edited by Beverly Guy-Sheftall, 232–240. New York: New Press; Deborah King. 1988. "Multiple Jeopardy, Multiple Consciousness: The Context of a Black Feminist Ideology." *Signs: Journal of Women in Culture and Society* 14(1): 42–72.
12. Franklin 2015.

References

Abdulahad, Tania, Gwendolyn Rogers, Barbara Smith, and Jameelah Waheed. 1983. "Black Lesbian/Feminist Organizing: A Conversation." In *Home Girls: A Black Feminist Anthology*, edited by B. Smith, 293–319. New York: Kitchen Table Press.

Collins, Patricia Hill. 1990. *Black Feminist Thought: Knowledge, Consciousness, and the Politics of Empowerment*. London: HarperCollins.

Combahee River Collective. 1983. "A Black Feminist Statement." In *Words of Fire: An Anthology of African-American Feminist Thought*, edited by Beverly Guy-Sheftall, 232–240. New York: New Press.

Cornwell, Anita. 1983. *The Black Lesbian in White America*. Tallahassee, FL: Naiad Press.

Franklin, Donna. 2015. *Ensuring Inequality: The Structural Transformation of the African American Family*. New York: Oxford University Press.

King, Deborah. 1988. "Multiple Jeopardy, Multiple Consciousness: The Context of a Black Feminist Ideology." *Signs: Journal of Women in Culture and Society* 14(1): 42–72.

Landry, Bart. 2000. *Black Working Wives: Pioneers of the American Family Revolution*. Berkeley: University of California Press.

Moore, Mignon R. 2008. "Gendered Power Relations among Women: A Study of Household Decision-Making in Black, Lesbian Stepfamilies." *American Sociological Review* 73: 335–356.

Moore, Mignon R. 2011. *Invisible Families: Gay Identities, Relationships and Motherhood among Black Women*. Berkeley: University of California Press.

Schwartz, Pepper. 1994. *Peer Marriages: How Love Between Equals Really Works*. New York: Free Press.

Chapter 13

"Kantsaywhere"

Black African Women Inside the Australian Racial Crucible

Mandisi Majavu

Colonial myths about Africa are characterized by narratives of humanity at its lowest—practices of promiscuity, gynecological aberrations, infanticides, general perversion, and bestiality supposedly all happen alongside cannibalism.[1] This colonial narrative about Africa portrays African womanhood as oversexed, primitive, ugly, and beastly.[2] Perhaps no other figure epitomizes the history of the Western imagination about African womanhood—that is, the connections between grotesquerie, animalism, and hypersexuality—than Sara Baartman, the "Hottentot Venus."[3]

Through a totalizing colonial discourse, it was claimed that the shape of Sara Baartman's body represented deviant sexuality, and her sexuality evidenced productive savagery. This discourse dovetailed perfectly with the longstanding racist argument made by slave owners who argued that African women's supposed savagery and deviant sexuality could be put to productive use.[4] Thus, during enslavement, African women were regarded as having bodies suited to reproduction; whether that was in providing sexual services to white men, producing children to keep the slave system afloat, or basically providing the labor necessary to ensure white leisure.[5]

In the 21st century, however, African female reproductive capacities shifted from being viewed as a benefit to Western societies to being regarded as a burden on the national economy of Western countries.[6] In Australia, the discursive focus of this chapter, young African women from refugee backgrounds are cast within a policy-oriented discourse that portrays them primarily as teenage mothers and social security dependents.[7] For instance, Ngum Chi Watts writes that teenage pregnancy among African teenagers has become a social problem for both the African Australian community and mainstream Australian society.[8] Through this discourse, African women are blamed for supposedly contributing to the disintegration of Australian society by giving birth to fatherless, state-dependent children, and thus burdening the welfare system with undue excess.[9]

Furthermore, this refugee discourse not only casts African womanhood within the discursive framework of the 'single mother' trope, but portrays young African women from refugee backgrounds as psychologically

DOI: 10.4324/9781003199113-17

damaged and promiscuous. Through this narrative, an oppressive image of a sexually unrestrained refugee Other is created. Hence, Muchoki asserts that there is a connection between migration and increased sexual health risk, while Ngum Chi Watts claims to have found in her research that motherhood gives an orphaned "refugee girl" an identity and a sense of purpose.[10]

The discursive groundwork that underpins research on African womanhood and sexuality in Australia is the cultural deficit model. This intellectual tradition is rooted in the Eurocentric worldview that takes for granted the alleged inferiority of poor people and Black people, while, concurrently, assumes that whiteness has "some ethereal qualities" that Blackness does not possess.[11] This uncritical acceptance of white norms is one of the defining features of research on African womanhood and sexuality in Australia.[12] Through the cultural deficit model, African masculinity is portrayed as violent, while African womanhood is portrayed as "unfit" to raise children. The cultural deficit model does not challenge the ideology of whiteness, but instead, views "bad breeding" as the source of poverty, criminality, low educational attainment, unemployment and other social ills.[13]

The discourse that foregrounds "bad breeding" as the source of social ills has, historically, tilted toward a eugenic agenda in which birth control becomes a medical and social tool to regulate the sexual reproduction of Black women, the poor and immigrants.[14] It is a historical fact that sexual reproduction in Australia has been used in the service of a white supremacist project—which was characterized by its commitment to fend off alleged "pathogenic colored races."[15] This racist project of "the breeding out of color" was taken up enthusiastically by Australian scientists who promoted a "scientific breeding programme" that aimed to remove Aboriginality and Blackness without "throwbacks."[16] As Edward Curr, an Australian politician, put it, the white race in Australian was destined to "exterminate the blacks of Australia."[17]

Since their arrival in Australia, according to Anderson, white settlers speculated about the racial difference between Aboriginal peoples and whites. They wondered where the Aboriginal people fit into the assumed racial hierarchy. The consensus was that Australia was once occupied by Tasmanians, whom it was argued were of "Negrito stock," until they were exterminated and assimilated by invaders known as Australians. T. H. Huxley—Charles Darwin's propagandist, proclaimed that Tasmanian people "constitute a special modification of the Negroid type."[18] Although it was concluded that the "full-blooded Tasmanian" died in 1877, white settlers continued to refer to Aboriginal people as Black people.

This is the context within which the racist project of the breeding out of Blackness in Australia was conceptualized and developed. The racist project to remove Aboriginality and Blackness without throwbacks resulted in the "Stolen Generations" phenomenon. From 1910 until 1970, it is estimated that "between one in three and one in ten Aboriginal children were forcibly removed from their families, thus creating stolen generations."[19] Auber Octavius Neville—the Chief Protector of Aborigines, who presided over the project to breed out Aboriginality and Blackness in the early 20th century in Australia, declared that all "colored children" should be treated as orphans.[20] Therefore, Neville proposed an institution where "colored children" should be housed and raised—a place where matters of racial hygiene would form a fundamental core of these children's socialization. Australian scientists believed that through a "scientific managed breeding" program, it was possible to produce a strong white race in Australia—"one more pure, virile, and cleanly even than in its European homeland."[21]

The Australian child welfare policy of removing Aboriginal children from their families was part and parcel of this eugenics project. The Stolen Generations phenomenon is the outcome of "human harvesting"—a eugenics project that claims that the evolution of race is selective.[22] This racist project views racial segregation as paramount to the success of white racial improvement or generally combating racial degeneracy. In Australia, white middle-class women supported this racist project through the Racial Hygiene Association (RHA) of New South Wales, forerunner of the present-day Family Planning Association. According to Carey, the RHA was the largest and longest-enduring eugenics project in Australia, and it represents "the high point" for women's involvement in any eugenics project. Since the eugenics project concerned itself with reproductive protocols and with child rearing, the white middle-class women's movement at this time regarded it as their social responsibility and duty to protect white Australia from the threat of racial degeneration.[23] What this history reveals is that Australian scientists and politicians were not only content in building a white Australia, rather, historical evidence suggests that the objective was to build a eugenic utopia—analogous to Francis Galton's utopia "Kantsaywhere."[24] The consensus among those who were in support of this eugenics project was that "in Australia there was power to make the race we wished. It should not only be a white race, but a race of the best whites."[25] So committed to this project was the Racial Hygiene Association that it only changed its name to the Family Planning Association in 1960.[26]

The Experience of Black Parenting in 21st-Century Australia

The portrayal of Aboriginality and Blackness as unfit for parenthood has left a lasting legacy on Australian societal institutions.[27] The overarching theme of that legacy is interwoven with the cultural deficit discourse that regards African women as "unfit" to parent.[28] One of the long-standing racist stereotypes about Black mothers in the West is that along with their inferior and defective genetics, "Black mothers transfer a deviant lifestyle to their children that dooms each succeeding generation to a life of poverty, delinquency, and despair."[29] In Australia this sentiment is expressed via the African refugee trope and through the racist narrative of "African gangs."[30] Consequently, through the intervention of social welfare institutions, state agents, socializing agents, and other agents of power (for example social workers and psychologists), the family life of Africans in Australia is invaded in order to supervise everyday family relations, while simultaneously, surveilling the parental strategies of African mothers.[31] African women feel that state agents in Australia behave as though African women's ability to contribute to the Australian society as "good" mothers, and thereby "good" citizens has to be continuously demonstrated and proven to the satisfaction of state agencies.[32] Through the Australian Child Protection Services, strict measures are deployed to control Black parenthood. In her research, Ramsay found that the stereotypical notions of incompetent black parents emerged as central to the operations of child welfare interventions in Australia. Kaur claims that African parents often adopt an authoritarian style in their parenting role and "attempt to control their children based on traditional collectivist values."[33]

This climate has resulted in children and young people from refugee backgrounds being overrepresented among the users of family services programs, according to the Victorian and Adolescent Monitoring System.[34] Ramsay cautions however that due to poor recording of the backgrounds of children, it is difficult to say with certainty that African children are actually overrepresented in the Australian child protection system. Although the Australian child welfare system is not federated, child protection interventions are administered in a similar procedure across different Australian states. The child welfare system is responsible for investigating child negligence and abuse, and has the power to decide whether allegations of child negligence and abuse warrant the removal of the child from the home. According to the Victoria State Government policies, the Child Protection Services' mandate includes taking matters to the Children's Court if it suspects child negligence and abuse. Moreover, the Child Protection Services have the authority to supervise children on legal orders granted by the Children's Court.[35] African parents in Australia resent the power that Child Protection Services has over them.

For instance, in my PhD research,[36] black male participants argued that the Australian Child Protection Services functions like a "family-smashing device"—to use Caplow's phrase—to break up black families.[37] A black male participant in my PhD research pointed out that "the Child Protection Services is hostile to African parents." Another male participant rhetorically asked:

> The question I have for the Child Protection Services is this: on what basis are they saying we are unfit to parent? Because when we were at

refugee camps protecting our children, they were not there. African children were surviving with their families without Child Protection Services. That is until we brought them to this country.

My PhD work researched African masculinity in Australia and New Zealand, and thus did not include women's voices on these issues. However, research done on African women about parenting in Australia does not contradict my findings. For example, Ramsay's research found that African mothers from refugee backgrounds are positioned as a threat to normative kinds of parenting, which is grounded on whiteness.[38]

Conclusion: Toward a Transnational Black Feminist Framework

This chapter builds on Hobson's notion of a transnational Black feminist discourse to highlight a diasporic connection between women of African descent based on a shared sense of struggling against the racist ideology of Black female deviance.[39] From Australia to Canada, Black female bodies have historically been labeled as oversexed, primitive, disruptive, and unfeminine. Black mothers in the West have traditionally struggled against a racist stereotype that portrays them as deviants who pass on defective genetics to their children.[40] Black women in the diaspora have not only suffered unequal access to opportunities and employment but also have to struggle against the racist discourse that casts them as inhabiting unacceptable bodies.[41] The challenge for a black feminist discourse is to articulate a liberating discourse that recognizes and theorizes the shared sense of lived experience of black women in the West, which is characterized by white domination.[42] Although no single explanation can accurately express the diverse lived experience of Black people in the diaspora,[43] a transnational black feminist discourse ought to provide us with an opportunity to make illuminative comparisons between the experiences of differently situated Black women in the West.[44] Ultimately, what this chapter argues is that colonial discourses about Black womanhood and Eurocentric images about Black womanhood and sexuality, as well as race, slavery, colonialism and the African refugee trope, overlap.[45]

Notes

1. Richard Phillips. 1998. "Writing Travel and Mapping Sexuality: Richard Burton's Sotadic Zone." In *Writes of Passage: Reading Travel Writing*, edited by James Duncan and Derek Gregory, 70–91. Routledge; Anna Laura Stoler. 2002. *Carnal Knowledge and Imperial Power: Race and the Intimate in Colonial Rule*. Berkeley: University of California Press.
2. Janelle Hobson. 2005. *Venus in the Dark: Blackness and Beauty in Popular Culture*. New York: Routledge; Shirley Anne Tate. 2015. *Black Women's Bodies and the Nation: Race, Gender and Culture*. London: Palgrave Macmillan.

3. Hobson 2005.
4. Jennifer Morgan. 2002. "'Some Could Suckle over Their Shoulder': Male Travelers, Female Bodies, and the Gendering of Racial Ideology, 1500–1770." In *Skin Deep, Spirit Strong: The Black Female Body in American Culture*, edited by Kimberly Wallace-Sanders, 37–65. Ann Arbor: University of Michigan Press.
5. Tate 2015.
6. Lisa Collins. 2002. "Economies of Flesh: Representing the Black Female Body in Art." In *Skin Deep, Spirit Strong: The Black Female Body in American Culture*, edited by Kimberly Wallace-Sanders, 99–127. Ann Arbor: University of Michigan Press.
7. Debbie Weekes. 2002. "Get Your Freak on: How Black Girls Sexualise Identity." *Sex Education: Sexuality, Society and Learning* 2(3): 251–262.
8. Mimmie Claudine Ngum Chi Watts. 2012. "Contraception, Teenage Pregnancy, Culture and Motherhood among African-Australian Teenagers with a Refugee Background in Greater Melbourne, Australia." PhD dissertation, La Trobe University, Australia.
9. Nena Foster. 2007. "Reinscribing Black Women's Position within HIV and AIDS Discourses." *Feminism & Psychology* 17(3): 323–329.
10. Samuel Muchoki. 2012. "Sexuality and Sexual Health of African-Australian Men with Refugee Backgrounds from the Horn of Africa: The Need for a New Research Agenda." *ARAS* 33(1): 132–150; Watts 2012.
11. Michael Jr. Boucher and Robert Helfenbein. 2015. "The Push and the Pull: Deficit Models, Ruby Payne, and Becoming a 'Warm Demander.'" *Urban Rev* 47: 743.
12. Ibid.
13. Ibid.
14. Dorothy Roberts. 1997. *Killing the Black Body: Race, Reproduction, and the Meaning of Liberty*. New York: Pantheon Books.
15. See: Warwick Anderson. 2005. *The Cultivation of Whiteness: Science, Health, and Racial Destiny in Australia*. Melbourne: Melbourne University Press.
16. Ibid.
17. Ibid., 199.
18. Ibid., 197.
19. Ibid., 248.
20. Anderson 2005.
21. Ibid., 140.
22. See: David Starr Jordan. 1906. "The Human Harvest." *Proceedings of the American Philosophical Society* 45(182): 54–69.
23. Jane Carey. 2007. "'Not Only a White Race, but a Race of the Best Whites': The Women's Movement, White Australia and Eugenics between the Wars." In *Historicising Whiteness: Transnational Perspectives on the Construction of an Identity*, edited by Jane Carey, Leigh Boucher, and Katherine Ellinghaus, 162–170. Melbourne: RMIT Publishing.
24. Nicholas Gillham. 2009. "Cousins: Charles Darwin, Sir Francis Galton and the Birth of Eugenics." *Significance* 6(3): 132–135.
25. Carey 2007, 162.
26. Rob Watts. 2016. *States of violence and the Civilising Process: On Criminology and State Crime*. London: Palgrave Macmillan.
27. Roberts 1997.
28. Georgina Ramsay. 2017. "Central African Refugee Women Resettled in Australia: Colonial Legacies and the Civilising Process." *Journal of Intercultural Studies* 38(2): 170–188.
29. Roberts 1997: 8.
30. See: Mandisi Majavu. 2018. "The 'African Gangs' Narrative: Associating Blackness with Criminality and other Anti-Black Racist Tropes in Australia." *African and Black Diaspora: An International Journal*. Doi: 10.1080/17528631.2018.1541958.

31. Georgina Ramsay. 2016. "Black Mothers, Bad Mothers: African Refugee Women and the Governing of 'Good' Citizens through the Australian Child Welfare System." *Australian Feminist Studies* 31(89): 319–335; Ramsay 2017.

32. Ramsay 2016.

33. Jatinder Kaur. 2012. *Cultural Diversity and Child Protection: Australian Research Review on the Needs of Culturally and Linguistically Diverse (CALD) and Refugee Children and Families.* Queensland, Australia. www.unisa.edu.au/contentassets/463f611a5f8645c0 9e089cd8cb43c7e0/cultural_diversity_child_protection_kaur2012_a4.pdf 13

34. Victorian and Adolescent Monitoring System. 2011. *Refugee Status Report: A Report on How Refugee Children and Young People in Victoria Are Faring.* Victorian and Adolescent Monitoring System. www.education.vic.gov.au/Documents/about/research/refugeestatusreport.pdf

35. Victoria State Government. N.d. *Child Protection. Department of Human Services Website.* Victoria State Government Website. www.dhs.vic.gov.au/for-service providers/children,-youth-and-families/child-protection.

36. See: Mandisi Majavu. 2016. "The Fact of the 'Uncommodified Blackness' Image: The Lived Experience of Black African from a Refugee Background in Australia and New Zealand." PhD Dissertation, University of Auckland, New Zealand.

37. Stephen Bahr. 1979. "The Effects of Welfare on Marital Stability and Remarriage." *Journal of Marriage and Family* 41(3): 533, citing Caplow 1976.

38. Ramsay 2017, 2016.

39. Hobson 2005.

40. Roberts 1997.

41. Maxine Leeds Craig. 2002. *Ain't I a Beauty Queen? Black Women, Beauty, and the Politics of Race.* New York: Oxford University Press.

42. Hobson 2005.

43. Jacqueline McLeod. 1999. "Introduction." In *Crossing Boundaries: Comparative History of Black People in Diaspora*, edited by Darlene Clark Hine and Jacqueline McLeod, xix–xxv. Bloomington: Indiana University Press.

44. Thomas Holt. 1999. "Slavery and Freedom in the Atlantic World: Reflections on the Diasporan Framework." In *Crossing Boundaries: Comparative History of Black People in Diaspora*, edited by Darlene Clark Hine and Jacqueline McLeod, 33–44. Bloomington: Indiana University Press.

45. Jennifer Devere Brody. 1998. *Impossible Purities: Blackness, Femininity, and Victorian Culture.* Durham, NC: Duke University Press.

References

Anderson, Warwick. 2005. *The Cultivation of Whiteness: Science, Health, and Racial Destiny in Australia.* Melbourne: Melbourne University Press.

Bahr, Stephen. 1979. "The Effects of Welfare on Marital Stability and Remarriage." *Journal of Marriage and Family* 41(3): 553–560.

Boucher, Michael Jr., and Robert Helfenbein. 2015. "The Push and the Pull: Deficit Models, Ruby Payne, and Becoming a 'Warm Demander.'" *Urban Rev* 47: 742–758.

Brody, Jennifer Devere. 1998. *Impossible Purities: Blackness, Femininity, and Victorian Culture.* Durham, NC: Duke University Press.

Carey, Jane. 2007. "'Not Only a White Race, but a Race of the Best Whites': The Women's Movement, White Australia and Eugenics between the Wars." In *Historicising Whiteness: Transnational Perspectives on the Construction of an Identity*, edited by Jane Carey, Leigh Boucher, Katherine Ellinghaus, 162–170. Melbourne: RMIT Publishing.

Collins, Lisa. 2002. "Economies of Flesh: Representing the Black Female Body in Art." In *Skin Deep, Spirit Strong: The Black Female Body in American Culture*, edited by Kimberly Wallace-Sanders, 99–127. Ann Arbor: University of Michigan Press.

Craig, Maxine Leeds. 2002. *Ain't I a Beauty Queen? Black Women, Beauty, and the Politics of Race*. New York: Oxford University Press.

Foster, Nena. 2007. "Reinscribing Black Women's Position within HIV and AIDS Discourses." *Feminism & Psychology* 17(3): 323–329.

Gillham, Nicholas. 2009. "Cousins: Charles Darwin, Sir Francis Galton and the Birth of Eugenics." *Significance* 6(3): 132–135.

Hobson, Janelle. 2005. *Venus in the Dark: Blackness and Beauty in Popular Culture*. New York: Routledge.

Holt, Thomas. 1999. "Slavery and Freedom in the Atlantic World: Reflections on the Diasporan Framework." In *Crossing Boundaries: Comparative History of Black People in Diaspora*, edited by Darlene Clark Hine and Jacqueline McLeod, 33–44. Bloomington: Indiana University Press.

Jordan, David Starr. 1906. "The Human Harvest." *Proceedings of the American Philosophical Society* 45(182): 54–69.

Kaur, Jatinder. 2012. *Cultural Diversity and Child Protection: Australian Research Review on the Needs of Culturally and Linguistically Diverse (CALD) and Refugee Children and Families*. Queensland, Australia. www.unisa.edu.au/contentassets/463f611a5f8645c09e089cd8cb43c7e0/cultural_diversity_child_protection_kaur2012_a4.pdf

Majavu, Mandisi. 2016. "The Fact of the 'Uncommodified Blackness' Image: The Lived Experience of Black African from a Refugee Background in Australia and New Zealand." PhD Dissertation, University of Auckland, New Zealand.

Majavu, Mandisi. 2018. "The 'African Gangs' Narrative: Associating Blackness with Criminality and Other Anti-Black Racist Tropes in Australia." *African and Black Diaspora: An International Journal*. doi: 10.1080/17528631.2018.1541958

McLeod, Jacqueline. 1999. "Introduction." In *Crossing Boundaries: Comparative History of Black People in Diaspora*, edited by Darlene Clark Hine and Jacqueline McLeod, xix–xxv. Bloomington: Indiana University Press.

Morgan, Jennifer. 2002. "'Some Could Suckle Over Their Shoulder': Male Travelers, Female Bodies, and the Gendering of Racial Ideology, 1500–1770." In *Skin Deep, Spirit Strong: The Black Female Body in American Culture*, edited by Kimberly Wallace-Sanders, 37–65. Ann Arbor: The University of Michigan Press.

Muchoki, Samuel. 2012. "Sexuality and Sexual Health of African-Australian Men with Refugee Backgrounds from the Horn of Africa: The Need for a New Research Agenda." *ARAS* 33(1): 132–150.

Ngum Chi Watts, Mimmie Claudine. 2012. "Contraception, Teenage Pregnancy, Culture and Motherhood among African-Australian Teenagers with a Refugee Background in Greater Melbourne, Australia." PhD dissertation, La Trobe University, Australia.

Phillips, Richard. 1998. "Writing Travel and Mapping Sexuality: Richard Burton's Sotadic Zone." In *Writes of Passage: Reading Travel Writing*, edited by James Duncan and Derek Gregory, 70–91. London: Routledge.

Ramsay, Georgina. 2016. "Black Mothers, Bad Mothers: African Refugee Women and the Governing of 'Good' citizens through the Australian Child Welfare System." *Australian Feminist Studies* 31(89): 319–335.

Ramsay, Georgina. 2017. "Central African Refugee Women Resettled in Australia: Colonial Legacies and the Civilising Process." *Journal of Intercultural Studies* 38(2): 170–188.

Roberts, Dorothy. 1997. *Killing the Black Body: Race, Reproduction, and the Meaning of Liberty*. New York: Pantheon Books.

Stoler, Anna Laura. 2002. *Carnal Knowledge and Imperial Power: Race and the Intimate in Colonial Rule*. Berkeley: University of California Press.

Tate, Shirley Anne. 2015. *Black Women's Bodies and the Nation: Race, Gender and Culture*. London: Palgrave Macmillan.

Victorian and Adolescent Monitoring System. 2011. *Refugee Status Report: A Report on How Refugee Children and Young People in Victoria Are Faring*. Victorian and Adolescent Monitoring System. www.education.vic.gov.au/Documents/about/research/refugeestatusreport.pdf

Victoria State Government. n.d. *Child Protection. Department of Human Services Website*. Victoria State Government Website. www.dhs.vic.gov.au/for-serviceproviders/children,-youth-and-families/child-protection

Watts, Rob. 2016. *States of Violence and the Civilising Process: On Criminology and State Crime*. London: Palgrave Macmillan.

Weekes, Debbie. 2002. "Get Your Freak On: How Black Girls Sexualise Identity." *Sex Education: Sexuality, Society and Learning* 2(3): 251–262.

Chapter 14

Black Feminist Piety

A Framework for Engaging Islam in Black Feminist Sociology

Ashley Garner

While seated on a New York City bench as just another body in the lunch crowd, I am reminded again of Nella Larsen's Passing. *I haven't read* Passing *in nearly a decade and much of what I can recall the most vividly is simply the way it unsettled me; yet, since converting to Islam and deciding to observe hijab, I find myself thinking about "passing" more and more. This morning, I tied my hijab into a turban—a style I turn to for reasons as trivial as wanting to wear earrings or, more significantly, on days where my iman (faith) is low, when I am looking for the comfort of being read as "just another Black woman with her hair wrapped." With my neck exposed, I offer a gentle "salam alaikum" to a non-Black Muslim woman passing by, and as if on cue, she doesn't return the greeting. I have passed successfully. For me, and the Black Muslim women I have interviewed and befriended, to "pass" is to segment yourself and your presentation. It is to acknowledge that there is a tension between the US construction of your faith and how you are racialized and gendered. It is making your home on terrain that can often leave you unsettled.*

Introduction

Patricia Hill Collins's *Black Feminist Thought* is perhaps one of the most well-known examples of writing Black feminist sociology. In the second edition, Collins moved away from defining something as Black feminist or not, aiming instead for "fluidity" in terms of who has a seat at the proverbial Black feminist table. The push to expand whom we typically count among Black feminist scholars and knowledge producers jumpstarted my enabled consideration of how Collins's tenets could be retooled to engage with Black women's religious participation in ways not originally addressed in *Black Feminist Thought*. In this chapter, I present Black feminist piety, a framework for studying Black religious women as knowledge producers who draw their knowledge base from gendered and racialized ways of enacting religiosity. I organize Black feminist piety (BFP) using core themes of "patriarchy," "conversion," and "(non)citizenship." Each of these themes separately enjoy prevalence in gender, religious, and race studies,

DOI: 10.4324/9781003199113-18

respectively. However, these conversations are often insular, relying only on the frames that dominate a given subfield,[1] rather than moving toward a truly intersectional analysis. I wrote BFP with a desire to insert the role of religiosity into Black feminist frames examining how religion impacts the racialization, gendering, and subjugation of Black women.

While I ultimately believe BFP can be used to frame scholarship on a range of faith traditions, I present Black Muslim women because (1) religion research generally centers Christianity,[2] (2) gender scholars interested in religion gravitate toward identifying agency in the face of "conservative religion," which in many cases is or includes the study of Islam[3] and (3) race scholars, like most sociologists, struggle to take seriously the role of religion in shaping racialization and racial identity at all.[4] Taken together, Black Muslim women bear the brunt of hegemonic frames—they might not be studied at all as non-Christians, the complexity of their experiences can be lost in the feminist desire to identify their capacity to be "agentive," or their status as Black women is parsed away from their religiosity.

In the sections that follow, I highlight how predominant frames within mainstream feminism and womanism lead to reproducing familiar conclusions about Black Muslim women study after study. After, I provide examples from my own exploratory research on Black Muslim women in the Northeast to show how work using a BFP framework destabilizes existing frames to break from accepted ways of studying religion. I structure this chapter around Collins's *Black Feminist Thought* because, for many, her book serves as an entrée to Black feminism and is emblematic of the Black feminist epistemology. Producing a Black feminist sociology demands rejecting binary definitions of Black women's intellect and feminism as Collins held; and, that act must include rejecting the insistence to recode religious people as "secular," which sociologists have done historically.[5] Black feminist sociology has the tools to dig into the complexities of Black religious women's every day; BFP offers a framework for wayfinding in terrain that Black and feminist studies have struggled to take seriously.

I must also position myself as a Black feminist convert to Islam. My experiences with conversion in my mostly Baptist, African American family and also in my day-to-day where strangers stop me in the street, the train, or doctor's office asking, "Where are you from?" undoubtedly inform this chapter. In these interactions, I deal not only with open frustration when I, as a hijab-wearing woman, cannot provide any answer other than "New Jersey, but my family's originally from the South." I also understand that as a Black woman I am expected to put them back at ease. This frustration extends to non-Black Muslim friends who, annoyed that my presence demands so many interruptions, urge me to respond that I am Yemini or Sudanese or some other acceptably foreign origin of Muslimness still in line with my racial presentation. My Black feminist politics are shaped by the interactions between religious markers, how I am racialized, and gendered social expectations.

Black Muslim Womanists?

Race and religion research often center Christianity. Womanist studies, which continue to be productive sites for examining Black women's relationship with religion, are no exception. Womanist scholar Stacey Floyd-Thomas describes womanism as the processes of Black women looking to themselves for their own liberation through (1) radical subjectivity, (2) traditional communalism, (3) redemptive self-love and (4) critical engagement.[6] Womanism breaks from Black liberation and feminist theologies that saw all Blacks as men and all women as white.[7] Debra Mubashshir Majeed captured that the "natural tendency in Black America to *speak* of African American religion and *mean* Christianity," pervades womanism.[8] Indeed, throughout the edited *Deeper Shades of Purple* where Majeed's chapter appears, I read many examples that equated womanism with Christianity. Even with Majeed's "Muslim Womanist Philosophy," I do not believe womanism offers the space to explore religiosity in an array of forms, chiefly for Islam since it is often positioned in opposition to Protestantism and democracy.[9]

Outside of womanism, mainstream feminism tends to unhesitatingly adopt all things secular while simultaneously labeling religious women as unfeminist and brainwashed. The feminism as secularism versus anti-feminist religiosity binary is limiting. In fact, the conditions created by secularity are fundamental to the proliferation of "conservative" religious movements,[10] yet our ability to understand that relationship is limited by imposing a false dichotomy.[11] Even as strides have been made toward etching the contours of a US-specific Islamic feminism,[12] debates continue regarding the extent that "Islamic Feminism" as a theoretical tool is able to engage race or is even interested in moving beyond the secular.[13]

Agentic or Not?

Muslim women are often presented from the agency perspective, in which instances where women are perceived to be resisting or subverting aspects of religious practice are highlighted.[14] For example, Saba Mahmood highlights the tendency to cite reasons women dress in accordance with *hijab* as a means of resisting the commodification of their bodies and for avoiding sexual harassment.[15] These examples are heralded within feminist networks and can be especially important for Black women whose bodies, through the use of controlling imagery, have historically been overly sexualized as "jezebels" and/or marked as asexual "mammies."[16]

Mahmood also found that these studies sometimes exclude the pre-dominant reasons their participants give for wearing hijab, such as piety, modesty, and virtue. The choice, whether conscious or not, to locate their decision outside of religiosity is puzzling considering the obsession with an agency-centered perspective. The implicit message is that agency cannot be tied to piety. Even in the midst of fruitful conversations about piety,[17] scholars interested in race and religion have reason to be disheartened since race scholarship has largely been dismissive of religion.[18] Just as merely sampling Black women is not synonymous with Black feminist scholar-ship, including religious women in a context wherein the only frames for interpretation are subversive versus submissive is not productive.[19]

Adding an axis of religion to Black feminist sociology challenges scholars to approach their analysis from more than a one-dimensional "every action is empowerment" perspective. Furthermore, BFP, like Black feminism on the whole, requires that scholars examine both the assumptions and stand-points of themselves and their subfields that produce slight variations on taken-for-granted conclusions of religious women.

Black Feminist Piety

Black feminist piety redefines the fixity of feminist definitions of agency and resistance by problematizing claims that agency consists primarily of acts that challenge social norms rather than those that seek to uphold norms. Saba Mahmood took this claim as far as challenging the assertion that "all human beings have the innate desire for freedom."[20] While it is irresponsible to conclude that Black women do not have the innate desire for freedom given the histories of racial violence committed under this guise, I do think an ambiguous, monolithic "freedom" is an example of how scholars can unwittingly "misattribute . . . forms of consciousness or politics that are not part of [their subjects] experience."[21] For example, Salafism refers to the strict adherence of living according to the Qur'an, *sunnah*, and the first three generations of Muslims.[22] Salafism often dis-courages engaging in politics, but Salafi women who opt to disengage do not do so primarily in order to resist the unjust treatment of Blacks sanc-tioned by American policy but because they believe their focus should instead be devoted to Islamic study. However, in conversations I've had with Salafi women, often some mixture of the two is given. It is my belief that it is more useful, and frankly more accurate, to begin analysis at this fault line rather than stopping at "freedom" or "subversion" in order to allow analyses of how power is constructed and explained within religious communities.

Examples of what I describe are found throughout anthropologist Carolyn Moxley Rouse's *Engaged Surrender*. For her participants, *tafsir*, or religious exegesis, strengthened their understanding of Islam by aiding women in becoming better Muslims.[23] However, *tafsir* often had political consequences. Like the example of Salafi women, we must recognize that while intentions are often rooted in Islam, how the consequences of these actions are interpreted and acted upon might be fuzzy. Instead of concluding that *tafsir* about equity between husband and wife, for example, was reached as a means of subverting Islamic gender hierarchies, an analysis consistent with BFP might investigate *why* and *how* the wife rationalized her interpretation and to what end that interpretation served rather than the interpretation alone. Essentially, analyses under this framework use common conclusions like subversion as starting rather than endpoints.

Rouse saw *tafsir* as a major reason why Black women gravitate toward Islam since there is no divinely appointed individual translating between the believers and Allah making Islam a "community with clear rules for engagement."[24] Interpretation of the Qur'an is in the hands of the believer, her respective mosque community, and the international religious scholars to whom they feel most aligned. Becoming a better *Muslimah* then is tied up with gaining detailed knowledge of the *Sunnah* and *hadiths*. This meant that while women were able to partly control how the community viewed sociopolitical issues by quoting *hadith* and following up these quotations with their *tafsir*[25] should dissenting opinions arise, it also meant that the "playbook" is written, unchanging, and increasing their knowledge of the "playbook" is fundamental to their religious journeys.

I echo Rouse by lifting up the importance of exegesis for Black religious women, but I found myself wondering how exegesis can be critical to BFP when it is also a barrier to claims-making abilities? In other words, sisters less knowledgeable of religious texts have less power to control how the community views pressing issues. However, in doing this research, I was reminded that all *tafsir* need not be politically useful since, regardless of outcome, it is still necessary to pay attention to the context surrounding the activity. A BFP analysis sees the *purpose* of exegesis as ensuring that the entire community becomes better Muslims, and then proceeds to analyze the implications of an empowerment limited to women involved in constant engagement with religious texts. Do those women not actively involved in *tafsir* perceive some lack in terms of their influence? If so, do they respond to that lack in religiously relevant ways, like increasing their study or in other ways? To what extent do the women who are more studied use their knowledge about issues within their community to shape what it means to be a better Muslim? And, what are the within-community implications when there is a limited or concentrated engagement with religious knowledge? These are examples of questions that use a BFP framework that go beyond misrecognition of religiously motivated actions. More importantly, these questions take seriously the impact that a woman's perception of her closeness with her Creator through seeking religious knowledge can have on herself, her community, and how she interacts with society.

Religion is the screen through which women filter their relationships with feminism, classism, and racism similar to how Collins describes the work Black women do to repackage their feminism and make it more palatable to their communities. The dialectical opposition/activism relationship Collins describes in *Black Feminist Thought*, however, is disrupted because an Islamic "filter" opposes certain aspects of secularity while also functioning as the means through which activism is realized. We must remember that one's capacity for action is enabled and created by specific relations to subordination—a truism that Black feminist scholars have long acknowledged.

Core Themes

On Patriarchy

Under BFP, our understanding of how patriarchy operates, particularly within everyday interactions, must be reformulated. Within this system of relational domination, patriarchy is experienced as a shared responsibility rather than a singularly oppressive force. Our critique of patriarchy must reflect this standpoint. One reason for this redefinition is because submission to one's Creator and to Their will, for many religious women is to be strived toward. Submission is an embodied practice with spillover effects into many other aspects of one's life, ultimately cementing a pious identity.[26] Additionally, Rouse found that Black converts to Islam desire proscriptive gender roles, which lay out which duties are expected from both husband and wife, therefore liberating women from having to bear the full burden of domestic affairs.

Controlling imagery greatly alters the theological "filter" through which Black *Muslimahs* engage with their realities. The "matriarch" image that Collins identifies describes the Black woman whose lack of femininity emasculates Black men causing them to abandon their families. The "matriarch" is central to state justifications for Black economic disadvantage and distorts the realities of political and economic inequality resulting from racial violence and discrimination.[27] For *Muslimah*, the "rules of engagement" with imagery shifts. Patriarchy under a BFP framework acknowledges that for Black women the gender role distinctions may provide a preferable alternative to the state of the family as shaped by racism. In my research, during discussions about saving for a new car, one participant chided me for using my own money—she reminded me that in Islam my money is mine alone and my husband's money is ours. Instead, she said I should remind my husband that it is my responsibility to take care of the house and his responsibility to spend to ensure I have everything I need to do that well, including a reliable vehicle. Here, reading the desire to preserve proscriptive gender roles as merely a function of the embeddedness of patriarchal values within religion would be a misstep. Engaging patriarchy as a shared responsibility is an attempt to untangle all of the ways Black women redistribute the impacts of patriarchy and racism—sharing their burden.

On Conversion

Conversion enables Black women to reposition themselves within personal and social narratives. Conversion to Islam offers an ability not to subvert controlling imagery but to exist between images. The monolithic image of a Muslim woman in the West is an Orientalized Arab, passive, chaste woman.[28] BFP simultaneously considers how Black women's bodies are sexualized and seen as "fair game" and how religious signifiers, like *hijab*, complicate this imagery by invoking the Orientalized image. Black *hijabis* reside in liminal space where they partially avoid tropes of asexual mammy, sexualized jezebel, and Orientalized chastity. As we saw in the opening vignette, however, liminality is not always a consistent good. The zone of nonexistence associated with liminality also works to "de-negroify" and "de-Islamicize" Black hijabis since their Blackness renders them less Muslim and their Islamic markers render them less Black.[29] For some of the women I spoke with, an unanticipated benefit of conversion or deciding to dress modestly, made it so their bodies were no longer the first thing noticed. One woman I interviewed noted that men no longer harassed her because they recognized the *noor*, or light, from Allah on her face. This sister also regularly lamented that Black women were the least desirable marriage partners in her mosque, which highlights the challenges of liminality.

For the Black women raised during the Civil Rights Era, conversion was "almost always tied to political consciousness, the desire for social change through resistance, and individual empowerment" in addition to reasons directly linked to piety.[30] Yet, a BFP perspective reminds us to historicize our conclusions before importing to studies on Black converts contemporarily. That is, understanding that Rouse's participants might have been speaking from a unique, generational perspective especially since the way religious communities' view what it means to be political is contested. New, unexplored rationales for conversion rooted across race, gender, and religion might be predominant. Precluding this analysis, however, is the frame within religious studies linking Black Muslim conversion to a proud connection between oneself and Black radical tradition,[31] which might now be dated or incomplete.

On (Non)Citizenship

(Non)citizenship refers to a structural denial of full citizenship rights to Black Americans. Until institutions are transformed and Black women are no longer treated as noncitizens, Collins believes that empowerment in the structural domain is impossible.[32] In relation to (non)citizenship as experienced by *Muslimahs*, Rouse writes, "For African-Americans to socially acknowledge their Islamic faith through certain types of dress is like carrying a United States exit visa; it is a sign of marking the closure of access to certain social and material rewards."[33] However, implied here is that Black women already had access to these rewards. In building her argument for noncitizenship, Collins and countless other scholars have argued that Black people are not only routinely marginalized but that US institutions depend on their marginalization.[34] Islam exacerbates this denial. Critical religious studies have offered a similar conclusion in relation to converts writing that these women are more likely to already experience marginality so embracing Islam presents less of a social loss.[35] However, studies published in race journals on the denial of citizenship rights to Muslims have been almost exclusively on Arab and South Asian communities.[36] Given both the dependency on religious markers to signal Muslimness and that traditional religious markers do not always fully signal group membership for Black women, it is fair to assume that experiences of noncitizenship are likely contextual. Black Muslim women situationally stand as "outsiders within" their racial and religious communities providing an understudied alternative understanding of how (non)citizenship functions.

A study on disadvantage within Black Muslim neighborhoods suggested one way of measuring Muslims' integration within American society was their residential proximity to non-Hispanic whites.[37] This piece cited housing discrimination as the reason why Black Muslims remained in urban, racially segregated zones but did not investigate religious rationales. A BFP framework would consider neighborhood choice in relation to individual religious practice and structural barriers that exist for certain religious and racial communities. Many pious Muslims walk to the mosque each Friday and, for men, multiple times every day. Moving into a majority non-Hispanic white neighborhood that lacks an accessible mosque is often religiously impossible. A BFP framework understands how religion might augment one's own definition of "healthy citizenship." Being a (non)citizen also means that one's choice to favor a neighborhood for its religious opportunity rather than its educational and economic opportunities is not readily understood by the very same scholars studying your community or policymakers whose initiatives lie beyond the bounds of what you deem religiously permissible.

Conclusion

The scholarship on religious women has been primarily interested in "naming" debates—as I've shown, while the frames vary by race, feminist, or religious studies, they constrain our ability to truly engage with the complexity of the role of religion. As researchers, our role to interpret must be balanced with understanding the fullness of the population. We do not have to accept participants' subjectivity at face value but must always be reworking the boxes that exist for interpretation given that our initial interpretations are a result of our own place in social structures and intellectual discourses.

Patricia Hill Collins identifies her break with a binary definition of Black feminist thought as one of the major improvements between the first and second editions. In following her example, Black Feminist Piety urges scholars to move away from the less fruitful attempts at labeling the actions of Muslim and religious women broadly, as resistance or agentic, authentic or inauthentic, subversive or submissive, feminist or anti-feminist, Black feminist or Black womanist. It pains me that much of what we know about Black religious women can fit neatly into one of those dichotomies. We must break with the sociological tendency to write off religious praxis as "folk." Black feminism has long had the tools to do better. Black feminists like Patricia Hill Collins drew our collective attention to how the greater visibility of Black women and their selective inclusion in workplaces or other venues made it more difficult to challenge the embeddedness of racism and sexism in our social structure.[38] Similarly, as our social and political landscape renders Muslims more and more visible, it is imperative that Black feminism become the home for critical, empirical sociology on Black Muslim women. Core themes of patriarchy, conversion, and (non)citizenship highlight where race, gender, and religious studies have traditionally failed these women and the redemptive possibilities offered by Black feminist sociology and Black feminist piety.

Notes

1. Ori Avishai and Courtney Irby. 2017. "Bifurcated Conversations in Sociological Studies of Religion and Gender." *Gender & Society* 31(5): 647–676.
2. Penny Edgell. 2012. "A Cultural Sociology of Religion: New Directions." *Annual Review of Sociology* 38: 247–265.
3. Avishai and Irby 2017.
4. M. O. Emerson, Elizabeth Korver-Glenn, and Kiara W. Douds. 2015. "Studying Race and Religion: A Critical Assessment." *Sociology of Race and Ethnicity* 1(3): 349–359.
5. Jurgen Habermas. 2010. *An Awareness of What Is Missing: Faith and Reason in a Post-Secular Age.* Cambridge: Polity Press; see also Ulrike Auga. 2015. "Decolonizing Public Space: A Challenge of Bonhoeffer's and Spivak's Concept of Resistance, 'Religion' and 'Gender.'" *Feminist Theology* 24(1): 49–68.
6. Stacey M. Floyd-Thomas. 2006. *Deeper Shades of Purple: Womanism in Religion and Society.* New York: New York University Press.
7. Ibid.; See also Akasha Hull (Gloria T.), Patricia Bell Scott, and Barbara Smith. 1982. *All the Women Are White, All the Blacks Are Men: But Some of Us Are Brave.* New York: Feminist Press at CUNY.

8. Debra M. Majeed. 2006. "Womanism Encounters Islam: A Muslim Scholar Considers the Efficacy of a Method Rooted in the Academy and the Church." In *Deeper Shades of Purple*, edited by Stacey M. Floyd-Thomas, 45. New York: New York University Press.
9. Pew Research Center Forum on Religion & Public Life. 2011. *The Future of the Global Muslim Population*. Washington, DC: Pew Research Center Forum on Religion & Public Life.
10. Saba Mahmood. 2005. *Politics of Piety: The Islamic Revival and the Feminist Subject*. Princeton, NJ: Princeton University Press.
11. Ibid.
12. Aysha A. Hidayatullah. 2014. *Feminist Edges of the Qur'an*. New York: Oxford University Press.
13. Majeed 2006.
14. For examples: Pamela J. Prickett. 2015. "Negotiating Gendered Religious Space: The Particularities of Patriarchy in an African American Mosque." *Gender & Society* 29(1): 51–72; Anna C. Korteweg. 2008. "The Sharia Debate in Ontario." *Gender & Society* 22(4): 434–454; John P. Bartkowski and Jen'nan Ghazal Read. 2003. "Veiled Submission: Gender, Power, and Identity among Evangelical and Muslim Women in the United States." *Qualitative Sociology* 26(1): 71–92.
15. Mahmood 2005.
16. Patricia Hill Collins. 2000. *Black Feminist Thought*. 2nd ed. New York: Routledge.
17. See: Daniel Winchester. 2008. "Embodying the Faith: Religious Practice and the Making of a Muslim Moral Habitus." *Social Forces* 86(4): 1753–1780; Aliya Hamid Rao. 2015. "Gender and Cultivating the Moral Self in Islam: Muslim Converts in an American Mosque." *Sociology of Religion* 76(4): 413–435; Rachel Rinaldo. 2014. "Pious and Critical." *Gender & Society* 28(6): 824–846.
18. Emerson, Korver-Glenn, and Douds 2015.
19. Mary Jo Neitz. 2014. "Becoming Visible: Religion and Gender in Sociology." *Sociology of Religion* 75(4): 511–523.
20. Mahmood 2005, 5.
21. Lila Abu-Loghud. 1990. "The Romance of Resistance: Tracing Transformations of Power through Bedouin Women." In *Art in Small-Scale Societies: Contemporary Readings*, edited by Richard L. Anderson, 203–219. Berkeley: University of California Press.
22. Alexander Meleagrou-Hitchens. 2018. *Salafism in America: History, Evolution, Radicalization*. Washington, DC: GW Program on Extremism.
23. Carolyn M. Rouse. 2004. *Engaged Surrender: African American Women and Islam*. Oakland: University of California Press.
24. Ibid.
25. An example response may resemble: "In 'x' *hadith* the companions of the Prophet Muhammad, peace be upon him (pbuh), state that the Prophet Muhammad (pbuh) states 'y' on 'z' particular issue meaning that . . ."
26. Mahmood 2005.
27. Collins 2000.
28. G. Mossiere. 2016. "The Intimate and the Stranger: Approaching the 'Muslim Question' through the Eyes of Female Converts to Islam." *Critical Research on Religion* 4(1): 90–108. Doi: 10.1177/2050303216630067.
29. Kambiz Ghaneabassiri. 2010. *A History of Islam in America: From the New World to the New World Order*. New York: Cambridge University Press.
30. Rouse 2004, 17.
31. Mossiere 2016.
32. Patricia Hill Collins. 2008. *Violence: A Micro-Sociological Theory*. Princeton, NJ: Princeton University Press.

33. Rouse 2004, 8.
34. See also: Moon-Kie Jung and Yaejoon Kwon. 2013. "Theorizing the US Racial State: Sociology Since Racial Formation." *Sociology Compass* 7: 927–940; John D. Márquez and Junaid Rana. 2017. "Black Radical Possibility and the Decolonial International." *South Atlantic Quarterly* 116(3).
35. Mossiere 2016.
36. See: Saher Selod. 2014. "Gendered Racialization: Muslim American Men and Women's Encounters with Racialized Surveillance." Ethnic and Racial Studies 42(4): 552–569; Bradley J. Zopf. 2018. "A Different Kind of Brown: Arabs and Middle Easterners as Anti-American Muslims." Sociology of Race and Ethnicity 4(2), 178–191.
37. Samantha Friedman, Recai M. Yucel, Colleen E. Wynn, and Joseph R. Gibbons. 2019. "Muslim-Non-Muslim Locational Attainment in Philadelphia: A New Fault Line in Residential Inequality?" *Demography* 56(4): 1327–1348.
38. Patricia Hill Collins. 1990. *Black Feminist Thought: Knowledge, Consciousness, and the Politics of Empowerment.* Boston, MA: Unwin Hyman.

References

Abu-Lughod, Lila. 1990. "The Romance of Resistance: Tracing Transformations of Power through Bedouin Women." In *Art in Small-Scale Societies: Contemporary Readings*, edited by Richard L. Anderson, 203–219. Berkeley: University of California Press.

Auga, Ulrike. 2015. "Decolonizing Public Space: A Challenge of Bonhoeffer's and Spivak's Concept of Resistance, 'Religion' and 'Gender.'" *Feminist Theology* 24(1): 49–68.

Avishai, Orit, and Courtney A. Irby. 2017. "Bifurcated Conversations in Sociological Studies of Religion and Gender." *Gender & Society* 31(5): 647–676.

Bartkowski, John P., and Jen'nan Ghazal Read. 2003. "Veiled Submission: Gender, Power, and Identity among Evangelical and Muslim Women in the United States." *Qualitative Sociology* 26(1): 71–92.

Collins, Patricia Hill. 1986. "Learning from the Outsider Within: The Sociological Significance of Black Feminist Thought." *Social Problems* 33(6): 14–32.

Collins, Patricia Hill. 1990. *Black Feminist Thought: Knowledge, Consciousness, and the Politics of Empowerment.* New York: Routledge.

Collins, Patricia Hill. 2000. *Black Feminist Thought.* 2nd ed. New York: Routledge.

Collins, Patricia Hill. 2008. *Violence: A Micro-Sociological Theory.* Princeton, NJ: Princeton University Press.

Edgell, Penny. 2012. "A Cultural Sociology of Religion: New Directions." *Annual Review of Sociology* 38: 247–265.

Emerson, M. O., Elizabeth Korver-Glenn, and Kiara W. Douds. 2015. "Studying Race and Religion: A Critical Assessment." *Sociology of Race and Ethnicity* 1(3): 349–359.

Floyd-Thomas, Stacey M. 2006. *Deeper Shades of Purple: Womanism in Religion and Society.* New York: New York University Press.

Friedman, Samantha, Recai M. Yucel, Colleen E. Wynn, and Joseph R. Gibbons. 2019. "Muslim–Non-Muslim Locational Attainment in Philadelphia: A New Fault Line in Residential Inequality?" *Demography* 56(4).

Ghaneabassiri, Kambiz. 2010. *A History of Islam in America: From the New World to the New World Order.* New York: Cambridge University Press.

Habermas, Jurgen. 2010. *An Awareness of What Is Missing: Faith and Reason in a Post-Secular Age.* Cambridge: Polity Press.

Hidayatullah, Aysha A. 2014. *Feminist Edges of the Qur'an*. New York: Oxford University Press.

Hull, Akasha (Gloria T.), Patricia Bell Scott, and Barbara Smith. 1982. *All the Women Are White, All the Blacks Are Men: But Some of Us Are Brave*. New York: Feminist Press at CUNY.

Jung, M.-K. and Kwon, Y. 2013. "Theorizing the US Racial State: Sociology Since Racial Formation." *Sociology Compass* 7: 927–940.

Korteweg, Anna C. 2008. "The Sharia Debate in Ontario." *Gender & Society* 22(4): 434–454.

Mahmood, Saba. 2005. *Politics of Piety: The Islamic Revival and the Feminist Subject*. Princeton, NJ: Princeton University Press.

Majeed, Debra M. 2006. "Womanism Encounters Islam: A Muslim Scholar Considers the Efficacy of a Method Rooted in the Academy and the Church." In *Deeper Shades of Purple*, edited by Stacey M. Floyd-Thomas. New York: New York University Press.

Márquez, John D., and Junaid Rana. 2017. "Black Radical Possibility and the Decolonial International." *South Atlantic Quarterly* 116(3).

Meleagrou-Hitchens, Alexander. 2018. *Salafism in America: History, Evolution, Radicalization*. Washington, DC: GW Program on Extremism.

Mossiere, Geraldine. 2016. "The Intimate and the Stranger: Approaching the 'Muslim Question' through the Eyes of Female Converts to Islam." *Critical Research on Religion* 4(1): 90–108. doi: 10.1177/2050303216630067

Neitz, Mary Jo. 2014. "Becoming Visible: Religion and Gender in Sociology." *Sociology of Religion* 75(4): 511–523.

The Pew Research Center Forum on Religion & Public Life. 2011. *The Future of the Global Muslim Population*. Washington, DC: The Pew Research Center Forum on Religion & Public Life.

Prickett, Pamela J. 2015. "Negotiating Gendered Religious Space: The Particularities of Patriarchy in an African American Mosque." *Gender & Society* 29(1): 51–72.

Rao, Aliya Hamid. 2015. "Gender and Cultivating the Moral Self in Islam: Muslim Converts in an American Mosque." *Sociology of Religion* 76(4): 413–435.

Rinaldo, Rachel. 2014. "Pious and Critical." *Gender & Society* 28(6): 824–846.

Rouse, Carolyn M. 2004. *Engaged Surrender: African American Women and Islam*. Oakland: University of California Press.

Selod, S. 2014. "Gendered Racialization: Muslim American Men and Women's Encounters with Racialized Surveillance." *Ethnic and Racial Studies* 42(4): 552–569.

Winchester, Daniel. 2008. "Embodying the Faith: Religious Practice and the Making of a Muslim Moral Habitus." *Social Forces* 86(4): 1753–1780.

Zopf, Bradley J. 2018. "A Different Kind of Brown: Arabs and Middle Easterners as Anti-American Muslims." *Sociology of Race and Ethnicity* 4(2): 178–191.

Part 4

Black Feminist Sociological Methodologies and What They Teach Us

Chapter 15

Love, Loss and Loyalty

A Black Feminist Reading
of Black Girlhood

Kenly Brown

Introduction

On a warm April afternoon, with bubble tea and fried chicken fingers nestled in the grass beside us, Paradise and her best friend Ashley sit across from me as cars speed through a busy intersection.[1] The cool breeze provides momentary relief from the heat as each of us jokingly clears our throats for this interview we pushed back for the last month due to work schedules and familial obligations. Paradise is 17 years old with auburn hair and long lashes that highlight her deep brown eyes and light brown complexion. She has on Victoria's Secret yoga pants and slides. Ashley is 18 years old wearing whitewashed jeans and a black tank top with her hair in a tight bun. Her bright smile accentuates her deep brown complexion. For the next two hours, we laugh, cry, and sit in silence. Toward the end of our time together, Paradise leans on Ashley's shoulder and says, "God isn't gonna give me anything that I can't handle. I feel like I'll push through."

***

This fieldnote excerpt is from one of my first interviews in a three-year ethnography about a California alternative school, H.B. Stowe Academy, that teachers, students, and community residents colloquially referred to as a "dumping ground" for the "bad kids."[2] Here, I witnessed Black girls relentlessly maneuver external vulnerabilities to exclusion and violence to create internal forms of support and community. Paradise's refrain, *God isn't gonna give me anything that I can't handle*, encapsulates a historical experience for Black women and girls. Saidiya Hartman's *Wayward Lives, Beautiful Experiments: Intimate Histories of Social Upheaval* exhumes scattered and displaced archives of Black women and girls in the 20th century to illuminate, similar to Paradise and Ashley's experiences, an "untiring practice of trying to live when you were never meant to survive."[3]

I met Paradise in her second-period Spanish class. I introduced myself to students in the course to share my initial research project to learn how Black girls perceive and maneuver discipline and punishment in schooling.

DOI: 10.4324/9781003199113-20

At the end of the class period, she introduced herself to me as a writer. She said she wanted to be part of the study to share her experiences with other Black girls because "there is not a lot out there about us." Over time, my research evolved from an inquiry about Black girls' perception of discipline and punishment in an alternative school to how Black girls survive interpersonal and institutional violence to make it to tomorrow. Paradise understood, as a Black girl becoming a Black woman, that no one would ensure her survival more than herself.

Written at the intersections of Black girlhood studies and ethnography, this chapter captures Paradise's coming of age story on the cusp of becoming the effaced, fixed, and criminalized Black woman. I draw upon a larger ethnographic study that includes participant and direct observation, semi-structured interviews, and informal conversations with students and staff collected over a three-year period. I spent over 1000 hours in a California continuation school, H.B. Stowe Academy, which enrolled approximately 80 students in the academic years of 2016–2017 and 2017–2018. Of those 80 students, 30 students attended regularly throughout the school year. Black girls made up about half of those regular attendees each year.

This close examination of Paradise's life reveals how a duality of experiences emerge during Black girlhood as girls who are seemingly structurally fixed in place cultivate identities and strategies of survival rooted in their lived experiences. Paradise's narrative contributes to Black feminist sociology by illustrating how experiences in childhood begin to shape how Black women resist, survive, and strategize in their womanhoods. In this chapter, I describe the significance of Black feminist ethnography as a way to expound upon the insights and interiority of Black girlhood through the conceptual work of Jennifer C. Nash's "felt life of Black feminism" to frame the felt life of Black girlhood in love, loss, and loyalty.[4]

Black Feminist Ethnography

Conventional ethnographic methods in sociology and anthropology systematically study culture and how people make meaning to create a shared set of values, norms, and materials. In *Writing Ethnographic Fieldnotes*, Emerson, Fretz and Shaw describe ethnographic field research as "firsthand participation in some initially unfamiliar social world and the production of written accounts of that world that draw upon such participation."[5] It is important to note a lack of familiarity with social worlds "unfamiliar" to one's own has resulted in insidious outcomes using data collected on multiply-marginalized people. A Black feminist read of and engagement with ethnographic methods (e.g., participant observation, direct observation, in combination with interviews) centers a familiarity in that people understand the stakes of their reality based on circumstances and experiences they live through.

Irma McClaurin's edited anthology *Black Feminist Anthropology* centers the elided work of Black feminists' anthropological ethnographies and theories foregrounded in Black intellectual thought and feminism.[6] Informed by this pioneering anthology, a Black feminist ethnographic methodology and praxis requires me to work against typologies and pathologies ascribed to marginalized communities. Joyce Ladner's *Tomorrow's Tomorrow* was the first urban ethnography to center the lives of Black girls. To delve into their lives in the Pruitt-Igoe housing project in St. Louis, Ladner subverted the deviance-model often used to examine the lives of Black girls to develop a sociohistorical account of the Black community that took seriously the nexus of age, race, and gender. Ladner acknowledges her initial approach to field work was "equipped with a set of ideas and labels that I intended to apply to these women. This, of course, meant that I had gone there only to validate and elaborate on what was *alleged* to *exist*."[7] As she spent time, shared resources, and connected with Black girls and young women, she learned that her training as a sociologist and the books she read on the Black community, did not illuminate and engage the complexities of Black life. Instead, Ladner situated her experiences and perceptions learned over time as a Black girl and woman who grew up in the Black community to ground her study in the ways that girls and women cope, strategize, and resist in a discriminatory and oppressive country.

Ethnographic methods from a Black feminist perspective operate beyond an outcome-based and deficit-centered paradigm. Nikki Jones in *Between Good and Ghetto: African American Girls and Inner-City Violence* took up Ladner's position to analytically resist a deviance-centered way to study Black girls and women. Accordingly, Jones took an opposing position to other mainstream ethnographers: "In contrast to the perspective apparent in many popular ethnographic works on Black populations, I began this research confident that the humanity of Black people was not a subject for debate."[8] Her research questions did not vilify or monolithically explore why Black girls were violent. Rather, she organized her research question out of a concern that several girls and women she built relationships with had: how to stay safe in order to secure their personal well-being.

Black feminist ethnography is about how Black girls embody and feel their position in their social worlds. In *Shapeshifters*, Cox explores the constellation of survival, aspirations, perspectives, and love that abounds among Black women and girls in a homeless shelter in Detroit. Cox describes ethnography as "thick description [that] allows Black girls to address the fullness of their lives, not just those aspects that could be defined as putting them at some ill-defined risk or as responsible for preventing their success."[9] Moving away from a position to defend the behaviors of Black girls and women, Cox compares how dancers embody their choreography to "move from a place of intuitive knowing" to how girls and women "stay in their bodies to rewrite the socially constructed meanings shackled to them."[10] Accordingly, Cox captures the interior experiences of Black girls and women that exist outside of external pleas to be seen as a person in a world that perceives Black girls as "nascent dangerous Black women"—making the life of Black girlhood an embodiment of experiences and feelings situated in relationships and encounters in their daily lives.[11]

The Affective Life of Black Girlhood

Black girls' interpersonal relationships with one another and other people they encounter shape their affective feelings and experiences. Gregg, Seigworth and Ahmed define affect as "encounters with forces and passages of intensity that bear out, while occasionally leaving bare, the singularly and intimately impersonal—even subpersonal and prepersonal—folds of belonging (or non-belonging) to a world."[12] Thus, affect is a material consequence of how Black girls feel in their social worlds and physical bodies. Jennifer C. Nash describes Black feminism as a *felt life*[13] where "black feminism has treated racism and sexism as felt experiences and how black feminists have theorized what it feels like to do labor that is both desired and devalued."[14] While Nash theorizes the felt life in the realm of the academy and law, I use the felt life as a way to write about the affective life of Black girlhood.

When Paradise shared her story, she took a moment to ruminate thoughtfully, courageously, and vulnerably on her life. A moment she had not been afforded in a long time while surviving violence, loss, and instability at home. It is here where I had the privilege, not a right, to sit and listen to pieces of her life. Black girlhood studies, Black feminisms, and ethnography inform *how* I write this chapter in the affect and in the words of a Black girl. As a Black woman doing work with Black girls, I capture what the mainstream canon of sociology cannot. I write her story as a witness, mentor, and a Black woman who cares for Black girls. Her life is affectively lived in struggle, love, and persistence.

According to Jennifer C. Nash, affective knowledge is undergirded by a politics rooted in love, where mutual vulnerability and witnessing illustrate Black women's capacity to survive. Because our vulnerability is tied to one another, we cultivate spaces where we can witness each other in struggle even when external systems minimize or erase us. Nash's love politics of witnessing and vulnerability informs my methodology for understanding and writing about Paradise's coming of age narrative situated in the loss of loved ones and the loyalty of an intimate friend. After several interviews, dinners, and walks with Paradise, she shared with me events in her young life that led her to a passion for writing and an intimate friendship with Ashley.

"Nobody Care About Black Women"

Paradise and I spent time together talking about her aspirations to own a business where patrons could "get their hair, nails, and shopping done in one go," publish a book, and have a family with a man "who really loves me for me." She spoke in a tone familiar with life's pitfalls and hope for something different from how she grew up. In her aspirations to build a successful career and healthy relationship, she also recognized her vulnerability. The following excerpt is from a fieldnote during Paradise's Spanish class where she reacts to multiple social media posts about the death of 19-year-old Kenneka Jenkins in Chicago, Illinois:

> *The school bell rings at H.B. Stowe Academy to alert students second period has begun. Ms. Jackson's Spanish class organize their chairs around the table to gather markers and stock paper to continue to create vocabulary flashcards in preparation for a quiz the next day. One of the students brought up news about the death of Kenneka Jenkins, a 19-year-old woman who attended a party with her friends and was found dead in a motel refrigerator in Chicago. As the students chimed in to share what they heard about her death via Instagram and Snapchat, Paradise, shouted, "That's why I am so upset! I am seeing her on my Instagram, but nobody is doing anything. Nobody care about Black women."*

Paradise's words hung in the classroom as our breaths were suspended in the air. Paradise leaned back in her chair angry and fed up. Paradise was upset that law enforcement was moving slowly to investigate what happened and why her friends abandoned her at this party. At the time, Paradise was 17 years old—two years younger than Kenneka. The coroner's office eventually ruled Kenneka's death as accidental. Paradise understood how volatile and precarious life can be for a Black girl.

By the age of six, Paradise recognized that she was all she had. Paradise is the youngest child in her family of three sisters and two brothers. Due to a significant age gap, she had a different experience with her mom who was going through a severe drug addiction. Paradise's maternal grandmother, Granny, sexually exploited her daughter. Granny sold Paradise's 14-year-old mother to a drug dealer's cousin. Before her mom's 15th birthday, she became pregnant with Paradise's oldest sibling. As her mom grew up, she struggled with an addiction and would beat and neglect Paradise's siblings. Paradise shared with me that she "is the most forgiving one" out of her sisters and brothers because she has sympathy for her mother because "we were born into this and we learn how to survive it." Paradise said she could *feel* the intergenerational abuse in her bones because she survived abuse herself.

At the age of three, Paradise moved in with her dad because her mom was unable to care for her. During this time, she became close to her Auntie Paradise (after whom she was named). When Paradise was four years old, her Auntie died in a car accident. Paradise poetically concluded, "She died because her heart popped." Even though Paradise was young when she lost her Auntie Paradise, she recounted the events of the morning she learned about her passing:

> *I woke up and I was like walking out of my dad's room and my cousin was crying. And then he was like, [Paradise] died. And I was like, "What? No, she's not. She's not dead." And then I had went downstairs, and then my dad was like, "I gotta tell you something." And he sit me in his lap and then my grandma, my grandpa and my granny they were all crying. And her son was crying and I was like, "What's going on?" [and] he was like, "She passed away." I was like no she didn't, no she didn't. So, then I ran up to her room because everyone was right next to my dad's room and she just wasn't there and I started crying because she was like my mom.*

By the age of four, Paradise experienced significant loss. Her Auntie's death not only left her emotionally devastated, but it also left her vulnerable to violence that every woman and girl in her family endured. Her dad used drugs to cope with the pain of losing his sister, and this put Paradise in danger. When she was six years old, her dad punched her in the legs several times when his girlfriend's son lied and said she dropped a bottle in the other room, "He lied on me because I wouldn't do sexual things to him." Once her mom saw the bruises a couple of days later, Paradise went back to live with her mom and stepdad. Even though Paradise was out of physical harm's way, her mom "was still doing drugs but she was at least working." Paradise continued to be estranged from her mom while her stepdad took care of her. She "felt like the world didn't want me."

To cope with the loss of her Auntie Paradise and pain from an addiction her mom battled, Paradise journaled and wrote fiction to process her loss. She creatively developed a complex female protagonist who navigated familial trauma and turned hustles into goldmines. She used her gift of writing to anchor her to this world and give herself purpose. Similarly, cultural critic bell hooks used writing to tether herself to a world that tried to throw her away: "I am a young poet, a writer. I am here to make words. I have the power to pull myself back from death—to keep myself alive."[15] Paradise would regularly tell me that loss felt particularly painful because she knew what it felt like to be loved. It was not until she met her best friend Ashley that she had an unconditional loving relationship with someone after the passing of her Auntie.

"She Is My Wifey"

Sitting on the fresh trimmed grass with Paradise and Ashley, we cultivated a space to process how Black girls learned how to survive, live, and thrive even when the line between life and death is slippery. When Paradise shared the death of her paternal Auntie, Ashley tilted her head to the side to look into her friends' eyes. Paradise's bottom lip began to quiver. Ashley gently put her hand on Paradise's arm to move closer to her. Ashley laid her head on her shoulder. As Paradise's voice faded away, tears welled at the rim of our eyes as Ashley began to share the loss of her godmother.

Ashley's godmother was her confidante and the person she depended on for support and someone to talk to: "She just knew everything about me. She could tell when I'm mad, tell when something is bugging me, [she just knew me]." When Ashley was 15 years old, her godmother fell in the shower and died soon after from complications. Ashley lost her best friend, "that was my absolute, besides her (gesturing toward Paradise), that was like my absolute best friend too. When she died, it just really, it just really felt like now I don't have anybody because I'm not really that close to my mom."

Paradise and Ashley live in the loss of maternal figures in their lives, both who have passed and those living in the present. The way they held each other in that moment described in the opening fieldnote, cultivated a space to grieve and express gratitude for one another. Friendship for Black girls is not only about protection against violence and indiscriminate loyalty, but it is a lifeline and a way to be seen in a world when feeling overlooked. Paradise and Ashley went to middle school together, but they were not best friends because, according to Ashely, "I already had a best friend when I met her. Obviously, we are not best friends no more." There is a loyalty understood between best friends: there can only be one. Once they both enrolled in their traditional high school, Coolidge High School they became best friends. When Paradise transferred to H.B. Stowe Academy before Ashley, Ashely walked Paradise to school—an extra mile—everyday to drop her off. Physical proximity did not dictate the parameters of their friendship because as Ashley said, "She know me better than I know me."

A year after graduation, Paradise found out she was pregnant. I learned about the pregnancy from Ashley when I texted her to organize a dinner to catch up. Ashley texted me back after I sent her several heart emojis, "Don't tell her I told you. Act surprised." I messaged Paradise right away to get dinner to catch up. She told me the news and asked if we could get burgers and fries because that was her new craving of the week. Paradise shared with me how her family took the news about her unborn child. Her dad said, "You ruined your life." Her mom told her, "You can't kill a life." Her on-again-off-again boyfriend questioned if the baby was his. Paradise already felt apprehensive about the pregnancy because "I am supposed to take care of everyone. But who takes care of me?" She said the only person who was supportive of her initially was Ashley.

When Ashley and I met for dinner, she said, "Paradise lost so many people in her life. She wasn't grounded to the world. This baby's gonna ground her because she has someone to take care of [who will love her unconditionally]." Ashley understood and witnessed her friend's difficulty to feel part of a world that that left her feeling alone. Ashley's understanding reflects a central tenet of Black feminism Nash describes: "This act of witnessing, for self and for others, naming what others seek to ignore or normalize, is black feminist assert, a practice of love, of tenderness, and of politics world-making."[16] Paradise and Ashley created an interior world to be there for one another through difficult times.

Paradise is a young woman and mom to a beautiful son. When I met her newborn, Ashley was right there in the hospital room as the godmother. This chapter is for girls like Paradise and Ashley who want to share her story for the next Black girl who feels lonely and abandoned with a desire to feel anchored and seen in this world. This is why I am a Black feminist ethnographer.

Conclusion

The affective experiences of Paradise illuminate not only her vulnerability—and that of other women and girls in her family—but also how the witnessing and loyalty of a longtime friend can provide a sense of stability. This love politics is often overlooked in studies of Black girls. Their coming-of-age story is one that is familiar for many of our most vulnerable Black girls. This chapter contributes to Black feminist sociology as an illustration of the ways Black girls and women move through the world, revealing how their efforts to survive, strategize, and resist emerge early on in their childhoods. A Black feminist love politics allows us to see how interpersonal relationships and interactions emotively register and materialize in the life of Black girlhood.

Paradise's narrative and relationships illuminate the implications of how historical and structural violence move through the lives of Black girls who create alternative support systems. Paradise understands how her encounters with others are informed by those who came before her. In Paradise's coming of age journey, she learned she is part of a long lineage of Black women whose fight for life, love, and joy, returning to Hartman's provocative statement, is an "untiring practice of trying to live when you were never meant to survive."[17] To a be a Black girl in the United States, Paradise understood the stakes of her decisions and the relationships she built to survive and enjoy life in spite of a system that seeks her demise.

Notes

1. All names and places in reference to the ethnographic study are pseudonyms.
2. Continuation education literature also uses "dumping ground" as a way to describe continuation schools (Kelly 1993, and Nygreen 2013).
3. Saidiya Hartman. 2019. *Wayward Lives, Beautiful Experiments: Intimate Histories of Social Upheaval.* New York and London: W.W. Norton & Company.
4. Jennifer C. Nash. 2019. *Black Feminism Reimagined: After Intersectionality.* Durham, NC: Duke University Press.
5. Robert Emerson, Rachel Fretz, and Linda Shaw. 2011. *Writing Ethnographic Fieldnotes,* 1. Chicago, IL: University of Chicago Press.
6. Irma McLaurin (ed.). 2001. *Black Feminist Anthropology: Theory, Politics, Praxis, and Poetics.* New Brunswick, NJ: Rutgers University Press.
7. Joyce Ladner. 1995. *Tomorrow's Tomorrow: The Black Woman,* xxi. Lincoln: University of Nebraska Press (author's emphasis).
8. Nikki Jones. 2009. *Between Good and Ghetto: African American Girls and Inner-City Violence.* New Brunswick, NJ: Rutgers University Press.
9. Aimee Meredith Cox. 2015. *Shapeshifters: Black Girls and the Choreography of Citizenship,* 59. Durham, NC: Duke University Press.
10. Ibid., 29.
11. Ibid., 18.
12. M. Gregg, G. J. Seigworth, and S. Ahmed (eds.). 2010. *The Affect Theory Reader,* 3. Durham, NC: Duke University Press.
13. Nash 2019 notes the ways in which affect theory conventionally nominalizes race and Black feminist works.
14. Nash 2019, 30.
15. Bell hooks. 1996. *Bone Black: Memories of Girlhood,* 182. New York: Henry Holt and Company.
16. Nash 2019, 119.
17. Hartman 2019, 228.

References

Cox, Aimee Meredith. 2015. *Shapeshifters: Black Girls and the Choreography of Citizenship.* Durham, NC and London: Duke University Press.

Emerson, Robert, Rachel Fretz, and Linda Shaw. 2011. *Writing Ethnographic Fieldnotes.* Chicago, IL: University of Chicago Press.

Gregg, Melissa, Seigworth, Gregory, and Ahmed, Sara (eds.). 2010. *The Affect Theory Reader.* Durham, NC: Duke University Press.

Hartman, Saidiya. 2019. *Wayward Lives, Beautiful Experiments: Intimate Histories of Social Upheaval.* New York and London: W.W. Norton & Company.

hooks, bell. 1996. *Bone Black: Memories of Girlhood,* 182. New York: Henry Holt and Company.

Jones, Nikki. 2009. *Between Good and Ghetto: African American Girls and Inner-City Violence.* New Brunswick, NJ and London: Rutgers University Press.

Kelly, Deidre. 1993. *Last Chance High School: How Girls and Boys Drop In and Out of Alternative High Schools.* New Haven, CT: Yale University Press.

Ladner, Joyce. 1995. *Tomorrow's Tomorrow: The Black Woman.* Lincoln: University of Nebraska Press.

McLaurin, Irma (ed.). 2001. *Black Feminist Anthropology: Theory, Politics, Praxis, and Poetics*. New Brunswick, NJ: Rutgers University Press.

Nash, Jennifer C. 2019. *Black Feminism Reimagined: After Intersectionality*. Durham, NC and London: Duke University Press.

Nygreen, Kysa. 2013. *These Kids: Identity, Agency, and Social Justice at a Last Chance High School*. Chicago: University of Chicago Press.

Chapter 16

Black Feminist Epistemological Methodology

Bridging Theory and Methods to Research Health and Illness

Jennifer Elyse James

Mary: I try to think healthy. And just keep it fair-minded and ask God to keep it going and keep my health not so heavy, not to be a burden on me. To keep me in the frame of mind where I don't have to be so harsh on myself. But I found myself one day, I really cried hard. I really cried hard. I asked God, "Why me?" I was angry with myself throughout that day. I was just blue. The voices in my mind laughed. And I wondered, "Why can't I laugh with the voices?"

JJ: What were they laughing at? Were they laughing at you? At cancer?

Mary: They were laughing because I was crying.

Mary is a 49-year-old Black woman with advanced cancer. When I met her, she was just finishing her first course of chemotherapy. She is seen in an oncology clinic at County Hospital, where she has received most of her health care for many years. While her cancer care is fairly straight forward, her experience of illness is complicated by the voices that she hears; voices which are closely tied to her interactions with the health care system and her ability to form relationships with her providers. When I began a qualitative research project studying the lives and health of Black women with advanced cancer, I knew I wanted to use Black feminist theory (BFT) and challenge the boundaries of academic literature by studying health and health care in a way that centers the lived experiences of Black women. I wanted to do work that was better able to both capture the complexity of a woman like Mary and engage her in the analysis of her narrative.

This chapter describes a new methodology I developed and piloted for a project on the lived experiences of Black women with advanced cancer.[1] I argue there is a need for a defined Black feminist epistemological methodology, which acts as a bridge between the epistemological commitment of BFT and the traditional qualitative research methods of interviews and observations.[2]

DOI: 10.4324/9781003199113-21

BFT as a Methodology: Application to Black Women's Experiences of Advanced Cancer

Black women have been historically underrepresented as both researchers and the subjects of research. In health research in particular, Black women are often only included in research that is comparative and too often it feels that we are being constantly told how we are less than, worse off, or failing. Too little research holds our thoughts and experiences as central.

BFT and the theory of intersectionality have particular relevance in the study of health. The National Black Women's Health Project founder Byllye Avery described the health care system as "laced with institutional racism" and Black women as "the ones at the bottom that capitalism feeds on."[3] By looking at the combined impact of class, race, and gender on health, scholars and activists can "develop a more comprehensive understanding of the complex social processes that influence wellbeing."[4]

Patricia Hill Collins argues that when Black women are in charge of our own self definitions, "four dimensions of Black feminist epistemology— lived experience as a criterion of meaning, the use of dialogue, the ethic of personal accountability, and the ethic of caring—come to the fore front."[5] I will describe each of the four tenets in-depth and explain how I have applied them methodologically.

Centering Lived Experience

The first core tenet is that alternative epistemologies are built upon lived experience and not upon an objectified position. Instead of the tradition of turning subjects into objects of study, Collins believes that only those who experience a particular standpoint can select the topics for investigation and the methodologies to be used. This tenet of lived experience is the basis for much of my epistemological framing for my project. My work is based in the lived experience of Black women and, in service of that, I chose intentionally broad and open research questions and decided to approach them qualitatively. I wanted my research to be centered on the lived experiences, perspectives, values and knowledges of Black women living with a potentially terminal cancer diagnosis. I am striving to privilege the wisdom of my participants over traditionally privileged medical knowledge. I created intentionally open interview guides to allow my research participants to set the pace and direction of the interview.

Creating a Collective Dialogue

Second, Collins advocates the use of dialogue rather than adversarial debate. The goal is not for one opinion or truth to shout down another; rather, the goal is for a conversation to exist between them and work in conjunction to develop new knowledge. When I began to explore the concept of collective dialogue in research I could only find work that positioned interviews *as* collective dialogue.[6] While I appreciate the work many scholars have done to make interviews more closely match these values, I disagree that interviews—as they are traditionally understood, even within the most progressive traditions—are in and of themselves collective dialogue. It is rare for the interviewer to insert herself intentionally in to the interview. In fact, researchers are taught specifically not to do that in the name of objectivity. Our insertion comes at the point of analysis and writing. So, while we have contributions from both parties at different stages of the research, it is not developed in a collective way.

bell hooks writes, "Dialogue implies talk between two subjects, not the speech of subject and object. It's a humanizing speech, one that challenges and resists domination."[7] This concept of collective dialogue has historical legacies in the Black community. Scholars have traced this idea of collective dialogue as the site of knowledge production and claims assessment back to slavery. In their foundational work *Women's Ways of Knowing*, Mary Field Belenky, Blythe McVicker Clinchy, Nancy Rule Goldberger, and Jill Mattuck Tarule assert that connectedness is an essential component of the knowledge validation process. Black women rarely work out knowledge claims in isolation; it is a community process. One example of this dialogue is the tradition of call-and-response in the Black community.[8] The most prevalent example of call-and-response can be found in worship services. The sermon is punctuated with "hallelujah" and "amen" and "Yes, Lord!" The preacher and the congregation work together to create the worship experience. It is a spontaneous, interactive process, not a passive one. All participants are active and all have a voice. A dialogue is created collectively. According to poet and essayist June Jordan, "our language is a system constructed by people constantly needing to insist that we exist."[9] Interruption, affirmation, and exclamation are an essential part of speaking patterns in the Black community.

My collective dialogue intervention involves creating a space where I echo back to participants what I am hearing from them and attempt to create a space of humble vulnerability where we can both speak about our impressions. I audio record and transcribe verbatim all interviews with participants. During and after the interview, I take extensive field notes. Using both transcripts and my notes, I write up a summary of each interview, my impressions, analysis, thoughts, questions, and confusions about the participant and our conversation. During the follow up interview, I read this summary—usually one to two pages—to the participant. I encourage her to interrupt me, correct me, or contradict me. Through this process, I can share with participants what they would otherwise not see until publication; how their story will be told, what themes are emerging, and the analytical work involved in generating new knowledge.[10]

The collective dialogue process also serves the purpose of validating themes of my research. Collins suggests that Black feminist thought must be validated by "ordinary African-American women."[11] For Collins, Black feminist scholarship needs to resonate with Black women and speak to their lives and experiences. Our knowledge cannot be produced in a vacuum from within the ivory tower, validated only after publication. Rather, I seek to prioritize this validation as a deliberate and intrinsic *part* of data collection and to incorporate collective dialogue into my research methodology.

Establishing an Ethic of Caring

The third tenet of Black feminist epistemology is the ethics of caring. This approach does not require the researcher to attempt to separate participant experience from her own experience or assume that it could be possible to separate knowledge from feelings. It is appropriate to express individual uniqueness and emotion in dialogue.

Collins describes three major components of the ethics of caring: the value placed on individual expressiveness, the appropriateness of emotions, and the capacity for empathy. While many positivist researchers—or as Collins terms them, "separate knowers"—try to extract individual personality from their ideas to avoid "bias," "connected knowers" see the value that individual personality brings to the table. We all have biases, feelings, and assumptions about our research that inevitably intertwine and influence how we approach our work. The ideas that I share and the analysis I conduct cannot and should not be separated from my person. Part of my goal in creating the collective dialogue with my participants is to bring that to the table. I allow us to dialogue about our reactions to each other. I make a deliberate analytical choice to not separate feelings from my work, but instead treat them as data and analyze them alongside the words of the participants in my study.

Committing to Personal Responsibility

Finally, Black feminist epistemology requires personal accountability of the researcher. Since knowledge is built upon lived experience, the assessment of knowledge is also an assessment of an individual's character, values, ethics, and concrete practices. This tenet shapes several aspects of my work, including the writing style and location of publications I choose. I take seriously bell hooks's critique that "in this capitalist culture, feminism and feminist theory are fast becoming a commodity that only the privileged can afford."[12] That is, I want my work to be not only by a Black woman and about Black women, but to be able to be consumed and understood by Black women, across levels of education. I strive to make my research available to participants in my study in an accessible and identifiable way. I also encourage research participants to pick a code name that will be used when my research is published. I want to ensure that a participant can pick up a book or article published from the project and know when I am quoting or referring to her.

Black Feminist Epistemological Methodology in Practice: Mary's Story

The following is an example of how I used this methodology with a participant who asked me to call her Mary. Mary was the sixth participant in my research study. At this point I had become more comfortable with this process, but Mary had a unique personal story, and I found this collective dialogue quite challenging. What follows is the collective summary I wrote about Mary, exactly as I read it to her in our second interview. Following the summary, I will describe the process and how I utilized each of the core tenets during our interactions.

Mary describes herself as a "happy-go-lucky woman who ended up with cancer at 48 years old." She's a small woman. Much shorter than I am. She described herself as "chunky," but I wouldn't use that label—maybe just a little round.

She was having problems for seven years before they found her cancer. She knew something was wrong with her, and she said she went back and forth to a lot of doctors. They said gastritis, this, that. She kept having pain and lost a bunch of weight. When she was finally diagnosed, she said, very poetically, "I think one tear dropped out of my eye. It didn't really hit me and really, it still hasn't hit me too much."

It sounds like a lot of people in her life have had cancer. She thinks the cause of her cancer is diet related—particularly eating too much meat. She described her childhood and her mother gardening—they always ate vegetables. She had a lot of nostalgia when she described this time. It sounded like a simpler time, a happy time. A healthy time.

I was surprised she didn't mention genetics as a potential cause of cancer since both of her parents died of cancer. This was a red flag for me but not an association she made. She did mention that she had a fear of chemotherapy because of her mom and a fear of being in a rest home because of her dad. Both seemed like very rational fears. She mentioned her sister told her she had to do chemo and was the one who really convinced her. She seemed grateful for that.

It was a hard decision for her to have chemo. She really didn't want to get the chemotherapy and said even on the day she was supposed to start she was late because something in her mind was telling her not to take it. She thought it would do to her what it did to her mother. But, she survived it. It was hard on her—she had to come up to the hospital a lot, she had to wear a machine and couldn't shower, and she had bad side effects— dehydration, sick to her stomach, affected her kidneys, fingertip problems. But, despite all that, she said it wasn't an inconvenience because it helped her live longer.

She described some dementia or memory issues that frustrate her and that for the last eight or so years since she had a surgery, she has been hearing voices. She said they are mean to her. She described one day when she was feeling blue and crying about her cancer. She said the voices in her mind laughed and she thought, "Why can't I laugh with them?" It made her angry that they were laughing because she was crying, and I found that heartbreaking.

She mentioned she's received some psychiatric care in the past but also mentioned she isn't very fond of her current therapist. This was concerning for me. I hope she is getting proper care, and I worry about the source of these voices. Is this something that can be treated? Is this the sign of a bigger problem?

Mary seemed incredibly insightful to me, and I wondered if sometimes she doesn't get taken as seriously as she should or if she ever feels disrespected by the medical community. She seems to really want to help people with her story—offered a lot of advice to other women about getting checked out and going through chemo—wants to support other women.

She said she was mad at herself, but I couldn't really understand why. She said she spent one day crying and asking God why me. It's when the voices laughed at her. She was angry with herself for questioning God. She shouldn't ask "Why me?"—but she feels like she shouldn't have cancer. It's just something he has to deal with. She can't be angry with God because he didn't give her the cancer. I found this heartbreaking. Why shouldn't she feel angry?

I used all four core tenets of Black feminist epistemological methodology over the course of my interviews with Mary. The core tenet of centering the lived experience is one that I anticipated taking place primarily in the planning stage of my research. And, in many ways it did. I intentionally framed my research questions to be centered on the lived experience of Black women and did not compare their experiences to men or to white women. I chose to center their knowledge in my analysis and use the perspectives of their providers as background information, focusing on their lives and perspectives, rather than the biomedical scope of their disease. Additionally, I planned interview guides that were incredibly open and unstructured to allow participants to focus on the aspects most important to them and to the telling of their stories. However, it was not enough for me to go into my research with the intention of centering the lived experiences of Black women. I had to continually make that goal clear to the participants in my study so that they felt they had permission to tell me about their lives.

I had the intention of creating a collective dialogue with Mary, which started with the summary I read to her. There are a few places where I spoke to things that I knew could potentially challenge Mary or our dynamic. One example is around the voices she hears and her psychiatric care. When Mary told me in our first interview that she hears voices and that she seemed to not be getting stable psychiatric care I became very concerned. I struggled prior to our second interview with how to describe the voices she had been hearing. I did not want to pathologize her, and I was worried I could alienate her. I tried to balance my need for deeper exploration as a researcher with my desire to respect her humility and vulnerability for sharing a difficult part of her life with me.

When I first read the collective dialogue summary to Mary she said, "That's incredible. It is. It is so touching and so meaningful. It described me so well." I thanked her and asked her if and how it should be adapted to better tell her story. We had the following exchange:

Mary: The voices is real. That's what I've got my report here from the doctor stating what he said that he's seen inside of me. So it's hush-hush and I can't really talk about it. . . . But I do have to get major surgery because they tried to hide something.

JJ: The doctors did?

Mary: Yeah, they planted something inside of me they tried to hide. It's in my doctor's write up. They did something sneaky.

JJ: They made a mistake and they didn't tell you?

Mary: No, it wasn't a mistake. They did this purposefully. Because how could you make a mistake and put something in somebody that don't belong in there? And they stole one of my ovaries.

JJ: How're you feeling about having to go back into surgery then?

Mary: Scared. And I don't want the same doctors to do it because they might implant something else in me.

JJ: I'm very intrigued by your story. I want to ask you more but I— you may not want to talk about it too much so I'm trying not to press you.

Mary: Yeah. It's amazing. They are investigating it. I shouldn't say this but I hope they—no I *should* say this—I hope they come out with a good outcome and teach the doctors a lesson. You cannot go around sticking things into people that don't belong into them.

JJ: Sort of similar but stepping back, do you have trouble trusting doctors because of all of this?

Mary: I'm skeptical about certain ones. And I know everybody is not like that. But they do got people in every position that got some wrongness to them. You know, doctors, lawyers, police. Just like all the police doing all these things to people. . . . I think that whatever happened gave me cancer. Whatever they did gave me cancer. Because they had something in me for eight years. That's what I feel, they gave me cancer. It destroyed my life.

When I had first asked Mary about the voices she said, "I shouldn't be talking about it." But, after our collective dialogue, Mary's response was to offer more explanation. She wanted to connect with me on this issue because of the way I broached it with her and because I was explicit with her that I wanted to collaborate with her in the telling of this part of her story. We were able to have an extensive conversation about her distrust in medicine and her theories of the true cause of the voices she hears. This is analytic work that Mary and I were able to do together. Through our collective dialogue, we were able to make a connection between distrust in medical care and the voices she hears, themes that would have remained separate if not for the process of sharing my reactions and insights from our first interview. I asked her again later in the interview if she trusts doctors. She said, "I don't know what to think. Some doctors I trust. Like women I trust. No women did this to me, it was men. All men did this to me. They did something that they shouldn't have and they are going to pay for it."

Throughout this collective dialogue I demonstrated the ethic of caring that I argue is essential to Black feminist epistemological methodology. I highlighted my own biases and assumptions about the origins of Mary's cancer, her response to a loss of faith, and the voices she has been hearing, while attempting to still leave a space for Mary to disagree with me. I was clear that there were aspects of her story and her reaction to her cancer that I found heartbreaking. I approached Mary from a perspective of empathy, but I also did not hide the places where my own experiences and knowledge may have conflicted with hers. Rather than attempting to distance myself from my feelings about Mary or my assumptions about her health, I brought them into the analytic process by allowing her to comment on them.

Mary chose her own code name for this project. She has already heard these words and has a sense of how she will be described in my writing. Mary knows that I will not simply be retelling or describing the voices she hears, but wondering about their origin and relating it back to the care she receives at County Hospital. I can take personal responsibility for my analytical work and the way I am presenting participants in this study, and I can do so with the knowledge that they have willingly collaborated with me in that process.

It would be easy to dismiss Mary's story or to view her only through the lens of mental illness. It would have been easy to side-step the topic of the voices as it is uncomfortable and could be seen as unrelated to her cancer narrative. Yet, through collaborating with Mary and lifting up my concern as a part of our analytic work, I was able to learn a deeper narrative. These voices that Mary hears are directly tied to her ability to seek care. Through exploring this topic through collective dialogue and the ethic of caring, we were able to work through central themes of trust in the health care system, relationships with healthcare providers, and medical decision-making. Mary is facing her fears every time she steps foot in the clinic and puts her life in the hands of providers that she doesn't know if she can trust.

Conclusion

If we are working in service of a goal of broadening what counts as knowledge, who produces knowledge, and who consumes knowledge, we must invite research participants into the process of knowledge production and dissemination. It is not only researchers who create knowledge; it is the participants who share from their own experiences and wisdom. By leaving out both collective dialogue and the ethics of caring—or making them deliberately separate from the data collection process—it is easy for researchers to marginalize research participants. As writer and activist Audre Lorde said, "The master's tools will never dismantle the master's house."[13] Through the creation of a Black feminist epistemological methodology, I hope to offer up new tools to be used in the study of Black women.

Notes

1. In the years since I began my project, other scholars have worked to develop methodologies grounded in BFT. I am particularly excited by the Black feminist methodology developed by Ashley Patterson, Valerie Kinloch, Tanja Burkhard, Ryann Randall, and Arianna Howard. 2016. "Black Feminist Thought as Methodology: Examining Intergenerational Lived Experiences of Black Women." *Departures in Critical Qualitative Research* 5(3): 55–76, and the Research Justice framework put forth by Black Women Birthing Justice (2018). Yet, both of these tremendous methodologies rely on the ability of Black women to show up at community gatherings and invest time in the research process. Black Feminist Epistemological Methodology was developed in order to introduce a methodological commitment to study Black women who may be unable to participate in more community-based methodologies due to health limitations.
2. I draw on Sandra Harding's (1987) work and the way she defined and distinguished among the concepts of epistemology, methods, and methodology. Epistemology describes who can know, what can be known, and how knowledge is developed. Methods are the techniques for gathering and analyzing data, such as interviews and observations. Methodology is the bridge between the two. It is how the researcher chooses to use the methods based on the epistemological positions she is taking. Methodology is where we work out the implications of epistemology.
3. S. Morgen. 2006. "Movement-Grounded Theory: Intersectional Analysis of Health Inequities in the United States." In *Gender, Race, Class and Health: Intersectional Approaches*, edited by A. J. Schulz and L. Mullings, 403. San Francisco, CA: Jossey-Bass.

4. A. J. Schulz, N. Freudenberg, and J. Daniels. 2005. "Intersections of Race, Class, and Gender in Public Health Interventions." In *Gender, Race, Class and Health: Intersectional Approaches*, edited by A. J. Schulz and L. Mullings, 373–393. San Francisco, CA: Jossey-Bass.

5. P. H. Collins. 2000. *Black Feminist Thought: Knowledge, Consciousness, and the Politics of Empowerment*, 266. New York: Routledge.

6. M. L. DeVault and G. Gross. 2012. "Feminist Qualitative Interviewing: Experience, Talk, and Knowledge." In *Handbook of Feminist Research: Theory and Praxis*, 206–236. Thousand Oaks, CA: Sage Publications, Inc.

7. bell hooks. 1989. *Talking Back: Thinking Feminist, Thinking Black*. Boston, MA: South End Press.

8. Collins 2000.

9. J. Jordan. 1985. *On Call: Political Essays*, 130. Boston, MA: South End Press.

10. Many feminist researchers share the transcripts of interviews or drafts of manuscripts with research participants. However, I have found in the past that most participants do not read lengthy transcripts. Many participants in my study had low literacy and significant time constraints that would make this process unreasonable.

11. Collins 2000.

12. bell hooks. 1994. *Teaching to Transgress: Education as the Practice of Freedom*, 71. New York: Routledge.

13. Lorde, Audre. 1984. "The Master's Tools Will Never Dismantle the Master's House." In *Sister Outsider: Essays and Speeches*, 110–114. Berkeley: Crossing Press.

References

Collins, Patricia Hill. 2000. *Black Feminist Thought: Knowledge, Consciousness, and the Politics of Empowerment*. New York: Routledge.

Devault, Marjorie L., and Glenda Gross. 2012. "Feminist Qualitative Interviewing: Experience, Talk, and Knowledge." In *Handbook of Feminist Research: Theory and Praxis*, edited by Sharlene Nagy Hesse-Biber, 206–237. 2nd ed. Thousand Oaks, CA: Sage Publications, Inc.

Harding, Sandra G. 1987. *Feminism and Methodology: Social Science Issues*. Bloomington, IN: Indiana University Press.

hooks, bell. 1989. *Talking Back: Thinking Feminist, Thinking Black*. Boston, MA: South End Press.

hooks, bell. 1994. *Teaching to Transgress: Education as the Practice of Freedom*. New York: Routledge.

Jordan, June. 1985. *On Call: Political Essays*. Boston, MA: South End Press.

Lorde, Audre. 1984. "The Master's Tools Will Never Dismantle the Master's House." In *Sister Outsider: Essays and Speeches*, 110–114. Berkeley: Crossing Press.

Morgen, Sandi. 2006. "Movement-Grounded Theory: Intersectional Analysis of Health Inequities in the United States." In *Gender, Race, Class and Health: Intersectional Approaches*, edited by A. J. Schulz and L. Mullings. San Francisco, CA: Jossey-Bass.

Patterson, Ashley, Valerie Kinloch, Tanja Burkhard, Ryann Randall, and Arianna Howard. 2016. "Black Feminist Thought as Methodology: Examining Intergenerational Lived Experiences of Black Women." *Departures in Critical Qualitative Research* 5(3): 55–76.

Schulz, Amy J., Nicholas Freudenberg, and Jessie Daniels. 2005. "Intersections of Race, Class, and Gender in Public Health Interventions." In *Gender, Race, Class and Health: Intersectional Approaches*, edited by A. J. Schulz and L. Mullings, 373–393. San Francisco, CA: Jossey-Bass.

Chapter 17

Creating Oppositional Knowledge as a Black Feminist

Assata Richards

As a Black feminist scholar, my intuition and my intellect drive my work. This belief and confidence to publicly assert myself as a principled-based researcher was something I had to learn outside of my academic training as a sociologist. This chapter shares my journey as I reinserted myself back into research, demonstrating how following my instincts and my ethics led me to richer and more rewarding work. And since my journey is not over, I want to share the meaningful outcomes, as well as the challenges that remain.

Five years after beginning my career as a tenure-track faculty member, I decided to leave academia to place myself and my work in direct conversation with and proximity to those I was researching and explicitly committed to—Black communities and their residents. This idea seemed controversial to my colleagues in the Eurocentric field of sociology that obsessively studies people and their patterns, yet seem allergic to actual human interaction. While I, too, recognized the value of critical distance as a necessity for credible sociological research, two events had reminded me that distance comes at a high cost: Hurricane Katrina and the death of my father. Because of these events, I began to radically reshape my professional identity to position myself in community, opting for moments of distance instead of a lifetime of it.

Hurricane Katrina happened a year after I became an assistant professor. I watched this devasting event unfold over 12 heartbreaking days from some 1,300 miles away. Occupied with the demands of my new position, I felt helpless and unable to return to my hometown of Houston to provide direct assistance. Moreover, I wanted to do more than volunteer in the relief effort. I wanted to utilize my specialized skills as a researcher and a social movement scholar to develop effective strategies to ensure displaced residents a structural opportunity to return home. I was unable to do that from my office on campus. The loss of life in New Orleans, the loss of community, and the loss of African American history and culture still haunt me.

DOI: 10.4324/9781003199113-22

From my office I was also unable to care for my father, as I had hoped to, in his final phase of life. When he was first admitted to the hospital with heart failure, I returned to Houston to attend to him with a promise to relocate him to live with me as soon as possible. I felt hopeful and incredibly blessed to be financially and emotionally positioned to care for him, which symbolized our relationship and my life coming full circle. My father's love had anchored me as a child in a turbulent world, and, as his daughter and oldest child, I wanted to support his healing physically, mentally, and emotionally. Yet my father transitioned on an October evening in 2006 as I was sitting in my office at the university revising a research paper for publication before returning to Houston.

My father's unexpected passing and the tragedy of Hurricane Katrina filled me with overwhelming doubt that my chosen path and the considerable training that I had received in white male—oriented institutions would allow me to produce "serious, diligent, and thoughtful intellectual work" powerful enough to significantly contribute to Black women and our communities. Doing so would require a paradigm that could uproot and replace the "taken-for-granted assumptions" and values embedded in traditional research that inherently produce inequity in our work.[1] Community-based participatory research (CBPR) is that paradigm because it is a principle-oriented approach that minimizes the gulf between research and action, as well as scholar and community.

When I first learned of CBPR, I was simultaneously excited and relieved. I was on the path to emancipate myself from the tight grip of traditional training and yet still stand firm in my identity as a researcher, and the ten principles of CBPR offered me guidance on how to practice sociology in a way that was "self-reflective, engaged and self-critical,"[2] which was something I had not received in my doctoral training. CBPR gave me a framework for (1) creating knowledge in deep relationship with communities that honored Black feminism's intention of collective action and (2) producing science from a critical theoretical perspective, which I assert aligns with Black feminism. Therefore, I contend that adherence to these guidelines stimulates the "alertness needed for oppositional knowledge projects" that is a fundamental goal of Black feminism.[3] In this chapter, I discuss the ten principles of CBPR through sharing three projects that I have undertaken to animate this idea.

Principles of Community-Based Participatory Research and Black Feminism

CBPR encourages the mindfulness that research involves several critical decision points that impact how our intellectual work aligns with the values of Black feminism. Moreover, each principle builds our

Table 17.1 Principles for Community-Based Participatory Research

Principle One: Focus on topics that are relevant to local communities.
Principle Two: Recognize, distinguish, and respect community as a unique and vital partner in the research process.
Principle Three: Facilitate collaborative, equitable partnership in all phases of the research.
Principle Four: Embrace the skills, strengths, resources, and assets of local individuals and organizations.
Principle Five: Openly address issues of race, ethnicity, racism and social class, and embody cultural humility.
Principle Six: Balance between research and social action.
Principle Seven: Promote co-learning and capacity building that attend to social inequalities.
Principle Eight: Develop cyclical and interactive processes.
Principle Nine: Disseminate knowledge gained to the broader community and involve all partners in the wider dissemination process.
Principle Ten: Offer a long-term commitment to all partners and support sustainability.

capacity to recognize inequities and advance justice in our work of producing knowledge. Table 17.1 specifies the principles that CBPR scholars employ to maintain their commitment to conducting research with a thoughtful approach that creates knowledge advancing social change.

These ten principles address how we produce knowledge, how we determine who consumes knowledge, and the role that power plays in both dynamics. These guidelines provide a value-based approach to developing and conducting research that encourages scholars to challenge the assumptions and practices of traditional research. In the following section, I will detail three projects that utilize research to inform social action on issues that impact the quality of life of Black women and their communities. I will demonstrate how CBPR has allowed me to engage research as a creative power to strengthen communities as reservoirs of mutual support for Black women and others similarly situated in structures of domination. Through these distinct projects, I will detail the challenges I faced at various stages of the research process and the rewards I received from maintaining a commitment to embody the consciousness of Black feminism in my research practice.

Collaborating With African American Leaders

One of my first CBPR projects involved working with a group of African American residents who wanted to create more opportunities for walking and biking in their neighborhoods to improve their health and strengthen their sense of community. A faculty member from a local university, who had already secured a national grant for a larger project, invited me into the project to collect survey data. I immediately attended to the power dynamic in my relationship with the residents and employed the third principle of CBPR, which directs scholars to facilitate collaborative, equitable partnership in all phases of research rather than exercise power over communities in ways that reinforce the belief that those who create knowledge cannot be trusted. Before submitting anything to the faculty member, I discussed my project budget with the residents, shared a draft of the contract between my organization and the university, and developed a memorandum of understanding between my organization and the residents. By making myself vulnerable through radical transparency, I was able to establish trust with residents, as well as shift some power from the university to the community.

Specifically, sharing the budget required my willingness to share with the community leaders how much the university was paying me for my intellectual work, which was uncomfortable for me because of the economic realities of the community. To address this imbalance in the budget, I included funds to train and hire residents to serve as community researchers on the project, as well as pay each resident to complete a survey. This suggestion was new to the leaders, who assumed that resident involvement required a willingness to give their time and their information voluntarily. The resulting conversation allowed us to collectively analyze how a request for residents to volunteer as their only means of participation assumes that everyone has access to the same amount of discretionary time and financial resources.

Compensating the community researchers and the survey respondents allowed me to exemplify, through the project, a value for Black women and their community as agents of knowledge. This was my way of activating the seventh CBPR principle, which is to promote co-learning and capacity building that attends to social inequalities rather than contribute to academics' continued exploitation of Black women in their communities. This principle embodies the belief in Black feminism that an interdependence exists between the taken-for-granted knowledge of Black women in communities and the specialized knowledge of Black women scholars. Consistent with the empathy that is part of Black feminism, CBPR encourages scholars to intentionally build reciprocal relationships that provide opportunities for an exchange of knowledge, skills, and resources as an integral part of the research process.

To communicate their role in the project and pride in their work, the residents created badges for themselves. Although I am sharing these findings for the first time in a publication, the residents routinely presented our collaborative research process and the valuable data that we collected

to fellow residents, local and national potential funders, and elected offi-
cials to advocate for needed resources to improve their community and the
lives of their neighbors.

My relationships with community members involved in the project
were not only more genuine and equitable through my employment of
CBPR principles, but the quality of the data also exceeded (the potential funder's) expectations. With four residents employed as community
researchers, we collected nearly 600 surveys throughout the neighborhood.
The primary data clarified the community understanding of mobility patterns and indicated that residents preferred walking rather than biking.
Also, the residents reported that they were currently walking two to three
times a week and reported a desire to walk more if city leaders built more
sidewalks, as well as if safety increased. This collaboration offered me several opportunities to employ CBPR and effectively utilize my skills as a
researcher to inform social action to improve the quality of life of Black
women and their community.

Collaborating With African American and Latino Mothers

I employed CBPR to guide my work in another project involving a large
nonprofit's efforts to improve the health of economically challenged children in predominantly African American and Latino communities, as a
means of supporting their academic success. Initially, a team of university
researchers designed the project, and one of the nonprofit's funders rec-
ommended that I assist the team in better understanding the healthcare
priorities of the students and their parents. My role involved developing a
strategy to administer surveys to approximately 1,000 students attending
schools located across 14 communities and an estimated 2,500 parents.

Because the community of focus was not actively involved in initiat-
ing the research, CBPR was instrumental in guiding my involvement in
the project and advocacy for greater equity in a project that employed a
very traditional research approach. For instance, the funder and nonprofit
had defined the research agenda, and the university-based researchers were
responsible for developing the survey instrument, analyzing the data, and
writing a report sharing the findings, as well as proposing a set of recommendations to better address the needs of the students through the services
of the nonprofit's school-based clinics. Though my power was limited in
the grand scheme of the project, I fully exercised my agency to advocate
for students and parents to be more central drivers in the project—both
in terms of defining the priorities of the research and having compensated
roles in acquiring and validating data. I was implementing the first and
second principles of CBPR, which direct scholars to focus their research
on topics that are relevant to local communities and recognize, distinguish,

and respect communities as unique and vital partners in the research process rather than sites for our work.

The project became more equitable through my insistence that the university researchers and the nonprofit increase the involvement of the community of focus in the research process. Consequently, we conducted focus groups with students and parents from the target schools to offer them the opportunity to validate the instrument. Both groups provided valuable amendments to the wording of the survey and suggested new questions and responses to reflect the needs for nonmedical services to support academic success.

I negotiated compensation for the students and parents who participated in the focus groups, and I allocated additional funds in the project budget to hire and train community members to collect the data and enter it into the primary database. Since I was successful in accessing these additional funds, I recruited students and parents from the focus groups to serve as community researchers to support their continued valuable involvement in the research process.

I held weekly training with the team, composed of African American and Latino women and girls, which focused on research methodology, data analysis, and culturally competent community engagement strategies. By positioning local individuals—students and parents—as skilled, strong, and resourceful instead of as powerless victims of the injustices they faced, the fourth principle of CBPR, I supported these women and their daughters in "see[ing] their true class interests" to build solidarity and community with each other.[4] Together we established collective goals that we achieved through accountability and interdependence. And through the research process, the women and girls of color were engaged, informed, compensated, and better positioned to impact change in their communities. Many expressed continuous gratitude for the additional income that the project provided their families.

The ninth principle of CBPR directs scholars to disseminate knowledge gained to the broader community and involve all partners in a broader dissemination process rather than concentrating effects on sharing our work in conventional ways with consumers of traditional research. This principle reflects a belief that we collectively own the valuable knowledge that we create in partnership with communities. Although invited to participate in formal presentations to share the project's findings, the women and students declined. Instead, the mothers requested support in utilizing the data to speak to school administrators and teachers about their concerns for their children. The students asked for assistance in using the data to discuss their needs with their parents. For these women, making presentations about the findings of the project was less important. Therefore, the mothers and students determined the highest and best use of the data. These mothers and students wanted to use their newly gained knowledge to speak directly to the individuals who were closest to them in the decision-making process. This experience reminded me that I do not always occupy the same structural position as the women and the communities at the center of my work, which requires me to acknowledge that I do not benefit in the same way from research. Therefore, CBPR challenges me to engage Black women in assisting me in deepening the meaning of knowledge, diversifying the recipients of knowledge, and discovering new pathways to share knowledge, which is a manifestation of the overarching belief that Black women are indeed creative agents.

Collaborating in Service to an African American Community

After collaborating on a series of projects, I initiated a partnership with a university-based researcher to employ the principles of CBPR to inform the work of a community-led effort to protect, preserve, and revitalize a historic African American community that was facing gentrification. Specifically, the project involved developing and administering an in-person survey to determine the needs of the residents in the community, who were vulnerable to displacement. As a third-generation resident of this community, I felt the project was deeply personal. As a Black feminist scholar with a set of valuable skills, I felt immensely obligated to "do serious, diligent, and thoughtful intellectual work" that contributed to the lives of Black women and others in my community.[5] The sixth principle of CBPR was instrumental in guiding me in seeking a balance between research and social action to counter the existing practice of developing a project that prioritizes developing an interesting dataset and publishable findings, which I strongly believed to be inappropriate and detrimental to this community. As a Black feminist, this CBPR principle held me accountable and responsible for "producing work to purposely . . . dismantle unjust intellectual and political structures."[6] Therefore, the expressed goal of the project was to produce data to address the social, economic, and political problems facing this African American neighborhood through contributing to the self-determination of the stakeholders and residents of the community.

To achieve this goal, I had to be willing to face challenges that might threaten my integrity and erode the benefit of the project to the community. One of the first significant challenges involved the research funders' discomfort with me serving in the role of co-principle researcher and resident leader. Additionally, I faced resistance from the community stakeholders, who were reluctant to recognize the value of the project and to prioritize the research data in our collective efforts. As with the funders, they had become overly reliant on me functioning in the role of a community organizer. They resisted my attempt to situate myself as a thought leader in developing evidence-based strategies supporting residents' social mobility to protect them from displacement.

Also, there was a lack of appreciation for how my lived experiences and scholarly expertise were significant contributions to the project. Analyzing the skepticism that I faced through the consciousness and framework of Black feminism, I had to affirm within myself the belief that my acquired skills as a scholar and my lived experience as a young single mother both gave me the power to create knowledge reflective of the priorities of my community and useful for effective social action. Furthermore, I had to find the courage to advocate for myself as I had done for others. I specifically addressed the amount of time I was investing in our collective work without any support for my small nonprofit organization, which was unsustainable and inequitable based on the resources being made available to other community stakeholders. More importantly, I fought to bring my full self into our collective work, which for me meant shifting our attention and resources to the residents who were experiencing the most significant effects of gentrification but were absent from our leadership table.

It is essential to acknowledge the critical support that I received from my African American female collaborator on the project, who leveraged her position at the university to advocate for my expertise with CBPR to the funders. Her advocacy for me increased my belief in myself and strengthened my commitment to employing an approach to research that aligned with my identity as a Black feminist. However, as a Black feminist functioning outside of a traditional organization, it was incredibly difficult maintaining an equitable collaboration throughout the research process with my co-investigator, situated at a large academic institution. Despite our expressed commitment to CBPR, we were operating from distinctively different organizational contexts. After not receiving an email response from me within an expected timeframe, she demanded that I adopt her university's standard approach of committing a certain percentage of my time each day to our project. I explained to her that our contractual agreement stipulated that the funder paid me an hourly fee to complete a set of tasks, which I had yet failed to do. Additionally, I felt extremely uncomfortable with the flawed belief that a grant could sufficiently compensate me for the inherent value of my time and lived knowledge that I was investing in the project.

To move forward, we both recommitted ourselves to caring for and supporting each other in ways that worked best for us based on our individual needs. The fifth CBPR principle encouraged me to openly address the confusing issues of race, ethnicity, racism, and social class that impacted our relationship and team dynamics (rather than ignore these systems of oppression). As a Black feminist sociologist, this principle was a valuable reminder to me of the need to contribute to the consciousness of Black women and others inside and outside of the academy to increase their understanding of the interlocking nature of oppression that impacts their lives on multiple levels. Patricia Collins writes, "African American women and other individuals in subordinate groups become empowered when we understand and use those dimensions of our individual, group, and disciplinary ways of knowing that foster our humanity as fully human subjects."[7]

This situation led to us employing the eighth principle of CBPR, which directs scholars to develop cyclical and interactive processes (rather than reproducing the hierarchical systems that place us in positions over and beneath others). This principle mandated that my co-investor and I commit ourselves to actively replace the norms, values, and practices that we had inherited from academic institutions. As a Black feminist scholar, I was able to contribute to a culture of producing work through a set of practices that nurtured and sustained the collective humanity of the members of the project. Furthermore, I was able to request the agency I needed as a Black feminist doing work in an African American community that was seeking to increase the self-determination of its residents.

Achieving fairness and equitable treatment for myself strengthened my commitment to the principles of CBPR. Consequently, the project hired and trained a team of residents to assist with developing the survey instrument and administer it in door-to-door surveys, which created full-time employment for the team for more than a year. These community researchers completed questionnaires with some 4,000 residents, who were compensated $50 each for their information and time. The $50 exceeded the residents' expectations and conveyed value for their time, as well as compassion for their economic circumstances. After completing the data collection, several of the community researchers transitioned to other research projects. Additionally, several increased their civic involvement in the neighborhood and began to use their experiences to advocate for others, as well as themselves.

An Invitation to Black Feminists

The collective heartbreaking tragedy of Hurricane Katrina and the personally devastating sudden death of my father unearthed truths within me that mandated I reconceptualize my work as a Black feminist scholar. I needed to narrow the divide between me and the communities of people that mattered deeply to me. Employing the principles of CBPR through the consciousness of Black feminism, I am bridging the physical and intellectual gaps that my academic training manufactured, as well as resolving contradictions in the "the political economy of the production and the consumption of knowledge itself."[8] This value-oriented approach to research encourages me to prioritize forming equitable partnerships based on respect and trust with communities to create knowledge that informs social action. Collaborating with academic researchers, community leaders, local residents, mothers, and students has been profoundly meaningful, not only because of the data that we gathered but because of the empathetic way in which it was gathered, which I invite more Black feminists to experience as a way of working. CBPR gives me the tools I need to resist and replace oppression with equity that offers a compassionate way of being with myself and with others.

Lastly, the tenth principle of CBPR is a reminder to place a value on the relationships that I establish through my work. This principle directs me to make a long-term commitment to those I collaborate with through research rather than treat relationships with communities as transactional. This principle recognizes that creating new knowledge is not enough to realize the social change we desire. Eradicating social injustice requires sustained collective effort. CBPR invites Black feminists to build community with Black women outside of the academy and invest the necessary resources in establishing mutually beneficial relationships. Patricia Hill Collins reminds Black feminists of the intrinsic reciprocity in this approach when she writes, "By making the community stronger, African-American women become empowered, and that same community can serve as a source of support when Black women encounter race, gender, and class oppression."[9]

Notes

1. Patricia Hill Collins. 1988. "The Social Construction of Black Feminist Thought." *Signs* 14: 772.
2. Ibid., 181.
3. Ibid., 137.
4. Patricia Hill Collins. 2000. *Black Feminist Thought: Knowledge, Consciousness, and the Politics of Empowerment*, 287. 2nd ed. New York: Unwin Hyman.
5. Patricia Hill Collins. 2016. "Black Feminist Thought as Oppositional Knowledge." *Departures in Critical Qualitative Research* 5: 134.
6. Ibid.
7. Patricia Hill Collins. 1990. *Black Feminist Thought: Knowledge, Consciousness, and the Politics of Empowerment*, 58. 1st ed. Boston, MA: Routledge.
8. Collins 2016, 134.
9. Collins 1990, 223.

References

Collins, Patricia Hill. 1988. "The Social Construction of Black Feminist Thought." *Signs* 14: 772.

Collins, Patricia Hill. 1990. *Black Feminist Thought: Knowledge, Consciousness, and the Politics of Empowerment.* 1st ed. Boston, MA: Unwin Hyman.

Collins, Patricia Hill. 2000. *Black Feminist Thought: Knowledge, Consciousness, and the Politics of Empowerment.* 2nd ed. New York: Routledge.

Collins, Patricia Hill. 2016. "Black Feminist Thought as Oppositional Knowledge." *Departures in Critical Qualitative Research* 5: 133–144. https://doi.org/10.1525/dcqr.2016.5.3.133

Chapter 18

Doing It for Ourselves
Research Justice and Black Feminist Sociology

Julia Chinyere Oparah

Through a community-based study of Black women and the maternal healthcare crisis, this chapter explores the power and potential of research justice as a tool to democratize Black feminist sociology. Starting with the seminal work of Patricia Hill Collins, I trace the transformative impact of Black feminism on the intellectual trajectories of those of us schooled within "second wave" Black feminist sociology in the 1990s and early 2000s. Building on this foundational work, Black women academic and community researchers using the "research justice" paradigm are pushing the discipline to evolve. This work has manifested most powerfully in the community-driven research efforts that undergird the Black women's birth justice movement. I argue that the next wave of Black feminist sociology will engage deeply with community-based critiques of the politics and process of knowledge production, put research capacities into the hands of those most directly impacted by interlocking structures of dominance, and challenge the commodification of the outcomes of our research endeavors.

Early Encounters

I entered a sociology PhD program in the early 1990s with a clear agenda: I wanted to counter the erasure of Black women's activism from scholarly accounts and to correct the representation of Black women in Britain as triply oppressed, silenced, and passive. Unlike many of my peers in the program, I had the benefit of being grounded in a grassroots movement and supported by other Black women activists who also wanted our story to be told. During the daytime, I was coordinator of Osaba Women's Center, a community organization that served as an anchor for Black families surviving racism, government neglect, drugs, unemployment, and gender-based violence. In the evenings, I drove to Warwick University, which was located on the outskirts of Coventry but symbolically named for the wealthier market town of Warwick, eight miles southwest of campus.

DOI: 10.4324/9781003199113-23

Leaving the dilapidated housing projects and blight of my neighborhood and entering the world apart of the university was a constant reminder that I would have to struggle to make my education relevant and to hold onto the clarity and confidence with which I entered.

My experience of sociology coursework was probably no different from that of other Black women on both sides of the Atlantic entering PhD programs at that time.[1] I gained a new language to talk about the relationships between people and social structures, got excited about social movement theory, and battled the professors on how much attention we should pay to what the founding social theorists had to say (or not) about slavery, racism, and empire. I was angry and frustrated that all the authors in my theory class were dead white men, grateful for the allyship of a South Asian student who tackled Marx's position on colonialism, thrilled when we were introduced to (white) feminist methodologies, and then disappointed when they turned out to have little of use to say about race. Above all, I hungered for fellow Black women sociologists—I was the only Black woman in my cohort—and for the possibility of a different sociology, one that I didn't have to spend my time critiquing, debunking, and dismantling. I needed a sociological lens and toolkit that would aid in the production of knowledge that could serve the communities of resistance that I was embedded in. I needed a usable sociology that took Black women's lives seriously.

And then I encountered *Black Feminist Thought*.[2] Collins shared that disorienting experience of entering the white academy, seeking to seize its opportunities to serve Black communities.[3] When she wrote about the "Eurocentric, masculinist knowledge validation process,"[4] it was is if she had been there in the classroom with me, reading the texts that erased Black British women's activism and agency and refusing the versions of social theory that relegated Black women to the status of workers, bodies, or an unmentioned absence. Her analysis of Black women's "outsider within" standpoint gave me permission to honor the voices and perspectives of Black women activists in my own research.[5] Collins's seminal work on the "matrix of domination" provided the theoretical tools I needed to unpack the tensions and complexities I encountered within the Black women's movement in Britain. Her discussion of the ethics of care, accountability to community, and research as dialogue served as a roadmap for me as an emerging researcher seeking to conduct research within communities that I was a part of and deeply committed to. Collins's epistemology laid the groundwork for an ethical engagement with the communities that are holders of the knowledge we seek to document, one that is grounded in solidarity and caring. In so doing, she allowed me to bring my whole self to my work as a sociologist, and to enter field research encounters with a critical eye and an open heart.

Evolutions

I share this personal intellectual genealogy because it captures an important moment in the evolution of Black feminist sociology transnationally. Many of the Black feminist PhDs who entered academe in the new millennium will never have encountered that first edition of Collins's canonical text, with its grey and blue cover. Instead, they will have met the book after Collins made significant revisions to address themes and critiques in the rapidly growing literature.[6] The revised edition, and Collins's later work, would make greater efforts to tackle subaltern genders and sexualities, to acknowledge the specificity of the "Black" in Black feminist thought, noting the work of African, Caribbean, and other diasporic voices, and to engage Black millennial popular culture.[7] As Black feminist sociology has evolved, previously marginal voices, including some of the authors in this volume, have challenged some of its underlying assumptions.[8] Black queer and trans scholars have critiqued Black feminism's uninterrogated allegiance to binary notions of gender and have developed a queer Black feminist sociology that works to reveal and dismantle the violence caused by the surveillance and policing of Black non-normative genders and sexualities. African and Caribbean feminist scholars have pointed out the marginalization of non-US and non-Anglo Black scholars in the Black feminist "canon" and have argued for a transnational Black feminism that explores horizontal solidarities across geographic and linguistic borders. And emerging millennial scholars have pushed their more established colleagues to take digital youth cultures and social media activism seriously.

Despite these impressive advances, I believe that Black feminist sociology has yet to fulfil the promise embedded in Collins's early epistemological inquiry. For sure, we have developed radical intersectional analyses, worked in solidarity with social movements to defend Black lives, extended the canon—first beyond white males, and then beyond US borders—and created an intellectual "home" where Black students and PhDs can thrive and produce relevant knowledge. Yet, the answer to the critical question "Who can produce knowledge?" remains troubling. With few exceptions, Black feminist sociologists have become absorbed into the knowledge production machine in ways that leave untouched the power dynamics between researcher and researched. Whether graduate student, postdoctoral fellow, or faculty, we are still usually the ones who set research agendas, determine how research should be conducted, analyze data, write up our findings, determine how they should be disseminated, and reap the financial and career benefits. Even where we are engaged in activist scholarship in the service of social movements, we often serve as the social historian or allied researcher, working *alongside* community colleagues rather than *sharing* the experience of conducting research and producing knowledge.

This concentration of sociological expertise and methodological tools in the hands of a group of trained experts creates what is known as a "knowledge elite." Knowledge elites typically enjoy and defend access to resources that other community members do not, from postdoctoral fellowships and academic salaries to research grants and invitations to international conferences. That those resources are hard won and the result of much sacrifice in the case of Black women graduate students and academics makes it only harder to consider relinquishing some of the power, privilege, and perks that come along with membership. In the next section, I will explore how a group of Black birth justice activists used a research justice approach to upend traditional research power relations and suggest some implications for democratizing Black feminist sociology.

Democratizing Research

In 2011, a small group of Black women came together in an Oakland, California, home to talk about their experiences of childbirth and the maternal healthcare system. We were mothers, grandmothers, doulas, youth and community organizers and reproductive justice advocates whose birth experiences ranged from highly medicalized hospital birth to unassisted homebirth. Despite our differences, we shared an urgent sense that there was something broken in the maternal health system, that Black women's lives and the lives of our infants were unnecessarily being placed at risk, and that the medical coercion and abuse that we had experienced firsthand must be challenged. At that first meeting, the group decided to form a grassroots organization, adopting the name Black Women Birthing Justice (BWBJ) and creating a definition of birth justice that has become a part of the mainstream reproductive justice lexicon:

> We believe that Birth Justice exists when women and transfolks are empowered during pregnancy, labor, childbirth and postpartum to make healthy decisions for themselves and their babies. Birth Justice is part of a wider movement against reproductive oppression. It aims to dismantle inequalities of race, class, gender and sexuality that lead to negative birth experiences, especially for women of color, low-income women, survivors of violence, immigrant women, queer and transfolks, and women in the Global South. Working for Birth Justice involves educating the community, and challenging abuses by medical personnel and overuse of medical interventions. It also involves advocating for universal access to culturally appropriate, women-centered health care. It includes the right to choose whether or not to carry a pregnancy, to choose when, where, how, and with whom to birth, including access to traditional and indigenous birth-workers, such as midwives and doulas, and the right to breastfeeding support.[9]

Negative experiences of maternal healthcare can be life-threatening. Approximately 700 people die from pregnancy-related causes each year in the US, more than any other industrialized nation, and tens of thousands more suffer life-threatening complications. According to the Centers for Disease Control Foundation, over 3 in 5 of these deaths were preventable. While maternal mortality rates are declining across the globe, the maternal mortality rate in the US increased between 2010 and 2014 despite higher rates of healthcare spending than countries with better maternal outcomes. Black women and infants in particular face high rates of preventable death and morbidity: Black pregnant individuals are four times as likely to die from pregnancy-related causes than white individuals. Black infants have higher rates of premature birth and low birthweight than any other racial group and are twice as likely as white babies to die before their first birthday.[10]

Concern about these racial disparities has led to significant funding to support medical research and related public health interventions aimed at tackling maternal and infant mortality. Yet these efforts have done little to transform Black women's birth experiences and outcomes. Most medical research into maternal health outcomes is conducted by evaluating birth, medical, and death records. These data may enable valuable analyses about patterns of morbidity and mortality, but separated from the lived experiences of the pregnant individuals whose bodies are mined to produce expert knowledge, they do little to improve the lives of those most affected by the patterns they document.

Black bodies have long been used for medical research, resulting in what Harriet Washington describes as "medical apartheid"—the exploitation of Black people, living and deceased, as subjects for research to benefit white physicians and patients.[11] Building on Washington's analysis, I introduced the concept of "obstetrical apartheid" to explain the racist heroism of the "medical giants," from François Prevost to J. Marion Simms, who developed the tools and science of obstetrics.[12] Lauded as heroes and founding figures, these physicians made medical advances by conducting violent, often fatal medical experiments on enslaved Black women. Today research subjects are protected from overt research violence by protocols and ethics review boards. Yet the colonial relations of research established at the inception of medical research in the US continue to undergird research norms. Ethical review protocols, put in place to protect "human subjects", conceive of research participants as individuals who must be protected from physical and psychological harm. They seldom address group rights to participation, or protection from group exploitation and marginalization. In the absence of such considerations, Black women are rarely consulted about how research about our reproductive lives should be conducted, analyzed, and disseminated and our voices and lived experiences are seldom included in the research. Our medical and death records are mined for data without our explicit consent, standing in as proxy for our bodies, and allowing researchers to become "experts" on Black maternal health without ever speaking to or consulting a Black woman. Our voices, our agency, and our interpretations of how we live in our bodies, carry and push out our babies are silenced and ignored. In these ways, Black women continue to experience contemporary research injustice rooted in the logics of medical apartheid.[13]

In the context of histories of research abuse, "over-researching," and lack of meaningful participation experienced by communities of color, some indigenous scholars have called for a politics of "refusal," whereby communities simply refuse to participate in the colonial logics of Western knowledge production.[14] Reclaiming sovereignty through refusal is a powerful stance, yet one that leaves us without new ways of producing knowledge. Rather than turning away from research because of its origins as a tool of colonialism and patriarchal racism, an understanding of the troubled history of research injustice has inspired anti-racist and indigenous researchers to turn toward decolonial methodologies. At the center of these transformative approaches to research are questions of participation and epistemology. Influenced by Linda Tuhiwai Smith's seminal text *Decolonizing Methodologies*, decolonial researchers have been emboldened to ask questions like: "Who knows our community's needs best?" "Who decides what counts as knowledge?" "Whose knowledge is recognized, validated, and cited?" and "Who is this knowledge for, anyway?"[15]

Birthing Knowledge

Given the history of research injustice, the members of Black Women Birthing Justice approached the idea of conducting a research project with some skepticism. While there was consensus that we wanted to document and lift up Black women's stories about their experiences of maternal healthcare, there was less agreement on what that meant. As an activist scholar who was familiar with using research to uncover injustice and motivate change, I suggested that we should call ourselves a research team and seek funding for a community-based research project. Other members of the group rejected the label "research" as too university-based and elitist and preferred to see the work of listening to and honoring women's stories as a form of community outreach and sharing among sisters. Sohng argues that participatory research encompasses both knowledge production and community organizing, and encourages researchers to view community outreach and development as important competencies.[16] For BWBJ, the concept of "research justice" provided a bridge between these two modalities and gave us a radically alternative understanding of research that all our members could embrace.

Coined by former Oakland community-based organization 'The Data-Center: Research for Justice, research justice seeks to replace traditional knowledge production norms with an approach that privileges political empowerment and cultural sovereignty.[17] According to DataCenter, research justice "is achieved when marginalized communities are recognized as experts, and reclaim, own and wield all forms of knowledge and information."[18] Research justice builds on participatory action research (PAR), a paradigm that seeks to break down hierarchies between experts and communities, researchers and research subjects by placing research capabilities into the hands of communities most directly impacted by social ills and driving community-led action as a result.

PAR originated in radical social movements in Latin America in the 1960s, and PAR principles have been adopted selectively in US academia, particularly in youth, education, and health research. A version of PAR, called community-based participatory research, has gained recognition among health researchers as a way to involve impacted communities in research and generate more sustainable and culturally sensitive outcomes. CBPR has been criticized for replicating the very hierarchies between knowledge haves and have-nots that PAR first set out to dismantle, due to its focus on participation as a way to support research agendas driven by academic and government researchers.[19] In contrast, research justice emphasizes community-driven research with community control "over all stages of the 'knowledge lifecycle'—from producing, analyzing, interpreting, packaging and deploying knowledge."[20]

Where knowledge elites validate only one form of knowledge, specifically knowledge written in scholarly language, dissociated from bodies and emotions and affiliated with academic institutions, the research justice paradigm legitimates other ways of knowing. Alongside "expert" or "scientific" knowledge, research justice elevates embodied, experiential, cultural, and sacred knowledge. According to Black indigenous scholar Andrew Jolivette, this allows for the infusion of "radical love, transformative justice and collective action" as interconnected methodological components.[21]

Love. Spirit. Action. Collective power. These were concepts that many of the members of BWBJ had not previously associated with research. Starting with these concepts meant that we could not simply apply the research methods that I had learned during my PhD program. The methodology texts I studied said nothing about bringing the sacred into the research process; they failed to mention the role that Black love might play in meaningful research relationships, and they seldom addressed questions of power and control. We had to design a new research process, one that would allow for embodied and metaphysical knowledge and would enable participants and co-researchers to co-create a container for the powerful emotions associated with birth, loss, and medical trauma.

So we threw out the textbooks and instead asked how we might elicit truth, nourish hearts, and create a space to begin healing journeys, both for ourselves and for our participants. We did not conduct individual interviews, deciding that the one-on-one dynamic of the interview would only serve to isolate women with their stories. We also rejected the traditional focus group model where the researcher asks a set of open-ended questions, facilitates discussion, and records responses. Instead we invited women to share their stories at a sharing circle. The circles used traditional research protocols to the extent they were useful: women read and signed consent forms, children were dropped off to childcare, and the circles were recorded and transcribed. But there, the similarity with traditional research methods ended. The circles became "a ceremonial act of mutual respect and co-sharing";[22] we began with a non-Christian invocation and grounding, inviting ancestors into the space and asking spirit to make space for deep seeing and healing. Participants were invited to speak for as long as they felt called to in response to one question: "What was your vision for your birth, and how did the reality compare?" After feedback from women who had experienced pregnancy and infant loss that hearing birth stories could be retraumatizing, we held a circle dedicated to women who had experienced loss, which included a ritual of altar building. Given the affirmation, patient listening, and support of a circle of women, participants shared at length; for some, telling their full birth story or sharing painful experiences of pregnancy loss for the first time. BWBJ co-researchers often shared their stories with the other participants, blurring the hierarchies between researcher and participant. Together we held space for love, joy, and pain. We awoke and touched parts of ourselves that had yet to heal, wept, shared, and laughed together.

As an academic researcher, adopting a research justice approach required far more of me than my previous research experiences. I found myself called on to go beyond my comfort zone emotionally and in turn found my emotional intelligence expanding as we held space for the deeper level of sharing enabled by the spiritual context. I had to encounter and address my own losses and trauma, seeking out emotional support as the moving and often painful stories triggered my own memories. I found my spiritual and intellectual worlds coming together, and experienced vulnerability, humility, and personal growth.

Once set in motion, the research justice approach disrupted the "researcher" role that I had been used to and forced me to let go of control. I was no longer making decisions about the research process according to my Black feminist principles and sociological expertise; instead decisions were made collaboratively and, at times, in ways that I didn't initially agree with. For example, I was very influenced by feminist critiques of quantitative methods, and I initially wanted to use only qualitative data. The collective wisdom ruled otherwise, since BWBJ members opined that supporting the stories with quantitative data gathered from a question-naire would help influence policy-makers. Ultimately, the more compre-hensive information that we obtained by putting the questionnaire data into conversation with the sharing circle transcripts and birthworker inter-views was so valuable that I was glad to have been outvoted. At the time, however, letting go of control over the research process was disorienting. My success as a Black feminist PhD student and then scholar had in so many ways relied on my ability to carve out and follow my own path, but this trailblazing and oppositional stance was not helpful in this context. Instead, I had to seek out and honor the collective wisdom of the group.

Timing was another challenge. As the only academic in the group, I could dedicate more time to the work than other members whose paid work and family responsibilities restricted their available time. This some-times meant that things moved more slowly than I wanted them to and I had to relax and resist seizing the reins out of frustration. The research project became a huge time commitment that spanned nearly five years of data collection and occupied many weekends. While I believed that we had reached saturation point after about 60 stories, the optimal number typically offered in qualitative research texts, the collective decided that it would be meaningful to be able to say that we had collected 100 stories. Again I was overruled, and again the collective wisdom turned out to be right: in the last few circles, we heard from our first HIV-positive par-ticipant, and were able to conduct a sharing circle with teen mothers that revealed specific challenges related to body image and breastfeeding. Tran-scribing and analyzing the data was also time-consuming. Student interns did much of the transcription, which meant that the work slowed to a standstill during exam times. Our goal was for the entire collective to be involved in interpreting and analyzing the data. In the end, we identified key quotes and had group discussions about them, following which I and another member wrote up the draft study and members gave feedback. In all, it took almost over a year to draft, discuss, and finalize the result: *Bat-tling Over Birth*.[23]

A research justice framework encourages us to interrogate the politics of knowledge dissemination and to challenge the commodification of socio-logical findings. Given that a sole author book contract with a university press can be the determining factor in a tenure decision, junior academ-ics seldom feel empowered to make social justice-informed choices about research dissemination. But failing to do so diminishes the radical potential of our work and limits who will access and use it to inform change. Our previous collaborative book project, *Birthing Justice*, was originally slated to be published by South End Press. However, when the independent fem-inist publisher ceased operations, the rights were purchased by Routledge and the book was published at a price that made it inaccessible for many community members and birthworkers. With this experience in mind, we decided to self-publish the results of our research online in an open-access format. Ultimately, our self-published website could not handle the numerous attempted downloads of the lengthy report, and we decided to publish with Praeclarus, a small independent press specializing in women's health topics, with the agreement that they would sell the paperback for no more than $20 as well as a cheaper Kindle edition. Digital media can also play a critical role in disseminating knowledge. We used a digital media campaign, with the hashtags #liberateblackbirth, #battlingoverbirth and #respectblackbirth, memes, tweets, blogs, webinars and a growing Facebook community, to raise awareness about the themes of the book, share the stories with a wider audience, and motivate readers to action.

Concluding Reflections

Black feminist sociologists occupy a contradictory positionality: on the one hand, we are "outsiders within" academia, motivated by our lived experiences of marginality to produce insurgent knowledge and serve movements for justice. On the other hand, as members of a knowledge elite, we are afforded access to legitimacy and resources as a result of our training, qualifications, and academic affiliations, and inculcated into a mode of engagement that diminishes community agency by consolidating decision-making power in the hands of the "expert" researcher. Turning a research justice lens on our work as insurgent sociologists allows us to examine critically the role of the academic researcher and foster horizontal research relationships based on mutual sharing of knowledge and expertise. Collaborating with impacted communities impacted by social injustice to set research agendas, and working together to co-create every part of the research lifecycle, ensures that the time, energy, and resources that we put into our research results in usable knowledge, owned and acted on by impacted communities.

As the authors in this volume so comprehensively demonstrate, Black feminist sociology, almost 30 years after Collins's foundational volume, is vibrantly alive and relevant. As we map out the meanings and possibilities of this work, we are called on to dismantle traditional modes of engagement and let go of some of the power and authority that comes with academic degrees and status. Only by working to democratize our research endeavors will we be able to fulfill the promise of Black feminist sociology as a radically transformative theory and praxis.

A research justice framework empowers us to rethink what we've learned about research, to share power, and to let go of control over the research process. This is not easy. We will be called to deepen our emotional intelligence and to do the spiritual and psychological work that allows us to be our whole, vulnerable selves in the research process. The hygienic, organized, and linear research process of the sociological textbook will be replaced with the messiness of human emotions and conflicts, laughter and tears. We will have to grapple with how to explain concepts like community sovereignty, sacred knowledge, and Black love to institutional review boards and dissertation and tenure committees. But only through this powerful and courageous work will we be able to mobilize the full potential of sociological research in the service of communities of resistance.

Notes

1. Angela Davis. 1994. "Black Women and the Academy." *Callaloo* 17(2): 422–431. https://doi.org/10.2307/2931740
2. Patricia Hill Collins. 1991. *Black Feminist Thought: Knowledge, Consciousness, and the Politics of Empowerment.* London: Routledge. [First published by Hyman Unwin in 1990]
3. Collins, Patricia Hill. 2005a. "That's Not Why I Went to School." In *The Disobedient Generation: Social Theorists in the Sixties,* edited by Alan Sica and Stephen Turner, 94–113. Chicago, IL: University of Chicago Press.
4. Collins, 1991.
5. This work is published under my former name, Julia Sudbury. Julia Sudbury. 1998. *Other Kinds of Dreams: Black Women's Organizations and the Politics of Transformation.* London and New York: Routledge.
6. Patricia Hill Collins. 2000. *Black Feminist Thought: Knowledge, Consciousness, and the Politics of Empowerment,* x–xiii. New York: Routledge.
7. Collins, Patricia Hill. 2005b. Black Sexual Politics: African Americans, Gender and the New Racism. New York: Routledge.
8. Buchanan, Bonaparte, and Butler in this volume.
9. Black Women Birthing Justice. N.d. "What is Birth Justice?" www.blackwomenbirth ingjustice.org/what-is-birth-justice. Accessed August 6, 2019.
10. Julia Chinyere Oparah et al. 2015. "By Us Not for Us: Black Women Researching Pregnancy and Childbirth." In *Research Justice: Methodologies for Social Change,* edited by Andrew Jolivette, 21, 117–138. Bristol: Policy Press.
11. Harriet Washington. 2006. *Medical Apartheid.* New York: Doubleday.
12. Julia Chinyere Oparah and Alicia Bonaparte. 2015. *Birthing Justice: Black Women, Pregnancy and Childbirth,* 10. New York: Routledge.
13. Ibid., 2015.
14. Audra Simpson. 2007. "On Ethnographic Refusal: Indigeneity, Voice and Colonial Citizenship." *Junctures* 9 (December): 67–80.
15. Linda Tuhiwai Smith. 2012. *Decolonizing Methodologies: Research and Indigenous Peoples.* London: Zed Books.
16. Lee S. Sohng. 1996. "Participatory Research and Community Organizing." *Journal of Sociology and Social Welfare* XXIII(4): 77–97.
17. Miho Kim Lee. 2015. "Foreword." In *Research Justice: Methodologies for Social Change,* edited by Andrew Jolivette, xvii. Bristol: Policy Press.
18. Andrew Jolivette. 2015. *Research Justice: Methodologies for Social Change,* 5. Bristol: Policy Press
19. R. Hagey. 1997. "The Uses and Abuses of Participatory Action Research." *Chronic Diseases in Canada* 18(2): 1–4.
20. Kim Lee 2015, xviii.
21. Jolivette 2015, 7.
22. Ibid.
23. Julia C. Oparah, Helen Arega, and Dantia Hudson. 2018. *Battling Over Birth: Black Women and the Maternal Health Care Crisis.* London: Praeclarus Press.

References

Black Women Birthing Justice. n.d. "What Is Birth Justice?" www.blackwomenbirthingjus tice.org/what-is-birth-justice. Accessed August 6, 2019.

Building U.S. Capacity to Review and Prevent Maternal Deaths. 2018. "Report from Nine Mortality Review Committees." www.cdcfoundation.org/sites/default/files/files/Report fromNineMMRCs.pdf. Accessed August 7, 2019.

Collins, Patricia Hill. 2000. *Black Feminist Thought: Knowledge, Consciousness, and the Politics of Empowerment.* New York: Routledge.

Collins, Patricia Hill. 1991. *Black Feminist Thought: Knowledge, Consciousness, and the Politics of Empowerment.* London: Routledge. [First published by Hyman Unwin in 1990].

Collins, Patricia Hill. 2005a. "That's Not Why I Went to School." In *The Disobedient Generation: Social Theorists in the Sixties,* edited by Alan Sica and Stephen Turner, 94–113. Chicago, IL: University of Chicago Press.

Collins, Patricia Hill. 2005b. *Black Sexual Politics: African Americans, Gender and the New Racism.* New York: Routledge.

Davis, Angela. 1994. "Black Women and the Academy." *Callaloo* 17(2): 422–431. https://doi.org/10.2307/2931740

Hagey, R. 1997. "The Uses and Abuses of Participatory Action Research." *Chronic Diseases in Canada* 18(2): 1–4.

Jolivette, Andrew. 2015. *Research Justice: Methodologies for Social Change.* Bristol: Policy Press.

Kim Lee, Miho. 2015. "Foreword." In *Research Justice: Methodologies for Social Change,* edited by Andrew Jolivette, xvii. Bristol: Policy Press.

Oparah, Julia Chinyere, Helen Arega, and Dantia Hudson. 2018. *Battling Over Birth: Black Women and the Maternal Health Care Crisis.* Amarillo, TX: Praeclarus Press.

Oparah, Julia Chinyere, and Alicia Bonaparte. 2015. *Birthing Justice: Black Women, Pregnancy and Childbirth.* New York: Routledge.

Oparah, Julia Chinyere et al. 2015. "By Us Not for Us: Black Women Researching Pregnancy and Childbirth." In *Research Justice: Methodologies for Social Change,* edited by Andrew Jolivette, 117–138. Bristol: Policy Press.

Simpson, Audra. 2007. "On Ethnographic Refusal: Indigeneity, Voice and Colonial Citizenship." *Junctures* 9 (December): 67–80.

Smith, Linda Tuhiwai. 2012. *Decolonizing Methodologies: Research and Indigenous Peoples.* London: Zed Books.

Sohng, Lee S. 1996. "Participatory Research and Community Organizing." *Journal of Sociology and Social Welfare* 23(4): 77–97.

Sudbury, Julia. 1998. *Other Kinds of Dreams: Black Women's Organizations and the Politics of Transformation.* London and New York: Routledge.

Washington, Harriet. 2006. *Medical Apartheid.* New York: Doubleday.

Chapter 19

For a Black Feminist Digital Sociology

Melissa Brown

Black girls twerking. Black women sex. Black sex at work. I do not know what the keyword hits on your blog look like, but some of the keywords that lead to my blog often make me wonder what the search engine user intended to find and whether Black feminist scholarship satisfied their queries. I created Blackfeminisms.com in 2016 to get a second use out of the notes I had taken for my comprehensive exams in social stratification and social psychology. I also felt frustrated by the dialogue forming among Black Twitter[1] that perpetuated falsehoods about Black feminism, Black women, and Black LGBTQ people. Blackfeminisms.com circumvents the intellectual gatekeeping of academic publishing imposed on Black feminist scholars to get their knowledge to whoever has access to an internet-based search engine. It is for the girls who like to cite their sources in the middle of their Twitter thread clapbacks or the ones who want to provide resources in their annual "diversify your syllabus" email to their professors. Yet, the activity measured in terms of referrers, keyword hits, and blog post views suggests that not everyone who comes across Blackfeminisms.com seeks knowledge by and about Black women.

When user racial bias encounters search engine algorithms, the results are the reinforcement of longstanding controlling images of Black women as hypersexual Jezebels.[2] However, as the performance metrics of Blackfeminisms.com suggest, when internet users with a Black feminist lens introduce digital content into the virtual public sphere, they disrupt this racial bias by redirecting views intended for the sexualization of Black women to an education that disconfirms the racialized sexual stereotypes embedded in the content the users had sought out. The emergence of digital technology affects Black women and Black LGBTQ people in complex and nuanced ways. This reality necessitates a type of sociology that not only provides tools for the analysis of digital society but also for the consideration of what we learn about the ways digital technology affects society, reinforcing existing inequalities as it also opens up new avenues to empower marginalized people.

DOI: 10.4324/9781003199113-24

I introduce *Black feminist digital sociology*, which draws on Black feminist thought as critical social theory as theorized by Patricia Hill Collins[3] and digital sociology as formulated by Deborah Lupton,[4] as a framework for sociological analysis of digital society from the positionality of the outsider within[5] and the use of digital tools for a Black feminist public sociology. Using my creation of Blackfeminisms.com as a virtual encyclopedia of academic scholarship by and about Black women, I work to redress the intellectual gatekeeping facilitated by the paywalls of scholarly publishers that restrict access to work by Black feminist scholars. Engaging Black feminist perspectives on digital technology, I use quantitative data automatically generated through Wordpress.com to examine how online accessibility to Black feminist scholarship weakens algorithmic bias. A Black feminist digital sociology addresses how Black women and Black LGBTQ people use digital technology and create or remix digital practices to shape social processes and institutions in contemporary society.

Black Feminist Interventions Into the Study of Digital Society

In Deborah Lupton's book *Digital Sociology*, she describes four major research activities of digital sociology: (1) digital practice as sociology professionals, (2) sociological analyses of the use of digital media, (3) the analysis of digital data and (4) the use of critical social and cultural theory to analyze digital media. The "digital divide" remains the most persistent mainstream framing of the relationship between race and technology in social science literature. Andre Brock and colleagues[6] describe this argument as one that conflates racial inequality with technological incompetency: "Either minority groups lack material access, lack mastery of digital practices and literacies, or lack value systems promoting the educational achievement necessary to acquire base proficiency in digital systems."[7] Indeed, my own research challenges these assumptions.[8] I used quantitative content analysis to examine how Twitter users engaged in "intersectionality as critical praxis," using #SayHerName, a campaign started by Kimberlé Crenshaw to address police violence against women.[9] My findings showed that Black women use Twitter and blogging sites to raise consciousness about police brutality against Black women, murders of Black transwomen, and incidents of domestic violence against Black women in the United States and the United Kingdom. This analysis shows that the adoption of Black feminist thought as a framework for the analysis of digital technology and producers of digital content offers important sociological insights about digital practices, users of digital technology, internet-based social networks, and the infrastructure of digital technology in the 21st century.

The methodology of digital divide research often includes statistical analysis of large-scale survey data, which limits the interpretation of findings to relationships among explanatory variables accounted for in the survey design. As a result, this analytical approach cannot account for how white supremacy and capitalism function together to create these disparities. A Black feminist intervention into digital sociology begins at the outsider within standpoint[10] to draw attention to how a multiple consciousness[11] informs the way people with marginalized race, gender, and sexual identities engage digital technology to facilitate their access to power.

Black feminist digital sociology provides a strategy for the analysis of race and technology that recognizes how the matrix of domination[12] maintains unequal social relations and the ways intersecting oppressions[13] creates an unequal distribution of power among producers and users of digital technology. My approach to Black feminist digital sociology draws on other Black feminist scholars of information and communication technologies whose work envisions counternarratives about Black people, particularly Black women, as participants in a digital society. Additionally, these scholars adopt concepts rooted in Black feminist thought to guide empirical analyses of digital technology users and the creation of digital content.

Black Cyberfeminist Thought

Kishonna Gray[14] provides a concise outline of the three major themes of Black cyberfeminist thought in *Digital Sociologies*. This first theme centers on how social structural oppression shapes technology and virtual spaces. It recognizes the white masculine bias of technology and virtual spaces, calling for the marginalized to "regain control of hegemonic imagery to be able to define themselves"[15] with internet technologies. The second theme centers on intersecting oppressions in virtual spaces to promote "a privileging of marginalized perspectives and ways of knowing" to address "the diverse ways that oppression can manifest in the materiality of the body and how this translates into virtual spaces."[16] Finally, the third theme speaks to how Black digital technology users navigate "the process involved in racializing public space within virtual settings,"[17] leading to distinctiveness forms of marginalization and resistance. The assumptions of Black cyberfeminist thought give Black feminist digital sociology a theoretical background that circumvents the inclusion of a non-Black comparison group as it asserts that the study of Black people in and of themselves creates new knowledge about society and digital technology.

Black Feminist Technology Studies

In *Algorithms of Oppression*, Safiya Noble offers Black feminist technology studies as "an epistemological approach to researching gendered and

racialized identities in digital and analog media studies" that also provides "a new lens for exploring power as mediated by intersectional identities."[18] Noble draws on Black feminist thought as a conceptual starting
place for the interrogation of classification systems used in technologies like commercial search engines and library databases. According to
Noble, the algorithms of internet software draw on classification systems
that source information shaped through a white colonial gaze of Black
women that characterize them as Mammies, Jezebels, Sapphires and
other controlling images.[19] These algorithms also exclude Black women
and girls from imagery associated with dominant cultural assumptions of
womanhood and girlhood. This duality of invisibility and hypervisibil-
ity in how classification systems depict Black women and girls prompts
Noble to call for an ethics of algorithms that account for how people
of color understand and see themselves in the creation of information
technologies. Black feminist digital sociology constitutes a sociological
approach to Black feminist technology studies in its focus on the exploration of how intersectionality mediates the relationship between power
and social relations for people with marginalized race, gender, and sexual
identities.

A Computational Digital Autoethnography of Blackfeminisms.com

To analyze Blackfeminisms.com, I use computational digital autoethnography (CDA), a Black feminist methodology created by Nicole Marie
Brown[20] wherein researchers use computation methods to analyze a corpus
of their digitized data. Brown[21] uses topic modeling on a digital corpus of
written text including posts, comments, pictures, and links produced over
a nine-year period to identify themes related to Black feminist articulations of love, violence, and death as material or symbolic. For this analysis,
I use quantitative content analysis to calculate the frequency of keyword
phrases in each category I identified in a digital corpus of text I produced
between 2016 and 2020.

The website includes 29 pages: Eight pages of resources that have annual
lists of academics books written by Black women scholars or that cover
Black women or Black feminism; seven pages of educational materials
such as a 30-day minicourse on Black feminism; five pages about myself
and the website itself; and three pages on my research projects or writing.
That website also includes 138 posts about a wide range of topics: (1)
research by Black feminist academics or on Black women, (2) pop-culture
depictions of Black women, (3) art and entertainment produced by or
centering Black women and (4) Black feminism as a theoretical framework
and critical praxis. I wrote all the posts and pages myself aside from one
post of an essay written by Irma McClaurin, and two pages, including the

Black feminist archive by Irma McClaurin and the #SayHerName bibliography by Apollo Rydzik.

The data described here comes from Wordpress.com, a service that offers tools to host and manage websites. Wordpress.com provides users a dashboard through Jetpack, a plugin created by WordPress that enables users to monitor the security and performance of their websites. Provided metrics include: (1) the number of visits and views to pages and blog posts, (2) the frequency of keyword phrases that led to the website and (3) the frequency of webpages that refer to your website through direct links or hyperlinks embedded in that webpage. Wordpress.com enables users to download CSV files of this data, which I then imported into Microsoft Excel in August 2020. Jetpack provides performance metrics calculated per day, per week, per month, per year, and all time. This analysis draws from metrics for all visitors and views since the blog started in June 2016.

Since June 2016, the blog has received 211,523 visitors and 306,207 views. A total of 45 percent of views come to Blackfeminisms.com through Google Search. Another 11 percent of views come through links to the blog shared on Facebook, and 5 percent come through links posted to Twitter. The remaining 38 percent come from other search engines, social networking sites, hyperlinks in other blog posts, and links shared by users of university electronic learning systems. Search engines crawl websites for words and phrases that match up to those entered by an internet user into the search engine of their choice. The search engine then pulls links to websites that contain these keywords somewhere in the text of the page and display the results in a web browser window. Wordpress.com does not provide the keywords for most search results due to limitations imposed by search engines that block what website management software can access to protect the privacy of their users. The data on keywords accessed from Wordpress.com includes a list of 498 keyword phrases that led to 3,186 views, roughly 17 percent of the 18,779 views to the website that resulted from referrals by search engines that linked to the website.

The Search Trafficking of Black Women

The following section illustrates the application of CDA to digital data from Blackfeminisms.com to illuminate how search engine crawlers and web indexing reveal the ways internet users encounter a Black feminist academic virtual space. Table 19.1 shows the categories I identified based on the 498 keyword phrases available in my dataset. For this chapter, I focus on all types except "miscellaneous."

As shown in Table 19.1, 49 percent of the keyword phrases referred to Black feminist scholarship or activism. The five search terms with the highest number of views included "Black feminism" (N = 526), "Black feminist" (N = 50), "Black feminist movement" (N = 45), "Black feminist

Table 19.1 Keyword Phrases by Category

Category	Keywords (N = 498)	Total Views (N = 3,186)
Black Feminism	49%	58%
Pornography and Erotica	25%	25%
Sociology	10%	6%
Controlling images	9%	6%
Popular culture	3%	2%
Miscellaneous	3%	4%

Note: This table excludes unknown keyword phrases (Total Views = 15, 593)

theory" (N = 42), and "Black feminisms" (N = 40). These keyword phrases turned up in search results linked to my summaries of work by Black women academics. For example, users who searched for Toni Morrison or her novel *Sula* linked to a blog post titled "Black Feminism in *Sula*," where I described how the novel's characters Nel and Sula embodied controlling images of Black womanhood.

Twenty-five percent of the keyword phrases concerned explicit sexual content. The five search terms with the highest number of views included "Black women sex," (N = 78), "Black girls twerking" (N = 43), "Black sex" (N = 42), "America sex" (N = 31), and "Black women twerking" (N = 30). These viewers linked to two blog posts: (1) "Batty-Werk: You-Tube and Black Girls Twerking as Personal Vlogging," where I summarize an academic article by Kyra Gaunt on the commodification, appropriation and sexualization of Black girls twerking on YouTube, and (2) "The Sexual Labor of Black Women in Pornography," in which I summarize concepts from *A Taste for Brown Sugar* by Mireille Miller-Young about how Black women performers in the pornography industry demonstrate sexual agency.

Ten percent of the keyword phrases named sociological writings or concepts I had summarized. The top five keyword phrases with the most views included 14 for "Massey and Denton," authors of *American Apartheid.* Ten views came from users searching for "racial zoning." Nine came from searches for *Sex and the Conquest* by Richard Trexler. Seven views came from searches for "pathologizing Blackness," which links to an essay I wrote where I summarized a chapter by Kevin McGruder titled "Pathologizing Black Sexuality: The U.S. Experience." Finally, six views resulted from users searching for Joanne Nagel, whose book *Race, Ethnicity, and Sexuality* I summarized.

Nine percent of keyword phrases pointed to stereotypes about Black women. The top five keyword phrases with the most views included: a direct link to a blog post on the emasculation of cis-heterosexual Black men (N = 5), "jezebel slavery" (N = 5), "jezebel definition for Black women" (N = 5), "the history of Black mothers" (N = 4), and "jezebel stereotype for flashcard" (N = 3). Search results lead to a blog post that defines the Jezebel, a blog post that debunks the Black matriarchy thesis, and a reading list that cites academic and journalistic perspectives on the Jezebel.

Finally, 3 percent of the keyword phrases came from search results about Black women in film, television, and popular culture. The top five keyword phrases with the most views included: "Black TV shows 2018" (N = 6), "TV shows with Black women" (N = 6), "feminist rappers" (N = 5), "lyrical content of today's female rappers" (N = 5), and "TV shows black feminism" (N = 4). These searches link to blog posts about shows that feature Black women leads and Black women rappers and dancehall artists with pro-woman, sex-positive lyrics.

Black Feminist Theory, Black Girls Twerking: The Virtual Construction of Black Womanhood

I applied Black feminist digital sociology as a conceptual framework for a computational digital autoethnography[22] of keyword data from a blog site that I have self-authored for four years. Through a quantitative content analysis of these keywords, I identified five categories that show what type of information people seek out on the internet about Black women and Black feminism through search engines. This analysis points to several ways that users construct Black womanhood in the text of keywords in search engines.

First, most views came from search engine users seeking information about educational information on Black feminism or sociological writings, which demonstrates the utility of digital technology for Black feminist public sociology projects. It constitutes a distinct form of Black cyberfeminism[23] and digital sociology as a professional practice.[24] Users in search of Black feminism find what they are looking for in a website called Blackfeminisms.com. Nevertheless, these users must come to the search engine with the knowledge of Black feminism or the idea that Black women do feminism to find the website. Still, Black feminist public sociology projects take different forms. For example, Tressie McMillan Cottom uses Twitter and has a podcast with another Black feminist scholar, Roxane Gay. Through these mediums, Cottom uses digital technology to amplify a Black feminist analysis of popular culture and current events to a networked audience. Given the hidden curriculum of academia, the use of social networking and blogging sites in this way represents an essential intervention in the gatekeeping that has long prevented Black women scholars from accessing specific opportunities or forming community.

Second, keywords in search engines reflect the ways controlling images of Black women as hypersexual or matriarchs continue to influence the types of depictions of Black women people seek out. At least one in four of the keyword phrases I categorized referred to Black women as the subject of pornography or twerk videos. One in ten keyword phrases sought out information about Black women as Jezebels or matriarchs, a concept rooted in the scientific racism of thinkers like Daniel Patrick Moynihan that shifts the blame for the disempowerment of Black families away from the system to those that it oppresses.[25] Like Noble,[26] I found that the way search engines function means that they continue to drive a considerable amount of traffic to websites that include showing Black women having sex. Additionally, these findings support Gaunt,[27] who contends context collapse emergent in internet-mediated communications leads to the sexualization and racialization of how Black women and girls embody themselves online, particularly as dancers in twerk videos. While Black women and girls share twerk videos as a type of personal vlogging, other internet users view this content through the prism of controlling images that distort these actions as lewd and hypersexual.

Finally, Black feminist digital sociology can create public intellectual projects that redirect the pornographic gaze[28] to Black feminist knowledge about sexuality. Though a search engine user seeks out the sexual content of Black women, the search engine turns over results to my website since it leaves it to the user to account for the context of each link. My decision to upload a summary of academic text about the sexualization of Black women to a website that search engines can crawl for keywords without recognition of the context leads to a scenario wherein less observant search engine users get directed to content that challenges rather than perpetuates the racial sexualization of Black women in pornography. This failure to account for context creates an avenue to education on the controlling images of Black women as hypersexual found in such content.

Pathways Forward for Black Feminist Digital Sociology

I still remember myself in my last year of undergraduate school when I picked up *Black Feminist Thought* for the first time. As I read about controlling images and sexism from Black men, the contradictions of my upbringing as a girl child of Jamaican immigrants raised in the Southern Baptist church made sense. The knowledge of Black feminism liberated me from the politics of respectability my family and the church had insisted I adopt. I created Blackfeminisms.com as a labor of love for Black women in similar pursuit of the knowledge to free themselves.

Black feminism centers the ways the matrix of domination[29] shapes the experiences of Black women to theorize agency and promote a humanistic, visionary pragmatism rooted in Black community politics.[30] Black feminist digital sociology brings this framework into the analysis of digital data and the development of virtual intellectual projects. Rather than frame digital technology as "the Great Equalizer" or perpetuate the rhetoric of the digital divide, this framework considers how new technologies exploit long-standing intersecting oppressions[31] to perpetuate ongoing social inequality. Instead, Black feminist digital sociology begins from an outsider within standpoint[32] to offer alternative perspectives about how digital technology shapes the social construction of race, gender, class, and sexuality in contemporary society.

The task of a Black feminist digital sociology includes examining digital technology use and practices to understand how the experiences of Black women and Black LGBTQ people figure into the social processes that define a contemporary digital society. I envision that other scholars will take up Black feminist digital sociology and expand it to encompass the digital practices of lesbian, bisexual, transgender, and queer Black women; Black women who live outside the North American continent; and Black girls of all ages. I also envision a Black feminist digital sociology canon that embraces Black feminist thought as cultivated by people outside the ivory tower. Black women in academia must engage in citational practices that draw on Black women of all walks of life in recognition of the ways the knowledge we gain from Black women comes first and foremost from lived experiences. This type of intellectual engagement also addresses the existence of Black feminist thought as a knowledge project in dialogue with community voices and cultural forms of knowing that the academy has historically sought to erase or coopt.

Beyonce, "Video Phone," 2008 single; full album 2018- I Am . . . Sasha Fierce

Notes

1. Meredith Clark. 2015. "Black Twitter: Building Connection through Cultural Conversation." In *Hashtag Publics: The Power and Politics of Discursive Networks*, 205–217. New York: Peter Lang Publishing, Inc.
2. Safiya Noble. 2018. *Algorithms of Oppression: How Search Engines Reinforce Racism*. New York: New York University Press.
3. Patricia Hill Collins. 1998. *Fighting Words: Black Women and the Search for Justice*. Vol. 7. Minneapolis: University of Minnesota Press.
4. Deborah Lupton. 2014. *Digital Sociology*. London and New York: Routledge.
5. Patricia Hill Collins. 1986. "Learning from the Outsider Within: The Sociological Significance of Black Feminist Thought." *Social Problems* 33(6): S14–S32.
6. André Brock, Lynette Kvasny, and Kayla Hales. 2010. "Cultural Appropriations of Technical Capital: Black Women, Weblogs, and the Digital Divide." *Information, Communication & Society* 13(7): 1040–1059. Doi: 10.1080/1369118x.2010.498897.
7. Ibid., 1041.
8. Melissa Brown, Rashawn Ray, Ed Summers, and Neil Fraistat. 2017. "#Sayhername: A Case Study of Intersectional Social Media Activism." *Ethnic and Racial Studies* 40(11): 1831–1846. Doi: 10.1080/01419870.2017.1334934.

9. Kimberlé Crenshaw, Andrea J. Ritchie, Rachel Anspach, Rachel Gilmer, and Luke Harris. 2015. "Say Her Name: Resisting Police Brutality against Black Women." African American Policy Forum, Center for Intersectionality and Social Policy Studies.
10. Collins 1986.
11. Deborah King. 1988. "Multiple Jeopardy, Multiple Consciousness: The Context of a Black Feminist Ideology." *Signs: Journal of Women in Culture and Society* 14(1): 47–72.
12. Patricia Hill Collins. 2000. *Black Feminist Thought: Knowledge, Consciousness, and the Politics of Empowerment.* London: Routledge.
13. Kimberle Crenshaw. 1991. "Mapping the Margins: Intersectionality, Identity Politics, and Violence against Women of Color." *Stanford Law Review* 43(6): 1241–1299. Doi: 10.2307/1229039.
14. Kishonna L. Gray. 2017. "'They're Just Too Urban': Black Gamers Streaming on Twitch." In *Digital Sociologies*, edited by J. Daniels, K. Gregory, and T. M. Cottom, Vol. 1, 355–368. Cambridge: Policy Press.
15. Ibid., 358.
16. Ibid., 359.
17. Ibid.
18. Noble 2018, 171–172.
19. Collins 2000.
20. Nicole Marie Brown. 2019. "Methodological Cyborg as Black Feminist Technology: Constructing the Social Self Using Computational Digital Autoethnography and Social Media." *Cultural Studies Critical Methodologies.* Doi: 10.1177/1532708617750178.
21. Ibid.
22. Ibid.
23. Gray 2017.
24. Lupton 2014.
25. Collins 2000.
26. Noble 2018.
27. Kyra D. Gaunt. 2015. "YouTube, Twerking & You: Context Collapse and the Hand-held Co-Presence of Black Girls and Miley Cyrus." *Journal of Popular Music Studies* 27(3): 244–273.
28. bell hooks. 2004. *We Real Cool: Black Men and Masculinity.* New York and London: Routledge.
29. Collins 2000.
30. Stanlie M. James and Abena P. A. Busia (eds.). 1993. *Theorizing Black Feminisms: The Visionary Pragmatism of Black Women.* London: Routledge.
31. Crenshaw 1991.
32. Collins 1986.

References

Brock, André, Lynette Kvasny, and Kayla Hales. 2010. "Cultural Appropriations of Technical Capital: Black Women, Weblogs, and the Digital Divide." *Information, Communication & Society* 13(7): 1040–1059. doi: 10.1080/1369118x.2010.498897
Brown, Melissa, Rashawn Ray, Ed Summers, and Neil Fraistat. 2017. "#Sayhername: A Case Study of Intersectional Social Media Activism." *Ethnic and Racial Studies* 40(11): 1831–1846. doi: 10.1080/01419870.2017.1334934
Brown, Nicole Marie. 2019. "Methodological Cyborg as Black Feminist Technology: Constructing the Social Self Using Computational Digital Autoethnography and Social Media." *Cultural Studies Critical Methodologies.* doi: 10.1177/1532708617750178

Clark, Meredith. 2015. "Black Twitter: Building Connection through Cultural Conversation." In *Hashtag Publics: The Power and Politics of Discursive Networks*, 205–217. New York: Peter Lang Publishing, Inc.

Collins, Patricia Hill. 1986. "Learning from the Outsider Within: The Sociological Significance of Black Feminist Thought." *Social Problems* 33(6): S14–S32.

Collins, Patricia Hill. 1998. *Fighting Words: Black Women and the Search for Justice*. Vol. 7. Minneapolis: University of Minnesota Press.

Collins, Patricia Hill. 2000. *Black Feminist Thought: Knowledge, Consciousness, and the Politics of Empowerment*. London: Routledge.

Crenshaw, Kimberle. 1991. "Mapping the Margins: Intersectionality, Identity Politics, and Violence against Women of Color." *Stanford Law Review* 43(6): 1241–1299. doi: 10.2307/1229039

Crenshaw, Kimberlé, Andrea J. Ritchie, Rachel Anspach, Rachel Gilmer, and Luke Harris. 2015. "Say Her Name: Resisting Police Brutality against Black Women." African American Policy Forum, Center for Intersectionality and Social Policy Studies.

Gaunt, Kyra D. 2015. "Youtube, Twerking & You: Context Collapse and the Handheld Co-Presence of Black Girls and Miley Cyrus." *Journal of Popular Music Studies* 27(3): 244–273.

Gray, Kishonna L. 2017. "'They're Just Too Urban': Black Gamers Streaming on Twitch." In *Digital Sociologies*, edited by J. Daniels, K. Gregory, and T. M. Cottom, Vol. 1, 355–368. Cambridge: Policy Press.

hooks, bell. 2004. *We Real Cool: Black Men and Masculinity*. New York and London: Routledge.

James, Stanlie M., and Abena P. A. Busia (eds.). 1993. *Theorizing Black Feminisms: The Visionary Pragmatism of Black Women*. London: Routledge.

King, Deborah. 1988. "Multiple Jeopardy, Multiple Consciousness: The Context of a Black Feminist Ideology." *Signs: Journal of Women in Culture and Society* 14(1): 47–72.

Lupton, Deborah. 2014. *Digital Sociology*. London and New York: Routledge.

Noble, Safiya. 2018. *Algorithms of Oppression: How Search Engines Reinforce Racism*. New York: New York University Press.

Part 5

Imagining Black Feminist Sociological Futures and What They Create for Us

Chapter 20

Allyship in the Time of Aggrievement

The Case of Black Feminism and the New Black Masculinities

Freeden Blume Oeur and Saida Grundy

Black Feminism and Its Discontents

In 2019, *Vox* reporter Jane Coaston announced that *intersectionality*—or the idea of mutually reinforcing systems of oppression—might be the most hated word in American conservatism. Even self-identified liberals have made their contempt for feminist theory and intersectionality known in their attacks on "grievance studies."[1] Perhaps the strangest bedfellow made by contemptuous reactions to intersectionality has been the New Black Masculinities (NBM). An emergent framework that includes "Black Masculinism" in African American studies and "Black Male Studies" in philosophy, NBM elucidates the suffering endured by Black men and boys.[2] This perspective challenges Black feminism for viewing Black men as perpetrators of violence but not as victims themselves. Intersectionality is viewed as a trap that wrongly blames Black men for aspiring to be patriarchs who seek power over Black women. The adherents of NBM indict Black feminists for profiting off careers that caricature and crucify Black men. They claim that Black men are silenced out of fear that speaking out against Black feminism will mean professional alienation.

Yet Black feminism is hardly the hegemony that NBM perceives. As the post-truth era views their politics with increasing suspicion, Black feminists time and again are forced to defend the legitimacy of their work. And with intersectionality now the lingua franca of gender studies programs, feminist scholar Jennifer C. Nash has lamented how Black feminists have tried to protect intersectionality as their exclusive property. Other commentators such as Robyn Wiegman are discouraged by how an apocalyptic outlook has overshadowed Black feminism's hopeful and liberatory politics.[3]

With Black feminism back on its heels, we ask: What explains this antipathy toward Black feminism? And how do we chart a path forward? As two avowed Black feminist sociologists who study Black masculinity, we rebuff the notion that supporting the very real cause of struggling Black men and boys requires casting off Black feminism. We demonstrate rather

DOI: 10.4324/9781003199113-26

that NBM rehearses what we call *Black male aggrievement*, an ideology that anchors conservative gender politics to its anti-racist motivations and claims injury at the hands of Black feminism as a field, and Black women in particular. Black male aggrievement, and the antagonism between Black feminism and NBM, has been nurtured by a neoliberal academy that delegitimizes critical scholarship and takes delight in conflict between progressive movements. Turning to our own research on schools, targeted to young Black men, we highlight how a conservative gender politics animates programmatic efforts to uplift young Black men. These efforts promote what the legal scholar Paul Butler calls Black male exceptionalism, the idea that Black men are more deserving of help than other groups. The "New" Black Masculinities and the "neo"-liberal ideologies that guide these initiatives are, in fact, rooted in an old brand of "progressive conservatism."[4] In a contemporary moment marked by the disposability of Black life and Black feminism's vulnerability, Black feminism—one grounded in a politics of caring and reparations—is needed more than ever.

Thriving, Dying and Defensive Black Feminism

Black feminism unearths, critiques, and attacks the forces of gendered racism. Not merely a challenge to white patriarchy, Black feminism is also critical of misogyny and sexual violence within the Black community. Groundbreaking early theorizing of intersectionality by Kimberlé Crenshaw[5] demonstrated how legal narratives obfuscate sexual violence against Black women. Attempts to call out sexism and sexual violence within the Black community have historically been met with silencing tactics in order "not to bring a good brother down."[6]

Black feminism has been described as both thriving and dying.[7] Popular memoirs by Black women—including Roxane Gay's *Bad Feminist* (2014)[8] and Tressie McMillan Cottom's *Thick* (2019)[9]—have helped sustained public interest in Black feminism, while exposing rifts between a perceived elite academic feminism and its grassroots politics. This expanded interest in Black feminism has been met with strong resistance to intersectionality, the tradition's most wide-reaching contribution. Detractors view it as a dressed-up version of identity politics and a form of white-bashing. Conservatives regard it as "dangerous" to claim that oppressed groups do, in fact, experience multiple forms of oppression.[10] Even still, Black feminism remains a "minority discourse" that constantly needs to justify its worth.[11] Black feminism has become increasingly vulnerable in the face of the Trump administration's relentless attack on higher education. And as faculty positions become scarce in our age of austerity, academics of all stripes claim the mantle of objective scientific research and dismiss Black feminist approaches as unscientific "me-search." The field's enduring marginalization has led to worries that demands for legitimacy have made

Black feminism appear overwhelmingly defensive[12] and worries over Black feminism's territorial policing of intersectionality, which has divided Black women from other feminist scholars of color.[13] With Black feminism at a crossroads, gender scholar Brittney Cooper wonders if it has a future at all.[14] The seeming demise of Black feminism comes amid the increasing precariousness of the lives of Black women and girls, who, according to the National Partnership for Women and Families 2018, experience disproportionately poor health outcomes and face high maternal mortality rates.[15]

Black Male Aggrievement

With Black feminism on the defensive, the advocates of NBM have come out swinging. They view Black feminism as a roadblock to a truly critical study of Black masculinity. The backers of NBM allege that while Black feminism claims in theory to account for Black men, gender is instead taken to be synonymous with women. Thus, "actually existing" intersectional accounts prioritize Black women's experiences and demean Black men and boys, who are viewed as aspiring (white) patriarchs. Under the rubric of Black feminism, Black men and boys are assailants and never victims of gendered racism and sexual violence. These proponents accuse the academy of legitimizing pseudo-theories of Black men rooted in what is actually racist misandry, or a fear and hatred of Black men.

We acknowledge the good intentions behind NBM. This framework addresses difficult topics, such as an overlooked history of how Black men have been victims of sexual assault. But we are concerned with the larger implications. While NBM is new in name, it relies on an old formula: a progressive anti-racist agenda anchored in an anti-feminist, conservative gender politics—Black male aggrievement. The legal roots of "aggrievement" help emphasize how NBM advocates make a claim to injury at the hands of Black feminism and Black women scholars. Instead of rejecting intersectionality, this ideology *repackages* it as a framework that is anti-racist but also anti-feminist (and, as we suggest later, even pro-capitalist).[16] By trading feminism for anti-racism, NBM ultimately views power as a two-dimensional field. It is marred by a zero-sum "seesaw" logic where Black men must be down if Black women are up. NBM resorts to a kind of elementary accounting of disadvantage. For example, in his critique of Black feminism, T. Hasan Johnson essentially reduces social measures to "privilege"—which results in awkward phrasings such as "rape and domestic violence privilege"—and creates graphs comparing "Black male privileges" to "Black female privileges."[17] This comparison flattens the impact of those structures, ideologies, and policies that advantage whites over others. Johnson rejects the notion of Black male privilege not by accounting for the myriad ways that Black men are disadvantaged compared to their white peers, but by enumerating ad nauseum the specific advantages Black men and women supposedly have "over" one another. And while NBM claims a dearth of evidence of Black male privilege, the historical record shows how "patriarchal assumptions and institutions . . . still dominate Black civil and political society."[18]

The seesaw logic of NBM posits a "Black male exceptionalism," or the claim "that by almost every index of inequality, Black males are on the bottom."[19] For instance, Tommy Curry, a leading figure in Black male studies, writes, "In our current political-disciplinary milieu, patriarchy is thought to direct its violence primarily toward women through misogyny, despite the historical and sociological findings that show Western patriarchy to be a structural system that directs its most lethal violence against racialized (outgroup) males while preserving the lives of females through paternalism."[20] But gender theorists have long argued that patriarchy poses harm to *everyone*, and Curry's framing creates an uncomfortable situation where readers are asked to choose the side of Black men by virtue of the degree of violence enacted on them.

NBM replaces Black feminism with dubious theories.[21] The various threads of NBM have found a guiding light in the sociologist Robert Staples, the main progenitor of the original Black men's studies of the 1970s. Like Staples, Tommy Curry argues that Black feminists have perpetrated "myths" about Black men and masculinity. Yet race and gender theorists have largely dismissed the work of Staples for its blatant sexism and contempt for Black women. For example, in 1979 Robert Staples argued that middle-class Black men "screen out" strong Black women as partners because they prefer more feminine, and therefore submissive, women. He even called it the "masculine perquisite" of Black men to desert female partners who are decision-makers in the home.[22]

Though claiming to defend the rights of all "Black males," NBM offers ultimately a myopic view of Black manhood and gender. As T. Hasan Johnson claims, intersectionality is only popular because of the relative lack of Black men in higher education:

> The rightness of intersectionality theory is not based on the merits of Black feminism per se, but on the predominant numbers of Black females who comprise Black academe, especially in gender studies where courses are mostly taught by women . . . to women . . . for women.[23]

By reducing intellectual contributions to bodies, and by focusing narrowly on a struggle between Black women and Black men, Johnson misses the larger intellectual landscape where many white and other non-Black scholars can use intersectionality as they wish while remaining shielded from criticism.

Johnson ignores how a discourse of Black intellectualism has tradition-ally been rendered male;[24] and a concomitant history of how Black male intellectuals, even when claiming to be a champion of women's rights, have dismissed the radical agency and intellectual contributions of Black women.[25] Indeed, it is revealing that the male adherents of NBM have mainly criticized Black women and *not* other male scholars who engage Black feminists' work. By pitting Black female and male scholars against one another, Johnson overlooks a tradition of Black male feminist scholar-ship where Black men—including Rudolph Byrd, Devon Carbado and Mark Anthony Neal[26]—have worked alongside Black women as allies. Johnson's assertion further reflects the cis-heteronormativity of NBM. Black feminism, for example, with its commitment to destabilizing the categories of woman, gender, and embodiment, has served as a rich intel-lectual and political base for queer Black scholarship.[27] And scholars of a nascent Black transgender studies have drawn inspiration from Black feminism's capacity to disrupt and reconfigure the meanings around racial-ized gender.[28]

The Wreckage of Neoliberalism

In this time of Black suffering and death, Black feminist sociology can reorient thinking about the purpose and potential of intersectionality. Intersectionality can help us understand the *particularities* of gendered rac-ism for each group under white patriarchy and how the violence suffered by Black men and Black women are connected. We should embrace inter-sectionality as a "recreative" framework, in the words of Rose M. Brewer,[29] which can help repair the damaged relationship between NBM and Black feminism. As Audrey Lorde famously warned, "we cannot afford to do our enemies' work by destroying each other."[30] Therefore, here we encour-age a less *epistemological* view of intersectionality, one that highlights the particular standpoints of Black women and Black men; and encourage a more *systemic* view of intersectionality, in which mutually dependent forces of inequality divide potential allies in the service of hegemony.[31]

It is not surprising that Black feminism and NBM are at odds today when higher education is under attack from a cruel brand of neoliberal-ism.[32] The neoliberal university premised on corporate logics, top-down decision-making and diminished faculty governance relishes tensions between Black feminist scholars and defenders of NBM. It can absolve itself of any responsibility to resolve conflict, knowing that "losses"—in courses, programs, and faculty—can be chalked up to necessary downsiz-ing and cost-cutting. Neoliberal ideologies built on divisiveness, competi-tion over scarce resources, and a post-race and post-feminist worldview have fed the gender conservative, cis-normative and zero-sum politics of Black male aggrievement. NBM, therefore, has been *seduced* by the neoliberal project. Like NBM, the neoliberal embrace among Black male elites is not altogether new. As Leah Wright Rigueur has documented, it can be traced back to the "progressive conservatism" of 1960s Black politics, which turned to entrepreneurialism, free-market solutions, and public-private partnerships as pathways to social mobility.

While overcited and frequently misunderstood, neoliberalism remains a complex and enormously damaging force that has restructured economic policies and advanced a worldview of colorblind racism and postfeminism. Better intersectional thinking is needed, therefore, to help sift through the wreckage of neoliberalism. Yet gender studies courses are increasingly on the chopping block, just as they are needed the most.[33] Moreover, Black men and women remain sorely underrepresented in higher education. According to data from the National Science Foundation, Black students in 2017 made up only 5.4 of the nearly 55,000 PhDs awarded nationwide.[34] In many fields, not a single doctorate went to a Black student. One direct consequence is that research on whiteness and masculinity remains largely in the hands of white scholars, whose "exclusionary practices" include squeezing out the contributions of researchers of color. Meanwhile, a Black feminist pedagogy based on collaboration and caring is threatened by the neoliberal university's "bare pedagogy," in the words of educational scholar Henry Giroux,[35] one premised on isolation and merciless competition. And still largely shut out from more secure tenure-track positions, scholars of color have flooded the expanding class of precariously situated contingent faculty.[36]

Black Male Uplift

Neoliberal ideologies have spread to every level and corner of US education. In an era of privatization, a number of odd bedfellows, such as corporations and faith-based organizations, compete for opportunities to "solve" the crisis of young Black men. Like the theories on which NBM rely, these initiatives reinforce social class and gender divisions even as they promote a more explicitly anti-racist agenda. We demonstrate this through an analysis of the federal initiative *My Brother's Keeper*, and discuss how this effort at Black male uplift resonates in our respective scholarship on Black male educational institutions: Blume Oeur's research on all-male public high schools and Grundy's study of Morehouse College, the US's historically Black college for men.[37]

On May 19, 2013, then President Barack Obama spoke at the Morehouse College Commencement. He charged the graduates with the daunting task of taking the helm of Black racial advancement: "Your generation is uniquely poised for success unlike any generation of African Americans that came before it. . . . Too few of our brothers have the opportunities that you've had here at Morehouse." His words quickly grew weighty: "There are some things, as Morehouse men, that you are obliged to do for those still left behind. . . . Excuses are the rhetoric of the incompetent," he railed. "Nobody cares if you suffered from discrimination."[38] Presented to these educated Black men was a clean-up job of the embarrassment to the race attributed to their disadvantaged counterparts.

How did we arrive here, where young Black men are upheld as the saviors of the race and lambasted as its most likely detriment? How has this paradox of promise- and peril-driven efforts come to promote Black male achievement? Our respective feminist scholarship has critiqued both the masculinist constructions of young Black men's "problems" and how responses to these supposed problems expose how intersectionality has been repurposed to oddly anti-feminist ends.[39] While efforts at Black male achievement most obviously penalize Black womanhood, they also injure Black men, particularly those at the margins of class and sexuality. And they endorse the notion that the advancement of the race is yoked to the advancement of Black men.

The Morehouse speech was a promotional stop for Obama, who a year later unveiled My Brother's Keeper (MBK), an initiative with the expressed goal of addressing the "persistent opportunity gaps" facing African American and Latino boys.[40] The criticism was swift. Over a thousand Black feminists signed an open letter to President Obama decrying a "vicious cycle in which the assumptions that girls are not in crisis leads to research and policy interventions that overlook them, thus reinforcing their exclusion from efforts like MBK."[41] What fell below the radar were the politically curious origins of MBK. Originating in the Department of Justice, the program's neoliberal ideas about personal responsibility, law and order, and Black male criminality have brought both Black and white conservatives to the same table as left-of-center Black community advocates. The launch of MBK was supported by such right-wing figureheads as Bill O'Reilly, who has famously railed that Black poverty rates are driven by the dissolution of Black families.[42] MBK's advisory board is littered with private sector conglomerates such as Prudential and Deloitte. Still, the corporatization of Black community-based initiatives has been widely embraced. As an example of "social justice capitalism," privatization has helped relieve community angst over what to do with Black boys.[43] A curious coalition has formed around Black boys in which Black community leaders and white neoliberal conservatives believe that corporate debts to Black communities are a form of economic justice. Accompanying this belief is the congruent idea that private sector action is more effective for African Americans than social welfare programs.

My Brother's Keeper is an exemplar of what Michael Dumas calls "neoliberal governmentality," where big-business innovations are offered as a way to "fix" the character flaws of Black male youth.[44] The same has been forged on the grounds of all-male public schools targeting Black boys.

When the City of Chicago rolled out its own city-wide MBK initiative in 2015, leading the way was Tim King, the CEO and founder of Urban Prep Academies, the most well-known of these schools. The schools' proponents have argued that Black-white achievement gaps require a radical intervention in the schooling of solely Black boys, despite feminists citing that the performance gap between white and Black girls is actually wider than that between white and Black boys.[45] Like MBK, Black male academies have garnered support from the left-leaning Open Society foundation as well as support from conservative organizations such as The Walton Family Foundation by falling in step with right-of-center ideologies about ending state-run schools and diminishing the power of teachers unions. In bringing together liberals and conservatives in these ways, Black male academies, like MBK, hit, as Kimberlé Crenshaw observes, a "political sweet spot among populations that both love and fear them."

The institutional cultures of Black male achievement are paradoxically a mashup of racial advancement ideologies and conservative practices about behavioral modeling, discipline, and morality. Blume Oeur (2018) demonstrates this in *Black Boys Apart: Racial Uplift and Respectability in All-Male Public Schools*, his year-long ethnographic study of two such male academies serving class-disadvantaged Black boys in the same city. Following a state takeover of the public-school system, one of these high schools, Northside Academy (pseudonym), assembled a board of trustees featuring many of the city's elite, which secured large funds unavailable to most public schools. The school also embraced its own version of progressive conservatism and cultivated a sense of tradition—in the form of a mandatory Latin curriculum and a strict uniform of blazers and ties—to show that their "gentlemanly" students possessed the disciplined minds and bodies that distinguished them from their more disadvantaged and "unworthy" peers. The school drew on the same principles behind MBK that linked old, conservative respectability politics with newer and trendier "grit" and "resilience" narratives to promote the idea that changes in personal character and temperament—as opposed to structural change—can lift up Black boys. These politics have intensified with the emergence of a "character education" industry over the past 15 years. This industry promotes the idea that in order to be successful, poor youth must cultivate non-cognitive skills such as perseverance, optimism, and self-confidence. These skills can help compensate for their lack of advanced technological skills compared to their international counterparts, who are normally Asian in the neoliberal imagination. In his Morehouse speech, Obama also drew on this belief in human capital development, a foundation of neoliberal ideology.[46] "In today's hyperconnected, hypercompetitive world," Obama asserted, "with millions of young people from China and India and Brazil—many of whom started with a whole lot less than all of you did—all of them entering the global workforce alongside you, nobody is going to give you anything that you have not earned."

Many of the cultural curricula for K-12 Black male academies were inspired by Morehouse College. As Saida Grundy shows in her forthcoming book, *Respectable: Politics and Paradox in the Making of the Morehouse Man*, a culture of Black male respectability at Morehouse narrowly constructs racial leadership within a promotion of neoliberal individualism. Grundy's interviews with graduates revealed that racial leadership was most often understood as a default status of individual accomplishment, buttressed by masculinist ideals of ambition and personal responsibility. When asked how Morehouse men improved conditions for Black men writ large, one respondent replied,

> The beginning [of improving Black communities] is not to be a Black man whose condition need be improved. Our broader responsibility is to not only be examples to the community but to empower people to do and be that in communities.

This promotion of neoliberal ideologies within notions of leadership lent themselves easily to prioritizing individual pathways to upward mobility. Business administration has long been the most popular major at Morehouse, and a culture of corporatization permeates student life and curricula. Similarly, the high-school boys in *Black Boys Apart* were groomed to be leaders of industry, or what Blume Oeur calls "ambitious entrepreneurs." At Morehouse, mandatory courses in business etiquette teach men to tie Windsor knots and recognize shrimp forks in preparation for interviews with coveted Wall Street firms. That several of their classmates advanced onto lucrative careers in finance was seen as proof of Morehouse's contributions to Black community leadership. In this thinking, having Black men in corporate leadership produces trickle-down race betterment when Black men steer capitalist enterprises, assumedly translating their success into anti-racist ends. Like a sequel to the embossed blazers and motivational messaging of the Black male high schools in Blume Oeur's research, a culture of respectability defined the Morehouse milieu. These institutions double-down on character education to further stave off the belief that Black men face barriers to mobility.

Allyship in the Time of Death

As feminist sociologists of Black masculinity writing in an era of deepening class inequality, a resurgence of ethnic nationalism, continued gender-based violence, and increasing anti-feminist sentiment, we insist that Black feminism is needed more than ever. This Black feminism is critical of all sexist behaviors without pathologizing men. In the words of Tarana Burke, Me

Too, the movement she founded, was never intended as a "vindictive plot against men."[47] The Black feminism we imagine is a deeply caring politics: one that shines light on the myriad forces that promote intra-racial divisions, and helps to rehabilitate those divisions. Jennifer C. Nash has called for "love in the time of death," or for Black feminists to embrace "radical intimacies" with other women of color.[48] We end with a call for a radical allyship needed to fight a white supremacy abetted and authorized by patriarchy, and protected by the post-race and post-feminist cloak of neoliberalism. For that reason, we embrace the Combahee River Collective's insight that anticapitalism gives Black feminism its "revolutionary potential."[49]

"What we must do," Audre Lorde writes, "is commit ourselves to some future that can include each other and to work toward that future with the particular strengths of our individual identities."[50] While we have been critical of the New Black Masculinities, we welcome opportunities to work with its proponents to find "some future." We accept the invitation of our Black feminist colleagues Aisha A. Upton and Jalia L. Joseph (writing in this volume) to explore new Black feminist futures and imagine an allyship of Black feminism and a *Newer* Black Masculinities united against all forms of state and intimate violence against Black populations.[51] We envision a Black feminist politics of caring and reparations that recognizes Black women and men as worthy of recognition and pursues holistic socioeconomic policies to address historical injustices. Even if Black feminism must, in the words of Jennifer C. Nash, "let go" of intersectionality as its exclusive property, it can hold on more firmly to a praxis that shows deep empathy for the many victims of gendered racism and capitalism.

Notes

1. James Lindsay, Peter Boghossian, and Helen Pluckrose. 2018. "Academic Grievance Studies and the Corruption of Scholarship." *Aero*, October 2. These researchers fabricated a number of studies in an attempt to expose the perceived absurdity of what they term "grievance studies," or research on race, gender, and sexuality. Their "studies" ridiculed intersectionality.
2. Tommy Curry. 2017. *The Man-Not: Race, Class, Genre and the Dilemmas of Black Manhood*. Philadelphia, PA: Temple University Press; T. Hasan Johnson. 2018. "Challenging the Myth of Black Male Privilege." *Spectrum: A Journal on Black Men* 6(2): 21–42.
3. Robyn Wiegman. 2012. *Object Lessons*. Durham, NC: Duke University Press.
4. Leah Wright Rigueur. 2017. "Neoliberal Social Justice: From Ed Brook to Barack Obama." *Social Science Research Council Items*, May 30. https://items.ssrc.org/reading-racial-conflict/neoliberal-social-justice-from-ed-brooke-to-barack-obama/
5. Kimberlé Crenshaw. 1991. "Mapping the Margins: Intersectionality, Identity Politics, and Violence Against Women of Color." Stanford Law Review 43(6): 1241–1299.
6. Devon Carbado. 1999. *Black Men on Race, Gender, and Sexuality*. New York: New York University Press; Saida Grundy. 2019. "The Flawed Logic of R. Kelly's Most Unlikely Supporters." *Atlantic*, January 10.

7. Jennifer C. Nash. 2019. *Black Feminism Reimagined: After Intersectionality*. Durham, NC: Duke University Press.
8. Roxane Gay. 2012. *Bad Feminist: Essays*. New York: Harper Perennial.
9. Tressie McMillan Cottom. 2019. *Thick: And Other Essays*. New York: New Press.
10. Christian Gonzalez. 2018. "The Illiberal Logic of Intersectionality." *Quillette*, May 8.
11. Alexander Weheliye. 2014. *Habeas Viscus: Racializing Assemblages, Biopolitics, and Black Feminist Theories of the Human*. Durham, NC: Duke University Press.
12. Hazel Carby. 1984. *Reconstructing Womanhood: The Emergence of the Afro-American Woman Novelist*. Oxford: Oxford University Press.
13. Nash 2019.
14. Brittney Cooper. 2015. "Love No Limit: Towards a Black Feminist Future (In Theory)." *Black Scholar* 45(4): 7–21.
15. National Partnership for Women and Families. 2018. "Black Women's Maternal Health: A Multifaceted Approach to Addressing Persistent and Dire Health Disparities." www.nationalpartnership.org/our-work/resources/health-care/maternity/black-womens-maternal-health-issue-brief.pdf
16. Keisha Lindsay. 2018. *A Classroom of Their Own: The Intersection of Race and Feminist Politics in All-Black Male Schools*. Champaign: University of Illinois Press.
17. Johnson 2018.
18. Manning Marable. 2001. "Groundings with My Sisters: Patriarchy and the Exploitation of Black Women." In *Traps: African American Men on Gender and Sexuality*, edited by Rudolph P. Byrd and Beverly Guy-Sheftal, 146. Bloomington: Indiana University Press.
19. Paul Butler. 2013. "Black Male Exceptionalism? The Problems and Potential of Male-Focused Interventions." *Du Bois Review* 10(2): 485.
20. Curry 2017, 231.
21. Just as the original Black Masculinities studies was nonfeminist, inaugural theorizing on masculinities within sociology adopted a feminist stance but paid insufficient attention to race.
22. Robert Staples. 1979. "The Myth of Black Macho. A Response to Angry Black Feminists." *Black Scholar* 10(6–7): 24–33.
23. Johnson 2018, 38; "Status and Trends in the Education of Racial and Ethnic Groups, 2017." Washington, DC: US Department of Education National Center for Education Statistics. In 2014, only 38% of all Blacks enrolled in college were men.
24. Hazel Carby. 1998. *Race Men*. Cambridge, MA: Harvard University Press.
25. Joy James. 1997. *Transcending the Talented Tenth: Black Leaders and American Intellectuals*. New York: Routledge.
26. Mark Anthony Neal. 2015. *New Black Man*. New York: Routledge.
27. Ronald Ferguson. 2004. *Aberrations in Black: Toward a Queer of Color Critique*. Minneapolis: University of Minnesota Press.
28. Treva Ellison, Kai M. Green, Matt Richardson, and C. Riley Snorton. 2017. "We Got Issues: Toward a Black Trans*/Studies." *TSQ* 4(2): 162–169; Buchanan
29. Rose M. Brewer. 1989. "Black Women and Feminist Sociology: The Emerging Perspective." *American Sociologist* 20(1): 57–70.
30. Audrey Lorde. 2007. *Sister Outsider: Essays and Speeches by Audrey Lorde*, 142. Berkeley: Crossing Press.
31. Hae Yeon Choo and Myra Marx Ferree. 2010. "Practicing Intersectionality in Sociological Research." *Sociological Theory* 28(2): 129–149.
32. Daniel Saunders. 2010. "Neoliberal Ideology and Public Higher Education in the United States." *Journal for Critical Educational Policy Studies* 8(1): 41–77.
33. Wright Rigueur 2017.

34. National Science Foundation. 2017. "Doctorate Recipients from U.S. Universities." https://ncses.nsf.gov/pubs/nsf19301/data

35. Henry Giroux. 2010. "Bare Pedagogy and the Scourge of Neoliberalism." *Educational Forum* 74(3): 184–196.

36. TIAA. 2016. "Taking the Measure of Faculty Diversity." www.tiaainstitute.org/sites/default/files/presentations/2017-02/taking_the_measure_of_faculty_diversity.pdf

37. Saida Grundy. Forthcoming. *Respectable: Politics and Paradox in the Making of the Morehouse Man.* Oakland: University of California Press.

38. Barack Obama. 2016. "Read President Obama's Commencement Address at Morehouse College." *Time.* June 2, 2016. https://time.com/4341712/obama-commencement-speech-transcript-morehouse-college/.

39. Lindsay 2018.

40. See https://obamawhitehouse.archives.gov/my-brothers-keeper.

41. "Why We Can't Wait: Women of Color Urge Inclusion in 'My Brother's Keeper." 2014. *African American Policy Forum*, June 17. http://aapf.org/recent/2014/06/woc-letter-mbk.

42. Bill O'Reilly. 2014. "Are You Your Brother's Keeper?" *Fox News.* February 26, 2014. www.foxnews.com/transcript/bill-oreilly-are-you-your-brothers-keeper.

43. Wright Rigueur. 2017.

44. Michael Dumas. 2016. "My Brother as 'Problem': Neoliberal Governmentality and Interventions for Black Young Men and Boys." *Educational Policy* 30(1): 94–113.

45. Carbado 1999.

46. Clayton Pierce. 2013. *Education in the Age of Biocapitalism: Optimizing Educational Life for the Flat World.* New York: Palgrave Macmillan.

47. Olivia Petter. 2018. "Tarana Burke." *Independent*, November 30.

48. Nash 2019.

49. Keeanga-Yamahtta Taylor. 2017. *How We Get Free: Black Feminism and the Combahee River* Collective. Chicago, IL: Haymarket Books, 69.

50. Lorde 2007, 142.

51. Aisha A. Upton and Jalia L. Joseph. 2021. "Exploring the Black Feminist Imagination" In *Black Feminist Sociology: Perspectives and Praxis*, edited by Zakiya Luna and Whitney Pirtle, 300–309. New York: Routledge.

References

Blume Oeur, Freeden. 2018. *Black Boys Apart: Racial Uplift and Respectability in All-Male Public Schools.* Minneapolis: University of Minnesota Press.

Brewer, Rose M. 1989. "Black Women and Feminist Sociology: The Emerging Perspective." *The American Sociologist* 20(1): 57–70.

Bridges, Tristan. 2019. "The Cost of Exclusionary Practices in Masculinities Studies." *Men and Masculinities* 22(1): 16–33.

Butler, Paul. 2013. "Black Male Exceptionalism? The Problems and Potential of Male-Focused Interventions." *Du Bois Review* 10(2): 485–511.

Byrd, Rudolph P., and Beverly Guy-Sheftall. 2001. *Traps: African American Men on Gender and Sexuality.* Bloomington: Indiana University Press.

Carbado, Devon. 1999. *Black Men on Race, Gender, and Sexuality.* New York: New York University Press.

Carby, Hazel. 1984. *Reconstructing Womanhood: The Emergence of the Afro-American Woman Novelist.* Oxford: Oxford University Press.

Carby, Hazel. 1998. *Race Men.* Cambridge, MA: Harvard University Press.

Choo, Hae Yeon, and Myra Marx Ferree. 2010. "Practicing Intersectionality in Sociological Research." *Sociological Theory* 28(2): 129–149.

Coaston, Jane. 2019. "The Intersectionality Wars." *Vox.* May 5. www.vox.com/the-highlight/2019/5/20/18542843/intersectionality-conservatism-law-race-gender-discrimination

Cooper, Brittney. 2015. "Love No Limit: Towards a Black Feminist Future (In Theory)." *Black Scholar* 45(4): 7–21.

Cottom, Tressie McMillan. 2019. *Thick: And Other Essays.* New York: New Press.

Crenshaw, Kimberlé. 1991. "Mapping the Margins: Intersectionality, Identity Politics, and Violence Against Women of Color." *Stanford Law Review* 43(6): 1241–1299.

Crenshaw, Kimberlé. 2014. "The Girls Obama Forgot." *New York Times.* July 30. www.nytimes.com/2014/07/30/opinion/Kimberl-Williams-Crenshaw-My-Brothers-Keeper-Ignores-Young-Black-Women.html

Curry, Tommy. 2014. "Michael Brown and the Need for a Genre Study of Black Male Death and Dying." *Theory & Event* 17(3): 1.

Curry, Tommy. 2017. *The Man-Not: Race, Class, Genre and the Dilemmas of Black Manhood.* Philadelphia, PA: Temple University Press.

Dumas, Michael. 2016. "My Brother as 'Problem': Neoliberal Governmentality and Interventions for Black Young Men and Boys." *Educational Policy* 30(1): 94–113.

Ellison, Treva, Kai M. Green, Matt Richardson, and C. Riley Snorton. 2017. "We Got Issues: Toward a Black Trans*/Studies." *TSQ* 4(2): 162–169.

Ferguson, Ronald. 2004. *Aberrations in Black: Toward a Queer of Color Critique.* Minneapolis: University of Minnesota Press.

Gay, Roxane. 2012. *Bad Feminist: Essays.* New York: Harper Perennial.

Giroux, Henry. 2010. "Bare Pedagogy and the Scourge of Neoliberalism." *Educational Forum* 74(3): 184–196.

Gonzalez, Christian. 2018. "The Illiberal Logic of Intersectionality." *Quillette.* May 8. https://quillette.com/2018/05/08/illiberal-logic-intersectionality/.

Grundy, Saida. 2019. "The Flawed Logic of R. Kelly's Most Unlikely Supporters." *Atlantic.* January 10. www.theatlantic.com/entertainment/archive/2019/01/why-some-women-still-support-r-kelly/579985/

Grundy, Saida. Forthcoming. *Respectable: Politics and Paradox in the Making of the Morehouse Man.* Oakland: University of California Press.

James, Joy. 1997. *Transcending the Talented Tenth: Black Leaders and American Intellectuals.* New York: Routledge.

Johnson, T. Hasan. 2018. "Challenging the Myth of Black Male Privilege." *Spectrum: A Journal on Black Men* 6(2): 21–42.

Lindsay, James, Peter Boghossian, and Helen Pluckrose. 2018. "Academic Grievance Studies and the Corruption of Scholarship." *Aero.* October 2. https://areomagazine.com/2018/10/02/academic-grievance-studies-and-the-corruption-of-scholarship/

Lindsay, Keisha. 2018. *A Classroom of Their Own: The Intersection of Race and Feminist Politics in All-Black Male Schools.* Champaign: University of Illinois Press.

Lorde, Audre. 2007. *Sister Outsider: Essays and Speeches by Audrey Lorde.* Berkeley: Crossing Press.

Marable, Manning. 2001. "Groundings with My Sisters: Patriarchy and the Exploitation of Black Women." In *Traps: African American Men on Gender and Sexuality*, edited by Rudolph P. Byrd and Beverly Guy-Sheftal, 119–152. Bloomington: Indiana University Press.

Nash, Jennifer C. 2019. *Black Feminism Reimagined: After Intersectionality*. Durham, NC: Duke University Press.

National Partnership for Women and Families. 2018. "Black Women's Maternal Health: A Multifaceted Approach to Addressing Persistent and Dire Health Disparities." www.nationalpartnership.org/our-work/resources/health-care/maternity/black-womens-maternal-health-issue-brief.pdf

National Science Foundation. 2017. "Doctorate Recipients from U.S. Universities." https://ncses.nsf.gov/pubs/nsf19301/data

Neal, Mark Anthony. 2015. *New Black Man*. New York: Routledge.

Obama, Barack. 2016. "Read President Obama's Commencement Address at Morehouse College." *Time*. June 2. https://time.com/4341712/obama-commencement-speech-transcript-morehouse-college/

O'Reilly, Bill. 2014. "Are You Your Brother's Keeper?" *Fox News*. February 26. www.foxnews.com/transcript/bill-oreilly-are-you-your-brothers-keeper.

Petter, Olivia. 2018. "Tarana Burke." *Independent*. November 30, 2018. www.independent.co.uk/life-style/women/metoo-founder-tarana-burke-ted-women-sexual-violence-rights-men-a8660416.html

Pierce, Clayton. 2013. *Education in the Age of Biocapitalism: Optimizing Educational Life for the Flat World*. New York: Palgrave Macmillan.

Saunders, Daniel. 2010. "Neoliberal Ideology and Public Higher Education in the United States." *Journal for Critical Educational Policy Studies* 8(1): 41–77.

Staples, Robert. 1970. "The Myth of the Black Matriarchy." *Black Scholar* 1(3–4): 8–16.

Staples, Robert. 1979. "The Myth of Black Macho. A Response to Angry Black Feminists." *Black Scholar* 10(6–7): 24–33.

"Status and Trends in the Education of Racial and Ethnic Groups, 2017." Washington, DC: US Department of Education National Center for Education Statistics.

Taylor, Keeanga-Yamahtta. 2017. *How We Get Free: Black Feminism and the Combahee River Collective*. Chicago, IL: Haymarket.

TIAA. 2016. "Taking the Measure of Faculty Diversity." www.tiaainstitute.org/sites/default/files/presentations/2017-02/taking_the_measure_of_faculty_diversity.pdf

Upton, Aisha A., and Jalia L. Joseph. 2021. "Exploring the Black Feminist Imagination" In *Black Feminist Sociology: Perspectives and Praxis*, edited by Zakiya Luna and Whitney Pirtle, 300–309. New York: Routledge.

Weheliye, Alexander. 2014. *Habeas Viscus: Racializing Assemblages, Biopolitics, and Black Feminist Theories of the Human*. Durham, NC: Duke University Press.

"Why We Can't Wait: Women of Color Urge Inclusion in 'My Brothers's Keeper." 2014. *The African American Policy Forum*. June 17. http://aapf.org/recent/2014/06/woc-letter-mbk

Wiegman, Robyn. 2012. *Object Lessons*. Durham, NC: Duke University Press.

Wright Rigueur, Leah. 2017. "Neoliberal Social Justice: From Ed Brook to Barack Obama." *Social Science Research Council Items*. May 30. https://items.ssrc.org/reading-racial-conflict/neoliberal-social-justice-from-ed-brooke-to-barack-obama/

Chapter 21

Theorizing Embodied Carcerality

A Black Feminist Sociology of Punishment

Brittany Friedman and Brooklynn K. Hitchens

Carcerality is embodied across generations. Black feminists know and encounter a multitude of parasitic vines that fight tirelessly to remain attached to their hosts. Every breath, every furtive thought, Black feminists remain the innovators reaching outside the matrices of their time. We feel the vines even when others cannot see them. Even when the prison is far, but especially when it is near. Our knowledge is unshakable. Vines violently latch onto familiar, intersectional nooses, incapacitating Black women and girls prior to any physical death. *Embodied carcerality* manifests the moment our birthed bodies are read and acted upon as Black.

In her work on criminal justice imagery, Brittany Friedman proposes embodied carcerality as a conceptual tool for understanding the production of carceral subjects through reifying one's physical representation as indistinguishable from a deviant object. She argues this reification process occurs through a series of interpersonal interactions, where a person's outward representation (movement, speech, appearance) is perceived as inherently dangerous and deserving of control, prior to any legally identifiable offense. Experiencing a continuous array of interactions representing one's physical attributes as synonymous with inherent danger is consequential because the process establishes the association as social fact. Such patterned relations can alter the cognitive and thus perceptual outlook of carceral subjects whereby external attempts to control people as objects can eventually feel normal. This interactive process produces embodied carcerality. It is the process that institutions use to both dispossess us and then convince everyone that our dispossession is the natural way of the world, rather than an injustice.[1]

Much like our ancestors continued to feel the slavers reach even if they had successfully run to freedom, Black women and girls too feel imprisoned even without being confined to a metal cage. We are witnesses, dually ensnared by our own subjugation and the condition of those we hold dear. Our embodied carcerality is further entrenched through intimate connections with friends, family, and communities similarly wading through the precarity of life and death. Black women and girls' intersectional bodies

DOI: 10.4324/9781003199113-27

are objectified and surveilled, yet we remain the backbone bracing those around us who are trapped within the same punishment continuum. Interconnected subjectivity rings true across the everyday Black experience as emancipation remains elusive with the 13th Amendment wholly intact. The imprisonment of those networked closest to us adds another layer of carcerality onto our already deep-seated, embodied pains. More vines to push through, more thorns to avoid, and more wounds that never fully heal. We are whiplashed with vicarious exposure, which Brooklynn K. Hitchens argues is its own form of racialized trauma and victimization, through the loss of family members, being spatially constrained to visit loved ones, and financially supporting our communities as its members are assembled in and out of the criminal justice system.[2] These added layers of criminal justice contact deepen the already established web that is embodied carcerality.

Within these embedded layers of embodied carcerality, what happens then, when we become individually ensnared within the criminal justice system ourselves? Mass imprisonment (jails and prisons) fostered the exponential reinstatement of physical incapacitation. We have witnessed material chains blossom like a familiar weed, returning once again as the matrix of our time. The imprisonment of the United States Black population structures how we live and die: whether in the civil sphere (e.g., political rights), social sphere (e.g., dominant group acceptance), or physical sphere (e.g., the body), and the interdependence between all three. Rose Heyer and Peter Wagner's work on prison policy reveals that our communities are disappearing with such spatial concentration that in 178 United States counties half of the Black population counted in the 2000 census was incarcerated.[3]

With each generation, we feel the matrices grip tighter. No longer wading through the vines, but instead we are snatched and relegated to a box at the root of the vine. Recent figures from the Sentencing Project and the Bureau of Justice Statistics reveal 1 in 18 Black women born in 2001 will likely spend time in a prison cage.[4] Black women continue to be imprisoned at twice the rate of white women, and 1.3 times the rate of Latinx women—disproportionately for nonviolent drug offenses.[5] Aleks Kajstura reports that in total 219,000 women are warehoused in local jails, state and federal penitentiaries, juvenile lockup, and immigrant detention, while another 1 million women are on probation and parole.[6] Alexi Jones reports that as of 2018 1 in 37 adults are under some form of correctional supervision, including imprisonment, electronic monitoring, probation, and parole.[7] But the reach of the carceral state stretches beyond imprisonment and supervision to extraction from the pocketbook. Jones's figure does not even include the surveillance of monetary sanctions that disproportionately punishes and generates revenue extracting from racial and ethnic minorities and those who are poor or low-income, as demonstrated in the scholarship of Alexes Harris, Mary Pattillo, Karin Martin and Brittany Friedman.[8]

We fill these cages and are subjected to violence, surveillance, and extraction more than all other women and girls. But as Shatema Theadcraft suggests, when we are harmed, few pay attention even if the harm leads to our death.[9] Uncovering the reasons for these travesties, requires us to see beyond a world that takes our carcerality for granted. By doing so, we can uncover the images that bind us and the requisite meanings mobilized to kill us. We turn to renowned feminist sociologist Patricia Hill Collins and use her typology of "controlling images" as theoretical foundation to understand how embodied carcerality infringes across different contexts.[10] We argue the familiar, everyday controlling images used to reify our physical existence with inherent danger are also weaponized to justify legally branding us with a criminal mark. This sociocultural and politicized branding is successful because those same interpersonal interactions that shape the cognitive makeup of the controlled, also shape the controllers, or penal actors. These agents of control are convinced that their perceptions of reality are correct because Black women and girls as deviant has become an established truth in our cultural imagination, which Regina Arnold argues reinforces the dual process of Black victimization and criminalization.[11] We argue the production of embodied carcerality establishes our innate deviance as social fact. Hence, we propose a new controlling image, "The Criminal," as the dominant image that structures all of the other controlling images in Collins's typology. The controllers need little evidence to suggest that one or more controlling images are "real" depictions of Black women and girls in order to enact punishment, as *assumed criminality is the underlying yardstick* justifying the original production of each image.

Embodiment From Image to Control

Examined through the lens of embodiment, Black feminist contributions to the sociology of punishment are essential tools to understand how what Nicole Gonzalez Van Cleve calls "racial degradation" is the intention, not the exception.[12] Black people are positioned as deviant in everyday interactions, even beyond the courtrooms of the most crooked counties. As Marquis Bey teaches us, our bodies are categorized as fixed objects where onlookers presume to know us with a single gaze. This consequential presumption has both obvious and less apparent manifestations. Unpacking the concept of embodied carcerality allows us to operationalize the effect of embodiment on the process of punishment. We advance this exercise by first questioning how controlling images engender a state of embodied carcerality through informal and formal means, and propose "The Criminal" as a dominant schema coproducing each controlling image. Second, we ask how "The Criminal" translates into the institutionalization of controlling images, and examine how they are *practiced* and enacted through criminal justice decision-making and thus further *inscribed* onto Black women and girls as reality.

The Criminal as Dominant Reference

Patricia Hill Collins's seminal *Black Feminist Thought* gifted us with the language to articulate the negative, socially constructed stereotypes we as Black feminists encounter on a daily basis. The "controlling images" of Black womanhood—the mammy, matriarch, welfare mother, and Jezebel—are debilitating caricatures designed to maintain Black women's subordination to whiteness.[13] Reified in media, popular culture, and academic scholarship, these images personify what Philomena Essed called the enduring "gendered racism" and intersectional oppression that are particular to the experiences of Black women and girls.[14] Rooted in efforts to sustain the dominance of slavery on the backs of Black women, these controlling images are attacks to Black female sexuality, motherhood, fertility, dignity, and ultimately freedom. Alexander Weheliye's work expands on these controlling images as "racialized assemblages," or ways of categorizing human groups as a means of subjection.[15]

As a conceptual tool, we believe embodied carcerality reveals how the relationship between controlling images and subjection is an interactive process that we experience in various contexts. Significantly, such controls not only initiate subjection but regulate a precarious existence in perpetuity. Informal interpersonal controls such as glares, harsh words, and outright being ignored are juxtaposed with formal systemic controls such as school discipline, stop and frisk, mandatory drug screenings, the imposition of fines and fees, or checking in with one's parole officer. The baseline image grounding this predicament is that of a dangerous, chaotic criminal where control is a treatment for natural deviance. As such, we extend the controlling images framework to highlight "The Criminal" as the dominant frame of reference, grounding the justification process for inscribing each controlling image onto bodies as everyday practice. The criminal image is rooted in the widely held belief that deviance is born, it is natural, and that it is just the way some are, which is a lasting remnant of early positivist criminology and its foundational backbone, biological racism.

In *Black Feminist Thought*, the *mammy* is the first of Collins's controlling images and reinforces the economic exploitation of Black women through depictions of deference and servitude.[16] The mammy figure is portrayed as the asexual, unattractive, faithful, and obedient domestic servant who acts as a surrogate mother devoted to the cultivation of white families, even at the expense of nurturing her own. Her worth is tied to her ability to support the development of whiteness, whether as a maid, wet nurse, or caretaker. Collins asserts that the mammy image typifies a "normative yardstick used to evaluate all Black women's behavior," particularly the extent to which they can adhere to white ideals of Black submission and docility.[17] The mammy as the epitome of compliance is only possible because her perceived propensity for criminality is low, and her commitment to loyalty is perceived to outweigh her "deviant" desires. Thus, the actual measurement by which Black women and girls are assigned images is determined by how likely they are to succumb to their supposed-deviant, criminal nature. Inherent danger and the perceived likelihood one will "give into" one's "nature" is the true yardstick, with controlling images reified by their juxtaposition to "the criminal." Because the mammy is not entirely "pure," she is still closely watched by the white families she cares for just in case she "cannot help herself" since she was "born that way."

The second controlling image is the *matriarch*—the unfeminine, overly aggressive woman who emasculates her husband and neglects her children. Collins explains that where the mammy figure is used to depict Black mothers in white homes, the matriarch figure is used to portray Black mothers in Black homes.[18] Disparaged as the "bad" Black mother who denigrates her lover or husband but cannot properly supervise her children, the matriarch archetype is used to stigmatize Black women for living in impoverished, female-headed homes and for the educational failure of Black children. The work of Susila Gurusami and Black feminists like Dorothy Roberts reveals how this social stigma continues to contort the lives of low-income Black mothers, particularly those who live in urban communities and are most vulnerable to adverse justice contact.[19] Beneath the matriarch archetype, Black mothers' worth is tied to their inability to uphold traditional ideals about the Black family structure and fulfill their "traditional womanly duties" as wives and mothers.[20] The matriarch is a powerful controlling image because of its proximity to inherent danger as seemingly unfit, neglectful, and thereby criminal. Her biggest offense is her perceived deviation from patriarchal norms as wife and mother, which suggests she has succumbed at least at the family level, to her criminal nature.

The *welfare mother* or *welfare queen* is the third controlling image and typifies the supposed laziness and deception of Black women. Portrayed as a woman who misuses or steals welfare payments through fraud or manipulation, the image of the welfare mother is used to stigmatize poor, often single, Black women who depend on government assistance. The welfare queen is perhaps the most vilified of the controlling images, and is most embedded in our cultural lexicon because she is antithetical to American values of hard work, individualism, and upward mobility. White sociologist Daniel Patrick Moynihan was integral in solidifying this mythical trope to symbolize a "tangle of pathology," which helped to embolden the punitive welfare state. The welfare queen archetype is measured as *that* much closer to the embodiment of the criminal because she is seen as a rational free rider, a leech who takes from the state but does not contribute, and thus a thief without regard for individual responsibility in a capitalist society.

The fourth controlling image is the *Jezebel*—the sassy, sexually aggressive, and lascivious whore whose sexual appetite justified the rape of Black women during enslavement and repeated mistreatment in contemporary society. Jezebels are what K. Sue Jewell termed "bad black girls,"[21] whose bodies are "always public, always exposed," according to Carol Henderson,[22] and "always troubling to dominant visual culture," according to Nicole Fleetwood.[23] The Jezebel is measured as the closest to inherent danger and thus the most poignant example of the criminal incarnate. This occurs because her existence challenges the patriarchal rendition of family, which is grounded in the liberal economic logic that Black women and girls cannot claim ownership of their own bodies.

Because the Criminal as a racialized and gendered trope uses innate danger or natural deviance as the dominant frame of reference, it emboldens the other controlling images with varying degrees of disciplinary power. During interpersonal interactions, Black women and girls are understood in relation to their perceived proximity to the Criminal controlling image. Depending upon where they fall on the spectrum, they are met with the informal and formal controls we have described that produce a state of carceral existence, or embodied carcerality. The consequence is death. Embodied carcerality guides us on this precarious journey, subjecting us to social, civil, and with ultimate finality, physical demise.

Organizing Against the Systemic Consequences of Controlling Images

Imagine deadly consequences as systemic vines, where social control occurs through embodiment. In this world, embodiment is the soil from which controlling images bloom as power. Expanding this approach to controlling images enriches our understanding of punishment as culturally practiced. It is through the process of reification between the read body as a racialized and gendered being, its proximity to "The Criminal," and varying controlling images, that explain Black women's and girls' persistent entanglement within a criminal justice web. The penal actors tasked with determining their fates also embody their roles as disciplinarians and actively engage in reification as a function of their jobs.

Cyntoia Brown's story illuminates the power of embodiment and controlling images for punishment outcomes. Her heavily publicized clemency revealed that as a young girl, Brown ran away from home and was eventually forced into prostitution. One night in particular sealed her fate. At 16 years old, a 43-year-old real estate agent named Johnny Allen solicited Brown for sex and as the night continued, she would come to fear for her life and fatally shoot Allen. Prosecutors claimed she planned to rob him and the shooting was all part of an elaborate premeditated plot. However, Brown maintained her innocence even through her recent release, which came through gubernatorial clemency on August 7, 2019.

Black feminists fought tirelessly for Brown's freedom, never letting the public forget what her original conviction represented. If we take Patricia Hill Collins at her word, then a fair trial for Brown was doomed from the start. As a young Black woman, her position as a sex worker would only serve as further evidence of her inherent sexual deviance and prowess as a Jezebel. It would never serve to vindicate her as a Black girl in peril who fought to survive. The victim image escaped the realm of possibility because before the court she was already assumed to be guilty, her body read as a lascivious whore, a man-eater searching for her next victim. It would be this viscerally engrained trope that would prevent penal actors from seeing Brown as a teenager with the right to fight back when fearing for her life. When evaluating Brown, penal actors engaged in a process of comparison, reading her body and using their own embodied knowledge to assess her proximity to the criminal image. To them, Brown embodied the Jezebel as inscribed by her alleged actions, appearance as Black and female, and troubled life history—all of which placed her as close to the criminal as one can get. Brown was originally convicted and sentenced to mandatory life without parole. Caging in perpetuity—a civil, social, and physical death in one sweeping blow.

Seek relief and ye shall find control—inseparable from sensory experience and perception—in a punishment continuum designed to precede, ensure, and finally outlast any single conviction into infinity. As Black women and girls, carcerality is in our bones, entangling our ancestral spirits like poison ivy. In the words of Christina Sharpe, we remain "in the wake" of a past life that never truly died. Vines latch deep into roots, engulfing the body through intergenerational trauma.

Even Still We Thrive.

Black feminists have organized for centuries against controlling images and these embodied consequences. Alexis Gumbs reminds us the scenes of Black feminist fugitivity spill far and wide across time and space.[24] When we look to our intergenerational efforts, we see there is freedom in the unknown. From Harriet Tubman, Ida B. Wells, and Audre Lorde to Toni Morrison, Angela Davis, Patricia Hill Collins, and Dorothy Roberts, our intergenerational triumphs comfort us. They instill the will to fiercely identify, battle, and dismantle the systems that celebrate our demise and question our humanity.

Notes

1. BrittanyFriedman. "Are Emancipatory Images Possible? On the Relationship Between Criminal Justice Imagery and Embodied Carcerality." Working Paper. Rutgers University Center for Cultural Analysis 2020–2021 Faculty Fellowship. Seminar Theme: What Is Photography? https://cca.rutgers.edu/annual-seminar/2020-2021-seminar-what-is-photography.
2. Brooklynn K. Hitchens. 2021. "Stress and Street Life: Black Women, Urban Inequality, and Coping in a Small Violent City." PhD dissertation, Department of Sociology, Rutgers, The State University of New Jersey.
3. Rose Heyer and Peter Wagner. 2004. "Too Big to Ignore: How Counting People in Prisons Distorted Census 2000." *Prison Policy.* www.prisonersofthecensus.org/toobig/. Accessed October 4, 2019.
4. Sentencing Project. N.d. "Criminal Justice Facts." www.sentencingproject.org/criminaljustice-facts/. Accessed October 4, 2019.
5. Jennifer Bronson and E. Ann Carson. 2019. "Prisoners in 2017 (NCJ 252156)." Bureau of Justice Statistics. Report 1–44. Sentencing Project. 2018. "Fact Sheet: Incarcerated Women and Girls, 1980–2016." Report 1–4.
6. Aleks Kajstura. 2018. "Women's Mass Incarceration: The Whole Pie 2018." *Prison Policy.* www.prisonpolicy.org/reports/pie2018women.html. Accessed October 4, 2019.
7. Alexi Jones. 2018. "Correctional Control 2018: Incarceration and Supervision by State." *Prison Policy.* www.prisonpolicy.org/reports/correctionalcontrol2018.html. Accessed October 4, 2019.
8. Brittany Friedman and Mary Pattillo. 2019. "Statutory Inequality: The Logics of Monetary Sanctions in State Law." *Russell Sage Foundation Journal of the Social Sciences* 5(1): 174–196; Alexes Harris. 2016. *A Pound of Flesh: Monetary Sanctions as Punishment for the Poor.* New York: Russell Sage Foundation; Karin D. Martin. 2018. "Monetary Myopia: An Examination of Institutional Response to Revenue from Monetary Sanctions for Misdemeanors." *Criminal Justice Policy Review* 29(6–7): 630–662.
9. Shatema Threadcraft. 2017. "North American Necropolitics and Gender: On #BlackLivesMatter and Black Femicide." *South Atlantic Quarterly* 116(3): 553–579.
10. Patricia Hill Collins. 1990. *Black Feminist Thought: Knowledge, Consciousness, and the Politics of Empowerment.* New York: Routledge Press.
11. Regina A. Arnold. 1990. "Processes of Victimization and Criminalization of Black Women." *Social Justice* 17(3): 153–166.
12. Nicole Gonzalez Van Cleve. 2016. *Crook County: Race and Injustice in America's Largest Criminal Court.* Palo Alto, CA: Stanford University Press.
13. Collins 1990.
14. Philomena Essed. 1991. *Understanding Everyday Racism: An Interdisciplinary Theory.* Newbury Park: Sage Publications; Brooklynn K. Hitchens. 2019. "Girl Fights and the Online Media Construction of Black Female Violence and Sexuality." *Feminist Criminology* 14(2): 173–197.
15. Alexander G. Weheliye. 2014. *Habeas Viscus: Racializing Assemblages, Biopolitics, and Black Feminist Theories of the Human.* Durham, NC: Duke University Press.
16. Collins 1990.
17. Ibid., 266.
18. Ibid.
19. Susila Gurusami. 2018. "Motherwork Under the State: The Maternal Labor of Formerly Incarcerated Black Women." *Social Problems* 66(1): 128–143. Brooklynn K. Hitchens and Yasser A. Payne. 2017. "Brenda's Got a Baby: Black Single Motherhood and Street Life as a Site of Resilience in Wilmington, Delaware." *Journal of Black Psychology* 43(1): 50–76; Dorothy E. Roberts. 1993. "Motherhood and Crime." *Iowa Law Review* 79: 95–141.

20. Collins 1990, 268; Daniel Patrick Moynihan. 1965. *The Negro Family: The Case for National Action*. United States Department of Labor.
21. K. Sue. Jewell. 1993. *From Mammy to Miss America and Beyond: Cultural Images and the Shaping of U.S. Social Policy*. New York: Routledge Press.
22. Carol Henderson. 2010. "Introduction." In *Imagining the Black Female Body: Reconciling Image in Print and Visual Culture*, edited by Carol Henderson, 1–19. New York: Palgrave Macmillan.
23. Nicole R. Fleetwood. 2011. *Troubling Vision: Performance, Visuality, and Blackness*. Chicago, IL: The University of Chicago Press.
24. Marquis Bey. 2019. *Them Goon Rules: Fugitive Essays on Radical Black Feminism*. Tucson: University of Arizona Press; Alexis Pauline Gumbs. 2016. *Spill: Scenes of Black Feminist Fugitivity*. Durham, NC: Duke University Press; Christina Sharpe. 2016. *In the Wake: On Blackness and Being*. Durham, NC: Duke University Press.

References

Arnold, Regina A. 1990. "Processes of Victimization and Criminalization of Black Women." *Social Justice* 17(3): 153–166.

Bey, Marquis. 2019. *Them Goon Rules: Fugitive Essays on Radical Black Feminism*. Tucson: University of Arizona Press.

Bronson, Jennifer, and E. Ann Carson. 2019. *Prisoners in 2017 (NCJ 252156)*. Washington, DC: Bureau of Justice Statistics. Report 1–44.

Collins, Patricia Hill. 1990. *Black Feminist Thought: Knowledge, Consciousness, and the Politics of Empowerment*. New York: Routledge Press.

Essed, Philomena. 1991. *Understanding Everyday Racism: An Interdisciplinary Theory*. Newbury Park: Sage Publications.

Fleetwood, Nicole R. 2011. *Troubling Vision: Performance, Visuality, and Blackness*. Chicago, IL: The University of Chicago Press.

Friedman, Brittany. "Are Emancipatory Images Possible? On the Relationship Between Criminal Justice Imagery and Embodied Carcerality." Working Paper. Rutgers University Center for Cultural Analysis 2020–2021 Faculty Fellowship. Seminar Theme: What Is Photography? https://cca.rutgers.edu/annual-seminar/2020-2021-seminar-what-is-photography.

Friedman, Brittany, and Mary Pattillo. 2019. "Statutory Inequality: The Logics of Monetary Sanctions in State Law." *Russell Sage Foundation Journal of the Social Sciences* 5(1): 174–196.

Gumbs, Alexis Pauline. 2016. *Spill: Scenes of Black Feminist Fugitivity*. Durham, NC: Duke University Press.

Gurusami, Susila. 2018. "Motherwork Under the State: The Maternal Labor of Formerly Incarcerated Black Women." *Social Problems* 66(1): 128–143.

Harris, Alexes. 2016. *A Pound of Flesh: Monetary Sanctions as Punishment for the Poor*. New York: Russell Sage Foundation.

Henderson, Carol. 2010. "Introduction." In *Imagining the Black Female Body: Reconciling Image in Print and Visual Culture*, edited by Carol Henderson, 1–19. New York: Palgrave Macmillan.

Heyer, Rose, and Peter Wagner. 2004. "Too Big to Ignore: How Counting People in Prisons Distorted Census 2000." *Prison Policy*. www.prisonersofthecensus.org/toobig/. Accessed October 4, 2019.

Hitchens, Brooklynn K. 2019. "Girl Fights and the Online Media Construction of Black Female Violence and Sexuality." *Feminist Criminology* 14(2): 173–197.

Hitchens, Brooklynn K. 2021. "Stress and Street Life: Black Women, Urban Inequality, and Coping in a Small Violent City." PhD Dissertation, Department of Sociology, Rutgers, The State University of New Jersey.

Hitchens, Brooklynn K. and Yasser A. Payne. 2017. "Brenda's Got a Baby: Black Single Motherhood and Street Life as a Site of Resilience in Wilmington, Delaware." *Journal of Black Psychology* 43(1): 50–76.

Jewell, K. Sue. 1993. *From Mammy to Miss America and Beyond: Cultural Images and the Shaping of U.S. Social Policy.* New York: Routledge Press.

Jones, Alexi. 2018. "Correctional Control 2018: Incarceration and Supervision by State." *Prison Policy.* www.prisonpolicy.org/reports/correctionalcontrol2018.html. Accessed October 4, 2019.

Kajstura, Aleks. 2018. "Women's Mass Incarceration: The Whole Pie 2018." *Prison Policy.* www.prisonpolicy.org/reports/pie2018women.html. Accessed October 4, 2019.

Martin, Karin D. 2018. "Monetary Myopia: An Examination of Institutional Response to Revenue from Monetary Sanctions for Misdemeanors." *Criminal Justice Policy Review* 29(6–7): 630–662.

Moynihan, Daniel Patrick. 1965. *The Negro Family: The Case for National Action.* Washington, DC: United States Department of Labor.

Roberts, Dorothy E. 1993. "Motherhood and Crime." *Iowa Law Review* 79: 95–141.

Sentencing Project. 2018. "Fact Sheet: Incarcerated Women and Girls, 1980–2016." Washington, DC. Accessed June 29, 2021 (https://www.sentencingproject.org/wp-content/uploads/2016/02/Incarcerated-Women-and-Girls.pdf).

Sentencing Project. n.d. "Criminal Justice Facts." www.sentencingproject.org/criminaljustice-facts/. Accessed October 4, 2019.

Sharpe, Christina. 2016. *In the Wake: On Blackness and Being.* Durham, NC: Duke University Press.

Theadcraft, Shatema. 2017. "North American Necropolitics and Gender: On #BlackLivesMatter and Black Femicide." *South Atlantic Quarterly* 116(3): 553–579.

Van Cleve, Nicole Gonzalez. 2016. *Crook County: Race and Injustice in America's Largest Criminal Court.* Palo Alto, CA: Stanford University Press.

Weheliye, Alexander G. 2014. *Habeas Viscus: Racializing Assemblages, Biopolitics, and Black Feminist Theories of the Human.* Durham, NC: Duke University Press.

Chapter 22

Too Intersectional

What Black Feminism and Disability Studies Can Build Together

Subini Ancy Annamma

> Here are the words of some of the women I have been, am being still, will come to be.
>
> —Audre Lorde, *Chosen Poems-Old and New,* 1982

With this quote, Audre Lorde reminds us that we are always evolving. Black feminist sociology, with its foundations in Black feminism, has been a wellspring of ideas bringing us closer to liberation from intersecting oppressions. In one of the foundational texts on Black feminist sociology, Patricia Hill Collins reminds us that Black feminist sociology has broken down borders between academic disciplines as well as between the academy and the streets.[1] Moreover, Black feminist sociology understands that dismantling interlocking oppressions requires stretching theory. In another foundational Black feminist sociology text, Rose M. Brewer stated,

> Alone, race, class and gender are rather sterile categories for black feminist thinking. They are infused with meaning developed out of many decades of social thought on class, race, and gender. However, *in interplay and interaction the concepts of race, class, and gender become rich.* Nonetheless, delineating the nature of the paradigm and the specifics of the intersection have proved to be rather difficult. This is because the metaframeworks of class, gender, and race, have to be revisioned.[2]

Using Brewer's and Lorde's words, I invite Black feminist sociologists to consider what metaframeworks of ours can be revisioned and suggest evolving to include a critical disability studies lens.

As opposed to a traditional view of disability that (1) understands disability as a biological deficit, (2) individualizes disability as an individual or family problem and (3) strives to fix or remediate disability; disability studies is the "socio-political-cultural examination of disability."[3] Hence, disability studies recognizes that disability is not a problem to be fixed, but that all bodies are different and what matters is what meaning we

DOI: 10.4324/9781003199113-28

bring to bear on those differences.[4] To be clear, disability studies continues to center whiteness, as shown in Chris Bell's academic critique[5] and Vilissa Thompson's #DisabilityTooWhite public intellectual callout. Consequently, I infuse Black feminist sociology with disability critical race theory (DisCrit).[6] I begin by sharing real world examples of state violence against Black Disabled[7] girls considered too intersectional, what critical race feminist Michele Goodwin describes as "when one possess(es) a host of 'bad' markers or social characteristics."[8] Often Black Disabled girls are imagined as both superhuman and out of control—this master narrative justifies violence, yet at times, they go unprotected by Black feminists. Next I ask, what can "*What can Black feminism and DisCrit learn from each other?*" In this section, I recognize how throughout time Blackness and disability have been linked to eliminate Black people's rights, often making them hesitant to identify as Disabled. Yet this reticence to claim Disabled as a political identity can miss the ways ableism and racism are intertwined and used to strip humanity from all Black girls. Finally, I introduce Black feminist scholars who can guide us revisioning our frameworks. I invite Black feminist sociologists to consider what happens when Black feminist sociology is animated with DisCrit. DisCrit does not seek to replace white supremacy and patriarchy as the center of the analysis—instead, this multidimensional framing articulates how racism and ableism work together to uniquely position all Black girls as less than and Disabled Black girls as in need of punishment. We can evolve as Black feminist sociologists to reflect on how we uphold notions of normalcy, refuse the erasure of Disabled Black girls, and articulate why ableism and racism must be recognized.

The Violence of Being Read as Too Intersectional

In September 2019, Kaia, a 6-year-old Black girl, was arrested and transported via police car to a juvenile detention center;[9] the cause was a tantrum thrown in school, where she allegedly kicked a teacher after the teacher grabbed her wrists in an attempt to calm her down. After a public outcry, the arresting officer, a Black man, was eventually fired. State Attorney Aramis Ayala, a Black woman, dropped the charges, stating, "I refuse to play any role in the school-to-prison pipeline at any age. . . . This is not a reflection on the children but more of a reflection of a broken system that is in need of reform."[10]

As Professor Monique Morris has noted, the education system often pushes out Black girls. Given that 12 percent of Black girls are suspended, compared to just 2 percent of white girls,[11] the consequences for the officer and Ayala's refusal to charge Kaia were a reprieve from that push out.[12] However, less discussed was that Kaia's disability made her a target for the state's policy on violence in school. Kaia's grandmother Meralyn Kirkland described a conversation with the arresting officer,

> Kaia was acting out in class, a side effect due to a lack of sleep because of a medical condition. So he says, "What medical condition?" I said, "You know she has a sleep disorder, sleep apnea," and he says, "Well, I have sleep apnea, and I don't behave like that."[13]

Kirkland linking Kaia's arrest directly to her disability was a needed intervention, cutting through the narrative of "out of control" Black girl. Yet Kirkland and Kaia's counternarrative was denigrated by the officer and ignored in many ensuing discussions. Meanwhile, 19 percent of Black Disabled girls are suspended,[14] putting them in even more danger of being criminalized in schools than their non-disabled peers. Kaia's story is not unique; Black Disabled girls are rarely protected and often punished.[15]

In February 2019, an 11-year-old Black girl in a segregated special education class was assaulted by a white male teacher, wherein her braids were ripped from her head.[16] Later, a video was released showing the Black girl being thrown to the ground by that teacher.[17] Though the teacher was put on leave and eventually resigned, no charges were filed. The girl's mother, Mikiea Price believed the police and district attorney had their minds made up prior to the investigation. In fact, the district attorney requested records from the county human services department about Price's parenting, which the department refused.[18] In a scathing letter a department attorney, wrote,

> You have not provided any reason why you would be seeking reports related to the alleged victim and her family, nor in what way those records would be relevant to the current investigation. (The student's) parents are not the alleged maltreaters. . . . There is no viable reason for your office to be seeking records related to them.[19]

The violence this Black Disabled girl experienced at school was exacerbated by the police. Similar to the role Ayala played in Kaia's story, this violence was interrupted because one individual/department refused the pathologizing narrative the system was perpetuating.

According to some adults, the incident started because the Black Disabled girl sprayed air freshener, the teacher requested the girl stop, and the Black Disabled girl refused. Rob Mueller-Owens, a white male teacher, was called; the Black Disabled girl was instructed to leave, and she again refused. This narrative situates this Black Disabled girl as obstinate, but the police report provides context.[20] Tammy Gue, another adult in the room, describe it as being "like a cat and mouse game" and that "Mueller-Owens was following this [Black Disabled girl] around the room." Gue goes on,

"Mueller-Owens grabs. . . , pivots, and throws them onto the ground." The police report goes on to state that the officer "asked Gue who initiated the physical contact and she said Mueller-Owens. She told me there was no justification for Mueller-Owens to push her out of the classroom." A student witness from police report stated:

> Rob [Mueller-Owens] tried to push [Black Disabled girl] out of the room but [Black Disabled girl] was able to stop this action with her foot. [The police] asked [student witness] how Rob was pushing [student] and she stated with both hands.

These narratives by a student witness and one adult completely contrast the other two adults in the room. Again, according to the police report, "Mueller-Owens said that [Black Disabled girl] 'was punching with such force that she was using her entire upper body to swing her fists and as she was punching, her head would swing left or right with her body.'" Another teacher witness stated, "She fully expected to see blood on Rob's face based on the severity of the attack on him by [Black Disabled girl] and was surprised when she did not see blood on Rob's face." The two educators attempted to superhumanize this 11-year-old Black girl, claiming she possessed extraordinary amounts of strength.[21] Black children are often subjected to superhumanization, which is dehumanizing because they are not imagined as victims. It is important to note that gender does not protect Black girls: "That is, beginning as early as 5 years of age, Black girls were more likely to be viewed as behaving and seeming older than their stated age."[22] Black girls are often imagined as dangerous and devious, withholding perceptions of ability and innocence. This is further exacerbated as often Black Disabled people are described as having "super human strength," as Annnamma, Ferri and Connor demonstrated in their explanation of how this language was used to justify the killing of Natasha McKenna.[23] Thus, being a Black Disabled girl situated this 11-year-old child as being both superhuman and out of control; justifying the use of force.

These incidents are not isolated moments, but part of a systemic context in which Black Disabled girls are in danger in schools. In the district where the 11-year-old Black Disabled girl had her braids ripped out, the numbers are disturbing. Black Disabled elementary students were six times more likely, Disabled Black middle schoolers were 27 times more likely, and Disabled Black high schoolers were 76 times more likely to be arrested than non-Black students.[24] Though Black students overall were overrepresented in arrests, the glaring disparities that Black Disabled students experienced cannot be ignored (See Table 1).

Further context is provided by looking at seclusion and restraints, two trends in schools that are rarely discussed but still used. The US

Table 22.1 Arrest Rates of Disabled Black Students at Madison Metropolitan School District (MMSD) Compared to All Non-Black Students

	Non-Black Students	*Disabled Black Students*
Elementary	0*	6x
Middle School	6x	27x
High School	21x	76x

Source: Office of Civil Rights Data, disaggregated by Nino Rodriguez

* Black elementary students without disabilities had the same rate of arrest as all non-Black students in all grade levels combined

Department of Education defines seclusion as "the involuntary confinement of a student alone in a room or area from which the student is physically prevented from leaving."[25] This does not include unlocked timeout rooms. This is a wholly different kind of restriction, one that locks a student in isolation. A restraint is "restriction that immobilizes or reduces the ability of a student to move his or her torso, arms, legs, or head freely."[26] In a recent article on the use of seclusion and restraint in Washington, DC in the 2015–2016 school year, Kaplan reported: "That year, every single student restrained or secluded was a person of color."[27] I followed up with Kaplan and he shared more specifics: 130 students in Washington DC had been secluded a total of 527 times. Over 95 percent (124 students) were Black. Kaplan found that 188 students were restrained 379 times. Over 93 percent (176 students) were Black. Finally, two students were mechanically restrained, and both were Black.

When I followed up to determine how many of these children had a disability label, Kaplan responded: 88 of the 130 of who had been secluded and 118 of the 176 who had been restrained were Disabled; meaning over two-thirds of students who had been secluded and restrained were Disabled and over 90 percent were Black. Kaplan's analysis reinforces what is happening across the country: Black Disabled students are disproportionately being secluded and restrained.[28] These numbers were not broken down by gender, but we can predict many of these Black Disabled youth are Black girls, given their overrepresentation in other forms of school punishment.

Ultimately, instead of a disability label providing protection, Black Disabled girls are being targeted *because* of their disability. In Kaia's case, instead of recognizing how sleep disorders impact children's behaviors, those behaviors were used as a rationale to criminalize. In the 11-year-old's case, being in a segregated special education classroom "justified" a physical attack in response to her behaviors. Both were punished through physical assault, while others are being secluded and restrained—all of these responses are severely traumatizing.[29] This state violence continues to put Black Disabled girls in danger of experiencing trauma at school. Yet because they are "too intersectional" or experience a myriad of oppressions, some Black feminist sociologists do not theorize, and some Black activists do not organize, around these Black Disabled girls. So, I ask, "*What can Black feminist sociology and DisCrit learn from each other?*"

Evolving: Building a Bridge

Lorde's opening quote reminds us to be ever-evolving as Black feminists. When asked to expand on her meaning, Lorde answered.

> A poem grows out of the poet's experience, in a particular place and a particular time, and the genius of the poem is to use the textures of that place and time without becoming bound by them. Then the poem becomes an emotional bridge to others who have not shared that experience. The poem evokes its own world.[30]

Our goals then—as poets, writers, scholars—is to bridge to others who do not share the same experience. Not all Black feminists are Disabled, but Black feminist sociologists can recognize and call out ableism and how it intertwines with racism, uniquely targeting Black girls and women. Black feminist sociologists, then, can follow Brewer's argument considering what metaframeworks can be revisioned. To do so, I explore what Black feminist sociology and DisCrit can learn from each other. In *Homegirls*, Barbara Smith wrote,

> The simultaneity of oppression is still the crux of a Black feminist understanding of political reality and . . . is one of the most significant ideological contributions of Black feminist thought. . . . We saw no reason to rank oppressions, or as many forces in the Black community would have us do, to pretend that sexism, among all the "isms," was not happening to us. Black feminists' efforts to comprehend the complexity of our situation as it was actually occurring. . . . Although we made use of the insights of other political ideologies, such as socialism, we added an element that has often been missing from the theory of others: what oppression is comprised of on a day-to-day basis.[31]

DisCrit's foundation in Black feminism meant that the "simultaneity of oppression" became a central tenet. Consequently, DisCrit learned from Black feminist sociology how intersectionality was not about a stacking of identities, but the ways oppressions converged and manifested in the day-to-day lives of Black girls.[32]

Drawing on the simultaneity of oppression, DisCrit recognizes how racism and ableism are mutually constitutive. Public intellectual and activist, TL Lewis, defines ableism:

> A system that places value on people's bodies and minds based on societally constructed ideas of normalcy, intelligence and excellence. These constructed ideas of normalcy, intelligence and excellence are deeply rooted in anti-Blackness, eugenics and capitalism. This form of systemic oppression leads to people and society determining who is valuable or worthy based on people's appearance and/or their ability to satisfactorily produce, excel & "behave." You do not have to be disabled to experience ableism.

In contrast to traditional disability studies work that centers whiteness and white people, Lewis's definition centers how normalcy is rooted in ideas of anti-Blackness, positioning all Black people as abnormal in learning, behavior, and intellect. Ableism and racism circulate in ways that reinforce normalcy as white, male, middle class, and cis-het. Said differently, ableism *enables* whiteness, consistently (re)orienting it as the norm, and concurrently ignoring when whiteness does not meet its own standards,[33] resulting in the celebration of white mediocrity.

Conversely, ableism debilitates Black people generally, and Black girls specifically. Debilitating processes, such as "the discourse, policies, and practices that limit access to being perceived as able and therefore worthy of support, often position Black girls as unwanted."[34] Employing debilitation this way rejects traditional uses that focus on the body or mind as biologically debilitated and highlight the processes that make spaces inaccessible. Those spaces are imbued with anti-Blackness and misogynoir,[35] which is enacted on Black girls through debilitating processes. Consequently, terms like *ghetto, difficult, loud, aggressive*, and others routinely applied to Black girls[36] are rooted in ableism and racism, debilitating Black girls. In a study with 70 high school—aged Black girls, Carter-Andrews, Brown, Castro, and Id-Deen found:

> Black girls described toxic racialized and gendered experiences with adults and peers in their schools . . . in both academic and extracurricular spaces. The girls were not immune from having their ways of being and knowing challenged and dismissed in environments where their identities and epistemologies should have been affirmed and valued.[37]

Consequently, the interdependence of racism and ableism that challenge their knowing and being make the world difficult to navigate for all Black girls; understanding that reality can strengthen the theorizing and analysis of Black feminist sociology. Being able to name ableism makes it more likely we can disrupt it as a tool of oppression that is rooted in anti-Blackness and white supremacy. Consequently, DisCrit can help Black feminist sociology engage in a substantive conversation on ableism that does not seek to replace racism, but understands the way they both work in tandem with sexism and classism to label, surveil, and punish Black girls.[38]

Black feminist sociology recognizes the social construction of race and gender, and the material impacts of being a Black woman.[39] DisCrit learned from Black feminist sociology to root itself in the material realities that result from social constructions of oppressed identities. Focusing on Black Disabled girls is necessary because they face dire material realities. They are overrepresented in school discipline, compared to non-Disabled Black girls. This is not to rank oppressions, but to recognize how ableism lands in lives differently. That is, ableism impacts all Black girls, *and* it hits Black Disabled girls hardest, literally. Similar, but of course not the same, to how cis-heteropatriarchy impacts all Black women, but is most dangerous for Black trans women. Black Disabled girls are constant targets and yet rarely afforded protection. Understanding ableism, then, requires that we understand how it lands in the lives of Black women and girls differently. Hence, Black feminist sociology would benefit from more consistent theorizing around and analyzing of the experiences of Black Disabled girls and women.

Rose M. Brewer notes that sociology as a field must contend with the "history and realities of racism, sexism, and classism,"[40] as it helps frame a systemic analysis of inequities that people of color face. Black feminist sociology required DisCrit to deeply engage with historical legacy of intertwining oppressions in order to strengthen its power to discern the processes that animate inequities. Moreover, the legal system has historically, and still currently, has been wielded as a weapon again Black women and girls.[41]

It has long been recognized that whiteness has functioned as a property right that confers intangible and material benefits to those who fit within its boundaries and punishes those who do not.[42] For Black women and girls, whiteness as property has been withheld along raced, gendered, and classed lines.[43] Critical race feminism has instructed DisCrit to theorize and analyze how property rights are secured and its borders tightened to keep out Black women and girls.[44]

Historically, Blackness and disability have been conflated, making many Black folks aware that being named as Disabled just for being Black facilitates the stripping of their rights. This historical trajectory has resulted in many Black people refusing to be associated with disability. Pickens notes, "Consider the historical relationship among blackness, womanhood and disability, which pitted the first two against the third."[45] Yet this reticence

misses the ways racism and ableism are intertwined, tightening the property boundaries of who we are willing to fight for socially and legally.[46] We
risk erasing Black Disabled girls from movements, while they are particularly susceptible to interpersonal and state violence. Thus, DisCrit allows
Black feminist sociologists to broaden our theorizing and analyzing, building coalitions that authentically include and are led by Black Disabled
women and girls.

Scholars That Refuse the Master Narrative of Too Intersectional

Ultimately there are many points of alignment wherein DisCrit has learned
from Black feminism, and Black feminist sociology can learn from Dis-
Crit. Black feminist sociology can continue to teach DisCrit lessons about
centering Black girls and women, and DisCrit can educate Black feminist
sociology around how to engage margins that have been underexplored.
Luckily for all of us, interdisciplinary scholars have taken up this call.

Therí Pickens has been leading the theorizing of the ways Blackness and
Disability are constructed.[47] She stated, "I call upon feminist, disability,
and black studies (or studies of race more broadly) as more than mere
enhancements to one another, but rather as conjoined enterprises that clarify the interrelated nature of form and content."[48] Her new book, *Black
Madness: Mad Blackness* pushes the boundaries of how we theorize about
the links between Blackness and disability.

Sami Schalk's new work *Bodyminds Reimagined: (Dis)ability, Race, and
Gender in Black Women's Speculative Fiction* allows for the deep engagement of Black women's lives in nonrealist contexts. Schalk notes,

> When Black feminist, critical race and gender studies scholars leave
> unchallenged the social construction of able-mindedness, accepting
> that able-mindedness is a necessary precursor to having racialized and
> gendered experiences of reality validated and recognized, we leave
> intact the very ableism being used against us.[49]

Schalk expands the boundaries for Black feminist sociology to engage in a
conversation about sexism, ableism, and racism in worldmaking.

Finally, Moya Bailey and Izetta Mobley wrote "Black Feminist Disability
Studies" as they unapologetically center Black feminism in disability studies. They argue,

> Rather than reformulate Crenshaw's model, we build on the intersec-
> tional work of scholars in both fields to suggest that disability, race,
> and gender are always already present and simply need to be attended
> to in our analysis. . . . To have a conversation and far more generative

theoretical projects that ultimately serve the goal of our collective liberation, this article moves unnecessarily disparate theoretical spaces toward each other.[50]

Each of these scholars is forging a pathing for Black feminist sociology and DisCrit scholars. They are mapping the margins for the rest of us, bringing the spaces that have been thrust aside into the center.[51]

Conclusion

In the cases of the Disabled Black girls who had been harassed, arrested, or assaulted in schools, some Black feminists either ignored the incidents or erased their disability when fighting for them. Yet, no Black girl or Black woman is "too" intersectional; this myriad of bad social characteristics is defined through systemic commitments to ableism rooted in white supremacy and fueled by anti-Blackness. Given that these are the very projects we work against, DisCrit and Black feminist sociology scholars must reflect on how we uphold notions of normalcy that ultimately (re)produce the very systems we seek to tear down. This reflection allows us to follow Lorde's words, evolving by returning to the Black Disabled girls' stories and reimagining the ways we can listen to and support them, so they can be brought into and lead coalitions, and we can all move toward justice. Ultimately, DisCrit and Black feminist sociology have much to learn from each other, and with these scholars lighting the way forward, we can all evolve from the women we were, the women we are, and move toward the women we will become.

Notes

1. Patricia Hill Collins. 1986. "Learning from the Outsider Within: The Sociological Significance of Black Feminist Thought." *Social Problems* 33(6): s14–s32.
2. Rose M. Brewer. 1989. "Black Women and Feminist Sociology: The Emerging Perspective." *American Sociologist* 20(1): 57–70. (Italics added for emphasis).
3. Simi Linton. 1998. "Disability Studies/Not Disability Studies." *Disability & Society* 13(4): 525.
4. Susan Baglieri and Janice H. Knopf. 2004. "Normalizing Difference in Inclusive Teaching." *Journal of Learning Disabilities* 37(6): 525–529.
5. Chris Bell. 2006. "A Modest Proposal." In *The Disability Studies Reader*, edited by L. J. Davis, 275–282. 2nd ed. New York: Routledge.
6. Subini Ancy Annamma, David Connor, and Beth Ferri. 2013. "Dis/ability Critical Race Studies (DisCrit): Theorizing at the Intersections of Race and Dis/ability." *Race Ethnicity and Education* 16(1): 1–31.
7. Wilmot, Annamma and Migliarini state: "We capitalize Disabled because we recognize that unlike conceptions of disability as deficit, we conceptualize Disability as a political identity with both material realities and a lineage of political resistance. Specifically, Black Disabled people have been fighting intersectional oppressions. . . . For more on Black Disabled as a political identity, see Vilissa Thompson's work *Black Disabled*

Woman's syllabus. . . . We also use Black Disabled women instead of Black woman with a disability because separating Disability implies a medical condition that one seeks to separate from the person." In S. Annamma, J. Wilmot, and V. Migliarini. (in press). "Everywhere and Nowhere: Expansive Notions of Disability to Counter the Erasure of Black Women and Girls." In *Investing in the Educational Success of Black Women and Girls*, edited by L. Patton Davis, V. Evans-Winters, and C. Jacobs.

8. Michele Goodwin. 2003. "Gender, Race, and Mental Illness: The Case of Wanda Jean Allen." In *Critical Race Feminism: A Reader*, 228–237, 229. New York: New York University Press.

9. Nicky Zizaza. 2019. "'A Literal Mug Shot of a 6-Year-Old Girl': Grandmother Outraged over Child's Arrest." www.clickorlando.com/2019/09/23/a-literal-mug-shot-of-a-6-year-old-girl-grandmother-outraged-over-childs-arrest/

10. A. Cutway. "Charges Dropped against 6-Year-Old Children Arrested at Orlando School. 2019." www.clickorlando.com/2019/09/25/charges-dropped-against-6-year-old-children-arrested-at-orlando-school-2/

11. US Department of Education Office for Civil Rights. 2014. "Civil Rights Data Collection Data Snapshot: School Discipline." Issue Brief No. 1. https://ocrdata.ed.gov/Downloads/CRDC-School-Discipline-Snapshot.pdf`

12. Monique Morris. 2016. *Pushout: The Criminalization of Black Girls in Schools*. New York: New Press.

13. "Officer under Scrutiny after Grandmother Says 6-Year-Old Arrested, Handcuffed." 2019. *Stamford Advocate*. para. 12. www.stamfordadvocate.com/national/article/Officer-under-scrutiny-after-grandmother-says-14461464.php

14. US Department of Education Office for Civil Rights 2014.

15. Subini Ancy Annamma. 2018. *The Pedagogy of Pathologization: Dis/abled Girls of Color in the School-Prison Nexus*. New York: Routledge.

16. Robert Chappell and Stephanie Díaz de León Madison. 2019. "Teacher on Leave after Alleged Beating of Girl, 11, Caught on Video." https://madison365.com/madison-teacher-on-leave-after-alleged-beating-of-girl-11-caught-on-video/

17. Fox 47 News Staff. 2019. "Video Posted Online Shows Blurry Whitehorse Middle School Incident." http://fox47.com/news/local/video-posted-online-shows-blurry-whitehorse-middle-school-incident

18. Negassi Tesfamichael. 2019. "Explained: What Do the Police Reports Say about What Happened at Whitehorse Middle School?" https://madison.com/ct/news/local/education/explained-what-do-the-police-reports-say-about-what-happened/article_f9756d57-5446-5e9a-9fae-3a71a5668d29.html

19. Ibid., para. 26.

20. Madison Police Department. 2019. https://bloximages.chicago2.vip.townnews.com/madison.com/content/tncms/assets/v3/editorial/a/90/a90429ed-1b3a-55e9-8a7b-38ec78d4b7bd/5c7ed2eea533c.pdf.pdf

21. Adam Waytz, Kelly Marie Hoffman, and Sophie Trawalter. 2015. "A Superhumanization Bias in Whites' Perceptions of Blacks." *Social Psychological and Personality Science* 6(3): 352–359.

22. Rebecca Epstein, Jamilia Blake, and Thalia González. 2017. "Girlhood Interrupted: The Erasure of Black Girls' Childhood." SSRN 3000695, 8.

23. Subini Annamma, Beth A. Ferri, and David J. Connor. 2018. "Cultivating and Expanding Disability Critical Race Theory (DisCrit)." *Manifestos for the Future of Critical Disability Studies: Volume 1*, 230–238. Toledo: Routledge.

24. Office of Civil Rights. 2012, disaggregated by Nino Rodriguez.

25. US Department of Education. 2012. "Restraint and Seclusion: Resource Document." 10. https://sites.ed.gov/idea/files/restraints-and-seclusion-resources.pdf

26. Ibid.

27. Kaplan, Josh. 2019. "When D.C. Schools Use Restraint or Seclusion, No Laws Govern Them. Allegations of Abuse Are Piling Up, para. 35." https://washington citypaper.com/article/177217/when-dc-schools-use-restraint-or-seclusion-no-laws-govern-them-allegations-of-abuse-are-piling-up/

28. US Department of Education Office for Civil Rights 2014.

29. Jennifer Smith Richards, Jodi S. Cohen, and Lakeidra Chavis. 2019. "The Quiet Rooms." https://features.propublica.org/illinois-seclusion-rooms/school-students-put-in-isolated-timeouts/

30. Charles H. Rowell and Audre Lorde. 2000. "Above the Wind: An Interview with Audre Lorde." *Callaloo* 23(1): 52–63.

31. Barbara Smith. 2001. "Introduction to Home Girls: A Black Feminist Anthology." In *Identity Politics in the Women's Movement*, edited by B. Ryan, 146–162, New York: NYU Press.

32. Andrea J. Ritchie. 2017. *Invisible No More: Police Violence against Black Women and Women of Color*. Boston, MA: Beacon Press.

33. Zeus Leonardo and Alicia Broderick. 2011. "Smartness as Property: A Critical Exploration of Intersections between Whiteness and Disability Studies." *Teachers College Record* 113(10): 2206–2232.

34. Annamma, Wilmot, and Migliarini. In press.

35. Moya Bailey. 2013. "New Terms of Resistance: A Response to Zenzele Isoke." *Souls* 15(4): 341–343.

36. V. E. Evans-Winters and Girls for Gender Equity. 2017. "Flipping the Script: The Dangerous Bodies of Girls of Color." *Cultural Studies Critical Methodologies* 17(5): 415–423; N. Jones. 2009. *Between Good and Ghetto: African American Girls and Inner-City*. New Brunswick, NJ: Rutgers University Press; E. W. Morris. 2007. "'Ladies' or 'loudies'? Perceptions and Experiences of Black Girls in Classrooms." *Youth & Society* 38: 490–515.

37. Dorinda J. Carter Andrews, Tashal Brown, Eliana Castro, and Effat Id-Deen. 2019. "The Impossibility of Being 'Perfect and White': Black Girls' Racialized and Gendered Schooling Experiences." *American Educational Research Journal* 56(6): 2531–2572.

38. Annamma 2018.

39. Frances M. Beal. 2008. "Double Jeopardy: To Be Black and Female." *Meridians* 8(2): 166–176.

40. Brewer 1989.

41. Beth Richie.2012. *Arrested Justice: Black Women, Violence, and America's Prison Nation*. New York: New York Univeristy Press.

42. Cheryl I. Harris. 1993. "Whiteness as Property." *Harvard Law Review*: 1707–1791.

43. Carter Andrews, Brown, Castro, and Id-Deen 2019.

44. Adrien Katherine Wing (ed.). 1997. *Critical Race Feminism: A Reader*. New York: New York University Press.

45. Therí A. Pickens. 2015. "Octavia Butler and the Aesthetics of the Novel." *Hypatia* 30(1): 169.

46. Goodwin 2003, 229.

47. Therí A. Pickens. 2019. *Black Madness: Mad Blackness*. Durham, NC: Duke University Press.

48. Pickens 2015, 169.

49. Sami Schalk.2018. *Bodyminds Reimagined:(Dis)ability, Race, and Gender in Black Women's Speculative Fiction*. Durham, NC: Duke University Press.

50. Moya Bailey and Izetta Autumn Mobley. 2019. "Work in the Intersections: A Black Feminist Disability Framework." *Gender & Society* 33(1): 19–40.

51. Kimberlé Crenshaw. 1991. "Mapping the Margins: Intersectionality, Identity Politics, and Violence against Women of Color," *Stanford Law Review* 43(6): 1241–1299.

References

Annamma, Subini Ancy. 2018. *The Pedagogy of Pathologization: Dis/abled Girls of Color in the School-Prison Nexus*. New York: Routledge.

Annamma, Subini Ancy, David Connor, and Beth Ferri. 2013. "Dis/ability Critical Race Studies (DisCrit): Theorizing at the Intersections of Race and Dis/ability." *Race Ethnicity and Education* 16(1): 1–31.

Annamma, Subini Ancy, Beth A. Ferri, and David J. Connor. 2018. "Cultivating and Expanding Disability Critical Race Theory (DisCrit)." In *Manifestos for the Future of Critical Disability Studies: Volume 1*, 230–238. Toledo: Routledge.

Annamma, Subini Ancy, J. Wilmot, and V. Migliarini, V. In press. "Everywhere and Nowhere: Expansive Notions of Disability to Counter the Erasure of Black Women and Girls." In *Investing in the Educational Success of Black Women and Girls*, edited by L. Patton Davis, V. Evans-Winters, and C. Jacobs.

Baglieri, S., and J. H. Knopf. 2004. "Normalizing Difference in Inclusive Teaching." *Journal of Learning Disabilities* 37(6): 525–529.

Bailey, M. 2013. "New Terms of Resistance: A Response to Zenzele Isoke." *Souls* 15(4): 341–343.

Bailey, M. and I. A. Mobley. 2019. "Work in the Intersections: A Black Feminist Disability Framework." *Gender & Society* 33(1): 19–40.

Beal, F. M. 2008. "Double Jeopardy: To be Black and Female." *Meridians: Feminism, Race, Transnationalism* 8(2): 166–176.

Bell, Chris. 2006. "A Modest Proposal." In *The Disability Studies Reader*, edited by L. J. Davis, 275–282. 2nd ed. New York: Routledge.

Brewer, R. M. 1989. "Black Women and Feminist Sociology: The Emerging Perspective." *American Sociologist* 20(1): 57–70.

Carter Andrews, D. J., T. Brown, E. Castro, and E. Id-Deen. 2019. "The Impossibility of Being 'Perfect and White': Black Girls' Racialized and Gendered Schooling Experiences." *American Educational Research Journal*. https://doi.org/10.3102/0002831219849392

Collins, Patricia Hill. 1986. "Learning from the Outsider Within: The Sociological Significance of Black Feminist Thought." *Social Problems* 33(6): s14–s32.

Crenshaw, K. 1991. "Mapping the Margins: Intersectionality, Identity Politics, and Violence against Women of Color." *Stanford Law Review*: 1241–1299.

Cutway, A. 2019. "Charges Dropped against 6-Year-Old Children Arrested at Orlando School. www.clickorlando.com/2019/09/25/charges-dropped-against-6-year-old-children-arrested-at-orlando-school-2/

Epstein, Rebecca, Jamilia Blake, and Thalia González. 2017. "Girlhood Interrupted: The Erasure of Black Girls' Childhood." Available at SSRN 3000695, 8.

Evans-Winters, V. E., and Girls for Gender Equity. 2017. "Flipping the Script: The Dangerous Bodies of Girls of Color." *Cultural Studies Critical Methodologies* 17(5): 415–423.

Goodwin, M. 2003. "Gender, Race, and Mental Illness: The Case of Wanda Jean Allen." In *Critical Race Feminism: A Reader*, edited by A. K. Wing, 228–237. New York: New York University Press.

Harris, C. 1993. "Whiteness as Property." *Harvard Law Review* 106: 1709–1791.

Jones, N. 2009. *Between Good and Ghetto: African American Girls and Inner-city Violence*. New Brunswick, NJ: Rutgers University Press.

Leonardo, Z., and A. Broderick. 2011. "Smartness as Property: A Critical Exploration of Intersections between Whiteness and Disability Studies." *Teachers College Record* 113(10): 2206–2232.

Linton, S. 1998. "Disability Studies/Not Disability Studies." *Disability & Society* 13(4): 525–539.

Morris, E. W. 2007. "'Ladies' or 'Loudies'? Perceptions and Experiences of Black Girls in Classrooms." *Youth & Society* 38: 490–515.

Morris, Monique. 2016. *Pushout: The Criminalization of Black Girls in Schools.* New York: New Press.

Pickens, T. A. 2015. "Octavia Butler and the Aesthetics of the Novel." *Hypatia* 30(1): 167–180.

Pickens, T. A. 2019. *Black Madness: Mad Blackness.* Durham, NC: Duke University Press.

Richie, B. E. 2012. *Arrested Justice: Black Women, Violence, and America's Prison Nation.* New York: New York University Press.

Ritchie, A. J. 2017. *Invisible No More: Police Violence against Black Women and Women of Color.* Boston, MA: Beacon Press.

Rowell, C. H. 1991. "Above the Wind: An Interview with Audre Lorde." *Callaloo* 14(1): 83–95.

Rowell, C. H., and Audre Lorde. 2000. "Above the Wind: An Interview with Audre Lorde." *Callaloo* 23(1): 52–63.

Schalk, S. 2018. *Bodyminds Reimagined:(Dis)ability, Race, and Gender in Black Women's Speculative Fiction.* Durham, NC: Duke University Press.

Smith, B. 2001. "Introduction to Home Girls: A Black Feminist Anthology." In *Identity Politics in the Women's Movement*, 146–162. New York: NYU Press.

US Department of Education Office for Civil Rights. 2014. *Civil Rights Data Collection Data Snapshot: School Discipline.* Washington, DC. March. https://www2.ed.gov/about/offices/list/ocr/docs/crdc-discipline-snapshot.pdf

Waytz, Adam, Kelly Marie Hoffman, and Sophie Trawalter. 2015. "A Superhumanization Bias in Whites' Perceptions of Blacks." *Social Psychological and Personality Science* 6(3): 352–359.

Wing, Adrien Katherine (ed.).1997. *Critical Race Feminism: A Reader.* New York: New York University Press.

Wing, Adrien Katherine (ed.). 2003. *Global Critical Race Feminism: An International Reader.* New York: New York University Press.

Chapter 23

We Major

Black Trans Feminism
Fights Back

Blu Buchanan and Ayotunde Khyree Ikuku

> Interviewer: *"What's the nastiest shade you've ever thrown?*
> *Juliana Huxtable: "Existing in the world."*
> —Juliana Huxtable, Interview for *Candy* (6th Issue)

This chapter is an invitation to take Black trans lives seriously; to move beyond hashtags and retweets to consider the experiences of Black trans women and femmes like ourselves. We aim to transform the shade of existing, as Juliana Huxtable discusses, into a political and social framework for transformation. Emerging from a conversation between two Black femme nonbinary scholars, this chapter charts the geographies of Black trans feminism and its theoretical interventions into the way we practice and theorize sociological knowledge. We draw from one part of the Black trans experience, from *our* roots as nonbinary femmes, but we hope it will open the door to a wider conversation with other Black trans community members who share an investment in our collective liberation. What can we learn through the lineages that weave their way through Black trans stories? What new interventions and insights can these perspectives bring to the potential un- or redoing of sociology?

We demand more than the inclusion of Black trans bodies as spectacles and signs of progress in sociological panels and presentations, which increase our visibility while simultaneously refusing to recognize our bodies, our knowledge, and our liberation. Instead, we articulate the features of a liberatory praxis that centers the material, affective, and political realities of Black trans women and femmes past and present. A praxis that asks, under what conditions—if any such exist—can Black trans feminism bridge the gap with the disciplinary project of sociology. First, we discuss four important pillars of thought within Black trans feminism, from realness to violence. Upon these pillars we then lay out three major interventions into sociology: a rigorous theory of abjection, a system of material reparations, and the consideration of abolition. Each of these interventions into sociology addresses its violence toward marginalized

DOI: 10.4324/9781003199113-29

bodies and communities. Each is meant to avoid neoliberal inclusion, to avoid the fetishizing of Black trans bodies and experiences as spectacle without transforming relations of power. Drawing on our community and accountability orientation, we articulate each intervention, its goals, and its consequences.

Recovering the Trans in Black Feminism

The feminist roots of our community are incredibly deep. Black feminist scholars like Patricia Hill Collins, bell hooks, and Claudia Jones have explored the unstable position of Black womanhood and femininity under white supremacy, both inside and outside the plantation. In Sojourner Truth's famous speech, often titled "Ain't I a Woman," she powerfully describes the precarity of "womanhood" as a category under anti-Black regimes of terror.[1] Anti-blackness, and the archive of slavery, make Black subjectivity—Black gender itself—a fugitive object of study. Unlike white feminists, Black feminist scholars approached the question of gender liberation from an unsettled social position; their legitimacy as women was fundamentally at odds with white supremacist understandings of womanhood and subjectivity. On a deeper level, white expectations of Black bodies ran counter to the idea of sexually dimorphic traits so important to developing the "biological" foundations of both the cis/trans and hetero/homo binaries. As C. Riley Snorton says, "To feel black in the diaspora, then, might be a trans experience."[2]

But while this ambiguous state, this queer orientation, might have engendered critical interventions that challenge the sex and gender binary itself, it instead frequently facilitated a retrenchment of these concepts. Black feminist scholarship often attempted to make claims on cis womanhood, and so has been slow to engage with more explicit gender and sexual transgressions and identities. These transgressive subjectivities have been celebrated within Black communities but often left out of the explicit scholarship of Black feminists. Into this gap, a new conversation about Black trans feminism has emerged.

This coalescing conversation between Black feminism and trans of color critique stands to benefit sociology by upending its anti-black, cis-centric foundations. Scholars Kai Green and Marquis Bey highlight the potential for a Black trans feminism in particular, "Black feminists illuminated a major problem with the category 'woman.' . . . I think Black feminists were asking for a reconstitution of the terms and the terrain, not simply for an assigned role or designated place on the already existing lands."[3] Black trans feminism follows Audre Lorde's call for refusing "the master's tools"—including the definitions and territories of predefined "womanhood."[4] In doing so Black trans feminism has the capacity to transform both Black feminism and sociology.

What Is Black Trans Feminism?

How do we stay alive and care for one another? Black trans feminism is an attempt to answer that question. Our feminism emerges from our position as Black trans nonbinary femmes, and the life-saving lessons we have learned from our elders.[5] Drawing from these elders, we explore the importance of undoing realness, community care, resisting disposability, and the uses of violence for collective freedom. From these connections, we draw out four aspects of Black trans feminism as a tradition and mode of thought.

To begin with, Black trans feminism refuses the concept of "realness." Who counts when we describe those who live at the intersections of Blackness, sexism, and trans antagonism? Historically sociologists often forefront these concerns, but Black trans feminism is uninterested in reinscribing claims of authenticity or passability to members of our community. Instead it is concerned first and foremost with the defense and support of marginalized genders. While the category "Black trans women and femmes" is helpful for understanding the position of particular people, we also acknowledge the permeability of this category—that we are primarily concerned with dismantling and abolishing the conditions under which "realness" is judged. This emerges from the Catch-22 imposed on us, with deadly results. If you are "real" then you are "lying" and deserve death. If you are not "real" then you are not a legible person and thus also deserve death. While sociology examines the rules of gender and race, Black trans feminism refuses to play by these rules altogether. It acknowledges the need to identify structures of domination, while simultaneously refusing to see these structures as immutable.

The second feature of Black trans feminism, community care, is shared with other kinds of Black feminism. It is perhaps best encapsulated by the words of CeCe McDonald, a Black trans woman and prison abolitionist who was incarcerated after defending herself and others from a trans antagonistic attack, "I love you [her letter writers] because you all invested in me what I could have not done on my own. Your own time, dedication, and emotions. And wherever it may have come from, it has given me the motivation and inspiration to fight for all of us."[6] Here McDonald both acknowledges the support and labor of her network of letter writers and simultaneously her responsibility to that work. Resisting the atomization and the individualization of neoliberal and white versions of "feminism," Black trans feminism refuses to collapse into individual practice, into pieces small enough to be "digestible" by antagonistic publics.

This also extends to developing a material network between marginalized peoples. The urgency of this aspect is rooted in our material realities— we often have neither the money nor the time to engage in the performative "women's empowerment" activities that have flourished under neoliberalism. It is a praxis informed by class and labor precarity, which rejects capitalist, consumer "feminism." The US Transgender Survey found that 1 in 5 Black trans respondents was unemployed (greater than the 15 percent average among trans people nationwide).[7] The same survey found that 38 percent of the total Black trans respondents were living in poverty—and this was higher when broken down to look at Black nonbinary people (46 percent) and Black trans women (44 percent). They also found that Black trans respondents were more likely (28 percent) than the average trans respondent (20 percent) to participate in labor in the underground economy (sex work, drug sales and other criminalized labor). Black trans feminism requires concrete, material actions that help one another and our communities—whether that means community safety walks, support with rent and food, or bail (to name just a few).

Those bonds, although imperfect, demonstrate how to create practices that resist disposability.[8] As a severely traumatized part of an already multiply-marginalized community, we recognize that we can and **will** do harm to others. Recounting her experiences with Marsha P. Johnson, Sylvia Rivera recounts a moment in which Marsha was violent:

> She came over to my house dressed like the Virgin Mary, in white and blue, and she was carrying a wooden cross and a Bible. She came in and started preaching the Bible to me and we had a few words. Then she took the wooden cross and hit me upside the head with it.[9]

In other documents, Sylvia contextualizes this moment, describing the death of Marsha's husband at the hands of police, the effects of untreated syphilis on Marsha's faculties, and her struggle to remain clear-headed in the year leading up to her death. Rather than absolving Johnson of responsibility Rivera instead hints at a moment when transformative, rather than punitive, justice is required.

Resisting disposability also means unraveling the language of "security." This lynchpin of punitive models supports the elite, further ostracizing those who were never valued to begin with. It does not serve us. Instead, humanizing intimate interpersonal conflict creates space for us to hold both our intra- and intercommunal trauma. As Miss Major outlines,

> You don't have to watch everybody, but love them and give them the space that they need. That doesn't mean hugging and smooching on them and holding them close—it means caring about what their existence is, helping as needed but leaving the room and the ability to grow or not grow, expand or not, on their own as they choose.[10]

Rather than reducing care work to sugary affection, nice feelings, or comfort, Black trans feminism commits us to mutual aid for one another's liberation.

This position on disposability lies in tension with the last aspect of Black trans feminism—the belief in the potential uses of violence. Black trans feminism embraces the necessity of community- and self-defense. Our feminism is most interested in clarifying the when and where of violence—the strategy-making and militancy of feminist interventions. Marsha P. Johnson is clear: "We [STAR] believe in picking up the gun, starting a revolution if necessary."[11] The absence of structural protections for Black trans women and femmes means we must often act in self-defense when we are attacked and work to proactively defend our communities by arming and defending ourselves—thus "violence" is a fact of Black trans life. While we struggle to end structural and interpersonal violence in our community, we also recognize the need to stay alive to do that work. Although it's also true that these moments of self- and community-defense are routinely used to lock us up, the fact remains that doing nothing, like silence, will not protect us.[12]

Demands and Interventions

Despite these realities, we are not passive recipients of violence. Black trans feminism is a call to action, for moving beyond reflexivity to concrete outcomes. Sociology has the potential to do more than simply describe inequality and stratification while commodifying marginalized bodies. Black trans feminism rejects, and undermines, the roots of sociology overall as a eugenic, patriarchal, and white supremacist discipline.[13] Our contrary reading demands the creation of a different set of goals, a different animating spirit, to the study of the social world. In this section, we challenge sociology to adapt its practices and theoretical orientations.

The first required intervention is an analytical orientation that examines abjection and how abjection supports the networks and systems both *within* and outside of the discipline. Abjection, a state of being cast off, is constituted by the object that must be refused—the radically excluded, not just from public participation but from meaningful recognition altogether. Drawing on Black thinkers like Hartman and Wilderson engaged in unpacking abjection, we call for a similar focus in sociology. This understanding of abjection is broad, intertwined with the everyday violence we experience. Long before we set foot inside sociological spaces, we experience abjection within wider society; and upon entering the sociological discipline, we face the continuation of that abjection.

This continued abjection manifests in the epistemic concerns of sociologists and the practices of sociology itself. The discipline writ large relies on the worthlessness and the jettisoning of us after extracting our labor and our epistemologies. As Schilt and Lagos point out, early studies of trans people in sociology focused on us as objects of study.[14] The "us" in many of these early studies were white people; among the first examples of trans-oriented sociology was Harold Garfinkel's work with Agnes, a trans woman, "a 19-year-old, white, single girl."[15] Schilt and Lagos argue that more recent attempts at bringing trans people into sociology have largely focused on attending to trans people as subjects, rather than objects. There remains a danger in focusing on individuals—white, able-bodied, rich—who are already more likely to be granted subjecthood. While sociology celebrates the incremental steps toward an "inclusive" study of trans personhood, it fails to examine how the *discipline* relegated trans people to nonpersonhood in the first place, and how and where this practice continues.

From a more practical perspective, if Black trans women and femmes manage to enter the discipline, they will face obstacles at every turn. Departmentally and on-campus, there is often nowhere for Black trans women and femmes to pee safely; requests to change these structures stigmatize us as "uncooperative," or worse yet, "activists." We are often confronted by persistent dehumanization by colleagues, including scholars of gender. We must, by dint of being Black and trans, be experts in trans studies, Black studies, **and** whatever research topic we pursue. On top of this, the increasing militarization and policing of higher education puts us at risk for harassment or death at the hands of police. These problems are not unknown; they are often simply deemed "too political" or controversial to address head on with the delicate political machinery of our discipline.

Black trans feminism also demands reparations from a discipline that has been involved in the ongoing death and incarceration of Black trans and cis women and femmes. Marsha P. Johnson, recounting the material realities of a Black trans sex worker, said, "I always get all of my money in advance, that's what a smart transvestite does. I don't ever let them tell me, 'I'll pay you after the job is done.' I say I want it in advance."[16] In this spirit, Black trans feminism demands its reparations upfront because "no woman gets paid after their job is done. If you're smart, you get the money first."[17] This sits alongside a broader call for reparations happening in the academy. In solidarity with, and alongside indigenous and First Nations peoples who have called for more than land acknowledgment from political and academic circles, Black trans feminism requires the transfer of wealth, land, and authority to the dispossessed within society.

Reparations themselves do not necessarily mean a radical restructuring of the discipline. The last sociological intervention advocated by Black trans feminism is abolition. This concept, of ending the institution of sociology, seems to be an especially hard intervention to grapple with, and so we have left it for last. By abolition, we do not mean abolishing the study of the social world, or necessarily the sociological imagination. Rather, we mean changing sociology as an institution so deeply it cannot be identified by its previous formation. It means celebrating and honoring the importance of ending certain relationships and ways of being. Black feminist sociologists, who have labored tirelessly to change the discipline, have shown us how to weaponize sociology to benefit the most marginalized; our present focus on abolition attempts to transform the entire discipline into a toolkit for deconstructing white supremacy everywhere.

But why abolition? Our community is often considered the "lowest rung" on the social ladder and as such have always been told to wait: for change, acceptance, recognition. Told to accept being tossed away for others' political gains. Thus Black trans feminism has a deep suspicion for any intervention that does not keep abolition at the forefront of its strategizing. To be clear, no single act will **cause** abolition—but if the vision driving our interventions is not abolitionist, it is likely to stop short of the material needs, desires, and yearnings of our people. This vision has the potential to, yet again, sacrifice those of us on the margins.

Conclusion

Black feminism and Black trans feminism are deeply intertwined intellectual and political projects. Black trans women and femmes have always been immersed in the traditions of their community, including Black feminism. Here we have tried first and foremost to build a bridge between Black women and femmes, cis and trans. As we have learned from Audre Lorde, Alice Walker, and Patricia Hill Collins, we invite others to engage the lessons provided by Mary Jones, Juliana Huxtable, Marsha P. Johnson, Miss Major and so many others. This call is not intended to inflame the differences between cis and trans women and femmes, but rather to offer an example of the organizing through difference proposed by Audre Lorde.[18] By locating our different positionalities, it is possible to organize ourselves in ways that recognize our relative structural power and powerlessness—to understand how we can work together toward our collective liberation.

Finally, we argue that these commitments manifest in a nonexhaustive set of practices and orientations. Understanding abjection, reparations, and abolition—these interventions are not necessarily new. But within this chapter we hope to breathe new life and vigor into these methods. Without them, Black trans people will remain a spectacle to be commented on, an object of study, or a measure of diversity to be leveraged by an overwhelmingly white, cis, patriarchal institution.

Acknowledgments

Special thanks to Tourmaline for doing the archival work to collect much of the relevant materials for this collection.

Notes

1. Sojourner Truth. 1851. "Ain't I a Woman?" www.sojournertruth.com/p/aint-i-woman. html
2. On page 8 of C. Riley Snorton. 2017. *Black on Both Sides: A Racial History of Trans Identity*. Minneapolis, MN: University of Minnesota Press.
3. Kai M. Green and Marquis Bey. 2017. "Where Black Feminist Thought and Trans* Feminism Meet: A Conversation." *Souls* 19(4): 438–454.
4. Audre Lorde. 2007 [1984]. "The Master's Tools Will Never Dismantle the Master's House." In *Sister Outsider: Essays and Speeches*, 110–113. Berkeley: Crossing Press.
5. Our theoretical perspective is drawn from the structural location of Black trans women and femmes, but as a mode of thinking it extends beyond the social structures which produce it.
6. CeCe McDonald. 2017. "'Go Beyond Our Natural Selves': The Prison Letters of CeCe McDonald," edited by Omise'eke Natasha Tinsley, *TSQ: Transgender Studies Quarterly* 4(2).
7. United States Transgender Survey. 2015. "USTS Black Respondents Report." www.transequality.org/sites/default/files/docs/usts/USTSBlackRespondentsReport-Nov17.pdf
8. By transformative justice, we mean, "Transformative justice [is] a liberatory approach to violence . . . [which] seeks safety and accountability without relying on alienation, punishment, or State or systemic violence, including incarceration or policing." www.usprisonculture.com/blog/transformative-justice/
9. On page 44–45 of Sylvia Rivera. 2013 "Queens in Exile, The Forgotten Ones." *Street Transvestite Action Revolutionaries: Survival, Revolt, and Queer Antagonist Struggle*. Bloomington, IN: Untorelli Press.
10. James Nichols. 2016. "Miss Major is a Trans Elder and Stonewall Icon . . . And She's Changing the World." *Huffington Post*. July 23, 2016. www.huffpost.com/entry/miss-major-transgender-elder_n_57927351e4b01180b52ef264
11. *Street Transvestite Action Revolutionaries*.
12. For more on this line of thinking, see Audre Lorde. 2017. *Your Silence Will Not Protect You: Essays and Poems*. London, UK: Silver Press.
13. As we have drawn deeply on Black feminist interventions, we recognize that these projects do not encapsulate everything sociology is—however, we also believe firmly that these interventions have yet to pierce the heart of the mainstream sociological project.
14. Kristen Schilt and Danya Lagos. 2017. "The Development of Transgender Studies in Sociology." *Annual Review of Sociology* 43(1): 425–443. www.annualreviews.org/doi/abs/10.1146/annurev-soc-060116-053348
15. Harold Garfinkel. 1967. *Studies in Ethnomethodology*. New York: Polity Press.
16. *Street Transvestite Action Revolutionaries*.
17. Ibid.
18. Audre Lorde. 2007 [1984]. "Age, Race, Class and Sex: Women Redefining Difference." In *Sister Outsider: Essays and Speeches*, 114–123. Berkeley: Crossing Press.

References

Garfinkel, Harold. 1967. *Studies in Ethnomethodology*. New York: Polity Press.

Green, Kai M., and Marquis Bey. 2017. "Where Black Feminist Thought and Trans* Feminism Meet: A Conversation." *Souls* 19(4): 438–454.

Huxtable, Juliana. 2013. "*Candy #6*." Interview by Casey Spooner. *The Now New Yorkers*. https://vimeo.com/69128412

Lorde, Audre. 2007 [1984a]. "The Master's Tools Will Never Dismantle the Master's House." In *Sister Outsider: Essays and Speeches*, 110–113. Berkeley: Crossing Press.

Lorde, Audre. 2007 [1984b]. "Age, Race, Class and Sex: Women Redefining Difference." In *Sister Outsider: Essays and Speeches*, 114–123. Berkeley: Crossing Press.

McDonald, CeCe. 2017. "'Go Beyond Our Natural Selves': The Prison Letters of CeCe McDonald," edited by Omise'eke Natasha Tinsley. *TSQ: Transgender Studies Quarterly* 4(2): 243–265.

Nichols, James. 2016. "Miss Major is a Trans Elder and Stonewall Icon . . . And She's Changing the World." *Huffington Post*. July 23, 2016. www.huffpost.com/entry/ miss-major-transgender-elder_n_57927351e4b01180b52ef264

Rivera, Sylvia. 2013. "Queens in Exile, The Forgotten Ones." In *Street Transvestite Action Revolutionaries: Survival, Revolt, and Queer Antagonist Struggle*. Bloomington, IN: Untorelli Press.

Schilt, Kristen, and Danya Lagos. 2017. "The Development of Transgender Studies in Sociology." *Annual Review of Sociology* 43(1): 425–443. www.annualreviews.org/doi/ abs/10.1146/annurev-soc-060116-053348

Truth, Sojourner. 1851. "Ain't I a Woman?" www.sojournertruth.com/p/aint-i-woman.html

United States Transgender Survey. 2015. "USTS Black Respondents Report." www.transe quality.org/sites/default/files/docs/usts/USTSBlackRespondentsReport-Nov17.pdf

Chapter 24

Exploring the Black Feminist Imagination

Aisha A. Upton and Jalia L. Joseph

Dreams and the imagination hold power. Activist and author Toni Cade Bambara eloquently stated, "When you dream, you dialogue with aspects of yourself that normally are not with you in the daytime and you discover that you know a great deal more than you thought you did."[1] In following the tradition of dreams as liberatory praxis, the dreams of Black feminist scholars open up space for understanding what sociologist Patricia Hill Collins calls "subjugated knowledge."[2] Despite the attempts to silence Black women's epistemologies, the dialogue continues zooming through space, cycling through time.[3] The push to continue these conversations acknowledges the Black feminist assertion that we deserve space, that by choosing to center our realities, we fight for our right to be liberated, that no one gets free without us.[4]

The articulation of this knowledge is subversive itself and often spills out from written words into activism. Both the concepts of the dream and the imagination help to explain how Black feminist sociological scholarship provides insight into knowledge production, in which memory is never lost and only the art of forgetting exists.[5] In resisting this "art of forgetting," Black feminist scholarship subverts the willfulness of the discipline to invisiblize the work of Black feminist scholars.

When we center Black women narratives, knowledge, and voices, what can we truly learn about their visions of liberation and freedom? How can stories from Black feminist writers shape and impact the broader sociological research? To this end, we review scholarship from contemporary Black feminist sociological scholars and demonstrate how Black women create revolutionary writing that sees a tangible connection through the real world, their own lived experiences, and their scholarship.[6] We suggest that through the work of contemporary Black feminist sociological scholarship, Black women's use of imagination, dreams, and subjugated knowledge creates a mode of theorizing, an "epistemological clapback" that challenges norms in white sociological tradition and masculinism in Black critical thought. Through this, we expand the use of the Black feminist canon and demonstrate the benefits of Black women's epistemologies in sociology.

DOI: 10.4324/9781003199113-30

Black feminist epistemologies exist at the center of decolonizing the imagination. According to writers Walidha Imarisha and adrienne marie brown,[7] in *Octavia's Brood*, "The decolonization of the imagination is the most dangerous and subversive form there is: for it is where all other forms of decolonization are born. Once the imagination is unshackled, liberation is limitless." In this sense, Black feminist theorizing is similar to the Afrofuturist speculative fiction of Black women authors such as Octavia Butler and N. K. Jeminisn, who bless us with ideas of what a collective liberated Black future can look like. Susana M. Morris, scholar and co-founder of the Crunk Feminist Collective, asserts that there is a symbiotic relationship between this speculative fiction and Black feminist epistemologies.[8] Morris says that "as Afrofuturism seeks to liberate the possibilities that open up when Blackness is linked to futurity, so does Black feminist thought seek to uncouple dominance from power as Blacks assert their agency."[9] Meanwhile, the subversive nature of this uncoupling aids in liberatory praxis through everyday resistance and larger social movements against oppressive systems and institutions. Through this chapter, we explore dreams and the imagination as a site of radical possibility for Black women as they relate to knowledge production and social action writ large.

We Dream of Stars and Galaxies

Black feminist theory and Afrofuturism are interconnected epistemologies in which dreams and the imagination flourish. Acknowledging the symbiotic relationship between the two reveals as much, similar to artist Mawena Yehouessi's description of Afrofuturism as "the recall for a forgotten/despised legacy, the struggle for present-time acknowledgment and the attempt to impose its rights to be as equally part of future forecasts."[10] Black feminist thought is the imagining of futures and proclamation of present self through a critical Black and critical gender conscious lens. To do this, Black feminist theorists act as seers of wisdom aimed with creating a new mechanism for understanding a Black future outside of the bonds of essentialist claims of masculinist Blackness and subversive white notions of gender. Sociologist bell hooks explains that Black feminist theorists aim to move beyond what the world sees us as, instead opting for a mode of understanding centered on the "liberated voice."[11] A voice that proclaims the multiplicities of a Black feminist future, one where Black women are continuously liberated, loved, and visible to ourselves by ourselves; one where we continue to dream, create, and imagine. A message which suggests we "stop letting others fuck with our future,"[12] but instead assert ourselves now fully without apology to imagine a world without reservation; a world immersed in using the Black feminist imaginary as a site of radical possibility.

Black feminist theory and Afrofuturism are "conversations with one another."[13] These conversations exist because Afrofuturism, much like Black feminist thought, aims to prioritize voices that have been left out. As we learn from both Patricia Hill Collins[14] and Robin D. G. Kelley,[15] the ability to see the future in the present without the entanglement of dominance expands the reality of Black possibility. This possibility is the radical Black imaginary, a historical lineage in which Black people move forward with the hope of a new era.[16] However, unlike the Black radical imaginary, the Black feminist imaginary requires pushing past unlearning whiteness and capitalism to recognizing the interconnectedness of whiteness and patriarchy that limit a Black future.

Additionally, Black feminist theory and Afrofuturism share the goal of disrupting the past centered in confronting our race memories.[17] Here, race memories refer to the collective memories of Black people that have more accurate depictions of our own historical events even though that narrative is not included in the white patriarchal history-making processes. Proclaiming a Black feminist future requires grappling with the depictions of the past because we are not removed from the historical trauma. That is not an unpleasant reality but a chance to rectify and envision the truth we know exists.

This proclamation of a Black feminist future is where the Black feminist imagination manifests. A Black feminist imagination embraces an imagined future that centers Black women's experiences in liberation and healing. A Black feminist imagination is not bound to the speculative or fantasy but rather "transcends genre,"[18] and is expressed in poems, short stories, and sociological theory. A Black feminist imaginary details the possibility of other, where Black women are not solely the other, the subjective being in which everyone uses for labor—physical, emotional, and mental. Rather it centers the "multidimensionality"[19] of Black womanhood and caters to knowledge that erupts from the spirit. The Black feminist imaginary is a spiritual reality, a connection to who we have been, who we are now, and what we envision ourselves as in the future.

Imagining the Beloved Community

One of the aspects that is central to a Black feminist imagination is the importance of community. As we learn from writers who encompass a Black feminist imagination, community can be a site of political contestation as well as a site of affirmation, identification, and political expression that challenges established hierarchies.[20] Community becomes a mechanism in which Black women write to speak to other Black women to heal. As bell hooks[21] details in *Sisters of the Yam*, "Celebrated fiction by Black women writers is concerned with identifying our pain and imaginatively constructing maps for healing" (23). For Joy James,[22] the Black community is an example of "complex humanity." Akin to the concept of the community is what Bambara calls the "gathering"—a storyword[23] used by the author to describe "the joy of gathering together to think deeply and act decisively on behalf of 'salvation.' "[24] Community becomes a pivotal site in which decolonization takes precedent through perseverance and survival.

In Bambara's *On the Issue of Roles*,[25] community represents a way

> to fashion revolutionary lives, revolutionary relationships . . . if your house isn't in order, you ain't in order. It is so much easier to be out there than right there. The revolution isn't out there. Yet. But it is here.[26]

The act of getting your house in order and starting the revolution at home—that is creating a prefigurative community—is the best way to get yourself in order. In this sense, dismantling hierarchies within your own community is an act of self-love and survival. Bambara wants us to know that while the revolution isn't happening out in the world yet, the community is the best place to start.

Octavia Butler, foremother of Afrofuturism and continuous curator of the Black feminist imaginary demonstrates this in *Parable of the Sower*[27] and the *Parable of the Talents*.[28] The protagonist Lauren Olamina consistently imagines communities built out of Earthseed: the belief that "*God is Change. Shape God.*"[29] After Lauren creates the first Earthseed community, Acorn, she tells Bankole, "The land is yours. The community is ours. With our work, and with Earthseed to guide us, we're building something good here."[30] People of diverse races, ages, and abilities comprise Acorn. Acorn represents a utopia in which all people are respected and embraced as valuable members, all capable of contributing to the greater good of the group. At a time when the country is in political and moral turmoil and when walled communities burn to the ground, community acts as a place for self-definition and self-value.[31] In *Parable of the Talents*, Butler further elaborates on the importance of community. In saying, "paradise is one's own place, one's own people, one's own world, knowing and unknown, perhaps even loving and loved," Butler is expressing that at the heart of the community is love. For Lauren this remains true, for even as Acorn is attacked by religious fanatics who are inspired by a president who plans to "make America great again," Earthseed lives on.[32]

In a collection of her short stories, *How Long Til' Black Future Month*, N. K. Jemisin[33] creates a multitude of universes. The story "The Ones Who Stay and Fight," tells the story of the city of Um-Helat, a diverse utopia that is characterized by the way that the people and the environment nurture each other. Jemisin describes the city as being full of people who "come from many others, and it shows in the sheen of their skin and kink of hair and plumpness of lip and hip."[34] This community that Jemisin creates is "not that barbaric America"[35]—instead, it is through observing the city of Um-Helat that

> you might be able to envision a world where people have learned to love, as they learned in our world to hate. Perhaps you will speak of Um-Helat to others, and spread the notion farther still, like joyous birds migrating on trade winds. *It's Possible.* Everyone—even the poor, even the lazy, even the undesirable—can matter. Do you see how just the idea of this provokes utter rage in some? That is the infection defending itself . . . because if enough of us believe a thing is possible, then it becomes so.[36]

Jemisin's creation of Um-Helat as a city with the ability to engage in radical love continues the narrative of constructing maps for healing. It is through this radical love that the city is able to separate itself from the barbaric America.

Black feminist literature and scholarship centers community. For these writers, community serves the essential functions of creating space for self-definition, self-value, and healing. The idea of keeping these communities separate from the outside world (or worlds) and safe shows that the love that goes into creating and sustaining these communities is a radical love—it highlights how love can be set as a limit to the reaches of white supremacist structures and antiblackness.[37]

Black Feminist Imagination in Sociology

The pathways of the Black feminist imagination are not lost on the sociological discipline. In the same way that speculative fiction like that of Butler and Jemisin impact the broader field of science fiction by highlighting the experiences (even, or especially, if they are otherworldly) of Black people, Black feminist sociologists already have a historical relationship to Black feminist writers and sociologists who provide pathways to the Black feminist imagination.

In sociology, the Black feminist imagination is not new. Anna Julia Cooper represents a pivotal figure who incorporated the Black feminist imagination into her theory and methods. In *A Voice from the South*, Cooper[38] explicitly references the imagination through the connection of the past to the future. She writes, "For each of us truth means merely the representation of the sensations and experiences of our personal environment, colored and vivified—fused into consistency and crystallized into individuality in the crucible of our own feelings and imagination."[39] Moreover, Cooper details that aspects of a person are not divorced from historical events nor is knowledge production. Here is the blueprint she provides for the Black feminist imagination in sociology, we must understand that we are not individually molded but rather we have a community of scholars who have come before us (and that will come after) that provide the blueprint we can follow.

Ida B. Wells also represents a Black feminist sociologist's active role constructing the Black feminist imaginary. In the 1892 pamphlet *Southern Horrors: Lynch Law in All Its Phases*, Wells describes what would be necessary for a future without lynch law. She states that people need to "employ the boycott, emigration, and the press" in order to stamp out the "last relic of barbarism and slavery." Moreover, in the later book *Red Record*,[40] Wells's closing chapter "The Remedy" directly asks the reader what they will do to "thwart anarchy and promote law and order."[41] Wells offers critical insights as to what readers can do because she envisions a future where lynching is not the law of the land, because "when the Christian world knows the alarming growth and extent of outlawry in our land, some means will be found to stop it."[42]

Similar to our sociological ancestors, we also see contemporary Black sociologists recognizing that Black feminist sociology is (and always has been) an interdisciplinary project. In the *Death of White Sociology*, sociologist Joyce Ladner[43] writes, "Black sociologists must develop new techniques and perspectives."[44] Following in this legacy and manifesting the Black feminist imagination as something that needs to be constructed outside of the bounds of what we do now, numerous Black feminist sociologists are creating new means to do sociological theorizing.

In *Black Feminist Thought*,[45] Collins uses the work of Toni Morrison, Toni Cade Bambara, Gwendolyn Brooks, Ann Allen Shockley, Rosa Guy, Sherley Anne Williams and a plethora of other Black feminist writers to provide support for her work. Rose M. Brewer[46] uses the work of Audre Lorde, Angela Davis and the Combahee River Collective in "Theorizing Race, Class, and Gender: The New Scholarship of Black Feminist Intellectuals and Black Women's Labor." Deborah King[47] incorporates the voices of Michelle Wallace, Sojourner Truth, Maria Stewart, Anna Julia Cooper, Josephine St. Pierre Ruffin, Frances Watkins Harper, Pauli Murray, Frances Beale, Audre Lorde and Angela Davis to construct multiple jeopardy in "Multiple Jeopardy, Multiple Consciousness."

These are only a few examples, but the central point remains the same through the contingencies of their revolutionary writing, we see an indisputable relationship in which Black feminist sociologists use Black feminist works to expand the Black feminist imaginary. The use of these texts creates a means of conducting research and establishing theories that breaks the white epistemological norms of sociology.

No Ends, New Beginnings

Our chapter highlights the power of dreams and the imagination in the work of Black feminist writers. It is our hope that we provide solid links between Afrofuturism and Black feminist sociology as connected epistemologies that allow for the Black feminist imagination. Further, we expand on Black feminist texts through an immersive Afrofuturistic lens in which we situate the redesign of "community" as imperative to decolonizing texts. Lastly, we put Black feminist sociologists in conversation with Black feminist writers to demonstrate how Black feminist sociology reveals the same forms of radical imagination and dreaming as derived from Black feminist classics.

A core tenet we posit of Black feminist sociology is to revel in the same modes of theorizing that assert who we are outside of the reach of white supremacy and patriarchy. This method necessitates that we create dreams for ourselves and for those that may read and be influenced by our work—our Black feminist community. Through this chapter, we demonstrate how Black feminist sociology immerses itself in the crucial work of decolonization, theory building, and radical Black feminist possibility through centering Black women. This placement of Black women at the center helps us dare to dream of possibilities and imagine a more liberated future.

Notes

1. Roseann P. Bell, Bettye J. Parker, and Beverly Guy-Sheftall. 1979. *Sturdy Black Bridges: Visions of Black Women in Literature*, 243. Garden City, NY: Doubleday.
2. Patricia Hill Collins. 2002. *Black Feminist Thought: Knowledge, Consciousness, and the Politics of Empowerment*, 11. New York and London: Routledge.
3. Ibid.
4. Combahee River Collective. 1986. *The Combahee River Collective Statement: Black Feminist Organizing in the Seventies and Eighties.* Albany, NY: Kitchen Table; Keeanga-Yamahtta Taylor. 2017. *How We Get Free: Black Feminism and the Combahee River Collective.* Chicago, IL: Haymarket Books.
5. Kodwo Eshun. 2003. "Further Considerations of Afrofuturism." *CR: The New Centennial Review* 3(2): 287–302.
6. Kimberly Nichele Brown. 2010. *Writing the Black Revolutionary Diva: Women's Subjectivity and the Decolonizing Text.* Bloomington: Indiana University Press.
7. Walisdah Imarisha and Adrienne Maree Brown. 2015. *Octavia's Brood: Science Fiction Stories from Social Justice Movements*, 4. Oakland, CA: AK Press.
8. Susana M. Morris. 2012. "Black Girls Are from the Future: Afrofuturist Feminism in Octavia E Butler's 'Fledgling.'" *Women's Studies Quarterly* 40(3/4): 153.
9. Ibid.
10. Mawena Yehouessi. n.d. "Afrofuturism: The Time Overlapse." *Blacks to the Future.* http://blackstothefuture.com/en/afrofuturism-the-time-overlapse
11. bell hooks. 1989. *Talking Back: Thinking Feminist, Thinking Black*, 9. Boston, MA: South End Press.
12. Brittney C. Cooper. 2015. "Love No Limit: Towards a Black Feminist Future (in Theory)." *Black Scholar* 45(4): 7–21.
13. Morris 2012.
14. Collins 2002.
15. Robin D. G. Kelley. 2002. *Freedom Dreams: The Black Radical Imagination.* Boston, MA: Beacon Press.

16. Charlene Carruthers. 2018. *Unapologetic: A Black, Queer, and Feminist Mandate for Radical Movements*. Boston, MA: Beacon Press.
17. Alice Walker. 2004. *In Search of Our Mothers' Gardens: Womanist Prose*. Boston, MA: Houghton Mifflin. Harcourt.
18. Brown 2010.
19. Kimberle Crenshaw. 1998. "Demarginalizing the Intersection of Race and Sex: A Black Feminist Critique of Antidiscrimination Doctrine, Feminist Theory, and Antiracist Politics." *Feminism and Politics*: 314–343.
20. Patricia Hill Collins. 2010. "The New Politics of Community." *American Sociological Review* 75(1): 7–30.
21. bell hooks. 1993. *Sisters of the Yam: Black Women and Self-Recovery*. Boston, MA: South End Press.
22. Joy James. 2013. *Seeking the Beloved Community: A Feminist Race Reader*. Albany, NY: SUNY Press.
23. Toni Cade Bambara. 1970. "On the Issue of Roles." In *The Black Woman: An Anthology*, 101–110. New York: Signet.
24. Brown 2010.
25. Bambara 1970.
26. Ibid.
27. Octavia E. Butler. 1993. *Parable of the Sower*. Vol. 1. New York: Open Road Media.
28. Octavia E. Butler. 1998. *Parable of the Talents: A Novel*. Vol. 2. New York: Seven Stories Press.
29. Butler 1993, 330.
30. Ibid.
31. Patricia Hill Collins. 1986. "Learning from the Outsider Within: The Sociological Significance of Black Feminist Thought." *Social Problems* 33(6): s14–s32.
32. Butler's use of "Make America Great Again" is based on Ronald Raegan's 1980 campaign slogan "Let's Make America Great Again"; however, the phrase is now linked to the 2016 campaign of Donald Trump.
33. N. K. Jemisin. 2018. *How Long 'til Black Future Month*. New York: Orbit.
34. Ibid., 5.
35. Ibid., 5.
36. Ibid., 12.
37. Linh U. Hua. 2011. "Reproducing Time, Reproducing History: Love and Black Feminist Sentimentality in Octavia Butler's 'Kindred.'" *African American Review* 44(3): 391–407.
38. Anna Julia Cooper. 1998. *A Voice from the South*. 1892. Reprint. Xenia, OH: The Aldine Printing House.
39. Ibid., 63.
40. Ida B. Wells. 1895. *The Red Record and Southern Horrors*. New York: Floating Press.
41. Ibid., 92.
42. Ibid., 94.
43. Joyce A. Ladner. 1998. *The Death of White Sociology: Essays on Race and Culture*. Baltimore, MD: Black Classic Press.
44. Ibid., xvii.
45. Collins 2002.
46. Rose M. Brewer. 2016. "Theorizing Race, Class, and Gender: The New Scholarship of Black Feminist Intellectuals and Black Women's Labor." In *Race, Gender and Class*, 58–64. New York: Routledge.
47. Deborah K. King. 1988. "Multiple Jeopardy, Multiple Consciousness: The Context of a Black Feminist Ideology." *Signs: Journal of Women in Culture and Society* 14(1): 42–72.

References

Bambara, Toni Cade. 1970. "On the Issue of Roles." In *The Black Woman: An Anthology*, 101–110. New York: Signet.

Bell, Roseann P., Bettye J. Parker, and Beverly Guy-Sheftall. 1979. *Sturdy Black Bridges: Visions of Black Women in Literature*. Garden City, NY: Doubleday.

Brewer, Rose M. 2016. "Theorizing Race, Class, and Gender: The New Scholarship of Black Feminist Intellectuals and Black Women's Labor." In *Race, Gender and Class*, 58–64. New York: Routledge.

Brown, Kimberly Nichele. 2010. *Writing the Black Revolutionary Diva: Women's Subjectivity and the Decolonizing Text*. Bloomington: Indiana University Press.

Butler, Octavia E. 1993. *Parable of the Sower*. Vol. 1. New York: Open Road Media.

Butler, Octavia E. 1998. *Parable of the Talents: A Novel*. Vol. 2. New York: Seven Stories Press.

Carruthers, Charlene. 2018. *Unapologetic: A Black, Queer, and Feminist Mandate for Radical Movements*. Boston, MA: Beacon Press.

Collins, Patricia Hill. 1986. "Learning from the Outsider Within: The Sociological Significance of Black Feminist Thought." *Social Problems* 33(6): s14–s32.

Collins, Patricia Hill. 2002. *Black Feminist Thought: Knowledge, Consciousness, and the Politics of Empowerment*. New York and London: Routledge.

Collins, Patricia Hill. 2010. "The New Politics of Community." *American Sociological Review* 75(1): 7–30.

Combahee River Collective. 1986. *The Combahee River Collective Statement: Black Feminist Organizing in the Seventies and Eighties*. Albany, NY: Kitchen Table.

Cooper, Anna Julia. 1988. *A Voice from the South*. 1892. Reprint. Xenia, OH: The Aldine Printing House.

Cooper, Brittney C. 2015. "Love No Limit: Towards a Black Feminist Future (in Theory)." *Black Scholar* 45(4): 7–21.

Crenshaw, Kimberle. "Demarginalizing the Intersection of Race and Sex: A Black Feminist Critique of Antidiscrimination Doctrine, Feminist Theory, and Antiracist Politics." *Feminism and Politics*: 314–343.

Eshun, Kodwo. 2003. "Further Considerations of Afrofuturism." *CR: The New Centennial Review* 3(2): 287–302.

hooks, bell. 1989. *Talking Back: Thinking Feminist, Thinking Black*. Boston, MA: South End Press.

hooks, bell. 1993. *Sisters of the Yam: Black Women and Self-Recovery*. Boston, MA: South End Press.

Hua, Linh U. 2011. "Reproducing Time, Reproducing History: Love and Black Feminist Sentimentality in Octavia Butler's 'Kindred.'" *African American Review* 44(3): 391–407.

Imarisha, Walidah and Adrienne Maree Brown. 2015. *Octavia's Brood: Science Fiction Stories from Social Justice Movements*. Oakland, CA: AK Press.

James, Joy. 2013. *Seeking the Beloved Community: A Feminist Race Reader*. Albany, NY: SUNY Press.

Jemisin, N. K. 2018. *How Long 'til Black Future Month*. New York: Orbit.

Kelley, Robin D. G. 2002. *Freedom Dreams: The Black Radical Imagination*. Boston, MA: Beacon Press.

King, Deborah K. 1988. "Multiple Jeopardy, Multiple Consciousness: The Context of a Black Feminist Ideology." *Signs: Journal of Women in Culture and Society* 14(1): 42–72.

Ladner, Joyce A. 1998. *The Death of White Sociology: Essays on Race and Culture*. Baltimore, MD: Black Classic Press.

Morris, Susana M. 2012. "Black Girls Are from the Future: Afrofuturist Feminism in Octavia E. Butler's 'Fledgling.'" *Women's Studies Quarterly* 40(3/4): 146–166.

Taylor, Keeanga-Yamahtta. 2017. *How We Get Free: Black Feminism and the Combahee River Collective*. Chicago, IL: Haymarket Books.

Walker, Alice. 2004. *In Search of Our Mothers' Gardens: Womanist Prose*. Boston, MA: Houghton Mifflin Harcourt.

Wells, Ida B. 1991. "A Red Record. 1895." In *Selected Works of Ida B. Wells-Barnett*. Introduction by Trudier Harris, 138–252. New York: Oxford University Press.

Wells, Ida B. 2014. *Southern Horrors: Lynch Law in All Its Phases*. New York: Floating Press.

Yehouessi, Mawena. n.d. "Afrofuturism: The Time Overlapse." *Blacks to the Future*. http://blackstothefuture.com/en/afrofuturism-the-time-overlapse

Placing Ourselves

Zakiya Luna and Whitney N. Laster Pirtle

Zakiya (aka Prof Luna)

At the end of my third year on the tenure track, my mother died. Over the years of her deteriorating health, we'd had time to connect and my best decision ever was to be intentional in working to better understand her as a whole person, ask the questions I had of her and hear her stories. Still, when she died a couple of months before I began a fellowship, much of that year was a fog. I did not attend ASA 2017. Leaving an institution even for a few months offers perspective. A few weeks before ASA 2018 in Philly, I had lunch with a senior White colleague. She made an off-hand comment about a situation in my first year and told me not to worry as "it didn't affect our relationship." I was tired enough of being diplomatic to offer the unfiltered truth: yes, it did.

Over the years, I had wondered far too often how many of these same colleagues would even *think* to engage with junior White women this way (the various forms of what literary scholar Koritha Mitchell refers to as "know-your-place" aggression to the yelling at me in front of students and so on).[1] Sure, I was not perfect because none of us is, but it takes energy to maintain compassion, and a professional demeanor and "never let them take your shine" as my cousin reminded me. As I had at other institutions, I navigated many dynamics as I carved out space for other communities such as developing campus interdisciplinary working groups and creating a faculty Write-on-Site that started with one session a week and over the years has grown to almost daily sessions and yearly writing retreats. I leaned more heavily on senior scholars outside my department and institution, adding to their labor. We know that while the specific details vary, the outlines of this story of Black women in the academy has been repeated in conferences, edited volumes, journals, and social media (#BlackintheIvory). While some of us continue to survive, that pre-ASA 2018 lunch made clear: I still needed more spaces to *thrive*.

I committed to using the upcoming time in Philadelphia to create more of that. Re-entering ABS was a way to re-enter community—and it had changed in glorious ways since my prior membership: so many vibrant young people, a queerer sensibility and delightful emphasis on praxis. The ABS edited volume *The New Black Sociologists* was inspiring but raised a question for me: where was the equivalent of McClaurin's volume in Sociology?[2] When other people at the conference talked about their edited volume work it looked fun. Why couldn't *we* do that? I was not sure who the "we" was yet.

When a friend who was not as ASA alerted me to the Yams dinner, I emailed Whitney and was excited to be able to join a new group of Black women for a meal. I had heard about Whitney when she was hired at UCM (news about Black women hires makes the UC rounds). The first time we met was carpooling to that restaurant, where our table was by far the largest, and just a few tables over senior scholars who had been at ABS waved at us. We tried to maintain decorum amidst pure giddiness of being with each other (and one Yams' mom, whose presence was another subtle reminder of ancestral legacies). If these women would not be interested in being the "we," who would? I did not have to worry-there was interest. Because far too many of us need spaces to thrive and find the academy lacking. But *we* are the space to thrive.

Whitney

I have always felt a bit like an outsider in the academy. I grew up in a college town, but the connection I had to that college was that my parents had dropped out. Being an outsider within[3] in every academic stage meant I learned early on that it was imperative for me to find my people, and quick. My through-the-roof imposter syndrome in graduate school wasn't calmed until after my White and elite graduate program received funding from an external foundation during my six years there, and six faculty of color were hired, four Black, and each incoming graduate cohort was about half students of color, most of whom were Black women. In an instant, it seemed, we were able to create Black spaces and community in a PWI and PW discipline. I had three amazing Black men scholars on my dissertation committee and a community of primarily Black women graduate students uplifted each other, holding research, happy hours, prayer groups, and more.

I was so thankful to obtain a faculty position in a university that is well-resourced, not too large, and strong majority-minority student population. But the biggest struggle I had during the transition was finding *my* people. I went from having access to a strong Black community and mentors, in and out of the university, to being one of a handful of Black folks wherever I went. My sociology PhD program had more Black faculty and grad students then our entire institution when I started. There was a hole where my community used to be. So, I tried to build community where I could. I began working more closely with Black students on campus,

I got connected with women of color faculty on my campus, I joined any closed Facebook group for WOC I could, and when Black women sociologist groups were created I jumped right in desperately wanting to break bread with sisters that I had missed.

The void was about missing my people, but I missed them because of the ways they had always supported me in the academy. I missed when folks saw my side-eye and met it with a nod. I missed the scholarship that would push me past my comfortable spots. I missed walking into a room and being able to say "*girllll*" and have already said enough. And I had plenty of moments where I wished that could have happened. Where I needed to share an experience and I needed validation. One instance happened early during my tenure. I attended an all-campus faculty meeting and literally was unable to have a place at the table—the White man sitting next to me wouldn't physically move to make space.[4] I needed epistemological tools

Figure A.1 ASA 2019 Breakfast before #CiteBlackWomen panel

Pictured: Jomaira S, Aisha U., Lia J., Freeden B., Endia H., Whitney P., Rose B., Kenly B., Zakiya L., Jen J. (and Pax J)

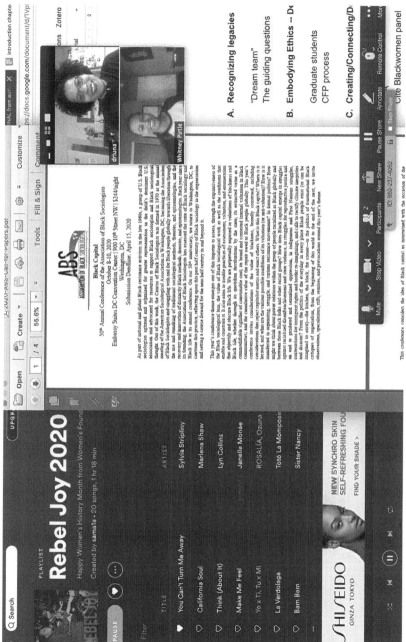

and a ready-to-ride crew behind me to 'come correct' and call out these harms. This book provided me with that.

Writing *BFS* has widened my networks and my thinking in so many ways. I have found sisters, friends, mentors, and mentees through this project. BFS has also blown my intellectual mind. I have learned so much about the legacies who helped pave the way and am so encouraged by next generation of Black scholars. BFS not only filled the void, but made my cup run over.

Notes

1. Koritha Mitchell. 2018. "Identifying White Mediocrity and Know-Your-Place Aggression: A Form of Self-Care." *African American Review* 51(4): 253–262.
2. Marcus A. Hunter, ed. 2018. *The New Black Sociologists: Historical and Contemporary Perspectives*. New York: Routledge; Irma McClaurin, ed. 2001. *Black Feminist Anthropology: Theory, Politics, Praxis, and Poetics*. New Brunswick, NJ: Rutgers University Press. Luna was introduced to this volume in UNC's Minority Undergraduate Research Apprentice Program, a pre-graduate research program for minorities that was eventually re-named for its first alumni to receive a PhD, Mignon Moore.
3. Patricia Hill Collins. 1986. "Learning from the Outsider Within: The Sociological Significance of Black Feminist Thought." *Social Problems* 33(6): s14–s32.
4. Whitney N. L. Pirtle. 2020. "We, Too, Are Academia; Demanding a Seat at the Table." *Feminist Anthropology* 2(2): 179–185.

Black Feminist Sociology and Black Freedom Now

Whitney N. Laster Pirtle and Zakiya Luna

A Note[1]

"If Black women were free," wrote the Combahee River Collective in 1977, "it would mean that everyone else would have to be free since our freedom would necessitate the destruction of all the systems of oppression."[2]

As Black feminist sociologists with expertise crossing fields of race and racism, health equity and reproductive justice, intersectionality, and social movements, learning how to get free grounds our work. Especially in this current moment. A moment in which viral pandemic kills a disproportionate number of Black people, and as more Black Americans are murdered by the police. A time in which Black folks are trying to stay alive, while fighting to stay alive.[3] Although the dominant narrative would suggest Black men, more than women, may be more affected by both COVID-19 and police brutality,[4] Black women shouldn't get lost in this time, especially if we all want to get free.

Skylar Herbert, a 5-year-old Black girl was not free to grow old, rather she became the first child in the US to die from COVID-19 related complications, in April of 2020; her parents first responders in Detroit.[5] Deborah Gatewood was a Black woman and health care worker at a Detroit hospital, who also died in April 2020 after she was turned away four times from her own workplace when she caught COVID-19.[6] The emergency room doctor gave her cough medicine, instead of taking her seriously, refusing to "trust Black women" as reproductive justice advocates have implored.[7] Honestie Hodges first made national headlines when she was only 11 after she was handcuffed by Grand Rapids, Michigan police who were looking for a white woman suspect. The officers were never disciplined because they broke no official policy; it was only at the expense of Honestie's police-caused trauma that the policy was changed. Still, she was not free. Just three years later, at age of 14, she too would pass away from COVID-19.[8] Breonna Taylor, an essential health care worker in Kentucky helping those with the coronavirus, died when police used a no-knock raid to break into the wrong home and shoot her.[9] None of the officers were indicted in her wrongful death.

Black women aren't free, and intersectionality teaches us that the conditions of our society are to blame. Black women live at the intersection of multiple systems of oppression: structural racism, structural sexism, and capitalism which constrain the opportunity to live freely and fully. These systems are often examined independently, and therefore Black women are erased from the analyses. Independently, using the pandemic as an example, structural racism[10] means Black Americans are at an increased risk for COVID-19,[11] while structural sexism[12] makes all women more vulnerable to COVID-19-related consequences,[13] and racial capitalism jointly limits the resources poor people of color have to mitigate the effects of COVID-19 risks.[14] But Black feminist writers have already told us that examining those systems independently is lazy and insufficient; Crenshaw instructs that "any analysis that does not take intersectionality into account cannot sufficiently address the particular manner in which Black women are subordinated."[15]

Black women incur mental, physical, and social injuries of inequality stemming from race, gender, class, sexuality, and so on.[16] Dorianne Mason wrote for Rewire that when the country sneezes, Black women get the flu.[17] These injuries are only amplified in times of health-related crises. Put plainly by Historian Treva Lindsey: "Black women are uniquely situated within overlapping systems of oppression to sustain disproportionate losses of both life and livelihood during this pandemic."[18]

Nursing professor Monica McLemore discussed how maternal health mortality is supposed to be a marker of a nation's wealth, but asked if Black women are twelve times more likely to experience maternal mortality, then is the US bankrupt?[19] The pandemic only amplifies pregnancy related inequities; for instance, due to the pandemic, a significantly higher number of Black and Hispanic women were choosing to wait to have children compared to White women as were queer-identified women in comparison to straight counterparts.[20] People seeking abortions experience delays or in cases of states like Texas, where abortion was deemed "non-essential" had to risk their lives to travel. Many left the state, placing themselves at further risk of a deadly disease, as in the case of a young Black woman profiled by CNN in a story about flying to California after Texas's March 2020 abortion ban.[21]

Black women are more likely to be in low wage "essential" jobs,[22] which makes them vulnerable to economic disruptions and reduces flexible resources to address health needs. In addition, Black women face race and gender discrimination within America's health care system that renders them both invisible and incompetent.[23] In Mason's piece, she tells us that the pandemic is just exposing that "our health-care system and health-care reform efforts have always carelessly or purposefully excluded us." We cannot forget that both Breonna Taylor and Deborah Gatewood were health care providers but died at the hands of the police and the pandemic.

The same intersecting systems that impact Black women's exposure to the pandemic also shape their increased exposure to police brutality and mass-incarceration, adding to the avalanche of injuries. Yet, similar to the lack of attention to race and gender disaggregation of COVID-19 data, there is an erasure of Black women when it comes to addressing police murder. In the *#SayHerName: Resisting Police Brutality against Black Women* report out of the African American Policy Forum, Crenshaw identifies this erasure: "Although Black women are routinely killed, raped, and beaten by the police, their experiences are rarely foregrounded in popular understandings of police brutality."[24]

For example, medical educator Rhea Boyd argues that police killing Black Americans is one of the oldest forms of structural racism in the US,[25] but she and many other Black women scholars have also studied how Black women experience compound risks and vulnerabilities within Black communities that exacerbate the violence they endure.[26] A recent study by sociologist Alyasah Sewell and colleagues found that living in lethally surveilled areas by police is linked to a host of negative physical health outcomes, including high blood pressure, diabetes and obesity, and at a greater rate for women than men—what the researchers name as gendered marginalization.[27] Even when the harm is indirect, through exposure to police violence online and within communities, there are negative health implications. Exposure to traumatic brutality viewed online increased rates of PTSD, but even more so in girls.[28]

It was not lost on us that between gasping for air and telling officers "I can't breathe" for the over eight excruciating minutes George Floyd yelled out, he also pleaded for his mother. Despite the virus's reach, many of us Black women heeded that call, joining millions on the streets to call out the continued state-sanctioned murder of Black men, women and trans people. Patricia Hill Collins's concept of othermothering[29] captures that call we feel to provide activism and advocacy on behalf of all children. But to care for our communities amidst the continuous loss is an unbearable grief placed on Black mothers,[30] aunties, sisters and others who make up the web of our families.

The Combahee River Collective statement also addresses the wear and tear of this work; that "the psychological toll of being a Black woman and . . . doing political work can never be underestimated."[31] Indeed, political mobilization among Black women is at an all-time high with whole sectors of the American republic asking us to save "us" all. Brittney Cooper directs her comments to White women

> "Instead of just thanking black women for protecting the nation from the voting patterns of white people, white feminists must organize white women" because "the world is on fire, and I don't know any black woman who has time for that."[32]

Black women's mobilizing in part laid the groundwork for a cultural shift that allowed for the historic nomination and eventual election of the first Black and Asian woman as Vice President, Kamala Harris. Yet, we must confront the limits of freedom in the hands of a former prosecutor. She cannot save us. How can any one Black woman save us if we are all not free?

The pandemic, police brutality, reproductive injustices, and Black women's erasure and autonomy within these narratives, is constraining our freedom, and killing Black bodies.[33] So we must ask, *what might freedom for Black women mean in our current health, police and political crises?* Freedom should include the ability to have enough material resources to make healthy decisions and have them actualized without penalty; to have a safe, secure non-violent home in which to shelter, to be treated with dignity and quality medical care when you need, to vote for yourself without the world on your shoulders. To be free to run without being hunted, to breathe without a knee in your neck, to sleep in peace and protection in your own home. For Black women's bodies to be their own.

If we all want to be free, we need radical healing that includes a critical consciousness, social justice framing, and the centering of intersectional analyses of Black women.[34] As Mason concluded in her article, "Truly investing in the health and well-being of Black women would reform our system and obviate the inevitable scramble to address public health crises like COVID-19."[35] But even when the vaccine ameliorated the threat of COVID-19, we are still left with the intersecting systems that constrain our ability to live free from other state-sanctioned harms even as people celebrated the announcement of Juneteenth as a US federal holiday.

Roxane Gay reiterates Cooper's point and put it plainly: no one is coming to save us.[36] Therefore, we must remember what Angela Davis taught us: freedom is a constant struggle.[37] We must consistently work to rebuild the system in order to amplify Black women's voices, center their experiences, and prioritize our freedom. Using Black feminist sociology as a framework to deconstruct the systems that constrain and harm Black women is how we all get free.[38]

Let's all get free.

Whitney N. Laster Pirtle and Zakiya Luna

Notes

1. This note is adopted from an op-ed Pirtle wrote for The Grio on July 1, 2020. https://thegrio.com/2020/07/01/black-women-need-to-be-free/.
2. Combahee River Collective. 1986 [1977]. *The Combahee River Collective Statement: Black Feminist Organizing in the Seventies and Eighties.* Albany, NY: Kitchen Table: Women of Color Press.
3. "Staying Alive, But Also Staying Alive" captures Ruha Benjamin's framing for the parallels between pandemic and police brutality during the summer of 2020, as she

titled her webinar talk https://aas.princeton.edu/news/staying-alive-also-staying-alive-reflections-how-pandemic-portal.

4. See examples of articles on men facing consequences more: Willem Roper. 2020. "More Men Dying of COVID-19 Than Women." *Statista*. www.statista.com/chart/21345/coronavirus-deaths-by-gender/. Accessed May 25, 2020; Santhanam, Laura. 2019. "After Ferguson, black men still face the highest risk of being killed by police." PBS: Health. www.pbs.org/newshour/health/after-ferguson-black-men-and-boys-still-face-the-highest-risk-of-being-killed-by-police. Accessed May 25, 2020.

5. Jasmin Barmore. 2020. "5-Year-Old with Rare Complication Becomes First Michigan Child to Die of COVID-19." *The Detroit News*. www.detroitnews.com/story/news/local/detroit-city/2020/04/19/5-year-old-first-michigan-child-dies-coronavirus/5163094002/. Accessed May 28, 2020.

6. Kim Soo. 2020. "Michigan Health Care Worker With Coronavirus Symptoms Dies After Being Turned Away From Hospital Four Times." *Newsweek*. www.newsweek.com/michigan-health-care-worker-coronavirus-symptoms-dies-after-being-turned-away-hospital-four-times-1499681. Accessed May 28, 2020.

7. SisterSong Women of Color Reproductive Justice Collective started the #TrustBlackWomen hashtag: https://trustblackwomen.org/our-roots/.

8. Glenn Riftkin. 2020. "Honestie Hodges, Whose Handcuffing Changed Police Policy, Is Dead at 14." *New York Times*. www.nytimes.com/2020/11/24/obituaries/honestie-hodges-dead-coronavirus.html. Accessed December 15, 2020.

9. Melissa Brown and Rashawn Ray. 2020. *Breonna Taylor, Police Brutality, and the Importance of #SayHerName*. Brookings Institute. www.brookings.edu/blog/how-we-rise/2020/09/25/breonna-taylor-police-brutality-and-the-importance-of-sayhername/. Accessed December 14, 2020.

10. Zinzi D. Bailey, Nancy Krieger, Madina Agénor, Jasmine Graves, Natalia Linos, and Mary T. Bassett. 2017. "Structural Racism and Health Inequities in the USA: Evidence and Interventions." *The Lancet* 389(10077): 1453–1463.

11. Judy Lubin. 2020. "Systemic Racism Is Making Coronavirus Worse in Black America." *Truthout*. https://truthout.org/articles/systemic-racism-is-making-coronavirus-worse-in-black-america/. Accessed May 29, 2020.

12. Patricia Homan. 2019. "Structural Sexism and Health in the United States: A New Perspective on Health Inequality and the Gender System." *American Sociological Review* 84(3): 486–516.

13. Helen Lewis. 2020. "The Coronavirus Is a Disaster for Feminism." *The Atlantic*. www.theatlantic.com/international/archive/2020/03/feminism-womens-rights-coronavirus-covid19/608302/. Accessed May 23, 2020.

14. Whitney N. Laster Pirtle. 2020. "Racial Capitalism: A Fundamental Cause of Novel Coronavirus (COVID-19) Pandemic Inequities in the United States." *Health Education & Behavior* 47(4): 504–508.

15. Kimberlé Crenshaw. 1989. "Demarginalizing the Intersection of Race and Sex: A Black Feminist Critique of Antidiscrimination Doctrine, Feminist Theory and Antiracist Politics." *University of Chicago Legal Forum* 140(1): 139–167.

16. Celeste Watkins-Hayes. 2019. *Remaking a Life: How Women Living with HIV/AIDS Confront Inequality*. Berkeley, CA: Univ of California Press.

17. Dorianne Mason. 2020. "When the Country Sneezes, Black Women Catch the Flu. What Happens With COVID-19 in the United States?" *Rewire News*. https://rewirenewsgroup.com/article/2020/03/23/when-the-country-sneezes-black-women-catch-the-flu-what-happens-with-covid-19-in-the-united-states/. Accessed May 22, 2020.

18. Treva Lindsey. 2020. "Why COVID-19 is Hitting Black Women So Hard. Women's Media Center: Health, Race/Ethnicity." *Women's Media Center*. https://womensmediacenter.com/news-features/why-covid-19-is-hitting-black-women-so-hard. Accessed May 23, 2020.

19. MacLemore shared her work in a Cite Black Women podcast wrote in *Scientific American*. Cite Black Women. 2020. "S2E5: Black Women and Health Equity: Spotlight on Black Maternal Health and COVID-19." https://soundcloud.com/user-211649525/s2e5-black-women-and-health-equity-spotlight-on-black-maternal-health-and-covid-19; Monica R. McLemore. 2020. "COVID-19 Is No Reason to Abandon Pregnant People." *Scientific American*. https://blogs.scientificamerican.com/observations/covid-19-is-no-reason-to-abandon-pregnant-people/?amp. Accessed May 28, 2020.

20. Laura D. Lindberg, Alicia Vande Vusse, Jennifer Mueller and Marielle Kirstein. 2020. "Early Impacts of the COVID-19 Pandemic: Findings from the 2020 Guttmacher Survey of Reproductive Health Experiences." New York, NY: Guttmatcher Institute. https://www.guttmacher.org/sites/default/files/report_pdf/early-impacts-covid-19-pandemic-findings-2020-guttmacher-survey-reproductive-health.pdf.

21. Kyle Almond and B. Wehelie. 2020. "She Tried to Get an Abortion during the Pandemic. Her State Wouldn't Allow It." Cnn.com. https://www.cnn.com/interactive/2020/06/health/abortion-access-coronavirus-cnnphotos/; Long 2020. Accessed December 16, 2020.

22. Leah Rodriguez. 2020. "Women of Color Are Experiencing the Biggest Economic Losses Amid COVID-19 Pandemic." *Global Citizen*. www.globalcitizen.org/en/content/women-of-color-disproportionately-unemployed-covid/. Accessed May 27, 2020.

23. Black women scholars continue to call out health care systems that harm their bodies through racialized and gendered biases that means Black women are seen as either invisible or incompetent. See; Tina K. Sacks. 2018. *Invisible Visits: Black Middle-Class Women in the American Healthcare System*. New York: Oxford University Press; Tressie McMillan Cottom. 2019. "I Was Pregnant and in Crisis. All the Doctors and Nurses Saw Was an Incompetent Black Woman." *Time*. https://time.com/5494404/tressie-mcmillan-cottom-thick-pregnancy-competent/. Accessed January 19, 2020.

24. Learn more about the campaign here: https://aapf.org/sayhernamereport/.

25. Rhea W. Boyd. 2018. "Police Violence and the Built Harm of Structural Racism." *The Lancet* 392: 258–259.

26. See Beth Richie. 2012. *Arrested Justice: Black Women, Violence, and America's Prison Nation*. New York: New York University Press.
    Nikki Jones. 2009. *Between Good and Ghetto: African American Girls and Inner-City Violence*. New Brunswick, NJ: Rutgers University Press.

27. Alyasah Ali Sewell, Justin M. Feldman, Rashawn Ray, Keon L. Gilbert, Kevin A. Jefferson, and Hedwig Lee. 2020. "Illness Spillovers of Lethal Police Violence: The Significance of Gendered Marginalization." *Ethnic and Racial Studies* 44(7): 1089–1114.

28. Brendesha M. Tynes, Henry A. Willis, Ashley M. Stewart, and Matthew W. Hamilton. 2019. "Race-related Traumatic Events Online and Mental Health Among Adolescents of Color." *Journal of Adolescent Health* 65(3): 371–377.

29. Patricia Hill Collins. 2002 [1990]. *Black Feminist Thought: Knowledge, Consciousness, and the Politics of Empowerment*. New York: Routledge.

30. Rochaun Meadows-Fernandez. 2020. "The Unbearable Grief of Black Mothers." www.vox.com/first-person/2020/5/28/21272380/black-mothers-grief-sadness-covid-19. Accessed May 29, 2020.

31. Combahee River Collective. 1986. *The Combahee River Collective Statement: Black Feminist Organizing in the Seventies and Eighties*. Albany, NY: Kitchen Table: Women of Color Press.

32. Brittany Cooper. 2017. "Stop Asking Black Women to 'Save America.' Start Organizing Your Own People." www.washingtonpost.com/news/posteverything/wp/2017/12/15/stop-asking-black-women-to-save-america-start-organizing-your-own-people/. Accessed December 16, 2020.

33. See Roberts's work on the contradictory ways arguments for "liberty" can harm, and kill, Black women's bodies. Dorothy E. Roberts. 1999. *Killing the Black Body: Race, Reproduction, and the Meaning of Liberty.* New York: Vintage Press.
34. The concept of radical healing has been spearheaded by Black women psychologists. See work here Jioni A. Lewis, Helen A. Neville, Della V. Mosley, Bryana H. French, Nayeli Y. Chavez-Dueñas, Hector Y. Adames, and Grace A. Chen "#SayHerName: Radical Healing for Black Women and Gender Expansive Folx." *Psychology Today.* www.psychologytoday.com/us/blog/healing-through-social-justice/202005/sayher name. Accessed July 1, 2020; Bryana H. French, Jioni A. Lewis, Della V. Mosley, Hector Y. Adames, Nayeli Y. Chavez-Dueñas, Grace A. Chen, and Helen A. Neville. "Toward a Psychological Framework of Radical Healing in Communities of Color." *The Counseling Psychologist* 48(1): 4–46.
35. Dorianne Mason. 2020. "When the Country Sneezes, Black Women Catch the Flu. What Happens With COVID-19 in the United States?" *Rewire News.* https://rewire newsgroup.com/article/2020/03/23/when-the-country-sneezes-black-women-catch-the-flu-what-happens-with-covid-19-in-the-united-states/. Accessed May 22, 2020.
36. Roxane Gay. 2020. "Remember, No One Is Coming to Save Us." *The New York Times.* www.nytimes.com/2020/05/30/opinion/sunday/trump-george-floyd-coronavirus.html. Accessed July 1, 2020.
37. Angela Y. Davis. 2016. *Freedom is a Constant Struggle: Ferguson, Palestine, and the Foundations of a Movement.* Chicago, IL: Haymarket Books.
38. Keeanga-Yamahtta Taylor, ed. 2017. *How we get free: Black feminism and the Combahee River Collective.* Chicago, IL: Haymarket Books.

References

Bailey, Zinzi D., Nancy Krieger, Madina Agénor, Jasmine Graves, Natalia Linos, and Mary T. Bassett. 2017. "Structural Racism and Health Inequities in the USA: Evidence and Interventions." *The Lancet* 389(10077): 1453–1463.

Barmore, Jasmin. 2020. "5-Year-Old with Rare Complication Becomes First Michigan Child to Die of COVID-19." *The Detroit News.* www.detroitnews.com/story/news/local/detroit-city/2020/04/19/5-year-old-first-michigan-child-dies-coronavirus/5163094002/. Accessed May 28, 2020

Boyd, Rhea W. 2018. "Police Violence and the Built Harm of Structural Racism." *The Lancet* 392: 258–259.

Brown, Melissa and Rashawn Ray. 2020. *Breonna Taylor, Police Brutality, and the Importance of #SayHerName.* Brookings Institute. www.brookings.edu/blog/how-we-rise/2020/09/25/breonna-taylor-police-brutality-and-the-importance-of-sayhername/. Accessed December 14, 2020

Collins, Patricia Hill. 2002 [1990]. *Black Feminist Thought: Knowledge, Consciousness, and the Politics of Empowerment.* New York: Routledge.

Combahee River Collective. 1986 [1977]. *The Combahee River Collective Statement: Black Feminist Organizing in the Seventies and Eighties.* Albany, NY: Kitchen Table: Women of Color Press.

Cooper, Brittany. 2017. "Stop Asking Black Women to 'Save America.' Start Organizing Your Own People." *The Washington Post.* www.washingtonpost.com/news/posteverything/wp/2017/12/15/stop-asking-black-women-to-save-america-start-organizing-your-own-people/. Accessed December 16, 2017

Cottom, Tressie McMillan. 2019. "I Was Pregnant and in Crisis. All the Doctors and Nurses Saw Was an Incompetent Black Woman." *Time*. https://time.com/5494404/tressie-mcmillan-cottom-thick-pregnancy-competent/. Accessed January 19, 2019

Crenshaw, Kimberlé. 1989. "Demarginalizing the Intersection of Race and Sex: A Black Feminist Critique of Antidiscrimination Doctrine, Feminist Theory and Antiracist Politics." *University of Chicago Legal Forum* 140(1): 139–167.

Davis, Angela Y. 2016. *Freedom is a Constant Struggle: Ferguson, Palestine, and the Foundations of a Movement*. Chicago, IL: Haymarket Books.

French, Bryana H., Jioni A. Lewis, Della V. Mosley, Hector Y. Adames, Nayeli Y. Chavez-Dueñas, Grace A. Chen, and Helen A. Neville. "Toward a Psychological Framework of Radical Healing in Communities of Color." *The Counseling Psychologist* 48(1): 4–46.

Gay, Roxane. 2020. "Remember, No One Is Coming to Save Us." *The New York Times*. www.nytimes.com/2020/05/30/opinion/sunday/trump-george-floyd-coronavirus.html. Accessed July 1, 2020

Homan, Patricia. 2019. "Structural Sexism and Health in the United States: A New Perspective on Health Inequality and the Gender System." *American Sociological Review* 84(3): 486–516.

Jones, Nikki. 2009. *Between Good and Ghetto: African American Girls and Inner-City Violence*. New Brunswick, NJ: Rutgers University Press.

Lewis, Helen. 2020. "The Coronavirus Is a Disaster for Feminism." *The Atlantic*. www.theatlantic.com/international/archive/2020/03/feminism-womens-rights-coronavirus-covid19/608302/. Accessed May 23, 2020

Lewis, Jioni A., Helen A. Neville, Della V. Mosley, Bryana H. French, Nayeli Y. Chavez-Dueñas, Hector Y. Adames, Grace A. Chen. 2020. "#SayHerName: Radical Healing for Black Women and Gender Expansive Folx." *Psychology Today*. www.psychologytoday.com/us/blog/healing-through-social-justice/202005/sayhername. Accessed July 1, 2020

Lindsey, Treva. 2020. "Why COVID-19 is Hitting Black Women So Hard." *Women's Media Center: Health, Race/Ethnicity*. https://womensmediacenter.com/news-features/why-covid-19-is-hitting-black-women-so-hard. Accessed May 23, 2020

Lubin, Judy. 2020. "Systemic Racism Is Making Coronavirus Worse in Black America." *Truthout*. https://truthout.org/articles/systemic-racism-is-making-coronavirus-worse-in-black-america/. Accessed May 29, 2020

Mason, Dorianne. 2020. "When the Country Sneezes, Black Women Catch the Flu. What Happens With COVID-19 in the United States?" *Rewire*. https://rewirenewsgroup.com/article/2020/03/23/when-the-country-sneezes-black-women-catch-the-flu-what-happens-with-covid-19-in-the-united-states/. Accessed May 22, 2020

McLemore, Monica R. 2020. "COVID-19 Is No Reason to Abandon Pregnant People." *Scientific American*. https://blogs.scientificamerican.com/observations/covid-19-is-no-reason-to-abandon-pregnant-people/?amp. Accessed May 28, 2020

Meadows-Fernandez, Rochaun. 2020. "The unbearable grief of Black mothers." *Vox*. www.vox.com/first-person/2020/5/28/21272380/black-mothers-grief-sadness-covid-19. Accessed May 29, 2020

Pirtle, Whitney N. Laster. 2020a. "Racial Capitalism: A Fundamental Cause of Novel Coronavirus (COVID-19) Pandemic Inequities in the United States." *Health Education & Behavior* 47(4): 504–508.

Pirtle, Whitney N. Laster. 2020b. "Black Women Need to Be Free" *The Grio*. https://thegrio.com/2020/07/01/black-women-need-to-be-free/. Accessed July 1, 2020

Richie, Beth. 2012. *Arrested Justice: Black Women, Violence, and America's Prison Nation*. New York: New York University Press.

Riftkin, Glenn. 2020. "Honestie Hodges, Whose Handcuffing Changed Police Policy, Is Dead at 14." *New York Times*. www.nytimes.com/2020/11/24/obituaries/honestie-hodges-dead-coronavirus.html. Accessed December 15, 2020

Roberts, Dorothy E. 1999. *Killing the Black Body: Race, Reproduction, and the Meaning of Liberty*. New York: Vintage Press.

Rodriguez, Leah. 2020. "Women of Color Are Experiencing the Biggest Economic Losses Amid COVID-19 Pandemic." *Global Citizen*. www.globalcitizen.org/en/content/women-of-color-disproportionately-unemployed-covid/. Accessed May 27, 2020

Roper, Willem. 2020. "More Men Dying of COVID-19 Than Women." *Statista*. www.statista.com/chart/21345/coronavirus-deaths-by-gender/. Accessed May 25, 2020

Sacks, Tina K. 2018. *Invisible Visits: Black Middle-Class Women in the American Healthcare System*. New York: Oxford University Press.

Santhanam, Laura. 2019. "After Ferguson, Black Men Still Face the Highest Risk of Being Killed by Police." *PBS: Health*. www.pbs.org/newshour/health/after-ferguson-black-men-and-boys-still-face-the-highest-risk-of-being-killed-by-police. Accessed May 25, 2020

Sewell, Alyasah Ali, Justin M. Feldman, Rashawn Ray, Keon L. Gilbert, Kevin A. Jefferson, and Hedwig Lee. 2020. "Illness Spillovers of Lethal Police Violence: The Significance of Gendered Marginalization." *Ethnic and Racial Studies* 44(7): 1089–1114.

Soo, Kim. 2020. "Michigan Health Care Worker With Coronavirus Symptoms Dies After Being Turned Away From Hospital Four Times." *Newsweek*. www.newsweek.com/michigan-health-care-worker-coronavirus-symptoms-dies-after-being-turned-away-hospital-four-times-1499681. Accessed May 28, 2020

Taylor, Keeanga-Yamahtta (ed.). 2017. *How We Get Free: Black Feminism and the Combahee River Collective*. Chicago, IL: Haymarket Books.

Tynes, Brendesha M., Henry A. Willis, Ashley M. Stewart, and Matthew W. Hamilton. 2019. "Race-related Traumatic Events Online and Mental Health Among Adolescents of Color." *Journal of Adolescent Health* 65(3): 371–377.

Watkins-Hayes, Celeste. 2019. *Remaking a Life: How Women Living with HIV/AIDS Confront Inequality*. Berkeley: University of California Press.